ACADEMIC ADVISING ADMINISTRATION

The second edition of *Academic Advising Administration: Essential Knowledge and Skills for the 21st Century* examines the evolving boundary-crossing role of the advising administrator in an increasingly complex and diversified higher education environment.

Written by scholar-practitioners in the field, chapters situate advising administration as a central and critical function that connects the curriculum and scholarship work of faculty members with the aspirations and goals of students. Through scholarly and practical content, combined with reflective questions, chapters challenge readers to examine the work of advising administration through the lenses of social justice, globalization, and the nature of the academy itself. The portrait of the advising administrator being developed in this second edition is that of a skilled practitioner; visionary and transformative leader; intellectual partner and collaborator; and academic advising "scholar-in-chief."

Intended equally for aspiring, new, and seasoned advising administrators, this book presents theories, scholarship, and practical applications that offer opportunities for personal and professional growth, self-reflection, and inspiration.

Susan M. Campbell is Chief Student Affairs Officer Emerita at the University of Southern Maine.

Calley Stevens Taylor is Vice President for Student Success & Engagement and Dean of Students at Cedar Crest College.

Mike Dial is Assistant Director of First-Year Advising at the University of South Carolina.

"A resource beneficial to new and seasoned advising administrators alike, this edition comprehensively engages readers across a broad base of knowledge, theories, tools, and practices. The editors and contributors highlight advising administrators as campus leaders, the 'scholar-in-chief' of academic advising, straddling the third space between academic and administrative roles within institutional structure and politics. This book supports advising administrators through changing technology, different advising models, data-driven decision-making, and so much more."

Lisa M. Rubin, *Associate Professor,*
Kansas State University

"The authors of the *Academic Advising Administration* 2nd Edition have done an exceptional job summarizing the contemporary literature on advising administration, with a critical focus on justice, diversity and inclusion. Several authors have provided a real service by drawing upon models and research from human resources and higher education, addressing advising's position in the liminal, third space between student and academic affairs. Critically, some authors moved beyond concentration on individual administrators/advisors to exploring the systemic impact of advising in the higher education eco-system. Focused predominantly on larger institutions with staffs of primary role advisors, much can also be found here for administrators at smaller institutions with faculty advisors."

Victoria A. McGillin, *Associate Vice President, John N. Gardner*
Institute for Excellence in Undergraduate Education

"Simply put – academic advising administrators at all levels should consider this book as their 'go to resource' for a clear understanding of both the explicit and implicit challenges they face as leaders who must be 'integrated practitioners,' 'scholar-in-chief,' and function as 'third space professionals.' The authors define a leadership space that exists across higher education contexts and cultures. 'Third Space' clearly places academic advising within the teaching/learning missions of our institutions. Each chapter is grounded in the language of academe and provides theoretical constructs, knowledge and tools that connect to daily practice. Embracing the methodologies and strategies presented will empower advising administrators to lay claim to their leadership role as the individuals best positioned on campus to cocreate a comprehensive academic advising culture that supports student learning and success."

Dr. Ruth A. Darling, *Associate Provost for Student Success,*
Emerita (The University of Tennessee),
NACADA Past President, Virginia Gordon Award Service to
NACADA Award

"This book recognizes and amplifies the liminal or 'third' space in higher education as a place of leadership, powerful platform, and lever for transformation. Further, this volume recognizes academic advisors as unique educators and advocates in that space to advance student learning, equity, and success and draws from current research, theory, policy, and 'voices from the field' to frame advising as a leading example of the scholarship of practice. The authors provide relevant, thoughtful, empirically driven yet student-centered strategies for academic advisors and advising administrators as critical agents of holistic student support and campus leadership, whether they are beginning their career in this role or are veterans."

Dr. Jennifer R. Keup. *Executive Director,*
National Resource Center for
The First-Year Experience and Students in Transition

ACADEMIC ADVISING ADMINISTRATION

Essential Knowledge and Skills
for the 21st Century

Second Edition

Edited by Susan M. Campbell,
Calley Stevens Taylor, and Mike Dial

NEW YORK AND LONDON

Designed cover image: Getty Images

Second edition published 2024
by Routledge
605 Third Avenue, New York, NY 10158

and by Routledge
4 Park Square, Milton Park, Abingdon, Oxon, OX14 4RN

Routledge is an imprint of the Taylor & Francis Group, an informa business

© 2024 BY NACADA: The Global Community for Academic Advising

The right of Susan M. Campbell, Calley Stevens Taylor, and Mike Dial to be identified as the authors of the editorial material, and of the authors for their individual chapters, has been asserted in accordance with sections 77 and 78 of the Copyright, Designs and Patents Act 1988.

First edition published by NACADA 2011

Library of Congress Cataloging-in-Publication Data
Names: Campbell, Susan M., 1941–editor. |
Taylor, Calley Stevens, editor. | Dial, Michael T., 1986–editor.
Title: Academic advising administration: essential
knowledge and skills for the 21st century/edited by Susan M. Campbell,
Calley Stevens Taylor, and Mike Dial.
Description: 2nd edition. | New York, NY: Routledge, 2024. |
Includes bibliographical references and index.
Subjects: LCSH: Counseling in higher education—Administration.
Classification: LCC LB2343.A297 2024 |
DDC 378.1/97—dc23/eng/20230519
LC record available at https://lccn.loc.gov/2023018864

ISBN: 978-1-64267-448-4 (hbk)
ISBN: 978-1-64267-449-1 (pbk)
ISBN: 978-1-003-43759-8 (ebk)

DOI: 10.4324/9781003437598

Typeset in Sabon LT Pro
by codeMantra

CONTENTS

FOREWORD

In the office where I spent my days as an advising administrator, this framed quote from the poem "The Summer Day" by Mary Oliver hung on the wall, so I saw it every day. It reminded me that each student I encountered was an individual seeking meaning for their life—their education and their eventual career. The quote also inspired me to consider my own journey toward a rich, whole-hearted life pursuing meaningful work.

As you work your way through *Academic Advising Administration: Essential Knowledge and Skills for the 21st Century* (second edition), you may feel overwhelmed by the demanding, complex, evolving nature of academic advising administration. The knowledge and skills needed to be effective in the role examined in this book include understanding and negotiating legal and ethical issues, managing organizational change, understanding advising structures, planning strategic communications, conducting assessment, and leveraging resources. Advising administrators need to develop their commitment to social justice in daily practice to ensure equitable and inclusive advising experiences for all students. They also use data to make appropriate decisions, cross-train advisors to ensure that students are well-served regardless of which staff member is at work that day, and diligently maintain their own professional knowledge base.

Advising administrators must know enough about Human Resource functions to recruit, select, hire, train, develop, and lead advisors and support personnel. The advising administrator must cross boundaries and break through silos to create wide-ranging institutional support for academic advising. They must know the needs of both the institution and its students and advocate for both. As a leader, the advising administrator must be effective both in the advising office and in the larger community, transcending barriers and building strong relationships with strategic partners across campus, what the authors call a "community of practice" in Chapter 8.

During the early weeks and months of the COVID-19 pandemic, advising administrators found themselves scrambling to develop options for distance advising opportunities. In some cases, the crisis led to advisors working from home when that may not have been an option before. This is just one example of the rapidly changing terrain that advising administrators encounter. Laws relating to higher education change, institutional policies and programs evolve, and every new hire in upper-level administration renews the need to justify the importance of academic advising and its connection to the institutional mission. It can be overwhelming, but support and information is available.

In my career, I frequently used resources from NACADA, especially conference sessions and publications, to guide program enhancement and my own professional development. This new edition continues NACADA's practice of providing updated information and thoughtful discussion of important advising-related topics. This book will be useful for advising administrators, new and experienced, and for advisors who wish to pursue advising administration. A note to advisors who wish to become advising administrators: experience as an academic advisor is essential to be a good advising administrator, but it is not enough. An additional set of skills are necessary to succeed in administration. For example, an administrator must have supervisory, budgeting, and program development skills, and it may be difficult to get experience in those areas while serving as an academic advisor. Reading this book is a great start. You may want to ask your supervisor to allow you to chair a search committee to learn hiring skills or supervise peer leaders to gain supervisory experience. Asking mentors for suggestions, volunteering to plan programs for students or advisors, attending advising administrator institutes, and taking on leadership roles in NACADA can all provide experiences useful in advising administration.

This book presents a deep examination of the multifaceted role of the academic advising administrator. Sometimes the role can feel isolated. For example, a director can make a personnel decision that their team questions, but confidentiality prevents transparent conversations. However, the complexity of the role also makes it deeply vital and rewarding. As an advising administrator, I was frequently in discussions where I could pull the conversation back to putting students' best interests at the center of the decision. I encouraged faculty members to research and write about student success. I coordinated an "Excellence in Advising" awards program for faculty and primary role advisors and saw advising rewarded in a way it had not been at my institution before. I interviewed prospective orientation leaders, judged homecoming events, and advised a fraternity. I worked with students who faced academic suspension and then returned to graduate with honors. I supervised academic advisors who went on to be directors of advising centers, professors, deans, and, in one case, a college president. I take pride in having been part of their stories. After 40 years working in higher education, I cannot imagine a position that would have allowed me to be more directly involved in so many student success stories and to be a more involved member of a university community. Advising administration is challenging but it is also full of rewards. For many of us, it is the quintessential definition of doing meaningful work as part of a rich journey and whole-hearted life.

Kathy J. Davis
Emeritus Director. Academic Advising and Transfer Center,
Missouri State University; 2018 NACADA Virginia Gordon
Excellence in the Field of Advising Award Recipient

ACKNOWLEDGMENTS

Three years may seem like a long time to organize and produce a volume that addresses all the dimensions of administrative life. However, as quickly as we made notes in the margins of manuscripts, the sociopolitical winds shifted, raising new issues and concerns for academic advising and the administrators who work tirelessly to ensure effective and meaningful experiences for students and advising teams. The result here is a thoughtful consideration— by content experts and scholarly practitioners in the field—of the environmental landscape of higher education; the functions and responsibilities of advising administrators; and the building, shaping, and sustaining of a learning-centered advising culture. This book is the result of collaboration with many colleagues who share, along with us as coeditors, a passion for academic advising and the potential it holds for supporting all students as they pursue their educational, career, and life goals.

This collaboration began with a gathering of colleagues who all share a vested interest, either as faculty members or as practitioners, in the administration of academic advising. Our sincere thanks to Rebecca Getz-Keller, Richie Gebauer, Claire Robinson, Casey Self, Leah Frierson, Karen Cole, Keven P. Thomas, Kim Smith, Stephanie Hands, Melissa Staddon, Carol Wilson, William Watts, and Dana Zahorik for their willingness to talk about critical issues in advising administration. We also thank Dr. Craig McGill and Dr. Lisa Rubin, faculty members in the masters and PhD programs in academic advising at Kansas State University, for sharing their course syllabi and knowledge with us as we sought to design an instructive and useful framework for this book.

We also thank all those who submitted a proposal for consideration for a chapter or a "Voices from the Field." The quality of the submissions made our work more difficult but increased our enthusiasm for the project. We are especially grateful to the authors whose work ultimately constitutes this book. From the first drafts through copyediting, we were impressed with your expertise and insights that offer important knowledge, provocative questions, and useful applications in the context of academic advising administration. We are also grateful for the authors of the "Voices from the Field," which so clearly complement and expand the information presented in the chapter with which they are associated.

We are also grateful for the time and energy that each reviewer gave to this project. Your comments and suggestions were always viewed as supportive, and more than one author commented on the extent to which the reviewers' comments strengthened their manuscripts. These reviewers and their institutional affiliations include:

Rene Couture, Arkansas Tech University
Melissa Cumbia, Virginia Tech
Kezia Daniels, Oral Roberts University
Thomas Grites, Stockton University
Andrea Hein, North Dakota State University
Sarah Howard, The Ohio State University
Jennifer Jensen, Lehigh University
Karla Knepper, Sinclair Community College
Michael Levinstein, Shippensburg University of Pennsylvania
Olivia Miller, University Missouri-Kansas City
Benjamin Norris, Frostburg State University
Brian Peters, North Carolina State University
Julia Qian, University of Notre Dame
Health Saito, University of Hawaii at Manoa
Ryan Scheckel, Texas Tech University
Kiana Shiroma, University of Hawaii at Manoa
Lauren Solina, Tennessee Board of Regents, TN College of Applied Technology at Murfreesboro
Sophie Spratley, University of Florida
Kevin Thomas, University of Central Arkansas

We are forever grateful for the assistance and support we received from NACADA: The Global Community for Academic Advising. In particular, we thank Ashley Thomas, managing editor, for her coordination, her gentle nudging, her content and editing expertise, and for her wise and humor-filled consultations, which were always freely given, whether we had a quick question or significant decision to make. As others have said—and we agree—without Ashley Thomas, there would be no book! Thank you, our friend!

Finally, we each have those we wish to acknowledge for their help in advancing this work.

Susan: It almost goes without saying that I am grateful to my husband, Dick, for giving me the space to do this work. He and I both know that while I talk about "really retiring," that is more easily said than done. I also want to thank my colleagues and friends to whom I constantly turn for guidance and feedback on my writing. I am grateful to Dr. Jayne Drake, Dr. George Steele, Dr. Ruth Darling, Dr. Brandon Smith, Dr. Charlie Nutt, and Dr. Peter Hagen for their honesty, even if I do not always like the feedback received. In all cases, their comments have helped to strengthen the outcome. Finally, to my coeditor colleagues, know that our collaborative approach to this work made even the heaviest lifts much lighter. Further, I love having made two new friends in the process.

Calley: First and foremost, I must express gratitude to my husband, Allen, for giving up so many nights and weekends with me while I worked on this book. My commitment to this project quickly became a family affair. As a former advising professional himself, Allen helped me process and hone my own perspectives on the topics we present in this book. I also owe thanks to Susan Fread and Dr. Ruth Darling for encouraging my involvement in NACADA publications, work that has become one of my most valued professional contributions. Thanks are also due to my mother, Linda, who offered thoughtful questions and tireless encouragement. To my colleagues at Cedar Crest College, especially Dr. Elizabeth Meade and Dr. Bob Wilson, I am honored to have their support, encouragement, and mentoring. And finally, thank you to my coeditors and new friends, who have made this project far more rewarding than I had anticipated.

Mike: I am forever grateful to my wife, Carrie, for all she does to support my scholarship. Many evenings and weekends have been spent in my home office, at a coffee shop, or visiting another quiet location while working on this book. Carrie unwaveringly creates space and time for me to pursue writing and editing. I'm grateful also for my own undergraduate and graduate academic advisors, Dr. Mick Mulvaney and Dr. Jenny Bloom, who encouraged and challenged me as a writer and scholar. Thanks to all my wonderful colleagues and supervisors past and present who have allowed me to stand in their doorways while chewing on ideas in collaboration. Finally, I am grateful to my coeditors who have made this project both incredibly meaningful and fun.

INTRODUCTION

The first edition of *Academic Advising Administration: Essential Knowledge and Skills for the 21st Century* was published in 2011. Before that, academic advising administration was typically included under the larger umbrella of student affairs administration. By 2011, the growth and importance of academic advising in the student experience, and its value in supporting student persistence and completion (Kuh et al., 2010; Light, 2001; Tinto, 1993, 2012) found those in advising administration calling for a publication that would serve the needs of those beginning in the field as well as veteran advising administrators more specifically. The first edition helped formalize the administration of academic advising as a distinct professional endeavor, a path initially paved by the adoption of the NACADA Concept Statement of Advising in 2006 and the report from the 2008 NACADA Task Force on the Infusion of Research in Advising. The former intentionally aligned academic advising with higher education's teaching and learning mission. The latter broadened scholarly inquiry to include empirical and applied research. The work of the 2008 Task Force situated the scholarship of advising (scholarly inquiry) within the broader umbrella of the scholarship of teaching and learning. In her 2018 article, "Scholarly Advising and the Scholarship of Advising," Troxel examined the scholarship of advising through the lens of the scholarship of teaching and learning. This work further advanced the important and necessary engagement of academic advisors in scholarly inquiry, as both consumers and producers. By extension, Troxel's (2018) work made more explicit the role of the administrator in supporting and promoting engagement in scholarly activities. Of course, the role of advising administrator

DOI: 10.4324/9781003437598-1

as "scholar-in-chief" is in addition to the myriad tasks associated with coordinating and supporting the delivery of academic advising.

The growth in graduate courses and degree programs on advising, at the masters and doctorate levels, indicates the increasing interest in academic advising and recognizes the role of the advising administrator as unique among other administrative positions in higher education. Thus, we come to the need to conceptualize academic advising administration as a distinct leadership position responsible for supporting and advancing student learning while also expanding the field of advising.

Undeniably, colleges and universities are complex organizations (Bastedo et al., 2016; Bess & Dee, 2012; Birnbaum, 1988; Kezar & Posselt, 2020; Manning, 2018). Working, managing, and leading within these organizations requires an ability to effectively navigate this complexity. Thus, understanding organizational theory as it applies to higher education and the associated decision-making processes is foundational to effective advising leadership and management. In addition, administrators must be able to adapt to rapidly changing circumstances to meet student needs; while adaptability may have been previously considered an individual characteristic, the COVID-19 pandemic revealed the imperative that adaptability become a job requirement.

The contemporary role of the academic advising administrator in higher education has arguably changed since the publication of the first edition of *Academic Advising Administration*. One area of particular note is the globalization of NACADA and the increasing recognition that advisors and advising administrators can learn from each other within and across international borders and cultural contexts. The interest in international perspectives on academic advising has been steadily increasing since the first joint international conference in Edinburgh, Scotland, in 2006. International organizations for academic advising have emerged and are affiliated with NACADA: The Global Community for Academic Advising, including United Kingdom Advising and Tutoring (UKAT) and LVSA (the Dutch National Association of Study Advisors). Academic advising is no longer U.S.-centric. Scholarship about the field needs to shape a more inclusive portrait of the advising administrator that acknowledges both similarities and differences and considers diverse institutional, cultural, and country contexts.

In addition, thanks to research and scholarship contributions, the role of equity and social justice in the administration and delivery of academic advising has gained visibility, importance, and commitment. The number and quality of research articles published in the *NACADA Journal* on the impact of academic advising on students of color has increased, as have discussions of mindfulness and equity across all levels of advising delivery.

Finally, not to be ignored is the ubiquity of technology in academic advising. Advising administrators find themselves making decisions about technology needs and uses, particularly as they relate to software as self-service, the promises and challenges technology offers in its impact on the student-advisor relationship, and the many legal and ethical issues therein.

Our Goals for This Book

A primary goal for this book is to situate and align academic advising administration with higher education's teaching and learning mission. In addition, this book is intended to elevate the role of the academic advising administrator as scholar-in-chief, responsible for supporting the development of self and others as practitioners and scholars to advance academic advising. In doing so, the position of the advising administrator as an integral member of any college or university's leadership team is strengthened. Ideally, this book will serve as a companion to other volumes that expand and extend the discussion of advising and advising administration in the areas of globalization, equity, and social justice, and offer guidance to administrators as they commit to being critical consumers of research as well as engaged scholars. Within this volume, through its chapters and "Voices from the Field" vignettes, the latter of which serve to further describe and situate chapter topics in a variety of contexts, we hope that our readers find opportunities for personal and professional growth, self-reflection, and inspiration.

More directly, we hope this book fills four needs. The first is to serve as a guidebook for new academic advising administrators or those interested in setting a goal to achieve such a role during their career. In this regard, the chapters in this book reflect knowledge areas critical to the success of professionals pursuing administrative careers in higher education generally and academic advising specifically. The second is to offer the field of academic advising a publication, at least parts of which can be used as a text for programs and courses in higher education administration that focus on academic advising. The third is to translate theory into practice through institutional and program vignettes that demonstrate and highlight the application of concepts and constructs. Finally, this volume aims to challenge and encourage seasoned advising administrators to critically reflect on, evaluate, and expand their own knowledge, skills, and practices.

There are three distinct parts in this book. Part I is focused on conceptualizing the evolving role of the academic advising administrator within the complex environment of higher education (Grites). This conceptualization includes the unique positionality of the advising administrator as a blended professional nestled within this complexity, necessarily navigating the cultures of the academy (McIntosh and Campbell). Kapinos and Stevens Taylor address the myriad structures for academic advising and offer guidance to administrators in understanding how such structures impact their roles, responsibilities, relationships, and decision-making practices.

Management, today and arguably into the future, has become more focused on leading change, particularly after pandemic realities significantly altered how academic advising is delivered. Nandedkar, Mbindyo, O'Connor, and O'Connor use transformational and servant leadership as anchors for interpreting and applying planned and unplanned models of change. In addition, the political and legal climate has become increasingly complex, signaling a need for the advising administrator to be acutely aware, perhaps more so than in the past, of legal and ethical issues that impact the content and practice of our work (Taffe-Reed and Lowery).

As blended professionals, academic advising administrators exist in both the administrative and academic spheres. To advance the field of academic advising, Troxel and Gabra situate the academic advising administrator as a scholar/practitioner as well as advocate for engagement in the scholarship of advising. Finally, Part I closes with a chapter by Etienne on socially just advising administration. The evolving role of advising administration, in a contemporary, global society, demands that administrators embrace principles of inclusion and social justice to ensure equity in the advising experiences of students as well as the experiences of those we lead.

Part II of this volume provides advising administrators with guidance on many of the functional responsibilities they can expect to be dealt or lead. Gebauer and Tharp reinforce the importance of developing internal and external partnerships. They broaden the concept and describe the nature of key partnerships and why they are valuable to the academic advising program. The next two chapters are inextricably related. Robbins and Vance provide guidance to the advising administrator in the design and implementation of an assessment plan. Although they also speak to advisor and delivery outcomes, their focus on student learning outcomes assessment informs what learning-centered advising is all about and why advising administrators must embed assessment into their practice. Kraft-Terry and Brown, while including assessment as a key element of program planning, take a broader view to guide the advising administrator in understanding the impact that careful, evidence-based planning and decision-making can have on positioning and improving an academic advising program. The importance of having a framework to guide program design and redesign is the focus of Whitney, Taub, and Aiken-Wisniewski's chapter, where they offer a scaffolded model of a practical, grounded approach to leading the design and implementation of advising programs.

Of course, the fiduciary and budgetary responsibilities of advising administrators cannot be ignored. Streufert, Cole, and Baker provide a concise and comprehensive exploration of finance within higher education and how administrators can use financial leadership to advocate for advising programs. Being able to strategically and effectively communicate with stakeholders is both critical and essential to advising administrators. Schmidt and Sullivan-Vance drive this point home by offering practical strategies administrators can use to establish a culture and habits of mind that support effective communication. To close Part II, Archambault distinguishes between succession planning and succession management, favoring the latter. The chapter offers insight into the succession management concept and how, when thoughtfully implemented, it provides flexibility and sustainability for both the advising program and the overall organization.

Academic advising and student success are inextricably linked (Campbell & Nutt, 2008; Drake, 2008; Karp, 2011), so Part III focuses on recruiting, developing, and retaining the advising team. Cardello explores building the advising team by providing effective practices for recruiting academic advisors. Advising is high-stakes, high-reward work. Training and professional development are the foundation upon which good advising is built. Given the important role that academic advisors play in students' academic success, Higgins, Gorgas, and Peabody advocate for the design and facilitation of learning-centered advisor onboarding and professional development programs. In addition to offering professional development opportunities, effective advising administrators set clear expectations and provide ongoing coaching and support to academic advisors through the shared process of performance management (Yarbrough, Lackey, and Spiers).

Today, advising may be seen by young professionals as a stepping stone to positions with progressively greater responsibilities in program or personnel management. Retaining high-potential, high-achieving advisors is integral to the success of individual advising units and the profession. Administrators may be able to facilitate greater longevity in advising roles by providing academic advisors meaningful opportunities to utilize more complex administrative skill sets within their student-facing roles (Robinson and Dial). Finally, advisors support students with increasingly complex needs, navigate exchanges with students' families or chosen support communities, and serve as intermediaries between several campus populations (leadership, faculty, students, other student support professionals, etc.). All the while, advisors take on secondary exposure to students' individual traumatic experiences including interpersonal violence, suicidal ideation, severe fluctuations in mental well-being, and race-related events. Brock focuses on the unique role advising administrators play in supporting advisor well-being through the challenges of this emotionally fraught work, as well as preventing burnout. Finally, while navigating myriad responsibilities and challenges, the advising administrator is responsible for establishing an environment and culture that provides advisors a psychologically safe space to develop and thrive as individual professionals and as a team. Morris, McKeown, and Dial describe how the advising administrator creates a space where high-potential advisors may become high-performing advisors.

A Few Notes

During the preparation of this book, the world witnessed dramatic changes in social and political landscapes, which in turn have implications and consequences for higher education. In Chapter 1, Grites describes how legislative and local action may lead to changes to laws and policies that directly impact advisors' work. For example, legislative actions at the state and local levels in the United States regarding critical race theory have begun to have implications (and consequences) for curriculum and instruction, at both institutional and individual levels. These actions may in turn impact advising administrators' work regarding equity and inclusion. Also in the United States, recent Supreme Court decisions regarding women's reproductive rights, while yet to be fully understood, may have implications for academic advising, particularly with regard to referring students to resources. All this is to say that advising administrators need to be aware of external (and internal) actions that have potential implications for our work with students.

One of the most important issues we have grappled with while preparing this book related to how much language matters and the significance of the evolving language of inclusivity and equity. The evolution we have witnessed seems to reflect insights gained through awareness and self-reflection. While an increased recognition of the role that language plays in this arena is positive, we know that it still presents a challenge, as many still struggle to find ways to capture the identity and experiences of our diverse world. As chapter drafts were submitted, we noticed that authors relied on many different terms and conventions when referring to underserved, underrepresented, and underacknowledged students (among others). In addition to these terms, other authors used "historically marginalized," "minoritized," and more recently, "new majority learners." We explored these terms with a number of scholars and asked ourselves, as editors, if we should adopt a single term for use throughout this book, even when authors expressed a strong preference and rationale for one over another. In the end, we decided to leave the phrasing of the authors intact, recognizing the ever-evolving nature of language and identity.

As much as we enjoyed putting together the list of topics to be covered in this book, it is safe to say that we enjoyed reading and reviewing the incredible works submitted on those topics far more. In every case, authors applied their expertise and practical experience in ways that have expanded the concepts of the topics, making them more relevant to contemporary academic advising administration. We again thank our advising colleagues for their willingness to share their thoughts, ideas, and content expertise with us and with all of you.

Academic advising administrators perform increasingly important and complex work daily. To those of you doing the work of advising administration and to those who aspire to one day serve in this capacity, we are grateful for you. The work is not always easy, but it is meaningful and has the potential to make a significant difference in the lives of individual students and for future generations of their families. It is likely that most advising administrators are more often presented with challenges and complaints than with appreciation and accolades. Know that your work matters to students, to the advisors in your care, and to the field of academic advising. Thank you for all that you do.

Susan M. Campbell, Calley Stevens Taylor, and Mike Dial

References

Bastedo, M. N., Altbach, P. G., & Gumport, P. J. (Eds.). (2016). *American higher education in the 21st century: Social, political, and economic challenges* (4th ed.). Johns Hopkins University Press.

Bess, J. L., & Dee, J. R. (2012). *Understanding college and university organization: Theories for effective policy and practice* (Vol. 1). Stylus.

Birnbaum, R. (1988). *How colleges work: The cybernetics of academic organization and leadership.* Jossey-Bass.

Campbell, S. M., & Nutt, C. L. (2008). *Academic advising in the new global century: Supporting student engagement and learning outcomes achievement.* Association of American Colleges & Universities.

Drake, J. K. (2008). Recognition and reward for academic advising in theory and in practice. In V. N. Gordon, W. R. Habley, T. J. Grites, & Associates (Eds.), *Academic advising: A comprehensive handbook* (2nd ed.) (pp. 396–412). Jossey Bass.

Karp, M. M. (2011). *How Non-Academic Supports Work: Four Mechanisms for Improving Student Outcomes* (CCRC Brief Number 54). Community College Research Center, Columbia University.

Kezar, A., & Posselt, J. (2020). Introduction: A call to just and equitable administrative practice. In A. Kezar & J. Posselt (Eds.), *Higher education administration for social justice and equity: Critical perspectives for leadership* (pp. 1–18). Routledge.

Kuh, G., Kinzie, J., Schuh, J. H., & Whitt, E. J. (2010). *Student success in college: Creating conditions that matter.* Jossey-Bass.

Light, R. (2001). *Making the most of college: Students speak their minds.* Harvard University Press.

Manning, K. (2018). *Organizational theory in higher education* (2nd ed.). Routledge.

Tinto, V. (1993). *Leaving college: Rethinking the causes and cures of student attrition* (2nd ed.). University of Chicago Press.

Tinto, V. (2012). *Completing college: Rethinking institutional action.* University of Chicago Press.

Troxel, W. G. (2018). Scholarly advising and the scholarship of advising. In W. G. Troxel & J. E. Joslin (Eds.), *New directions for higher education: Academic advising re-examined* (pp. 21–31). Wiley.

PART I

The Advising Administrator in the Context of the Academy

1

THE ADVISING ADMINISTRATOR IN THE CONTEXT OF THE ACADEMY

Thomas J. Grites

The role of an "advising administrator" has grown rapidly and has become more complex in the past five decades (Council for the Advancement of Standards in Higher Education, 2019; Grites & Gordon, 2009; Thurmond & Miller, 2006). Becoming a successful academic advising administrator means understanding various theories, approaches, research methodologies, and academic advising practices and programs. The intended result of such efforts is to confirm academic advising administrators' roles as leaders for achieving the successful programmatic and institutional outcomes of academic advising processes on campuses and, ultimately, student success.

This chapter examines the conditions administrators need to be aware of, including how administrators review and assess the effectiveness of their interrelationships and the possible strategies needed for implementation, modification, or elimination. This review spans the concept of academic advising from its broadest perspective to its day-to-day practice and covers the overall higher education landscape; legislative actions; institutional missions; strategic plans, policies, procedures, and practices that impact the advising process; peer relationships; the academic advising team; and, of course, students. The administrative factors addressed here may not exist at every institution, but they can inform academic advising administrators and serve as a reference for those aspiring to assume such a role.

The Higher Education Landscape

Enrollment declines, college rankings, accreditation reviews, individual student success metrics, and institutional retention and graduation rates

DOI: 10.4324/9781003437598-3

have led to better academic advising across this landscape (Arnold et al., 2019; Bailey et al., 2015; Carrasco, 2022b; Causey et al., 2020; Lederman, 2021; National Student Clearinghouse, 2021a, 2021b; Nietzel, 2021). In this environment, the role of the academic advising administrator has become one of understanding and managing expectations from others, as well as capitalizing on opportunities for themselves and their students. Administrators need to be familiar with the potential resources and applications for meeting expectations and enabling opportunities to capitalize on both.

These include, for example, current higher education literature on the theory, research, and practices related specifically to academic advising and as well as the ability to prepare (or defend) alternatives to the status quo. In short, academic advising administrators must scan the higher education landscape regularly to meet other institutional leaders' expectations while simultaneously identifying opportunities to improve what they already manage for individual students.

External and Internal Influences

Academic advising administrators cannot manage in a vacuum. Everything from state mandates to specific course equivalencies within academic curricula can influence academic advising programs. Below are some examples.

External Influences

Any number of external entities might have the authority to regulate certain aspects of the roles academic advising administrators play. For example, statewide policies regarding transfer credit articulation, course equivalencies, common course numbering, completion pathways, the balance of curricula, and other components, might establish parameters that must be considered in the operational functions of an academic advising program. Similarly, accreditors might have standards or regulations that dictate parts of curricula, and advising administrators are likely to have some oversight responsibility for ensuring that these conditions are met.

The advising administrator also needs to be aware of specific standards imposed by professional associations in areas such as business, nursing, teacher education, and/or social work, because they have certain control over their member institutions' curricula. Additionally, some higher education professional associations advocate for changes that could influence curricula. For example, the recent Joint Statement on the Transfer and Award of Credit (Gottlieb et al., 2021) offers eight "Key Considerations in the Transfer and Award of Credit" that include such factors as: identical standards for all prior learning, the learning modality, or the type of accreditation granted; removing obstacles for students to acquire transcripts; and providing "quality advising" as part of cross-institutional approaches. These associations normally do not have regulatory authority, but the advising administrator must be able to inform others about decisions regarding potential considerations on their campus and articulate the implications for students.

Internal Influences

How many times has one heard or made the following comments: "Our policy states..."; "But our procedure says..."; "We need to ask..."; or "We've always done it that way"? Any of these might be legitimate responses, so academic advising administrators must be comfortable discussing all of them and be able to respond accurately and appropriately to those over which they have some control or influence. Some of the topics they might encounter are described below.

The Faculty and the Curriculum

Lowenstein (2005) asserted that academic advisors teach students the meaning and "logic of the curriculum," (p. 65), thus the advising administrator must have a complete understanding of all academic curricula (i.e., their purpose, rationale, ownership, and control). Advising administrators must ensure that every academic advisor on the campus understands and practices these components. Because faculty members own the curriculum, the administrator may not be able to make curricular decisions such as waivers, substitutions, or course equivalencies; however, administrators must know the processes for such actions so that fair decisions result. After all, it is the curriculum that guides course selection, major selection, career aspirations, and degree or credential attainment—the ultimate criterion that helps define student success.

Other Stakeholders

Wes Habley's "hub" diagram illustrates a template to identify various stakeholders in the advising process (see Figure 1.1; W. Habley, personal communication, June 13, 2021). Including naysayers in planning is also an important aspect of the administrator's role. This visual compilation of components that relate to the academic advising process might suggest forming an academic advising council, developing advising syllabi, considering new protocols, and developing collaborative programs.

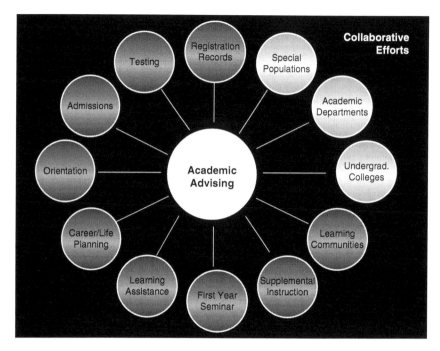

FIGURE 1.1 Habley's Hub Model for Academic Advising.

Note. The Hub Model for Academic Advising was created by Dr. Wes Habley who has granted permission for publication in this volume.

Additional offices or personnel to appear in the hub might include faculty senate, multicultural centers, transfer centers, and institutional research personnel.

The hub illustrates interactions between academic affairs and student affairs units. Though the reporting structure for academic advising administrators will determine the influence on the advising program, the strengths, expertise, and resources from the other units must be acknowledged and integrated.

Student Populations

Perhaps another "hub" with student population types at the center might be created to illustrate the necessary diversity, equity, and inclusion (DEI) dimensions among all student populations. This hub would be a ready visual reminder of the diversity that constitutes the entire student body and the importance of ensuring equity in their academic advising experience.

For example, the term *first-year students* traditionally refers to those entering higher education for the first time. However, transfer students are also first-year students at their new institutions who, in fact, might need even more transitional assistance. Similarly, a hub with student learning outcomes in the center could be used to illustrate the interconnectedness among advisors and other campus resources and programs that could enable these outcomes. For example, *using various technological tools* might be an outcome that is achieved via using degree audits, registration processes, learning management systems, in classrooms, career and job searches, tutoring modules, and others, which are enabled through multiple experiences and interfaces with those shown on the hub.

Political Nuances

Because the overall academic advising process permeates a broad spectrum of campus and off-campus constituencies, most of which will be protective of their respective responsibilities, an inclusive approach is desirable. Labor unions, faculty senates, deans' councils, both academic and student affairs vice presidents, and of course students should all be aware of and included in efforts to generate support for the advising process. For example, an advising administrator may have supervisory responsibilities that engage employees in clerical, custodial, or professional labor unions; similarly, those who work with faculty advisors must remain cognizant of collective bargaining agreements or faculty contract stipulations. The academic advising administrator's success here rests on the integration and collaboration of all potential influences on the advising program, both positive and negative. Of course, the integration of external mandates with those on one's own campus is not always easy, especially given the internal curricular aspects that sometimes appear to conflict with others. For example, one department might inadvertently schedule its required course in conflict with another department's required course; similarly, a sending institution might not be aware that the receiving institution does not offer any degrees that can be fully completed remotely or only at night and on weekends.

Management

It seems that most academic advising programs are under-resourced. Nevertheless, academic advising administrators still have responsibilities for managing, maintaining, and improving all resources that enable successful programs. Some of the most critical ones are discussed below.

Data Management

Advising administrators must master the important skill of data management, meaning they must find appropriate and relevant data and use it correctly. Data-driven decision-making is a reality. Almost every decision made in higher education requires data to substantiate its value, whether that request involves additional personnel; financial or physical space resources; or changes in policies, procedures, or programs.

Assessment Management

NACADA: The Global Community for Academic Advising has long advocated the need for both formative and summative measures when determining the efficiency and the effectiveness of the academic advising program. The primary assessment focus in the past two decades has been to determine the specific intended student learning outcomes and program outcomes that result from the advising process. This is no easy task, however, because there are not enough valid and/or reliable measures to verify anticipated results, especially in the noncognitive areas of student growth and development (see Chapters 9 and 10). However, a good reminder regarding assessment is that "a lack of assessment data can sometimes lead to policies and practices based on intuition, prejudice, preconceived notions, or personal proclivities—none of them desirable bases for making decisions" (Upcraft & Schuh, 2002, p. 20). Unfortunately, these approaches often occur.

Resource Management

Advising administrators manage multiple human, fiscal, and physical resources. The selection, training/professional development, assessment, and recognition of all academic advisors (i.e., human resources) are necessary components of any organization. Where both faculty and primary role advisors are used, these conditions can be difficult to manage equitably, so each aspect must be reviewed and compared periodically for equity and to assess expected results. For example, even the language used to describe the components noted above can be misunderstood; thus, the preference for the term "professional development" for all advisors is recommended. Professional development and evaluation of primary-role advisors is normally the purview of the advising administrator and should include areas beyond the curriculum (e.g., legal, ethical, and social justice issues).

Regarding fiscal resources, budget planning and analysis must use data to justify the need for—and importance of—the costs of improvement plans, their expected outcomes, and an implementation timeline. Similarly, requests for physical resources must have a clear rationale—be it to accommodate multiple people in individual offices, to ensure confidentiality, or to be proximate to other units that interface regularly with the advising office. Such resource requests should be shared with all affected units to facilitate their planning as well.

Integration of Resources

Collaboration with on-campus and external resources offers many opportunities for good academic advising to occur or be reinforced. Orientation, peak registration periods, career development, counseling, special units (e.g., veterans, transfers, tutoring, and disability services), and various professional associations provide such opportunities. Early exposure to college-level academic advising can begin the transition process from high school to college. If these opportunities are overlooked (or even ignored), the perception of academic advising will likely remain akin to that of the high school guidance counselor, because that is the role with which high school students are most familiar. This effort is not to disparage high school counselors, but to help students understand that the role of the higher education academic advisor is quite different, and the college advising process is one in which they will need to assume more personal responsibility.

Similarly, those who enter as transfer students also have the need for a smooth transition process, although they may not realize it immediately. After all, many feel as though they've already "been there, done that." Perhaps not until they realize that their new institution is also a new—and probably different—place, will they be more receptive to academic advising (Grites, 2013). McGill and Lazarowicz (2012) used Schlossberg et al.'s (1995) transition theory to describe the transfer experience as one that can be an "event, or non-event, that results in changed relationships, routines, assumptions, and roles" (Schlossberg et al., 1995, p. 27). Examples of these events include finding their way around campus, understanding new policies, or learning a new academic advising process.

Obviously, peak advising periods present an inordinate demand on advisors and should be reviewed for improved processes, policies, and practices. Those that will accommodate predictable demands more efficiently, while maintaining consistent effectiveness, should always be explored. This kind of effort requires the advising administrator to seek specific needs of the students represented by the various subgroups and offices noted earlier.

Advocacy and Leadership

The terms advocacy and leadership might seem synonymous, but there is a subtle difference between them, depending on the milieu in which the advising administrator functions. Administrators can advocate for any position, person, or issue they choose. The forum in which to do so will probably include offices or individuals with whom the administrator has already established communication channels. These relationships can make the tasks of developing and demonstrating the evidence to make their case easier. Administrators can self-proclaim their advocacy and proceed to engage themselves in their administrative roles as appropriate.

Formal leaders, on the other hand, are usually appointed or elected to leadership positions on committees, task forces, work groups, teams, or various ad hoc projects. Sometimes they can self-appoint, but they are usually selected or nominated by someone else. Academic advising administrators and leaders are probably selected because others have already recognized their leadership skills.

Engagement and Advocacy

Advising administrators must recognize that their advisee caseloads will diminish out of necessity. The trade-off is that the position probably requires many hours outside the office to contribute to other efforts that could affect the overall advising process. Ongoing communication with personnel in related offices can be critical to the success of the entire comprehensive academic advising process, to gain support for changes, and simply to share good will.

An important advocacy role for the advising administrator is to be aware of campus issues that reflect some of the broader issues that permeate higher education in general. All campus administrators need to be aware of, informed about, and engaged in issues that could conceivably have implications for the policies and procedures that academic advisors might be expected to implement. Some examples include test-optional admissions (Hoover, 2021); the alignment of academic programs with multiple sources of transferable credits (Gottlieb et al., 2021); and a resolution for "stranded" transfer credits for transfer students (Carrasco, 2022a; Gottlieb et al., 2021; Karon et al., 2020; Kilgore, 2020; Pingel, 2022).

One factor in the advocacy role is the reality that "you win some and you lose some." The latter result is most difficult when the issue is about a student or a staff member, but one of the many answers to any situation for which the advising administrator is advocating can be "No." The administrator's role must always be to understand the decision and its rationale, and to communicate it clearly and fairly to all parties affected, including personnel, students, parents, colleagues, or faculty members.

Institutional Success Versus Individual Student Success

Academic advising administrators must support both institutional and student success. They must be able to make a clear distinction between them and to communicate the differences to their advisors. This distinction is most evident in the context of retention, persistence, and graduation rates, all significant factors in institutional rankings, performance-based funding, grant proposals, and other awards. These metrics are calculated in the aggregate of student cohorts; thus, they constitute an institutional success measure. Yet they are most frequently referenced as the measures of "student success" or "outcomes."

Individual student success criteria are not captured in aggregated data. However, most academic advisors seek to achieve individual student success on a day-to-day basis, as their advisees articulate goals, ambitions, limitations, and preferences. These differences in the two meanings can create ethical dilemmas for advisors. For example, if a student considers leaving the institution—for whatever reason—how does the advisor respond? The administrator might be asked to help resolve the dilemma of loyalty to institutional success versus loyalty to the student's plans (see Chapter 5 in this volume and Lowenstein & Grites, 1993). Wallace and Wallace (2016) also examined who measures and defines student success and its conditions. They broached the ethical dilemmas that arise through the lens of advisors who ask themselves "Did I do the right thing?" Advisors might face conflicts between their own personal and professional values with any number of individual or institutional successes.

Some recognition of this discrepancy has been acknowledged by The Higher Learning Commission (2018), which asserted that the metrics used to measure student success range from retention, persistence, and graduation rates to a framework of "attainment of learning outcomes, personal satisfaction and goal/intent attainment, job placement and career advancement, civic and life skills, social and economic well-being, and commitment to lifelong learning" (p. 7). Furthermore, Smithers (2020) described this dilemma as one in which the three common metrics of retention, persistence, and graduation "also by definition define student failure," which the "concept of student success includes and exceeds" (pp. 12–13).

Silos and Partnerships

No matter how hard institutions and individuals have tried to eliminate the historic student affairs and academic affairs silos, little evidence substantiates the effectiveness of these efforts. How often is the reference to "the other side of the house" heard or stated? In times of enrollment declines, budget deficits, increasing operational costs, and institutional mergers and closings—amid expectations for improved retention, persistence, and graduation rates and workplace demands for better learning outcomes of graduates—institutions cannot afford to remain siloed. Even within academic affairs, individual academic departments, schools, and colleges sometimes create or modify their curricula with an inadequate awareness of the effects their decisions might have outside of their purview. Academic advising administrators must remain alerted to such changes and effects to avoid unforeseen, unintended, and unmanageable results to administer. Advising administrators can, and should, act as facilitators to bridge this long-standing gap.

Though a variety of administrative partnerships might be established on campus (e.g., with admissions, orientation programs, and academic departments), advising administrators might also become engaged in external partnerships such as articulation agreements. These agreements require communication between institutions, normally two-year and four-year colleges. Agreements range from dual admission, dual credit, or dual degrees of high school students to selective graduate school admissions. The administrator plays a key role in creating, maintaining, and assessing the management and effectiveness of both the internal and external agreements. The most essential aspect of this role is to ensure that all parties involved are kept informed about the most recent versions of these agreements.

Perhaps the most frequently overlooked "partnership" is the student's family. The Family Educational Rights and Privacy Act (FERPA) of 1974 precipitated a student-parent/guardian-to institution communication disconnect, unintentionally, in which academic advisors were forced to participate (USDE, 2021). This law essentially removed the *in loco parentis* role that college and universities had tended to play, and academic advisors adapted to this new standard. However, recent issues such as lack of campus engagement, exclusively online learning, lack of a functional at-home learning environment, and personal financing for higher education that resulted from the COVID-19 pandemic also resulted in increased academic and mental health concerns among college students (Selingo, 2021; Son et al., 2020). Furthermore, Leonhardt (2022) noted multiple negative results from precollege students that suggest these concerns will not soon dissipate. Perlmutter (2021) provided several compelling reasons for more such parental engagement by college administrators. Those who administer academic advising programs are certain to be consulted in many cases involving parents, especially those in course placement and planning, the rationale for certain degree requirements, transfer credit acceptance and applicability, the employment outlook, or even academic dishonesty charges. A return to stricter FERPA adherence may loom ahead.

The examples described above further illustrate the necessity of collaboration between academic affairs and student affairs units, irrespective of the academic advising administrator's reporting line. The curriculum must be maintained, and students must be identified and supported through the admissions processes, orientation programs, counseling interventions, and career education and development services. It is unlikely that all of these units will report to the same leader, so it seems imperative that silos be diminished and partnerships prevail to maximize the academic advising process.

Enrollment Management

The term enrollment management has essentially replaced the term "admissions" to become a significant and critical part of the common higher education vocabulary. Although this process—taken literally—is ongoing from prematriculation through graduation, many higher education administrators have held the myopic view that it applies primarily to the admissions process. However, the full scope of enrollment management regularly occurs via the academic advising process throughout the student's time on campus. Academic advising is the main and most consistent component of this effort. Every term, academic advisors help fill seats (and schedules) and find course alternatives for students. The academic advising administrator must assert the value in this process to make others more aware and supportive of its contribution to the enrollment management concept.

Scholar-Practitioner

Through modeling and supporting others via conference presentations, scholarship contributions (see Chapter 6), and leadership positions on or off campus, the advising administrator is a role model. Other administrators, peers, colleagues, and direct reports all expect administrators to guide them in their own work. Personal active engagement in the areas of professional development, along with the support for others to do the same, enables all advisors to engage in their own literature searches, in sharing their advising experiences and strategies with others outside their own campuses, and in contributing to the broader field of academic advising in general. Such active engagement in the profession provides perfect examples of exactly what we hope to achieve in our students as well: to become informed, engaged professionals in any and all workplace environments.

Final Thoughts

The role of the academic advising administrator is both challenging and critical. Students are always the top priority, but the circumstances under which this standard is maintained are often complicated and unpredictable. Ongoing professional development by and for the administrator is essential to create the optimal environment for a successful academic advising culture.

Student Growth and Development

Ultimately the primary goal of every academic advising unit, advising administrator, and all advising personnel is to strive for the success of each student, however they define it. Through the advising process, students should be able to realize the importance of what they can achieve through a college education, how to manage their choices to do so, and ultimately how to reach and achieve their successes. Some of these successes are not always obvious (e.g., building new friendships, overcoming adversity, and practicing collaborative and leadership skills). Such achievements are manifested in the process of development or growth that is expected to occur via the college experience.

The tasks needed to achieve these goals and to realize this development have become even more complicated. In fact, the institutional success measures mentioned above, namely retention, persistence, and graduation rates, seem to have become even more solidified as the sole metrics for determining student success; thus, the pressure for "good" advising has also become more important in achieving these measures.

This book, therefore, provides an array of theories, research, and practices to guide and support efforts for academic advising administrators to excel in their roles as local, regional, national, and international leaders in this exemplary field within higher education. The areas described in this chapter are merely introductions to and reminders of what academic advising administrators must strive to master within the context and environment of their institutions. Sharing these concepts, issues, and resolutions with peer administrators will serve to advocate for and demonstrate the value of a successful academic advising program on every campus.

Anticipate the Future

It is incumbent upon the academic advising administrator to remain informed about the potential changing policies, regulations, and mandates occurring across the higher education landscape. Other administrators—especially at higher levels—review such conditions regularly, and academic advising administrators need to stay informed of these as well. There is always some likelihood that they will be asked to respond to potential legislative actions, to adapt similar programs or processes, or to create new ones. Some of the recent and predicted future efforts include statewide transfer initiatives, reduced general education requirements, shorter degree timelines, noncollege-based degrees, the absence of admissions testing and remediation, institutional mergers, questions about the value of a degree, and others yet to be identified. For example, The Boyer 2030 Commission Blueprint (Association, 2022) offers 11 provocations for equity/excellence for R1 institutions, including "*holistic* advising that is student-centered and encompasses academic, career, and basic needs guidance" (p. 29) that encompasses "faculty; financial aid specialists; primary-role advisors; student affairs staff members; diversity, equity, inclusion, and justice (DEIJ) professionals; academic coaches; mentors; trained peers; and more" (p. 29). Also, 22 higher education professional associations have recently endorsed a Joint Statement on Importance of Clear, Fair Transcript Withholding Policies (American Council on Education, 2022), which will impact registration and transcript exchanges within and between institutions. Both examples could impact academic advising. It is important to note that NACADA was not involved in these policy discussions, so maintaining diligence about these potential issues for each campus can only assist in the planning aspect for academic advising administrators.

Not all academic advising administrators will encounter every aspect of the process described above, but the awareness and understanding of each could be useful when seeking program improvement, fostering one's own career advancement, expanding perspectives on the scholarship of advising, or simply furthering professional development. Along with regular NACADA publications and events, administrators are critical components of a hypothetical higher education "hub" as they strive to achieve both their student and institutional successes.

Reflection Questions

1 What factors are most critical in determining how long it takes to become an effective academic advising administrator?
2 Is the academic advising administrator considered a leader on campus? Why or why not? Who determines this designation?
3 What does your advising "hub" look like?
4 What are your top five priorities as an academic advising administrator?
5 How do you determine if your oversight responsibilities are too broad to remain effective?
6 How do you motivate your advisors to engage in professional development?

References

American Council on Education. (2022). *Joint statement on importance of clear, fair transcript withholding policies.* https://www.acenet.edu/Documents/2021-Joint-Statement-Award-of-Credit.pdf

Arnold, N., Voight, M., Morales, J., Dancy, K., & Coleman, A. (2019, June). *Informing improvement: Recommendations for enhancing accreditor data-use to promote student success and equity.* Institute for Higher Education Policy and Education Counsel. https://www.ihep.org/publication/informing-improvement-recommendations-for-enhancing-accreditor-data-use-to-promote-student-success-and-equity/

Association for Undergraduate Education at Research Universities. (2022). Fort Collins, CO. https://wac.colostate.edu/docs/books/boyer2030/report.pdf

Bailey, T., Jaggars, S. S., & Jenkins, D. (2015). *What we know about guided pathways*. Community College Research Center, Teachers College, Columbia University.https://ccrc.tc.columbia.edu/publications/what-we-know-about-guided-pathways-packet.html

Carrasco, M. (2022a, January 3). *A new plan to save stranded credits*. Inside Higher Ed. https://www.insidehighered.com/news/2022/01/03/pilot-will-settle-student-debt-and-release-stranded-credits

Carrasco, M. (2022b, January 7). *Fewer high school graduates go straight to college*. Inside Higher Ed. https://www.insidehighered.com/news/2022/01/07/fewer-high-school-graduates-enroll-college?utm_source=Inside+Higher+Ed&utm_campaign=39467653b5-DNU_2021_COPY_02&utm_medium=email&utm_term=0_1fcbc04421-39467653b5-197728941&mc_cid=39467653b5&mc_eid=58532d8913

Causey, J., Huie, F., Lang, R., Ryu, M., & Shapiro, D. (2020, December). *Completing college 2020: A national view of student completion rates for 2014 entering cohort (Signature Report 19)*. National Student Clearinghouse Research Center. https://eric.ed.gov/?id=ED609975" https://eric.ed.gov/?id=ED609975

Council for the Advancement of Standards in Higher Education for Academic Advising Programs. (2019). https://nacada.ksu.edu/Resources/Pillars/CASstandards.aspx

Gottlieb, M., Mitchell, T., & Jackson-Hammond, C. (2021). *Joint statement on the transfer and award of credit*. American Association of Collegiate Registrars and Admissions Officers, American Council on Education, and Council for Higher Education Accreditation. https://www.acenet.edu/Documents/2021-Joint-Statement-Award-of-Credit.pdf

Grites, T. J. (2013) Successful transitions from two-year to four-year institutions. *New Directions for Higher Education, 2013*(162), 61–68.

Grites, T. J., & Gordon, V. N. (2009). The history of NACADA: An amazing journey. *NACADA Journal, 29*(2), 41–55. https://doi.org/10.12930/0271-9517-29.2.41

Higher Learning Commission. (2018). *Defining student success data: Recommendations for changing the conversation*. https://download.hlcommission.org/initiatives/StudentSuccessConversation.pdf

Hoover, E. (2021, December 17). Extension of Harvard's test-optional policy fires "a shot across the bow" of higher ed. *The Chronicle of Higher Education*. https://www.chronicle.com/article/extension-of-harvards-test-optional-policy-fires-a-shot-across-the-bow-of-higher-ed?utm_source=Iterable&utm_medium=email&utm_campaign=campaign_3462122_nl_Academe-Today_date_20220103&cid=at&source=ams&sourceid=https://www.chronicle.com/article/extension-of-harvards-test-optional-policy-fires-a-shot-across-the-bow-of-higher-ed?utm_source=Iterable&utm_medium=email&utm_campaign=campaign_3462122_nl_Academe-Today_date_20220103&cid=at&source=ams&sourceid=

Karon, J., Ward, J. D., Hill, C. B., & Kurzweil, M. (2020, October 5). *Solving stranded credits: Assessing the scope and effects of transcript withholding on students, states, and institutions*. Ithaka S+R. https://sr.ithaka.org/publications/solving-stranded-credits/

Kilgore, W. (2020, August). *Stranded credits: Another perspective on the lost credits story*. American Association of Collegiate Registrars and Admissions Officers. https://www.aacrao.org/docs/default-source/research-docs/aacrao-stranded-credits-report-2020.pdf

Lederman, D. (2021, August 30). *An accreditor goes deeper on data*. Inside Higher Ed. https://www.insidehighered.com/news/2021/08/30/accrediting-agency-enables-closer-look-data-college-performance

Leonhardt, D. (2022, January 4). No way to grow up. *The New York Times*. https://www.nytimes.com/2022/01/04/briefing/american-children-crisis-pandemic.html

Lowenstein, M. (2005). If advising is teaching, what do advisors teach? *NACADA Journal, 25*(2), 65–73. https://doi.org/10.12930/0271-9517-25.2.65

Lowenstein, M., & Grites, T. J. (1993). Ethics in academic advising. *NACADA Journal, 13*(1), 53–61. https://doi.org/10.12930/0271-9517-13.1.53

McGill, C. M., & Lazarowicz, T. (2012). Advising transfer students: Implications of Schlossberg's transition theory. In T. J. Grites & C. Duncan (Eds.), *Advising transfer students: Strategies for today's realities and tomorrow's challenges* (pp. 131–133). NACADA: The Global Community for Academic Advising.

National Student Clearinghouse Research Center. (Spring 2021a). Overview: Spring 2021 Enrollment Estimates. https://nscresearchcenter.org/current-term-enrollment-estimates/

National Student Clearinghouse Research Center. (2021b, December 1). *High school benchmarks*. National Student Clearinghouse Research Center.

Nietzel, M. T. (2021, November 18). Updated figures show college enrollments falling further behind last year. *Forbes*. https://www.forbes.com/sites/michaeltnietzel/2021/11/18/updated-figures-show-college-enrollment-falling-further-behind-last-year/?sh=6c969121447d

Perlmutter, D. D. (2021, December 28). Admin 101: Why you should meet the parents. *The Chronicle of Higher Education*. https://www.chronicle.com/article/admin-101-why-you-should-meet-the-parents

Pingel, S. (2022, July 7). Lost and found: State and institutional actions to resolve stranded credits. Ithaka S+R. https://doi.org/10.18665/sr.316883

Schlossberg, N. K., Waters, E. B., & Goodman, J. (1995). *Counseling adults in transition: Linking practice with theory* (2nd ed.). Springer.

Selingo, J. (2021). *The new landscape for student well-being*. Vector Solutions. https://www.vectorsolutions.com/resources/whitepapers-guides/the-new-landscape-for-student-well-being/

Smithers, L. E. (2020). Every optimization is a policy failure: The catch (and release) of student success. *About Campus, 25*(5), 11–18. https://doi.org/10.1177/1086482220961129

Son, C., Hegde, S., Smith, A., Wang, X., & Sasangohar, F. (2020). Effects of COVID-19 on college students' mental health in the United States: Interview survey study. *Journal of Medical Internet Research, 22*(9), 1–14. https://doi.org/10.2196/21279

Thurmond, K. C., & Miller, M. A. (2006). The history of National Academic Advising Association: A 2006 update. *NACADA Clearinghouse*. http://www.nacada.ksu.edu/Resources/Clearinghouse/View-Articles/History-of-NACADA.aspx

Upcraft, M. L., & Schuh, J. H. (2002). Assessment vs. research: Why we should care about the difference. *About Campus, 7*(1), 16–20. https://doi.org/10.1177/108648220200700104

U.S. Department of Education. (2021). *Family Educational Rights and Privacy Act (FERPA)*. https://www2.ed.gov/policy/gen/guid/fpco/ferpa/index.html

Wallace, S. O., & Wallace, B. A. (2016). Defining student success. In T. J. Grites, M. A. Miller, & J. Givans Voller (Eds.), *Beyond foundations: Developing as a master academic advisor* (pp. 83–106). Jossey-Bass.

2

THE ACADEMIC ADVISING ADMINISTRATOR AS INTEGRATED PRACTITIONER

Emily McIntosh and Susan M. Campbell

Higher education organizations are complex; as academic advising administrators, we must appreciate and navigate within this environment (Bess & Dee, 2012; Birnbaum, 1988; Manning, 2018). The roles, responsibilities, and relationships to institutional decision-making and academic leadership often vary by institution. While expertise in academic advising is critical, navigating the complex environment of higher education to meet institutional goals can become challenging. In this regard, it may not be unusual for academic advising administrators—as representatives of the institution and linchpins between students and the curriculum—to feel caught or stuck between administration, academic departments, and students. In these instances, we may feel like organizational interlopers with managerial skills and content credentials, but without a firm footing in either administration or the academic work of the institution. Whitchurch (2013) legitimized the duality of this interloper role in her concept of the "Third Space" (p. 21). The work of academic advising administrators as "third space professionals" (Whitchurch & Gordon, 2017, p. 22) requires developing collaborative relationships with other academic departments, divisions, and faculty members. While sometimes feeling uneasy, this boundary crossing is necessary for advising administrators to support student learning success effectively. In reality, this unique, boundary crossing role helps situate academic advising administration within the institution and frame the administrator's professional identity.

This chapter examines the complexity and uniqueness of higher education as an organization and culture. As Veles and Carter (2016) suggested, "understanding the university's academic climate and academic culture is

DOI: 10.4324/9781003437598-4

paramount to understanding its core values, beliefs and strategic intent" (p. 522). We then consider and situate the role and identity of academic advising administrators as "integrated practitioners" and "third space professionals" (McIntosh & Nutt, 2022, p. 12) within the academy. What organizational perspectives contribute to our understanding of colleges and universities? What navigational lessons can be learned? How can we use these perspectives to help us understand and construct institutional roles and professional identities to advance academic advising administration and support students through effective academic advising?

The Complexity of Higher Education Organizations

While all organizations might lay claim to being "messy" or "complex," higher education is notable for being messy *and* complex. Colleges and universities have been described as organized anarchies with vague goals, unclear technology, and fluid participation (Birnbaum, 1988; Cohen & Marsh, 1986; Manning, 2018). Further, goals may differ by organizational position.

> What is a college? An educator might respond that a college is an institution offering comparatively advanced instruction leading to a degree. An administrator might answer that a college is an organization consisting of people in certain roles whose authority, responsibilities, and relationships are defined by legal documents, job descriptions, and organizational charts. A policy maker might look at a college as a goal-directed organization that serves a number of important societal functions, such as training...encouraging scientific development, or providing for social mobility.
>
> *(Birnbaum, 1988, xiii–xiv)*

Birnbaum's comments highlighted differences in the expectations and roles of organizational stakeholders that reveal the complexity of higher education, the professional expertise required to deliver instruction in the academy, and the tension that sometimes results from the complex collaboration that exists among stakeholders (Veles et al., 2019). This tension is typically most evident between those responsible for institutional direction—administrators—and those pursuing individual professional goals and achievements—faculty members.

Like most organizations, colleges and universities have administrative hierarchies and specified positions with responsibility for institutional direction, authority, and accountability for goal achievement. However, *unlike* other organizations, the responsibility and control of the organization's product content and process (i.e., curriculum and instruction) rests not with administrators but with the faculty members for whom institutional rewards, such as promotion and tenure, are inextricably intertwined with individual participation in discipline-based activities and external associations (Bess & Dee, 2012, 2014; Birnbaum 1988; Manning, 2018). In this regard, it makes sense that the personal and professional priorities for those responsible for curriculum and instruction may not always be the same for those in administration and vice versa.

What does this mean for the academic advising administrator, whose position is that of an administrative professional staff member—even if also holding faculty status—and whose role, regardless of span of control, is to advance institutional goals? What does this mean for a role and position that, in addition to management, leadership, and advocacy skills, requires expertise and professional engagement as a scholar-practitioner? Where does the advising administrator fit within the organization? There is much to unpack in these questions; therefore, developing an understanding about the complexity of higher education organizations is a good place to start. To begin, we draw from Birnbaum (1988) and Manning (2018) and their models of organizational functioning in higher education.

In his classic piece *How Colleges Work*, Birnbaum (1988) posited four models of organizational functioning in higher education: collegial, bureaucratic, political, and anarchical. Manning (2018) updated and expanded Birnbaum's work in *Organizational Theory in Higher Education*, adding the postmodern perspectives of feminist and gendered theories (including Queer Theory), Institutional theory, and Spiritual theory. Arguably, these models exist to some degree in all higher education organizations. However, the two most prominent, most visible, and most often directly experienced by academic advising administrators are the bureaucratic and collegial models. The underlying concepts in these perspectives help clarify the complexity of colleges and universities and illuminate the position, roles, and lived experience of the academic advising administrator as leader, manager, scholar, and institutional navigator.

Bureaucratic (and Managerial) Perspectives on Higher Education

Birnbaum (1988) defined the term "bureaucracy" in a descriptive and analytic way as, "The type of organization designed to accomplish large-scale administrative tasks by systematically coordinating the work of many individuals" (Birnbaum, 1988, p. 107). By this definition, colleges and universities are essentially social organizations with the work of the administrator involved with understanding and managing people toward achievement of institutional goals. The theoretical works of Weber (Gerth & Mills, 1948),

McGregor (1985), Roethlisberger and Dickson (2018), and Taylor (1967) serve here as a briefer course in organizational theory, each capturing unique organizational elements that advance our understanding of organizations and administrative work.

The concepts of rationality, impartiality, and objectivity serve as the foundation for bureaucracy, a perspective on organizations attributed to Max Weber (Gerth & Mills, 1948). For Weber (Gerth & Mills, 1948), the patriarchal system, prevalent at his time and dependent on the personal relationships and characteristics of those in control, was not a sustainable model. Today, evidence of Weber's perspective (e.g., functions, roles, authority, processes, and policies) continues to be visible in organizational charts and job descriptions. Frederick Taylor (1967) added to an understanding of organizational work in *The Principles of Scientific Management*, which addressed optimization of productivity through matching task skills with the skills of the person performing those tasks.

The idea of the organization as a social system began to emerge with the work of Roethlisberger and Dickson (2018). Originally conducted between 1924 and 1932, their studies revealed the importance of social relationships to worker motivation and productivity, adding new directions for organizational understanding, research, and the role of the administrator/manager. Finally, McGregor (1985) introduced perspectives on human nature as those related to work and productivity. McGregor's work shifted the focus from the match between work tasks and the skills of the worker to understanding the impact of manager-held human behavior assumptions regarding worker motivation, productivity, and support.

The bureaucratic and managerial aspects of higher education are simple facts of the administrator's life and provide a framework through which to organize our work and the work of others. Organizational theories that focus on structure analyze functions, positions, and authority to better align these with organizational needs (Bolman & Deal, 2017). Theories that inform us about the nature of organizations as social systems remind us, as Bolman and Deal (2017) suggested, that the needs of the organization and the needs of individuals are not mutually exclusive. These scholars argued that the savvy administrator could align strategy with action by asking questions that distinguish between structural and human behavior and relationship concerns.

Most advising administrators would agree that coordinating the work of individuals toward goal achievement is much easier when reporting relationships are direct and tightly coupled (i.e., the administrator has both authority and supervisory responsibility for the individuals doing the work). However, the advising administrator's authority seldom directly extends to include those responsible for curriculum and instruction.

The challenge is to determine how best to negotiate an effective bureaucratic or managerial role in an environment where the primary elements of the product (curriculum and instruction) are held by others (faculty members). Birnbaum's (1988) collegial perspective offered insight into the deep-seated, seemingly impermeable traditions of the academy, with which, ironically, academic advising administrators—even those without faculty status—have much in common.

Collegial Perspectives on Higher Education

While many regard bureaucracy as the earliest consideration of organizations, in fact, the earliest was the collegial perspective which means "colleges and universities have one of the longest lasting organizational structures in the world" (Manning, 2018, p. 37). Institutions of the Middle Ages presented the first evidence of "the uneasy coexistence of bureaucratic and collegial structures" (Manning, 2018, p. 37). This uneasy coexistence can best be appreciated by understanding the dimensions of organizational culture.

Edgar Schein (1985) defined culture as:
A pattern of basic assumptions—invented, discovered, or developed by a given group as it learns to cope with its problems of external adaptation and internal integration—that has worked well enough to be considered valid and, therefore, to be taught to new members as the correct way to perceive, think, and feel in relation to those problems.

(p. 9)

An important addition to this definition speaks to how these basic assumptions become unconscious behavioral guideposts and boundaries and "come to be taken for granted….and eventually drop out of awareness" (Schein & Schein, 2017, p. 6). Schein's work offered new insight into the process of organizational socialization and advanced inquiry into the study of culture in organizations, including higher education.

Kuh and Whitt (1988) were among the first to explore culture in colleges and universities. They addressed institutional culture and perspectives on institutional life, including discussions of the subcultures of faculty members, students, and administrators. These scholars summarized faculty subculture concepts and symbols noted by others, and their list reflected a set of values typically ascribed to the faculty culture.

The culture of the academic profession is based on the concepts and symbols of academic freedom, the community of scholars, scrutiny of accepted wisdom, truth seeking, collegial governance, individual autonomy, and service to society through the production of knowledge, the transmission of culture, and education of the young.

(Kuh & Whitt, 1988, p. 76)

Recently, Bergquist and Pawlak (2008) added that in higher education, culture "plays a major role in defining patterns of perceiving, thinking, and feeling about the nature and scope of education. A culture helps identify reactions to things that are important to people living and working in that culture" (p. ix).

The bureaucratic perspective is included in one of Bergquist and Pawlak's (2008) six cultures. The uneasiness that had been noted between the bureaucratic and collegial cultures was essentially accounted for by cultural differences, particularly regarding values and shared meaning (Bergquist & Pawlak, 2008). Shared values for the collegial culture include those related to academic disciplines, research, and scholarship (Bergquist & Pawlak, 2008) whereas for the bureaucracy or managerial culture, "the values are directed toward goals and measurement, organization, implementation, evaluation of work, fiscal responsibility, and effective supervision" (Bergquist & Pawlak, 2008, p. 43). While inherent tension exists between the bureaucracy and collegium, the roles are also generally viewed as complementary:

The faculty are generally responsible for the production of outputs that allow the organization to fulfill its missions.... Faculty perform specialized research and teaching roles.... Administrators, on the other hand, usually play important supportive roles.... They are responsible for providing services that assure that faculty, students, and staff members can perform their roles efficiently and effectively.

(Bess & Dee, 2014, p. 10)

What does this mean for the advising administrator who depends on engagement and collaboration with academic departments and individual faculty members in the design and delivery of academic advising? The tension between the bureaucracy and the collegium reflects a conflict between the competing priorities experienced by organizational stakeholders. Without a direct line of authority over the curriculum, the advising administrator must develop relationship tools to establish the collaborative relationships necessary to support the student academic advising experience.

Bergquist and Pawlak (2008) viewed the academy as a complex social system of multiple cultures. In their view, administrators should appreciate and engage with the cultures that exist and "determine how to work with and use the strengths and resources of the existing organizational culture to accomplish our goals" (p. x). We agree. First and foremost, as academic advising administrators, we need to understand the complexity of the organization in which we work. We need to understand ourselves as professionals in unique positions who must cross the cultural boundaries of the academy. These socially constructed boundaries are often immutable and impermeable, especially to those without formal academic appointments or formal recognition as scholars. This takes us to the *third space*, where we legitimize and position the role and professional identity of the academic advising administrator as *integrated practitioner*.

The Third Space, Third Space Professionals, and Integrated Practitioners

Whitchurch (2009) introduced and described the third space as "new *spaces* at the interface between academic and professional activity" (McIntosh & Nutt, 2022, p. 1) and "highlighted the role of *blended and unbounded professionals*, which spans both academic and professional domains" (McIntosh & Nutt, 2022, p. 1). We argue that the professional practice of the advising administrator can be positioned firmly within the domain of Whitchurch's (2008a) third space professionals. The advising administrator embodies the tenets of integrated practice, which are required of those working in third spaces in the academy (McIntosh & Nutt, 2022). The hallmarks of advising administration include advocating for students; negotiating relationships; working across recognized institutional structures, boundaries, and systems; and applying administrative and academic knowledge as well as scholarly approaches in their day-to-day work. This holds true in both U.S. and international advising settings.

The third space is inherently fluid and flexible. Professional identities, practices, and power dynamics are consistently debated and challenged. It is a paradigmatic space that "spans the notions of 'hybridity,' 'cultural politics,' and the concept of 'liminal spaces'" (McIntosh & Nutt, 2022, p. 2). The third space is fluid and ever-changing, continually being redefined and renegotiated.

The activities of the academic advising administrator align with and serve to establish the advising administrator as an integrated practitioner, whose role impacts students and the academy. Like other third space professionals, the career path to academic advising administration is not linear. Those in these administrative positions may have always been part of the professional, administrative staff of an institution or may, in addition to serving in an administrative capacity, also hold academic positions and faculty rank.

We further consider the positionality of academic advising administrators as leaders in their field and as advocates for student learning and success. We address the ambiguity of their positions as administrators who must effectively navigate both the academic and bureaucratic cultures of the academy and the challenges they face to establish advising as significant and scholarly. Collaboration between academic and professional departments and the embedding of best practices are key objectives of effective advising administration. However, transcending the barriers inherent in the siloed structure of the academy requires extraordinary personal qualities (McVitty, 2021) and impacts the roles and identities of advising administrators, many of whom often find themselves negotiating their sense of belonging and fit in academic and administrative spaces.

A Conceptual Framing of Academic Advising Administration in the Third Space

In exploring third space professionalism, Whitchurch (2009) introduced a conceptual framing of blended professionals (see Table 2.1). Her framework described the spaces that third space professionals occupy; the knowledges that they have and create; the relationships that they nurture; and the legitimacies they hold. For each category, Whitchurch considered the alignment between "Dimensions of Professional Activity," "Identity Dispositions of Blended Professionals," and "Theoretical Frames" or theory. The Theoretical Frames column notes additional sources Whitchurch used to inform her work. Whitchurch's framework outlined how positionality and identity in the advising space might influence and inform the enactment of the role in higher education organizations.

The Spaces We Occupy

Whitchurch (2009) explored the spaces occupied by third space professionals between academic and professional domains. She noted that these blended professionals can (a) "offer multiple understandings of the institution," (b) "accommodate the ambiguities of *third space* between professional and academic domains," (c) "re-define [and] modify professional space and boundaries," and (d) "work round formal structures" (p. 410). Drawing on Giddens (1991), Whitchurch (2009) reflected on identity as being "an individual's interpretation of their positioning in relation to others, rather than a fixed or core sense of belonging" (p. 410). She also noted that this activity involves navigating complicated conditions with multiple dimensions. In short, it takes a particularly skilled and insightful individual to work effectively in this way.

TABLE 2.1 Whitchurch's Conceptual Framing of Blended Professionals

Dimensions of Professional Activity	Identity Dispositions of Blended Professionals	Theoretical Frames
	An ability to:	Reflect:
Spaces	Offer multiple understandings of the institution	Idea of identity as a "project," involving an individual's interpretation of their positioning in relations to others, rather than a fixed core or sense of belonging (Giddens, 1992)
	Accommodate the ambiguities of third space between professional and academic domains	
	Redefine, modify professional space and boundaries	
	Work round formal structures	"supercomplex" conditions with multiple dimensions (Barnett, 2000)
Knowledges	Embed and integrate professional and academic knowledge	"weak boundaries" in relation to professional knowledges (Bernstein, 1970)
	Undertake research into institutional activity	
	Create an interactive knowledge environment	"relaxed" frames of reference (Bernstein, 1970)
		"elite" forms of professional who apply their expertise to complex individual tasks (Friedson, 2001)
Relationships	Enter and understand academic discourse/debate	"strong ties" to own internal networks (Granovetter, 1973)
	Form alliances with key partners	
	Facilitate autonomy of own staff	"weak ties" to external networks (Granovetter, 1973)
	Construct professional networks, internally and externally	
	Offer academic credentials	"communicative action", establishing "common definitions" oriented to "coming to an understanding with [others]", as opposed to "exerting an influence *upon others*" (Habermas, 1984).
Legitimacies	Achieve credibility in academic debate/space	
	Challenge the status quo	
	Manage the duality of "belonging" and "not belonging" to academic space	

Source: Whitchurch (2009). Reprinted with permission.

Academic advising administration typifies this spatial activity—working across both academic and professional domains, advocating on behalf of students, and negotiating relationships. As a result, the advising administrator must be comfortable with uncertainty and the ambiguities associated with the multiple and competing structures and cultures within the academy. Administrative practice modifies and redefines professional spaces and boundaries, especially in the creation of new knowledges (discussed below) as well as the leadership and advocacy of advising. This type of role modeling and leadership has sought to establish advising as a scholarly, informed activity, with the academic advising administrator becoming, in our words, the *scholar in chief*. In the United States, a "new professional class" (Pistilli & Gardner, 2022, p. 40) associated with discourses and concepts of social justice and student success has recently emerged. Advising is arguably part of this new professional class, where a new sense of belonging and identity for advising has been established, aligned with Giddens' (1999) work. Like other professionals in this new class, we certainly are impacted by the sense of "permanent oscillation and fluidity within and between enunciatory sites, physical locations, political positionings, effecting a web of interconnected conditions of possibility" (Routledge, 1996, p. 412).

The Knowledges We Have and Create

The second component of Whitchurch's (2009) framework considered the knowledges—amassed and created—by blended professionals. She posited that a key part of this role is to embed and integrate professional and academic knowledges (see Table 2.1). We argue that this integration is only achieved by those working collaboratively and across recognized boundaries to curate and consider the whole-student experience. A large part of this work is about fusing and melding knowledge from different areas, hence the focus on knowledges in the plural. Whitchurch stressed the importance of research to gaining and creating knowledge and situated scholarly activity as a fundamental part of integrated practice, thereby establishing the advising administrator as scholar in chief. Academic advisors are not the only higher education administrators to occupy third space roles; however, they are uniquely positioned to make the most of working in this space given that their experience and expertise is invariably academic-related and highly pedagogic in nature. As a result, building a strong and scholarly evidence base for academic advising helps to improve the reputation of advising as fundamental to pedagogic practice.

Fusing knowledges created and amassed through the advising process with known pedagogical practices and theories will inevitably strengthen the scholarly approach (McIntosh et al., 2020). In her framework, Whitchurch (2009) also suggested that blended professionals create an interactive knowledge environment; the advising administrator is a catalyst for advising knowledges and scholarly activity.

The Relationships We Nurture

The third component of Whitchurch's framework considers relationships nurtured between third space professionals and others both within and outside their organization. For example, Smith et al. (2021) noted that integrated practitioners have a fragile form of social capital—their identities are inextricably intertwined within the quality and status of the relationships they have with others across their organizational spheres. Here, Smith et al. focused on the importance of working with courage and determination to build these relationships and develop communities. Wenger (1998) referred to these communities as communities of practice where colleagues work in a thematic way, exploring mutual interests and needs. This is critically important for advising administrators who must reconcile internal needs, perspectives, and relationships with those who exist externally in broader academic advising networks such as NACADA. In developing relationships, Smith et al. (2021) pointed out the crucial role of advocacy. We argue that advocacy extends to advocating for ourselves, other advisors, and our students.

Whitchurch (2009) similarly noted that entering and understanding academic discourse and debate were critical activities for blended professionals, as were forming alliances with key partners and constructing professional networks. Indeed, these are the hallmarks of communities of practice, where advising spaces and relationships exist in a complex way across organizations, are fostered, and are nurtured. In this way, advising administrators in the third space must negotiate communities of practice as part of the conditions of their role. Advising administrators are champions for collaboration working within complex environments (Veles et al., 2019).

The Legitimacies We Hold

The final component of Whitchurch's (2009) framework considers the legitimacies of blended professionals in the third space. According to Whitchurch, blended professionals must have academic credentials and achieve academic credibility. Again, a nod to scholarly informed approaches is critical here, as the identity and legitimacy of integrated practice depends on active and engaged participation in various communities. Whitchurch (2009) posited that blended professionals must challenge the status quo and manage the conflicting "duality of 'belonging' and 'not belonging'" (p. 410) to academic spaces (see Table 2.1). When applied to the insights offered by Smith et al., there are some interesting tensions here which academic advising administrators often navigate in their practice. To understand this from a theoretical stance, Whitchurch (2008b) drew on the work of Habermas (1984) to focus on "communicative action" (Whitchurch, 2008b, p. 381) and "coming to an understanding with [others]" (Whitchurch, 2008b, p. 382) rather than imposing or exerting a viewpoint or influence upon them (see Table 2.1). Academic advising administrators frequently find themselves between or in and out of previously and historically defined spaces in the academy. Their career trajectories are often impacted by this, as queries around good fit and a sense of where administration belongs in the academy are often questioned.

Conclusion

This chapter began by reflecting on the usefulness of theory and the blurring of academic and professional boundaries. Theory has both organizational and personal applications. As academic advisors, we use theory to inform the philosophy that guides our individual work with students. Theory takes on new dimensions and directions for administrators as we navigate both within and beyond our boundaries and within an organizational landscape that is complex and increasingly global, yet unified by a commitment to and a belief in the purposes of the academy.

To understand the academy, we turned to Birnbaum (1988) and Manning (2018). Understanding the bureaucratic and collegial aspects of higher education organizations is important because these serve as the foundation upon which to construct a role and professional identity respectful of skills and content expertise. In fact, we recommend a broader consideration of organizational theory because no single organizational theory or perspective considers—or solves—every organizational concern. As Manning (2018) noted, new perspectives are needed given the current state of educational environments and globalization:

> Because of the rapid pace of change, including seismic changes occurring in countries such as China and India and regions such as the European Higher Education Area, new perspectives are warranted on the older theories about how colleges work.
>
> *(Manning, 2018, p. xiii)*

We advance the role of academic advising administrators as integrated practitioners with the knowledge and skills to navigate the third space between the academic and professional domains of colleges and universities. We posit that the role and function of the advising administrator does not fit neatly within the siloed boundaries in higher education organizations. In fact, the role requires fluidity and flexibility to accomplish divisional, departmental, and organizational goals. It requires crossing the boundaries of academic culture and partnering to support student success along with institutional milestones. As academic partners and third space professionals, advising administrators "need to develop a diverse range of skills" (Veles & Carter, 2016, p. 528). The third space, while not acknowledged as an organizational reality, is a *lived space* that demands further exploration, research, and scholarship, all within the context of a diversified academic workforce.

Reflection Questions

1 What spaces do you occupy as an advising administrator?
2 What are the key relationships between advising administrators across the organization? Can those be successfully established?
3 What unique and specialist academic and professional knowledges do we embed and integrate into our roles?
4 How do academic advising administrators manage the conflicting duality of belonging and not belonging to academic spaces?

References

Bergquist, W. H., & Pawlak, K. (2008). *Engaging the six cultures of the academy* (2nd ed.). Jossey-Bass.

Bess, J. L., & Dee, J. R. (2012). *Understanding college and university organization: Theories for effective policy and practice* (Vol. 1). Stylus.

Bess, J. L., & Dee, J. R. (2014). *Bridging the divide between faculty and administration: A guide to understanding conflict in the academy*. Routledge.

Birnbaum, R. (1988). *How colleges work: The cybernetics of academic organization and leadership*. Jossey-Bass.

Bolman, L. G., & Deal, T. E. (2017). *Reframing organizations: Artistry, choice, and leadership* (6th ed.). Jossey-Bass.

Cohen, M. D., & Marsh, J. G. (1986). *Leadership and ambiguity* (2nd ed.). Harvard Business School Press.

Gerth, H. H., & Mills, C. W. (Eds.). (1948). *From Max Weber: Essays in sociology*. Oxford University Press.

Giddens, A. (1991). *Modernity and self-identity: Self and society in the late modern age*. Stanford University Press.

Giddens, A. (1999). *The third way: The renewal of social democracy*. Polity.

Habermas, J. (1984). *The theory of communicative action: Reason and the rationalization of society*. Beacon Press.

Kuh, G. D., & Whitt, E. J. (1988). *The invisible tapestry: Culture in American colleges and universities*. Jossey-Bass.

Manning, K. (2018). *Organizational theory in higher education* (2nd ed.). Routledge.

McGregor, D. (1985). *The human side of enterprise: 25th anniversary printing*. McGraw-Hill.

McIntosh, E., & Nutt, D. (Eds.). (2022). *The impact of the integrated practitioner in higher education: Studies in third space professionalism*. Routledge. http://doi.org/10.4324/9781003037569

McIntosh, E., Steele, G., & Grey, D. (2020). Academic tutors/advisors and students working in partnership: Negotiating and co-creating in "the third space." *Frontiers in Education*. http://doi.org/10.3389/feduc.2020.528683

McVitty, D. (2021, March 30). Book review: The new power university by Jonathan Grant. *WONKHE*. https://wonkhe.com/blogs/book-review-the-new-power-university-by-jonathan-grant/

Pistilli, M. D., & Gardner, J. N. (2022). The emergence of the newest "professional class" in US higher education. In E. McIntosh & D. Nutt (Eds.), *The impact of the integrated practitioner in higher education: Studies in third space professionalism* (pp. 40–49). Routledge. http://doi.org/10.4324/9781003037569-6

Roethlisberger, F. J., & Dickson, W. J. (2018). *Management and the worker: An account of a research program conducted by the Western Electric Company, Hawthorne Works, Chicago*. (Reprint ed.). Forgotten Books.

Routledge, P. (1996). The third space as critical engagement. *Antipode, 28*(4), 399–419. https://doi.org/10.1111/j.1467-8330.1996.tb00533.x

Schein, E. H. (1985). *Organizational culture and leadership*. Wiley.

Schein, E. H., & Schein, P. A. (2017). *Organizational culture and leadership* (5th ed.). Wiley.

Smith, C., Holden, M., Yu, E., & Hanlon, P. (2021). 'So what do you do?': Third space professionals navigating a Canadian university context. *Journal of Higher Education Policy and Management, 43*(5), 505–519. https://doi.org/10.1080/1360080X.2021.1884513

Taylor, F. W. (1967). *The principles of scientific management*. W.W. Norton & Company.

Veles, N., & Carter, M.-A. (2016). Imagining a future: Changing the landscape for third space professionals in Australian higher education institutions. *Journal of Higher Education Policy and Management, 38*(5), 519–533. https://doi.org/10.1080/1360080X.2016.1196938

Veles, N., Carter, M. A., & Boon, H. (2019). Complex collaboration champions: University *third space professionals* working together across borders. *Perspectives: Policy and Practice in Higher Education, 23*(2–3), 75–85. https://doi.org/10.1080/13603108.2018.1428694

Wenger, E. (1998). *Communities of practice: Learning, meaning, and identity*. Cambridge University Press.

Whitchurch, C. (2008a). Shifting identities and blurring boundaries: The emergence of third space professionals in UK higher education. *Higher Education Quarterly, 62*(4), 377–396. https://doi.org/10.1111/j.1468-2273.2008.00387.x

Whitchurch, C. (2008b). Beyond administration and management: Reconstructing the identities of professional staff in UK higher education. *Journal of Higher Education Policy and Management, 30*(4), 375–386. https://doi.org/10.1080/13600800802383042

Whitchurch, C. (2009). The rise of the *blended professional* in higher education: A comparison between the United Kingdom, Australia and the United States. *Higher Education, 58*(3), 407–418. https://doi.org/10.1007/s10734-009-9202-4

Whitchurch, C. (2010). Convergence and divergence in professional identities. In G. Gordon & C. Whitchurch, (Eds.), *Academic and professional identities in higher education: The challenges of a diversifying workforce* (pp. 167–184). Routledge. https://doi.org/10.4324/9780203865255

Whitchurch, C. (2013). *Reconstructing identities in higher education: The rise of 'third space' professionals.* Routledge. https://doi.org/10.4324/9780203098301

Whitchurch, C., & Gordon, G. (2017). *Reconstructing relationships in higher education: Challenging agendas.* Routledge. https://doi.org/10.4324/9781315749358

VOICES FROM THE FIELD

Developing Third Space Leadership in Advising

Emily McIntosh

In 2008, I had the pleasure of hearing Celia Whitchurch present her preliminary work on the *third space* at a research seminar in the United Kingdom (UK). Having just finished my doctorate and being newly established in a professional support services role (the UK equivalent of an academic administrator), Whitchurch's work resonated with me. The concept of integrated practice and the ways of navigating and negotiating this oft-contested and misunderstood space mirrored my own experiences, working across both the academic- and professional-support services domains. My "academic-related" role brought with it all the challenges about space, identity, and effective ways of working that are discussed and debated at length in narratives of integrated practice. Being in a blended/academic-related role was new to me. Having brought experience of undertaking doctoral research and teaching history to undergraduates for more than five years, I was coming at this from the academic perspective. I remember wondering whether I had to surrender my academic credentials to work—and be successful in—a different type of role. How might I harness my existing experiences, reflecting on what works?

My academic experiences have always informed my advising practice. I have been strategic lead for academic advising/personal tutoring in two UK higher education institutions, a role equivalent to senior lead for academic advising. In the UK, *personal tutoring* is the term most often used to describe academic advising—a role usually fulfilled by academic colleagues. By working across boundaries and spaces, I have made sustained contributions to advising and tutoring in institutional, national,

DOI: 10.4324/9781003437598-5

and international contexts, informed by evidence-based approaches, the scholarship of advising, and my own practice-based research. I was recognized for this in 2021 when I was awarded a National Teaching Fellowship. I feel that I could not have done this, or worked effectively, without being an integrated practitioner. Establishing advising administration as integrated practice in the third space is important for the future strategic direction of this work. Yet, the third space and integrated practice has never been articulated and applied in advising and tutoring contexts.

My work in advising is rooted in integrated practice. I reflect on my personal philosophy of advising, and examples of my sustained leadership in institutional, national, and international contexts from a third space position. I use the conceptual framework for blended learning outlined by Whitchurch in 2009 to explore my professional role and identity. This *Voices from the Field* is structured into four parts where I focus on advising spaces, knowledges, relationships, and legitimacies, all of which have allowed me to develop my career in educational leadership with expertise in academic advising. I reflect on Whitchurch's four factors equally from both identity dispositions and theoretical frames.

Advising Spaces and Communities

Since hearing Whitchurch speak, my interest in and reflections on the third space and integrated practice have been impacted by the spaces that I occupy. While I have leadership responsibility for several educational priorities, these spaces have especially informed and contributed to my advising practice. In Whitchurch's (2009) framework, she considers that the concept of space is critical to achieving multiple understandings of an institution. I would also apply this to multiple understandings of the sector—given that most spaces that I have occupied play a key role in UK Advising and Tutoring (UKAT, the charitable body championing advising in the UK), and NACADA: The Global Community for Academic Advising (NACADA). The ambiguities between professional and academic domains are challenging for global higher education and can impact getting advising right. My membership in these spaces ensured that I could tackle these issues and bring about change. The infrastructure for advising at my own universities reflected my multiple understandings of institutions, enabling me to contextualize the immersive and educational experiences of being part of broader, international advising communities. At the same time, I have been able to champion advising by adapting and reshaping professional advising space and boundaries (Whitchurch, 2009).

Advising Knowledges

The advising knowledges I have developed in the third space have all shaped my philosophy of advising. My philosophy is that advising *is* teaching and, consequently, advising and tutoring is student-centred pedagogy. In a learner-centred approach, the role of advising and tutoring cannot be neglected, and it is through this role that learning conversations are facilitated. My approach aligns with Kift's (2015) holistic institutional and student mindset, informed by the wider literature on student success and advising scholarship. The literature on student success has impacted my thinking and enabled me to hone my strategic leadership of advising. I am inspired by higher educational frameworks that have developed my thinking about advising and tutoring and their place in higher education. The six principles of transition pedagogy (Kift & Nelson, 2005), Morgan's Student Experience Lifecycle Model (2011), the *What Works?* series (Thomas, 2012; Thomas et al., 2017), and the student lifecycle model, are all fundamental to learning and teaching systems. These structures provide pillars upon which to build an environment that promotes belonging and connectedness. These frameworks are human and learner-centred. They help to create systems of equity, inclusion, trust, and dialogue, which are fundamental for learning. Laycock (2009) emphasized the role of tutoring in helping students to establish "the connections between the different elements of the learning experience" (p. 121).

Advising Relationships

My relationships with my colleagues have helped me to develop my advising practice. I have had several developmental and supportive conversations with many colleagues in higher education who are also mindful of their role, purpose, and identity within a traditionally structured university system. These conversations have been with academic colleagues, professional support colleagues, and with those existing and operating within Whitchurch's conceptualization of the third space. Reflecting on my advising relationships and networks, it is easy to recognize that many of us have a strong sense of shared purpose and mission—and our shared values are immutable—they centre around the ability of advising to impact and support others, learning and teaching, academic development, and student support. We also share a sense that being between different *spaces* in the academy is neither comfortable nor easy.

Advising Legitimacies

My philosophy is at odds with the learning and teaching infrastructure in UK higher educational institutions, which are focused on the development and delivery of subject-based content and disciplinary norms. These traditional forms of pedagogy mean that tutoring has been a neglected area of student support and an under investigated area of inquiry. In the UK, advising has been supplementary to the curriculum, a transactional and passive process. As a leader in advising, I recognize the potential of advising to bring about transformational change in the delivery of learning and teaching; as such, I have considered the need to significantly reposition tutoring in the institutional consciousness as a vehicle to help meet increasingly diverse learner needs and student populations. I believe that institutional outcomes should not impede the academic imperative, which is to ensure improved outcomes for students, whether that be an increase in academic confidence and self-efficacy, equity and inclusion, development of learner autonomy, greater engagement, belonging, and responsiveness to feedback. These are all predicated on the legitimacy of advising to bring about change. Outstanding advising and tutoring can facilitate all of these outcomes for students.

Conclusion

Leadership in advising and tutoring requires a grasp of the challenges and opportunities of operating in a 21st-century higher education institution. One of the significant challenges concerns the lack of an agreed definition of tutoring in a UK context (Laycock, 2009; Walker, 2018, 2020) and differing models to describe how tutoring works on the ground (Earwaker, 1992; Lochtie et al., 2018). Indeed, tutoring has long been a system in flux and there has been an enduring lack of investment in its development (Grant, 2006; Luck, 2010). My work has sought to address these challenges and provide greater clarity about the landscape in which we are working.

References

Earwaker, J. (1992). *Helping and supporting students.* Open University Press.

Grant, A. (2006). Personal tutoring: A system in crisis? In L. Thomas & P. Hixenbaugh (Eds.), *Personal tutoring in higher education* (pp. 11–20). Trentham Books.

Kift, S. (2015, June). *Transition pedagogy: A whole student, whole-of-institution framework for successful student transitions.* [Keynote address]. International Conference on Enhancement and Innovation in Higher Education, Glasgow, Scotland.

Kift, S., & Nelson, K. (2005, July 3–6). Beyond curriculum reform: Embedding the transition experience. *Higher Education in a Changing World: Proceedings of the 28th HERDSA Annual Conference* (pp. 225–235). Higher Education Research and Development Society of Australasia.

Laycock, M. (2009, October 26). *Personal tutoring in higher education: Where now and where next?* Staff and Educational Development Association (SEDA).

Lochtie, D., McIntosh, E., Stork, A., & Walker, B. W. (2018). *Effective personal tutoring in higher education.* Critical Publishing.

Luck, C. (2010). Challenges faced by tutors in higher education. *Psychodynamic Practice, 16*(3), 273–287.

Morgan, M. (Ed.). (2011). *Improving the student experience: A practical guide for universities and colleges.* Routledge.

Thomas, L. (2012, July). *Building student engagement and belonging in Higher Education at a time of change.* Higher Education Academy. https://www.phf.org.uk/publications/works-student-retention-success-final-report/

Thomas, L., Hill, M., O'Mahony, J., & Yorke, M. (2017, April 11). *Supporting student success: Strategies for institutional change.* Higher Education Academy. https://www.heacademy.ac.uk/knowledge-hub/supporting-student-success-strategies-institutional-change

Walker, B. W. (2018). A defining moment for personal tutoring: Reflections on personal tutor definitions and their implications. *IMPact: The University of Lincoln Journal of Higher Education Research, 1*(1). https://e-space.mmu.ac.uk/626048/

Walker, B. W. (2020). Professional standards and recognition for UK personal tutoring and advising. *Frontiers in Education, 5.* https://doi.org/10.3389/feduc.2020.531451

Whitchurch, C. (2009). The rise of the blended professional in higher education: A comparison between the United Kingdom, Australia and the United States. *Higher Education, 58*(3), 407–418. https://doi.org/10.1007/s10734-009-9202-4

3

ADVISING STRUCTURES AND THE ADMINISTRATOR'S ROLE

Brian Kapinos and Calley Stevens Taylor

Now more than ever, advising administrators must navigate a variety of advising models that impact how they understand institutional advising goals, influence key stakeholders, respond to challenges, and develop collaborative solutions for the delivery, assessment, and evaluation of advising services. This chapter provides an overview of how diverse advising structures impact the work of the advising administrator and administrators' roles in navigating the complexities of higher education. To be successful, advising administrators must coordinate advising services, oftentimes with limited resources and limited authority over advising personnel, all while juggling enrollment goals, committee meetings, and providing training and development for advisors. Examples offered in this chapter are designed to provide an opportunity for advising administrators to consider how institutional types and advising models influence what is required to be effective institutional leaders. Aspiring and current advising administrators should use this chapter to gain perspective on how their role is impacted by different advising models and how variations in advising models might influence how they respond to some common challenges and opportunities.

Understanding the Administrator's Role Across Advising Models

Extensive literature describes institutional advising models, and has established their consistency within postsecondary institutions (Barron & Powell, 2014; Carlstrom & Miller, 2013; Crockett, 1982; Frank, 1988; Habley, 1983, 1993, 1997; Habley & McCauley, 1987; Hutson, 2013;

DOI: 10.4324/9781003437598-6

King, 2008; Pardee, 2004). Crockett (1982) and Habley (1983) first categorized the seven common models of advising according to their level of centralization. The structure of advising and the extent to which it is centralized or decentralized determines the planning and execution of the roles and responsibilities of an advising administrator (see Table 3.1).

In decentralized structures, academic and faculty advisors often have shared governance over advising and are located within academic units, allowing for more specialized advising (Pardee, 2004). Shared structures are quite common and often require tactful and intentional leadership from an advising administrator. In shared structures, academic advising is performed not only in a centralized administrative unit by primary-role advisors but also by faculty within individual academic divisions or departments (Pardee, 2004). There is only one centralized structure: the self-contained model, which utilizes advisors who are housed under one specific academic or administrative unit (King, 2008; Pardee, 2004).

Within each model, primary-role and faculty advisors are integrated into the student experience in different ways. It is essential that advising administrators familiarize themselves with the roles that each play within their institution's model. Understanding these roles is necessary when designing training, distributing resources, developing advising materials, and creating

TABLE 3.1 Primary-Role and Faculty Advisor Roles with Institutional Advising Models

Staff and Faculty Roles with Institutional Advising Models

Model	Organization	Primary-Role Advisors	Faculty Advisors
Self-contained	Centralized	Primary role	Minor role
Faculty only	Decentralized	Minor or no role	Primary advisors for students
Satellite	Decentralized	Strong role at the start	Faculty become primary advisors
Supplementary	Shared	Little role, professional development for faculty advisors	Primary advisors for students
Dual	Shared	Advise general education requirements	Advise major requirements
Split	Shared	Primary role with Undeclared/First Year	Primary advisors with students in the major
Total-intake	Shared	Primary role for all new students	Primary advisors once students declare a major

Note. Information taken from Pardee (2004) and Habley and McCauley (1987).

or revising advising program mission or outcomes. Administrators may also find it useful to understand how primary-role and faculty advisors complement each other across models, especially if they are presented with opportunities to propose or design changes to their institution's advising model.

Understanding the Intersection of Advising Models and Institutional Type

As advising administrators, understanding the identity and shared values of an institution is instrumental (Hurtado & Ruiz Alvarado, 2015) to developing and sustaining a successful advising model. As institutional types and advising models can influence the nature of an advising administrator's role, it is important for advising administrators to understand the relationships between them. Different institutional types impact how advising administrators navigate the intersection of the mission, vision, and culture of the institution, all while working within the confines of advising models, which may offer the administrator varying levels of authority over the coordination of advising services (Kapinos, 2020, 2021; Kramer, 1981). Table 3.2 summarizes the ways that advising administrators' roles vary by advising model.

The advising administrator must understand that several factors influence the selection of an advising model, including educational offerings, student population, selectivity, the role of faculty, and budgetary considerations, which are often associated with institutional type (King, 2008).

TABLE 3.2 Administrator Role within Advising Models

Model	Role within Advising Model
Self-contained	Manage all advising operations, lead advising staff, strong influence over advising operations
Faculty only	Minor role, support faculty advisors, professional development for faculty advisors
Satellite	Strong role within advising and academic department, support faculty advisors
Supplementary	Minor role, support professional development of faculty advisors
Dual	Manage advising operations of advising staff, general education advising
Split	Strong role with undeclared and first-year students, manage staff and advising operations
Total-intake	Strong role with first-year students, manage advising staff, support faculty advising post first-year

Note. Information taken from Pardee (2004) and Habley and McCauley (1987).

TABLE 3.3 Top Institutional Advising Models by Institutional Type

Institutional Type	Top Three Models (Ranked 1st, 2nd, and 3rd)		
Two-year public	Split model	Self-contained	Total intake
Four-year private	Faculty only	Shared supplementary	Shared/split
Four-year public	Split model	Self-contained	Total intake

Note. Information taken from Carlstrom and Miller (2013).

Table 3.3 provides an overview of the most common advising models in community colleges, as well as in public and private four-year institutions, all of which are further discussed below. Note that while private two-year institutions, technical colleges, and other institutional types are not fully reflected here, administrators working at these kinds of institutions will likely find some similarities between the characteristics of their institutions and those described in the table above.

Two-Year Public Community Colleges

In general, the mission of a community college is to be an open-access and affordable option for a wide range of diverse learners, to provide an educated workforce for the communities they serve (Cohen et al., 2013), and to promote vertical transfer opportunities to four-year institutions (Taylor & Jain, 2017).

The split, self-contained, and total intake advising models are the most common among community colleges (Carlstrom & Miller, 2013). Each model utilizes both primary-role and faculty advisors, and is designed to offer more intensive support for diverse student populations. These models, especially the split model, allow for faculty guidance and mentorship in the advising process, which can be important for very selective professional and career-related certificates and associate degrees. Advising administrators in these models usually supervise only primary-role advisors, with limited, if any, supervision of faculty advisors. Since most advising operations within community colleges are split or shared between academic and student affairs, it is imperative that advising administrators develop relationships with faculty advisors and academic affairs administrators (Carlstrom & Miller, 2013), especially if the administrator is housed within student affairs.

Four-Year Private Institutions

Private colleges and universities are tuition-dependent institutions, which generally focus on the formative aspects of education, promoting student development, and rigorous academic programs, all to support students' preparation for selective workforce opportunities or graduate education (Morphew & Hartley, 2006). Private institutions may concentrate on professional or pre-professional academic programs or may emphasize a liberal arts-based education while highlighting a commitment to academic excellence, experiential learning, and service leadership. These unique aspects of the mission and vision for private institutions make understanding the common advising models for these institutions extremely important to the success of an advising administrator.

A 2011 NACADA survey found that four-year private institutions heavily utilize faculty in advising and are more likely to employ the faculty-only model (Carlstrom & Miller, 2013). This significant faculty involvement highlights these institutions' commitment to immersing students in the academic experience and providing intensive faculty dedication to student mentorship (Yonker et al., 2019). Advising administrators at private institutions will find that demonstrating a commitment to the value and importance of faculty advising is central to their success. Supervision lines for advising administrators can be very limited at small private colleges and universities with few to no primary-role advising staff. However, large private institutions with large enrollments may have full advising centers, located either as stand-alone units or embedded within academic divisions, with an advising administrator supervising primary-role advisors. In these cases, administrators' expectations may be more similar to those traditionally found at four-year public institutions.

Four-Year Public Institutions

Four-year public institutions often promote a commitment to civic engagement and offer a quality baccalaureate or graduate education at an affordable price for in-state residents (Morphew & Hartley, 2006). They can range widely in size, from a few thousand students at small residential colleges to tens of thousands at large research-based universities. Public institutions, and, in particular, land-grant universities, are also charged with providing an affordable education and increasing college access (Geiger & Sorber, 2013). The faculty at small to midsize four-year public institutions often prioritize teaching and service as the core aspects of their work with students and the institution; at large public research universities, the faculty may focus on scholarship and research.

As in public two-year colleges, both primary-role and faculty advising are integral to the functions and culture of four-year public institutional advising models. Advising models at these schools often have a central advising office with generalist professional advisors and faculty serving as academic or program-specific advisors within their disciplines. Advising administrators will likely supervise primary-role advisors and report to student affairs or enrollment management, perhaps specifically to the dean of students or a vice president of enrollment management or student affairs; if located with academic colleges, they may report to academic deans.

The Advising Administrator's Positionality and Scope

The scope of authority granted to advising administrators may range from mid-level, such as a coordinator or director, to executive level, such as a chief student affairs officer (CSAO) or chief academic officer (CAO); however, each advising administrator must be "empowered … to accomplish the mission of the advising program" (King, 2008, p. 248). Positions in middle management vary in purpose and daily work but are generally responsible for leading specific components of an advising program, such as the supervision of staff and management of advising operations. When serving as coordinators or directors, administrators with mid-level positions may supervise primary-role advisors, support faculty advisors, or collaborate with other advising administrators at the institution. Middle managers may experience power differentials that play both up and down the administrative chain (Floyd, 2016), experience tension resulting from having an important responsibility with limited power to influence change, or feel isolated, even while enjoying opportunities to make a direct impact on others' lives (Pepper & Giles, 2015). Unlike executive-level administrators, mid-level administrators are more likely to work directly with students, with an assigned caseload or as a supplement to primary-role or faculty advisors, giving them insights into the needs of students, advisors, and the advising program.

Those who hold executive or senior leadership positions, such as academic deans, provosts, or CSAOs, play an important role in ensuring and operationalizing an institutional commitment to academic advising (Creamer & Scott, 2000). Though less likely to engage in the daily work of managing an advising program or advising individual students, administrators at this level help to ensure that academic advising is prioritized in institutional planning and budgeting, and that advisors are recognized for their efforts (Bultman et al., 2008). Executive or senior-level advising administrators should understand how advising and related processes "cut across all parts of the institution" (Bultman et al., 2008, p. 424), including those that may fall under the purview of other senior-level administrators and which promote collaboration and coordination. Because regular contact between upper-level administration and advising administrators is associated with greater familiarity with the institutional vision (Abelman et al., 2007), executive and senior-level administrators should strive to maintain substantial relationships with their institution's advising leadership; this may result in stronger connections between advising and the institutional vision.

In addition, different advising models require different resources. Moving from a faculty advising model to a primary-role advising model, or establishing an advising center, for example, requires financial planning and commitment (King, 2008). While mid-level administrators should be involved in any changes to an institution's advising model, executive-level administrators play a unique role in ensuring that advising is presented as a priority to other executive-level leaders, like the chief financial officer, the president, the board of trustees, or another governing body.

Administrative Locations and the Advising Administrator's Role

Academic advising programs may be housed within academic affairs, student affairs, enrollment management, or shared between divisions. Where advising services are located within the institutional structure can influence how the institution views advising (Cate & Miller, 2015) and drive the responsibilities, expectations, authority, and other dimensions of an advising administrator's role.

Academic Affairs

To support a culture that views advising as an academic pursuit, advising leadership must "be affiliated with the institutional structure that designs the curriculum" (Darling, 2015, p. 92). Advising administrators located in academic affairs benefit from being organizationally situated alongside faculty governance, curriculum committees, and the like. They may also find it easier to collaborate with faculty, academic deans, and provosts/CAOs, or use shared educational or pedagogical philosophies to find common ground. Advising administrators located in academic affairs may find it easier to engage faculty in support of developing advising pedagogy and outcomes, validating advising as a teaching and learning activity, or using advisors' knowledge of the student experience to inform academic policies or curricular decisions.

At the executive level, academic leaders such as deans and CAOs play an important role in framing advising as an educational experience that is central to the teaching mission of higher education (Bultman et al., 2008), and the decisions they make directly impact how advising is carried out (Menke et al., 2020). CAOs with advising functions in their portfolio should recognize their role in strengthening and integrating advising processes (Bultman et al., 2008) and should lead efforts to engage the whole community in collaborations that support advising functions (Bultman et al., 2008).

Enrollment Management

Advising services that are located within enrollment management functions, such as admissions offices, financial aid, and registrar's offices, may have increased opportunities to make systematic improvements in students' initial experiences with advising; support efforts such as student-friendly catalogs, degree-plans, and class schedules (Bultman et al., 2008); and advocate for alignment of policies and practices that influence academic decision-making, academic progress, and financial aid eligibility. They may also find it easier to advocate for the role of advising in enrollment, retention, and persistence.

However, while there are synergies between enrollment management and advising management, advising administrators in enrollment management units may experience pressure to prioritize processes and strategies that can distract from advising's core focus on human interaction (Joslin, 2018). Advising administrators serving in these units may find it useful to create relationships and develop allies within academic leadership and influential faculty; these relationships can help ensure that advising remains valued as an academic endeavor rather than a management function.

Student Affairs

Advising administrators in student affairs may have more opportunities for relationships with, or responsibilities for, a variety of programs that complement advising, such as coaching or orientation (Bultman et al., 2008), career services, or specialized programs that provide supplementary advising. Advising administrators in student affairs, who share responsibility for advising with faculty advisors, are especially suited to lead supplemental advising programs that address holistic topics such as academic, career, and life goals, which may be considered peripheral to faculty advisors (Allen & Smith, 2008).

Like CAOs, CSAOs with responsibility for advising or related programs, should endeavor to "[chart] the strategic direction of student affairs to align the division with the institutional priorities for advising [and] identify issues confronting students that will be addressed by advising" (Bultman et al., 2008, pp. 429–430). CSAOs must be able to facilitate intentional collaborations and integration of these services, with special attention to those that are of particular interest to faculty (Bultman et al.,

2008). However, CSAOs might find it difficult to advocate for recognition of advising as an educational experience if they or their programs are not seen as part of the institution's academic identity.

Unified Administrative Structures

At some institutions, the areas described above may be combined into other organizational structures. For example, student affairs and enrollment management may be combined into a single unit. In many community colleges, the positions of CAO and CSAO are held by a single individual (Bultman et al., 2008). For administrators in these comprehensive units, it is especially important to understand the relationship between traditional academic functions and traditional student affairs functions at the institution and consider the role that academic advising plays in bridging these sometimes disparate or siloed units. In this way, administrators in these combined units are uniquely suited to establish integrative advising cultures and programs that serve very diverse student populations and institutional needs.

Challenges and Opportunities within Advising Structures and Systems

The advising administrator must manage the complexity of an institution's advising system, including the quality, output, and delivery of advising services (Arndt, 1987; Tukey, 1996). Historically, an advising administrator's responsibilities were to meet with students for advising, work with faculty on matters of advising, and attend administrative meetings (Kramer, 1981; Spencer et al., 1982). These roles and responsibilities have become inherently more complex, and while the framing of an advising administrator's role within any given institution or unit can vary widely, there are some common challenges and opportunities that they are likely to encounter. These include navigating levels of authority and accountability, building relationships, technology and data management, and advisor training and development. How the administrator responds to, takes advantage of, or navigates these challenges and opportunities may be impacted by variations in institutional type or advising model.

Level of Authority and Accountability

The advising administrator may be faced with challenges inherent to positions that straddle academic and student affairs, such as having limited institutional authority to handle advising issues unilaterally (Kapinos,

2020), while also broadly holding responsibility over the coordination and quality of campus advising services (Kapinos, 2021). The disconnect between authority and responsibility presents challenges for advising administrators who need to respect existing boundaries and maintain control over the direction and scope of the advising program. This challenge is often seen in faculty-only and split models, and in large decentralized advising systems where little authority rests with any one advising administrator. The advising administrator will often have to be a "politician" serving as a strategic and intentional coordinator and consultant for advising issues while balancing the interests and preferences of faculty and administrators (Kapinos, 2020; Kramer, 1985). Without the authority to oversee all institutional advising services, advising administrators are challenged to ensure consistency in advising practices (Kapinos, 2021). Because middle managers are often constricted by traditional roles and are held increasingly accountable for outcomes and objectives over which they have little control (Gallos, 2002), advising administrators serving at the mid-management level may experience this more acutely. Leading from the middle requires recognizing stakeholders and understanding how to bring people together (Chebbi et al., 2020), which makes relationship-building imperative for mid-level advising administrators.

Building Relationships

An advising administrator must create an environment that is conducive to learning about advising and successfully establish relationships with stakeholders, develop support for advising initiatives, and leverage resources to ensure that advising services are delivered to students in a quality manner (Karp, 2013; Kramer, 1986). A successful advising administrator must navigate the complexity of building social capital with departments, directors, and faculty members to influence institutional advising operations. Positionality within the institution can impact how the advising administrator strategically develops relationships. For example, the advising administrator is often expected to perform tasks and operations such as improving student retention rates or increasing the registration numbers for the next semester. Administrators located in academic or student affairs may find that they have little authoritative control to manage the other offices and personnel required to complete tasks, such as admissions, financial aid, or registrar's offices, and would therefore benefit from using informal leadership methods such as building social capital with colleagues in these areas (see Chapter 8).

At institutions without faculty advisors, advising administrators should still establish strong and deliberate relationships with faculty members

(Hart-Baldridge, 2020). After all, one of the primary purposes of academic advising is to help students navigate and understand the curriculum, making advising inherently an academic function. Faculty members will be more responsive to institutional change when they are included in the decision-making process (McArthur, 2002). Advising administrators can unconsciously overlook this step when attempting to make institutional change, especially within centralized advising models where faculty are not relied upon to support advising operations. Feedback from senior faculty, program coordinators, or department chairs on advising-related initiatives will help support the change process and develop buy-in from other faculty members who may be resistant to change (McArthur, 2002).

Technology and Data Management

Advising administrators must recognize the importance of technology and data analytics (Steele, 2018). Technology is a vital tool that academic advisors and advising administrators use to connect with students, provide documentation, and identify trends associated with student enrollment, retention, and graduation rates (Pellegrino et al., 2021). For an advising technology system to succeed, it must be integrated into the campus-wide strategic plan to support students, and the advising administrator plays a vital role in ensuring this integration happens (Pasquini & Steele, 2016). Specifically, advising administrators in enrollment management areas may find that they are especially involved in managing advising technology and using data to drive programmatic decisions.

Advising administrators who oversee advising programs with high caseloads—for either faculty or primary-role advisors—may find that they are responsible for advocating for, and supporting, advising technology to manage student outreach and support (Kalamkarian et al., 2018). In centralized advising models, the advising administrator may be able to lead the adoption and implementation of such systems in the way that best suits their unit's needs, while those within decentralized advising models may find it beneficial to work with other advising administrators to identify shared needs and establish a framework for joint selection and implementation.

Advisor Training and Development

Finally, institutions expect to have competent staff who are ready to meet the needs of a diverse student population (Brown, 2008). However, the delivery of advisor onboarding and professional development is often complicated, as advising practitioners come from a variety of fields and backgrounds (Aiken-Wisniewski et al., 2015; McGill, 2019), and the extent to which an advising administrator can coordinate, expect, or even require professional development for advisors may depend on the advising model. In centralized systems, advising administrators have control over who attends and completes training and professional development, while in shared or decentralized structures, administrators need to develop partnerships with other advising administrators to promote participation in advisor training and development.

Conclusion

This chapter offered an overview of how advising administrators' expectations, roles, and responsibilities can be impacted by their institutional type and advising model. Advising administrators will often face challenges navigating their advising structures depending on their positionality within the organizational structure (Kapinos, 2021). Before accepting a position as an advising administrator, proposing a change to a new advising model, or advocating for advising resources, understanding the relationship between the advising model and the role of the advising administrator is essential. Although more challenges and opportunities exist for advising administrators than what has been described within this chapter, those presented here will help frame the context for advising administrators who are entering the profession or offer current administrators opportunities to reflect on ways that different institutional contexts impact their work.

Reflection Questions

1 As a current or future aspiring advising administrator, reflect upon your positionality within your organization structure alongside your institutional advising model.

   a What gaps do you see in the coordination of advising?
   b Where is your voice not present as an advising administrator within your organizational structure?
   c How can you lobby your campus leadership to understand your positionality within the organization and how it affects the coordination of advising services within your campus structure?

2 In more decentralized models, advising administrators will often need to work alongside other areas that may have supervision over advising services across your campus.

   a In such contexts, how could you start a conversation with your fellow advising administrators about how the advising model and leadership structure impact the coordination of advising services?

3 As an advising administrator in a faculty-only model, your leadership and supervision over advising services may be minimal.

a What strategies could you employ to influence the coordination and effectiveness of advising services in these environments?

4 In shared models, tension can sometimes arise between primary-role and faculty advisors, especially when their unique roles in the advising model are not clear.

a How can you effectively create an environment where faculty and primary-role advisors understand each other's value, roles, and responsibilities?

References

Abelman, R., Atkin, D., Dalessandro, A., Snyder-Suhy, S., & Janstova, P. (2007). The trickle-down effect of institutional vision: Vision statements and academic advising. *NACADA Journal, 27*(1), 4–21. https://doi.org/10.12930/0271-9517-27.1.4

Aiken-Wisniewski, S. A., Johnson, A., Larson, J., & Barkemeyer, J. (2015). A preliminary report of advisor perceptions of advising and of a profession. *NACADA Journal, 35*(2), 60–70. https://doi.org/10.12930/NACADA-14-020

Allen, J. M., & Smith, C. L. (2008). Importance of, responsibility for, and satisfaction with academic advising: A faculty perspective. *Journal of College Student Development, 49*(5), 397–411. https://doi.org/10.1353/csd.0.0033

Arndt, J. R. (1987). The academic advisor as environmental change agent. *NACADA Journal, 7*(2), 43–46. https://doi.org/10.12930/0271-9517-7.2.43

Barron, K. E., & Powell, D. N. (2014). Options on how to organize and structure advising. In R. L. Miller & J. G. Irons (Eds.), *Academic advising: A handbook for advisors and students Volume 1: Models, students, topics, and issues* (pp. 14–23). Society for the Teaching of Psychology. https://teachpsych.org/ebooks/academic-advising-2014-vol1

Brown, T. (2008). Critical concepts in advisor training and development. In V. N. Gordon, W. R. Habley, & T. J. Grites (Eds.), *Academic advising: A comprehensive handbook* (2nd ed., pp. 309–322). Jossey-Bass.

Bultman, J. E., Vowell, F. N., Harney, J. Y., & Smarrelli, J. (2008). Campus administrator perspectives on advising. In V. N. Gordon, W. R. Habley, & T. J. Grites (Eds.), *Academic advising: A comprehensive handbook* (2nd ed., pp. 415–437). Jossey-Bass.

Carlstrom, A. H., & Miller, M. A. (Eds.). (2013). *2011 NACADA national survey of academic advising* (Monograph No. 25). NACADA. https://nacada.ksu.edu/Resources/Clearinghouse/View-Articles/2011-NACADA-National-Survey.aspx

Cate, P., & Miller, M. A. (2015). Academic advising within the academy: History, mission, and role. In P. Folsom, F. Yoder, & J. E. Joslin (Eds.), *The new advisor guidebook: Mastering the art of academic advising* (2nd ed., pp. 39–52). Jossey-Bass.

Chebbi, H., Yahiaoui, D., Sellami, M., Papasolomou, I., & Melanthiou, Y. (2020). Focusing on internal stakeholders to enable the implementation of organizational change towards corporate entrepreneurship: A case study from France.

Journal of Business Research, 119, 209–217. https://doi.org/10.1016/j.jbusres.2019.06.003

Cohen, A. M., Brawer, F. B., & Kisker, C. B. (2013). *The American community college* (6th ed.). Jossey-Bass.

Creamer, E. G., & Scott, D. W. (2000). Assessing individual advisor effectiveness. In V. N. Gordon & W. R. Habley (Eds.), *Academic advising: A comprehensive handbook* (pp. 339–348). Jossey-Bass.

Crockett, D. S. (1982). Academic advising delivery systems. *New Directions for Student Services, 1982*(17), 39–53. https://doi.org/10.1002/ss.37119821705

Darling, R. (2015). The academic adviser. *The Journal of General Education, 64*(2), 90–98. https://doi.org/10.5325/jgeneeduc.64.2.0090

Floyd, A. (2016). Supporting academic middle managers in higher education: Do we care? *Higher Education Policy, 29*(2), 167–183.

Frank, C. P. (1988). The development of academic advising programs: Formulating a valid model. *NACADA Journal, 8*(1), 11–28. https://doi.org/10.12930/0271-9517-8.1.11

Gallos, J. V. (2002). The dean's squeeze: The myths and realities of academic leadership in the middle. *Academy of Management Learning & Education, 1*(2), 174–184.

Geiger, R. L., & Sorber, N. M. (Eds.). (2013). *The land-grant colleges and the reshaping of American higher education.* Routledge.

Habley, W. R. (1983). Organizational structures for academic advising: Models and implications. *Journal of College Student Personnel, 24*(6), 535–540.

Habley, W. R. (1993). The organization and effectiveness of academic advising in community colleges. *New Directions for Community Colleges, 1993*(82), 33–45. https://doi.org/10.1002/cc.36819938205

Habley, W. R. (1997). Organizational models and institutional advising practices. *NACADA Journal, 17*(2), 39–44. https://doi.org/10.12930/0271-9517-17.2.39

Habley, W. R., & McCauley, M. E. (1987). The relationship between institutional characteristics and the organization of advising services. *NACADA Journal, 7*(1), 27–39. https://doi.org/10.12930/0271-9517-7.1.27

Hart-Baldridge, E. (2020). Faculty advisor perspectives of academic advising. *NACADA Journal, 40*(1), 10–22.

Hurtado, S., & Ruiz Alvarado, A. (2015). Realizing the potential of Hispanic-serving institutions: Multiple dimensions of organizational transformation. In A-M. Núñez, S. Hurtado, & E. Calderón Galdeano (Eds.), *Hispanic-serving institutions: Advancing research and transformative practice* (pp. 25–46). Routledge.

Hutson, B. (2013). Faculty development to support academic advising: Rationale, components and strategies of support. *The Journal of Faculty Development, 27*(3), 5–11.

Joslin, J. E. (2018). The case for strategic academic advising management. *New Directions for Higher Education, 2018*(184), 11–20. https://doi.org/10.1002/he.20299

Kalamkarian, H. S., Boynton, M., & Salazar, A. L. (2018, July). *Redesigning advising with the help of technology: Early experiences of three institutions.* Community College Research Center, Columbia University. https://ccrc.tc.columbia.edu/publications/redesigning-advising-technology-three-institutions.html

Kapinos, B. (2020). Community college advising coordinators: A perspective from middle management. *Community College Enterprise, 26*(2), 46–67.

Kapinos, B. (2021). The perceptions community college advising coordinators have of their institutional advising models: An exploratory study. *NACADA Journal, 41*(1), 80–93. https://doi.org/10.12930/NACADA-20-22

Karp, M. M. (2013, May). Entering a program: Helping students make academic and career decisions. Community College Research Center, Columbia University. https://ccrc.tc.columbia.edu/publications/entering-a-program-academic-and-career-decisions.html

King, M. C. (2008). Organization of academic advising services. In V. N. Gordon, W. R. Habley, & T. J. Grites (Eds.), *Academic advising: A comprehensive handbook* (2nd ed., pp. 242–251). Jossey-Bass.

Kramer, H. C. (1981). The advising coordinator: Managing from a one-down position. *NACADA Journal, 1*(1), 7–15. https://doi.org/10.12930/0271-9517-1.1.7

Kramer, H. C. (1985). Advising systems and institutional coordination. *NACADA Journal, 5*(2), 41–49.

Kramer, H. C. (1986). Faculty development: The advising coordinator's changing scene. *NACADA Journal, 6*(2), 31–42.

McArthur, R. C. (2002). Democratic leadership and faculty empowerment at the community college: A theoretical model for the department chair. *Community College Review, 30*(3), 1–10. https://doi.org/10.1177/009155210203000301

McGill, C. M. (2019). The professionalization of academic advising: A structured literature review. *NACADA Journal, 39*(1), 89–100. https://doi.org/10.12930/NACADA-18-015

Menke, D. J., Duslak, M., & McGill, C. M. (2020). Administrator perceptions of academic advisor tasks. *NACADA Journal, 40*(2), 85–96. https://doi.org/10.12930/NACADA-20-12

Morphew, C. C., & Hartley, M. (2006). Mission statements: A thematic analysis of rhetoric across institutional type. *The Journal of Higher Education, 77*(3), 456–471. https://doi.org/10.1080/00221546.2006.11778934

Pardee, C. F. (2004). *Organizational structures for advising*. NACADA. https://nacada.ksu.edu/Resources/Clearinghouse/View-Articles/Organizational-Models-for-Advising.aspx

Pasquini, L. A., & Steele, G. E. (2016, February 29). *Technology in academic advising: Perceptions and practices in higher education*. Figshare. https://doi.org/10.6084/m9.figshare.3053569.v1

Pellegrino, L., Salazar, A. L., & Kalamkarian, H. S. (2021, April). *Five years later: Technology and advising redesign at early adopter colleges*. Community College Research Center, Columbia University. https://ccrc.tc.columbia.edu/publications/technology-advising-redesign-early-adopter-colleges.html

Pepper, C., & Giles, W. (2015). Leading in middle management in higher education. *Management in Education, 29*(2), 46–52. https://doi.org/10.1177/0892020614529987

Spencer, R. W., Peterson, E. D., & Kramer, G. L. (1982). Utilizing college advising centers to facilitate and revitalize academic advising. *NACADA Journal, 2*(1), 13–23. https://doi.org/10.12930/0271-9517-2.1.13

Steele, G. E. (2018). Student success: Academic advising, student learning data, and technology. *New Directions for Higher Education, 2018*(184), 59–68. https://doi.org/10.1002/he.20303

Taylor, J. L., & Jain, D. (2017). The multiple dimensions of transfer: Examining the transfer function in American higher education. *Community College Review, 45*(4), 273–293. https://doi.org/10.1177/0091552117725177

Tukey, D. D. (1996). Academic advising as a multisystem, collaborative enterprise. *NACADA Journal, 16*(1), 6–13. https://doi.org/10.12930/0271-9517-16.1.6

Yonker, J. E., Hebreard, D., & Cawley, B. D. (2019). Validating faculty advising through assessment. *NACADA Journal, 39*(1), 34–49. https://doi.org/10.12930/NACADA-17-034

VOICES FROM THE FIELD

Considerations in Working with Online Populations

Kristina Richards and Samantha Moreno

Understanding the unique needs of online students is critical to the success of any academic advising unit, particularly those supporting fully online student populations. This group of students balances several commitments outside of school, often consisting of full-time employment, parenting, and other major family responsibilities. Their time is limited and therefore accessing resources and obtaining critical information can be challenging even for the most organized student (Hoffman & Willinger, 2021; Richardson et al., 2021). It can be daunting to navigate the campus environment from a distance, which makes building a sense of connection with a trusted advisor more worthwhile.

In our role as advising administrators, we need to be mindful of the holistic student experience as we develop our organizations and service models. One model, the centralized student services model, is where advisors serve as a single point of contact and are cross-trained and well-versed in the services offered to students across all offices of the institution, so students do not have to contact multiple university offices to resolve an issue. The centralized model should easily refer students to the appropriate resources and offices for complex and escalated issues, such as financial aid and billing processes and policies. An important role for administrators is to cross-train advisors so that they can effectively assist students at all stages of the student-life cycle. This model empowers advising teams to employ a holistic approach in their work with students by considering all aspects of the student experience and guiding students in a meaningful way. Often, students engage with academic advisors where the purview of assistance may be limited to academic policies, programmatic details, and

DOI: 10.4324/9781003437598-7

registration support. This approach can be restrictive and frustrating for students who must navigate complex institutional systems. For online students, this can be an even larger barrier as time is limited and systems seem harder to access. Administrators working with fully online advising units should strive to implement advising structures that go beyond a transactional focus and become transformative, while aiming to holistically support students through their educational experiences.

Because every institution and its student population are unique, it is important to build an advising unit with the specific needs of the students they serve in mind. For example, advising administrators at institutions with significant first-generation student populations might consider having specialized advisors with extensive training preparing them to work with this group. Creating a sense of belonging and individualized support through a dedicated advisor, who can assist in most aspects of the student experience, can make all the difference for these learners. Student caseloads could be lower, allowing more time to provide personalized support in more frequent increments.

Similarly, advising administrators need to ensure advisors working with online students have an in-depth understanding of how the demographic of their online student population differs from their on-campus counterparts. A one-size-fits-all approach will not work for advisors who support students studying in a variety of learning modalities. Online programs tend to attract a larger number of non-traditional learners whose life experiences can differ greatly from those of traditional campus students. In our own practice, we have grown to understand that agility and the willingness to try new strategies are key to our success and evolution as a department. In our work with nursing students, for example, utilizing video recorded messages instead of a scheduled video conference yielded an uptick in student responsiveness and engagement. Students in nursing programs tend to work long and irregular hours, making it even more challenging to connect with faculty members and advisors than many other student populations. Having a dedicated advisor to whom most questions are directed allows students to feel connected to the university while having their needs met. Lessening the time needed to navigate complicated university systems has been invaluable to busy, working students and can make a difference in students being able to persist in their programs. Utilizing knowledge about this group of students and tailoring communication channels to their needs can increase response rates and engagement. Texting has also proven to be an effective communication channel with busy, online students, allowing advisors to communicate about deadlines, important dates, and announcements quickly and effectively. Texting also allows busy students to respond quickly and efficiently while they move between their various career, family, and educational responsibilities.

Recognizing and Advocating for the Specific Needs of the Online Student Population

One of the most significant ways advising administrators can impact online students is by advocating for their needs and working with the institution to remove unnecessary obstacles. Next to faculty members, academic advisors typically have more contact with students than any other staff member at their college or university. Naturally, advisors hear from students when institutional processes are broken or hard to navigate, making them ideal candidates to escalate issues and push for institutional change. Online students attending institutions with both on-campus and virtual options can be subjected to policies, unwritten rules, expectations, and communications geared primarily for their campus-based counterparts. Requiring immunization records from students, even those attending online and living outside the state and country, are an example of these kinds of policies. This can be a roadblock for online students that keeps them from starting their programs. Advocating to university leadership is a key role for the advising administrator and includes helping leaders understand how policies impact the online student experience, retention rates, and students' continuation of their studies. In the competitive world of online education, being responsive to student needs will help set a program apart from others in the field. Students seek institutions that strive to meet their needs and will often select the one that offers the most support and connection.

Navigating the Relationship with an Online Service Provider and Advisor

Should your institution choose an online service provider or have a separate and distinct unit for supporting students enrolled exclusively in online programs, cooperation between the online unit and academic advising/central student service units is a critical component for student success. While it can be daunting to "share a student," it can be done. After all, there are many units across the university that do this every day. To achieve cooperation, it is imperative for the advising administrator to work closely with the vendor to establish shared vision, mutual professional respect, trust, and understanding. It is also essential to communicate with the student in such a way as to ensure the student understands the role of the online service provider as compared to the role of the advising/central student service unit.

Ultimately, the cooperative team, led by the advising administrator, needs to continually put the student at the forefront. They must work together for the student to support as seamless an experience as possible. Developing cooperation between teams requires intentional decision-making and agreement between the leaders and teams. To begin, leaders will want to ensure that there is a strong mutual understanding of the purpose of the organizational structure and why it is imperative to student success. Once there is an agreed-upon larger purpose and understanding of online students, the team needs to unpack, understand, and create a student experience geared toward online students, including understanding each team member's role in the student's journey. Adding a specialist in project management can aid in creating student journey maps and identifying points of optimization in processes. A part of that process is to develop common language and narrative for the student. All support units must adhere to the process and regularly review whether the process is working or not.

Once the student journey and touchpoints have been agreed upon, the units need to determine escalation points for student issues. Escalation points should be the areas where the advising administrator wants someone in authority to answer questions or resolve issues. For example, the academic administrator will want the vendor to escalate complaints about faculty members to department chairs and not try to resolve the issue themselves. Further, advising administrators will need to establish protocols when a student has a question about an academic policy. Setting the escalation points establishes clear boundaries/guardrails in interactions with students. Another critical role for the advising administrator is to facilitate a regular review of processes as well as escalation points and to adjust as needed. This step requires a great deal of respect and trust, so relationship building between the advising administrator and online provider is critical. One way to increase trust through transparency, when working with students, is to employ a shared technology tool that can be used to track student interaction.

Conclusion

All students desire advising programs with streamlined processes, clear communication, and easy access to resources, faculty members, and staff; online students are no different. The role of the advising administrator is critical in developing and executing a robust centralized service model for online students. Whether it is contracting with a third-party service provider or building online support in-house, it is critical for advising administrators to partner with the campus student service units to determine how online students will access these resources and staff for a robust experience.

References

Hoffman, J., & Willinger, A. (2021). Transforming the practice of student affairs professionals: Creating an ecosystem of support that is inclusive of online learners. In J. Hoffman & P. Blessinger (Eds.), *International perspectives on supporting and engaging online learners* (pp. 13–27). Emerald Publishing Limited.

Richardson, M. D., Sheeks, G., Waller, R. E., & Lemoine, P. A. (2021). Pursuit of online services for online students. In Information Resources Management Association (Ed.), *Research anthology on developing effective online learning courses* (pp. 1850–1880). IGI Global. https://doi.org/10.4018/978-1-7998-8047-9

4

ACADEMIC ADVISING LEADERSHIP AND CHANGE MANAGEMENT

Ankur Nandedkar, Margaret Mbindyo, Rubab Jafry O'Connor, and Thomas Casey O'Connor

The Role of Academic Advising Administrators

The academic advising administrator serves the larger college or university community by contributing their consultative expertise regarding student transition and learning success (Chalmers, 2005). They are called upon to provide leadership as advising experts, scholars, and servants to the larger community. As the modern academic landscape evolves, administrators are being challenged to lead holistically and to encourage group values in advising to ensure an inclusive, equitable academic advising experience for all students (Fountain, 2021). Amidst an internal and external environment of continuous and global evolution, academic advising administrators must develop the knowledge and skills necessary to adapt and lead significant and relevant changes in their organizations. This chapter will explore the role of the academic advising administrator and offer preparatory considerations for navigation and leadership during times of change.

Extensive research on advising leadership shows that successful academic advising administrators go beyond mere administration (Lowenstein, 2005; Mbindyo et al., 2021; McClellan, 2010; Nandedkar et al., 2020). They prioritize sharing effective, high impact advising practices across campus and encourage innovation when appropriate. It is also essential that administrators assist frontline advisors in modeling desirable personal qualities like self-awareness, empathy, commitment, and competence in their daily interactions with both students and colleagues (Museus, 2021). Academic advising administrators shape the culture of the

DOI: 10.4324/9781003437598-8

institution through the decisions they make as well as the ways in which they enact their roles within the institution (Pargett, 2011). Their positions, with so many university touch points, enable them to perceive and participate in the daily evolution of the university.

There are many opportunities for advisors to play a key role in institutional and student development (Drake, 2011), and the ways an academic advising administrator deals with change has implications for how advisors respond. During times of change and transition, a good advising administrator should be able to support an advisor in leading their students (White, 2015). They must model effective leadership and problem-solving skills and demonstrate how to accomplish change for the common good of their units and their institutions. To be fully effective, administrators must be empowered to respond quickly and decisively to meet the fluid, interconnected needs and demands of all university stakeholders.

Empowering Academic Advising Administrators

Chitorelidze (2017) stressed that it is important for leaders to empower campus constituents at various levels. Doing so can aid them in effectively responding to the many pressing issues that academic institutions face in today's highly competitive world (Kezar et al., 2006; Lambert, 2006; Lau, 2010; Tsai, 2012). Dye (2011) described empowerment as the power that one has to produce, to prosper, and to promote growth in self and in others. Ultimately, the goal of any educational institution is to empower students so that they may prosper before and after graduation. Academic advisors can play a key role in student development when they are empowered to tailor their advising to the individual needs of the student. To achieve this, an empowered administrator will seek to create a dynamic, inclusive, and responsive environment to address the diverse needs of advisors and students. This type of environment encourages advisor morale as well as better student learning and wellbeing (Lee, 2009). Establishing a culture of empowerment throughout the advising organization is essential to keep pace with a rapidly changing educational landscape.

Empowerment can be defined "as giving employees more powers, responsibilities and authority to make decisions and solve problems through performing work independently [in] their own way and without the direct involvement of management" (Alfadli & Al-Mehaisen, 2019, p. 123). This definition suggests that one way the empowered academic advising administrator can encourage advisors is by allowing them to make decisions, solve problems, and think creatively as they advise students and manage their responsibilities. Supporting this autonomy has the effect of recalibrating the incentive structure such that the focus shifts from meeting the needs of one's employer to the development of students. Empowered academic advising administrators can therefore shape the student advising experience by challenging advisors to reflect on current approaches and to innovate within their own practices.

Leadership Models for the Empowered Academic Advising Administrator

Establishing an environment in which advisors feel empowered to reflect upon and potentially alter their advising practice requires an administrator who is versed in leadership models that advance empowerment. Two such models include Servant Leadership and Transformational Leadership (TL). These models' elements are consistent with the concepts of empowerment mentioned above; also, the literature on leadership has consistently shown these leadership styles to be effective (Drake, 2011; Mbindyo et al., 2021; Nandedkar et al., 2020; Paul & Fitzpatrick, 2015; van Dierendonck, 2011; Xie, 2020). A brief overview of these leadership styles is presented below, alongside ways in which their use can benefit the needs of all stakeholders and support the flexibility and adaptability required in times of change.

Servant Leadership Model

In his seminal study on servant leadership, Greenleaf (1977) observed that a servant leader is one whose aspiration to lead emerges from a desire to serve. This is distinct from one who seeks to lead out of an aspiration for power or control. Servant leadership skills include listening, empathy, healing, foresight, commitment to the growth of people, and building community (Crippen, 2004; Greenleaf, 1970; Spears, 2010). A servant leader seeks to aid in the growth of others in the hope that they, too, become servant leaders. In this process, individual growth becomes the organization's growth.

An academic advising administrator as a servant leader may seek to empower others by helping them develop holistically and enabling them to provide students with the necessary resources to achieve success during times of change (Spears, 2010). Servant leadership development gives administrators the opportunity to grow as leaders, develop others as leaders, and approach change as normal. With a focus on serving others, these leaders are more inclined to adapt their approach and persevere through difficult times. The aspiration to serve first, therefore, can be an engine of dynamism in times of change.

TL Model

In studying TL, Albritton (1998) postulated that the degree to which leaders are transformational is measured in terms of the leader's effect on followers. Transformational leaders are typically depicted as visionary, empowering, social, passionate, good communicators, and innovative (Hackman & Johnson, 2004). Administrators acting as transformational leaders can help increase both advisor and student satisfaction by actualizing those very attributes. Listening with genuine concern and appreciation, incorporating feedback, communicating decisions, and empowering advisors to act independently within the communicated framework builds a culture of trust that allows all stakeholders to share openly and act without fear.

During times of change, the transformational leader provides opportunities for others to feel supported and trusted and to excel in their work. Administrators who practice transformational behaviors have a demonstrated ability to achieve because they are able to inspire others to develop innovative problem-solving skills (Albritton, 1998; Yammarino & Bass, 1990). As that skill development occurs in a culture of trust and openness, experiences can be shared freely throughout the organization for the benefit of all. When individual growth transforms into team growth, the entire organization becomes more responsive to students and their evolving needs. As Pan et al. (2009) noted, having a vision for the advising unit and using various ways to motivate advisors and students may yield professional success for advisors and academic success for students.

Change Management and Academic Advising Administration

Managing change is crucial for an organization's long-term survival (De Matos & Clegg, 2013) and essential for an organization to thrive. When change occurs, current expectations are not put on hold. All involved must respond to the needs of the moment while keeping an eye on the future. In academic institutions, this means that the needs of currently enrolled students are every bit as important as next year's matriculating students. While this is perhaps challenging, implementing a carefully considered change management strategy can help ease the transition.

Change management is "the process of continually renewing an organization's direction, structure, and capabilities to serve the ever changing needs of external and internal" stakeholders (Moran & Brightman, 2000, p. 66). The changes that occur in an organization in response to environmental pressures are primarily categorized in two types: planned change and unplanned change (Cameron & Green, 2019). In planned change, leaders generally have sufficient time to prepare a comprehensive plan to execute the change (Cameron & Green, 2019); however, unplanned change can be sudden and may require action on the spur of the moment. The next two sections examine popular change management models and their implications for academic advising administration. As appropriate, specific scenario highlights important concepts for the academic advising administrator.

Planned Change Management Models: Lewin, Kotter, McKinsey, Maurer

Burnes (2004) emphasized that change is an omnipresent aspect of organizational life from a strategic and an operational standpoint, so managers must be aware of the organization's ability to handle the change effectively. One of the distinguishing features of planned change is that it provides time for the organization to prepare for the change. The models proposed by Lewin, Kotter, McKinsey, and Mauer effectively explain planned change.

Kurt Lewin's Organizational Change Model

Kurt Lewin's 1947 model is arguably the most popular change management model in the literature. It has three phases: Unfreeze, Change, and Refreeze; these refer to the three-stage process of change (Lewin, 1947). The phases and their implications for advising administration are presented in Table 4.1.

Implications for Academic Advising Administrators

Table 4.1 offers descriptions of Lewin's phases and insights into messages academic advising administrators might send to those they supervise during each phase. The practical implications explained in Table 4.1 also identify both opportunities and conflicts throughout the change process, thus providing advising administrators important lessons in change management to apply to their roles.

Kotter's Model of Change Management

John Kotter, a management professor at Harvard and accomplished change management expert, conducted a study of 100 organizations which were undergoing change and developed the eight-step model of change management process (Kotter, 1996). The details of the model are highlighted in Table 4.2.

TABLE 4.1 Kurt Lewin's Organizational Change Model

Phase #	Title	Description	Practical Implications
1	Unfreeze	This state is arguably the most challenging to implement because the primary goal is to "convince" the team that change is necessary and it is the way forward (Lewin, 1947).	An advising administrator must develop a compelling message by pointing to tangible factors such as declining enrollment, student dissatisfaction, and inefficient workflow. When leaders are unfreezing, individuals with strong personalities may provide counterarguments against the change. To successfully deal with such obstacles, administrators should motivate staff by drawing links between the benefits to the organization and the individuals. For example, suppose the advising unit within an institution installs new software for maximizing efficiency. Leaders can explain to people opposing the change that learning the new software's operations will strengthen their skill set and improve workflow efficiency. Administrators must show a willingness to listen to staff concerns and address them to correspond to the organizational change.
2	Change	Individuals involved in the change make the strategic shifts to their mindset while trying to overcome any insecurity and uncertainty they have about the future. It provides a platform to start and implement the plans to support the new direction (Lewin, 1947).	Emphasis should be on the benefits of the change. Individuals experiencing the transition would want to know "what's in it for me?" In addition to organizational benefits, leaders must specify the personal outcomes. Thus, it is critical to highlight individual rewards—including career growth and enhancement of skill set—that people should expect to receive long-term. While it is beneficial for administrators to empower employees, leaders should draw a line between giving employees flexibility and providing directions. In the software scenario above, if the leader empowers the employee to the extent that the employee can choose to occasionally return to the old way of doing things, the change process will fail. Thus, the employee must perceive the leader as supportive and championing the change. It will instill confidence and lead to employee engagement and workplace innovation.

(Continued)

Table 4.1 (*Continued*)

Phase #	Title	Description	Practical Implications
3	Refreeze	When progress is evident, it serves as indication that the organization is ready to refreeze. The critical signs that an organization is ready to embrace this phase are stability in the organizational processes, increased employee engagement, and higher productivity (Lewin, 1947).	The administration should observe whether employees have settled into new ways of doing things and whether the level of engagement is similar to the pre-change environment. Also, the administrators should acknowledge and reward team members when they adopt the change and improve productivity. Once productivity and engagement are enhanced, it is an appropriate time for the administrators to institutionalize the change.

TABLE 4.2 Kotter's Change Management Model

Step	Title	Description
1	Establish a sense of urgency	The goal of this step is to make a strong case that change is needed. It involves an analysis of the environment in which you look for potential threats or opportunities. It is recommended to establish dialogue with people to stimulate the change-related discussions and convince them.
2	Form a powerful guiding coalition	Employee empowerment and autonomy are the guiding factors of this stage. A cross-functional team that is highly autonomous can play an important role in the change process.
3	Develop a vision	It is critical for leaders to form a vision to initiate change and develop specific strategies required to implement that change.
4	Communicate the vision	The focus shifts from developing to communicating the vision. If the vision does not create a buy-in from a majority of the people, the efforts in developing the vision will be futile.

(*Continued*)

Step	Title	Description
5	Initiate action and remove barriers	Identify factors that create barriers—hierarchies, resistance cultures, change fatigue—and proactively work to remove the obstacles by supporting and rewarding people.
6	Generate short-term wins	Create subgoals and celebrate the successes achieved along the way to keep individuals engaged and enhance motivation.
7	Consolidate gains	Keep the momentum achieved in the previous stage. Analyze wins and failure in prior steps.
8	Institutionalize the change	The final phase is to ensure that change has been ingrained in the company's culture.

Note. Adapted from Kotter (1996).

Implications for Academic Advising Administrators

To understand the practical implications of this model for advising administrators, consider the following scenario: university administration wants to make a structural change in the way the institution delivers advising services. The administration has decided to move away from its current centralized approach to a decentralized model. They reorganize the advising team by assigning each advisor to be liaison for a specific college and relocate their office such that it is housed in their assigned college to serve students more effectively in discipline-specific areas.

The practical implications for advising administrators as it relates to the model steps are highlighted in Table 4.3.

McKinsey 7S Model of Change Management

The McKinsey 7S Model, created by Tom Peters and Robert Waterman, has subsequently been used to assess change management practices at various firms (Waterman et al., 1980). Their research identified seven elements of the organization which need to work in harmony for an organizational change to be successful (Alshaher, 2013; Waterman et al., 1980). The term 7S is included in the model because all identified elements begin with the letter "S":

- Strategy: The specific plan that outlines how organization will implement change.
- Structure: The vertical and horizontal connections among jobs that identify chain of command and establish accountability.
- Systems: The procedures utilized to accomplish routine activities in the organization.

TABLE 4.3 Implications of Kotter's Model

Step	Implications
Establish a sense of urgency	To accomplish change, advising administrators should proactively work with the institutional leadership team to understand the rationale supporting change. It will help them make a strong case for change in their division.
Form a powerful guiding coalition	It is also vital for an administrator to identify members of their division who will spearhead this change. It is helpful to look for employees from other divisions who are willing to assist.
Develop a vision	Administrators need to work with the coalition team to develop a vision that contains a strong rationale for the change.
Communicate the vision	Explain to the team why the change is important. It is advisable to include concrete examples of peer institutions that have implemented the change and benefits they received. It is critical to include anticipated benefits in the message while communicating to the stakeholders.
Initiate action and remove barriers	Identify roadblocks that can create problems while implementing change (e.g., staff shortage, logistical issues, and team member resistance) and work on removing those roadblocks.
Generate short-term wins	Divide the broader goals into sub-goals and assign timelines to each. This will keep the overall process on track.
Consolidate gains	As each sub-goal is accomplished, it is important to celebrate achievements while keeping flexibility for adjusting strategies if sub-goals are not achieved. Positive feedback will enhance employee engagement and motivation to change.
Institutionalize the change	Measure employee productivity on a weekly or monthly basis. When the new system is functioning and employee productivity is increased to match or exceed pre-change levels, it is then time to make changes permanent by infusing with organizational artifacts. This is done by renaming entities (offices, university brochures, website, etc.).

- Shared Values: The shared beliefs among employees that define work ethic in the organization and its culture.
- Style: The leadership style and decision making adopted by the administration.
- Staff: Employees and their general capabilities.
- Skills: The core competencies of employees that gives a competitive edge to an organization.

The first three elements—strategy, structure, and systems—are regarded as "hard" elements since they are more visible and can easily be influenced by management; the other four are described as "soft" elements, work at a deeper level, and are heavily influenced by organizational culture. Soft elements are equally as important to organizational functioning and change as the hard elements (Alshaher, 2013, pp. 1951–1952).

Implications for Academic Advising Administrators

Advising administrators should examine the institution's values and check whether or not they are consistent with the work done in the advising division. If inconsistencies exist, the processes will need to adjust to reflect institutional values. After the initial examination, administrators should analyze the hard elements of strategy, structure, and systems at the institutional level and find whether or not the design of the advising division is effective in its current state or if changes will better serve student needs. Next, analyze the soft elements for potential changes and contemplate if these soft elements are in harmony with each other and if they are consistent with the hard elements. For example, if the institutional strategy is the ongoing investment in staff and their professional development, how often are the division employees receiving such opportunities? If employees are devoid of such opportunities, how can the problem be solved to reflect the institutional strategy? Finally, after implementing change, the advising administrator should ensure that all seven elements are coherent to ensure long-term success.

Maurer's 3-Levels of Change and Resistance Model

Rick Mauer developed this change management model, which focuses on the top three reasons responsible for the failure of change processes in organizations. The three reasons highlighted are: lack of understanding about the change, negative emotional reaction to the change, and lack of trust in managers who champion the change (Maurer, 2020). The critical levels of resistance in Maurer's (2020) model are:

1 **I don't get it:** If employees don't understand the logic behind the change, why would they be willing to accept it?
2 **I don't like it:** Negative emotional reactions from employees are a major concern while implementing the change.
3 **I don't trust you:** Lack of trust between the parties often leads to change management strategies failure.

Implications for Academic Advising Administrators

Academic advising administrators should begin by examining the number of team members who are not on board with the reasoning for the change. It is critical to ensure most of the members are on board before serious efforts can begin. Often, explaining the rationale for the change and demonstrating evidence in success stories from peer institutions is enough to convince skeptics. If faced with strong emotional reactions, it is vital for the academic advising administrator to describe the outcomes if the status quo persists and explain how the change will benefit both the organization and the employees personally. Finally, trust-building is perhaps the largest challenge and should begin ahead of change implementation. If the pre-change assessment results show low levels of trust, administrators should invest in building trust with the team by adopting the following strategies:

- Listening to individual concerns and allowing team members to voice their opinions
- Treating everyone fairly
- Enhancing cooperation within and among various teams by resolving conflicts
- Building credibility by demonstrating past successes

Unplanned Change Management Models: Mitroff, Convergence/ Upheaval, and Punctuated Equilibrium

Unplanned changes are often the result of abrupt changes in the external environment. These changes are also referred to as *crisis management situations* and require fast-paced decision making and knowledge of available resources for successfully navigating the change process (Cameron & Green, 2019). The next sections examine models of unplanned change along with their implications for academic advising administration.

Mitroff's Crisis Management Model

Ian Mitroff, an accomplished crisis management expert, proposed a model of crisis management that consists of the following five phases:

i Signal detection entails systematically looking for warning signs of a crisis.
ii Prevention/preparation involves taking pre-emptive steps against crisis and keeping back up plans to manage crisis if it does take place.
iii Containment/damage limitation focuses on minimizing the impact of crisis by developing a detailed plan.

iv Business recovery stage consists of planning the recovery process by identifying the fundamental business process required to resume the business operation.

v Learning involves reflection and critical analysis of the lessons learned from experiencing a crisis (Mitroff & Pearson, 1993; Mitroff, 2005).

Implications for Academic Advising Administrators

Academic advising administrators must proactively look for any indicators of a potential crisis, such as increased student complaints, frequent errors made by staff members, or ineffective training procedures. Time is of the essence in any crisis management procedure. After identifying early indicators, administrators must swiftly develop a plan that includes the following:

- A cross-functional team of staff, faculty, administrators, and students;
- Analyzing various facets of the crisis;
- Establishing multiple channels of communications with the stakeholders;
- Identifying how business operations will continue.

Next, it is critical to share information with stakeholders about the procedures adopted to handle the crisis, minimize long-term damage, and leverage resources. Also, enact a system that allows the institution to run its operations with changes incorporated to combat the problem and reassure stakeholders that the business will regain momentum. Celebrating smaller wins achieved in the previous steps can help overcome challenges. In the final stage, the administrators should codify the lessons learned and share them with their team, creating long-term changes in the work processes and improving the institutional crisis management system.

Convergence/Upheaval and Punctuated Equilibrium Models

Two other popular models of unplanned change management are the Convergence Upheaval Model (Tushman et al., 1986) and Punctuated Equilibrium Model (Gersick, 1991). Both models share a common theoretical foundation; each suggests that radical organizational changes occur during a brief period of profound change, preceding and following extended periods of organizational stability (Shaw, 2018).

The Convergence/Upheaval Model argues that an organization experiences extended periods of convergence characterized by similar types of work routines, policies, and procedures; any changes that occur during converge are minor. When the organization encounters a crisis, the convergence cycle is broken by an upheaval—a period of significant change often executed in response to an emergency (Tushman et al., 1986). Similarly, according to the Punctuated Equilibrium Paradigm, organizational equilibrium is punctuated by periods of substantial change that interfere with more extended periods of stability (Gersick, 1991). When organizational equilibrium is punctured, a significant change occurs. As a result of the crisis, leaders need to engage in mental exercises and physical practice of deconstructing corporate norms to manage change (Shaw, 2018).

Implications for Academic Advising Administrators

Leadership competencies most useful under crisis management are fast decision making, effective communication, and risk-taking. One of the most critical tasks is forming a team of experienced employees that plays an essential role in crisis management. The academic advising administrator should then assess the overall risk and business impact in collaboration with the team. In the case of multiple threats, analyze each one separately. After the assessment, develop an action plan to mitigate risk using the change procedures. For example, in 2020, when the COVID-19 pandemic hit the U.S., most agencies, including K-12 and higher education institutions, switched to either completely remote learning or hybrid learning. The academic advising administrators formed crisis response teams, developed an action plan to continue in the safest way possible with the required changes in their business operations, and delegated responsibilities to the leadership team and crisis management team members. It is critical to communicate with stakeholders via various channels and provide frequent updates to enhance transparency and credibility. Finally, monitor the crisis continuously and adjust plans as the situations evolve.

Conclusion

As institutions of higher education work to meet the many and varied demands of rapid change, academic advising administrators will play a significant role in leading the necessary change management efforts. The unique position of an administrator within the broader institutional context requires deft navigation of organizational needs while leading necessary change strategies to meet the needs of an evolving student population. An administrator's mettle may be further tested in the face of unforeseen changes or moments of crisis. Success in times of change is only achieved if the advising administrator is empowered to act and to build flexibility into the operations of the advising team.

Empowerment is not simply an imposed institutional mindset. Empowerment will emerge through careful planning and preparation. Part of that preparation involves reflecting on change management models like the ones discussed in this chapter. Each offers a framework within which an academic advising administrator can begin to anticipate and prepare for change. When change does inevitably occur, the administrator will have considered and internalized the tools and strategies to act swiftly and decisively within a culture prepared for adaptation.

Reflection Questions

1 As an advising administrator, which type of transformational leadership behaviors would I, my colleagues, and my employees associate with me?
2 In my role as an advising administrator, how do I influence and inspire my direct reports?
3 Do the advisors in my unit feel exhausted or uplifted after interacting with me? Are they inspired to take any action?
4 Do I identify empathy and inclusion as critical leadership qualities? In my role as an advising administrator, do I understand what each person in my team is struggling with most? How do I know this? How do I show I understand?
5 What specific behaviors do I need to utilize to be an advising administrator who demonstrates servant leadership?
6 What is the difference between planned change and unplanned change? How should I prepare for such changes in my unit?
7 What can an advising administrator do to promote diversity and inclusion to better equip advisors to recognize and address inequity and prejudice in the workplace?

References

Albritton, R. L. (1998). A new paradigm of leader effectiveness for academic libraries: An empirical study of the Bass (1985) model of transformational leadership. In T. F. Mech & G. B. McCabe (Eds.), *Leadership and academic librarians* (pp. 66–84). Greenwood.

Alfadli, M. A., & Al-Mehaisen, S. M. (2019). The reality of administrative empowerment among the recently employed administrators in the intermediate schools. *International Education Studies, 12*(6), 120–133. https://pdfs.semanticscholar.org/b944/7be62e2dfba32010058cb7bb503947c5abbc.pdf

Alshaher, A. A.-F. (2013). The McKinsey 7S model framework for e-learning system readiness assessment. *International Journal of Advances in Engineering & Technology, 6*(5), 1948–1966.

Burnes, B. (2004). *Managing change: A strategic approach to organizational dynamics* (4th ed.). Prentice Hall.

Cameron, E., & Green, M. (2019). *Making sense of change management: A complete guide to the models, tools and techniques of organizational change* (5th ed.). Kogan Page.

Chalmers, L. (2005, September 01). An advising administrator's duty. *Academic Advising Today, 28*(3). https://nacada.ksu.edu/Resources/Academic-Advising-Today/View-Articles/An-Advising-Administrators-Duty.aspx

Chitorelidze, S. (2017). *Empowerment in academia: Non-academic professional staff's perspectives on employee empowerment* (Publication No. 13849410) [Master's thesis, University of Missouri-Columbia]. ProQuest Dissertations & Theses Global. https://doi.org/10.32469/10355/62353

Crippen, C. (2004). Servant-leadership as an effective model for educational leadership and management: First to serve, then to lead. *Management in Education, 18*(5), 11–16. https://doi.org/10.1177/089202060501800503

De Matos, J. A., & Clegg, S. R. (2013). Sustainability and organizational change. *Journal of Change Management, 13*(4), 382–386. https://doi.org/10.1080/14697017.2013.851912

Drake, J. K. (2011). The role of academic advising in student retention and persistence. *About Campus: Enriching the Student Learning Experience, 16*(3), 8–12. https://doi.org/10.1002/abc.20062

Dye, A. (2011). *Empowerment starts here: Seven principles to empowering urban youth.* Rowman & Littlefield Education.

Fountain, C. (Ed.). (2021). *Academic advising as a tool for student success and educational equity.* National Resource Center for The First-Year Experience & Students in Transition.

Gersick, C. J. G. (1991). Revolutionary change theories: A multilevel exploration of the punctuated equilibrium paradigm. *Academy of Management Review, 16*(1), 10–36. https://doi.org/10.2307/258605

Greenleaf, R. K. (1970). *The servant as leader.* Greenleaf Center for Servant-Leadership.

Greenleaf, R. K. (1977). *Servant leadership: A journey into the nature of legitimate power and greatness.* Paulist Press.

Hackman, M. Z., & Johnson, C. E. (2004). *Leadership: A communication perspective* (4th ed.). Waveland Press, Inc.

Kezar, A. J., Carducci, R., & Contreras-McGavin, M. (2006). *Rethinking the "L" word in higher education: The revolution of research on leadership.* Jossey-Bass.

Kotter, J. P. (1996). *Leading change.* Harvard Business School Press.

Lambert, P. A. (2006). *Faculty perceptions of empowerment, job satisfaction, and commitment to organization in three midwest universities* (Publication No. 30531699) [Doctoral dissertation, University of Missouri-Columbia). ProQuest Dissertations and Theses Global.

Lau, W. K. J. (2010). *Empowerment of non-academic personnel in higher education: Exploring associations with perceived organizational support for innovation and organizational trust* [Doctoral dissertation, University of Iowa]. https://doi.org/10.17077/etd.nua1b3wl

Lee, W-C. (2009, March 01). Promoting and practicing diversity in advising: Rationales and approaches. *Academic Advising Today, 32*(1). https://nacada. ksu.edu/Resources/Academic-Advising-Today/View-Articles/Promoting-and-Practicing-Diversity-in-Advising-Rationales-and-Approaches.aspx

Lewin, K. (1947). Frontiers in group dynamics: Concept, method and reality in social science; Social equilibria and social change. *Human Relations, 1*(1), 5–41. https://doi.org/10.1177/001872674700100103

Lowenstein, M. (2005). If advising is teaching, what do advisors teach? *NACADA Journal, 25*(2), 65–73. https://doi.org/10.12930/0271-9517-25.2.65

Maurer, R. (2020, February 17). *Why don't you want what I want? The three faces of resistance.* ZenBusiness. https://www.zenbusiness.com/blog/whatiwant1/

Mbindyo, M., O'Connor, R. J., & Nandedkar, A. (2021). Linking transformational leadership theory to the practice of academic advising – A conceptual paper. *Journal of Higher Education Theory and Practice, 21*(12), 172–182. https://doi. org/10.33423/jhetp.v21i12.4710

McClellan, J. L. (2010). Leadership and complexity: Implications for practice within the advisement leadership bodies at colleges and universities. *Complicity: An International Journal of Complexity and Education, 7*(2), 32–51. https:// journals.library.ualberta.ca/complicity/index.php/complicity/article/view/8916

Mitroff, I. I. (2005). *Why some companies emerge stronger and better from a crisis: 7 essential lessons for surviving disaster.* AMACOM.

Mitroff, I. I., & Pearson, C. M. (1993). *Crisis management: A diagnostic guide for improving your organization's crisis-preparedness.* Jossey-Bass.

Moran, J. W., & Brightman, B. K. (2000). Leading organizational change. *Journal of Workplace Learning, 12*(2), 66–74. https://doi.org/10.1108/13665620010316226

Museus, S. D. (2021). Revisiting the role of academic advising in equitably serving diverse college students. *NACADA Journal, 41*(1), 26–32. https://doi. org/10.12930/NACADA-21-06

Nandedkar, A., Mbindyo, M., & O'Connor, R. J. (2020). Advisor transformational leadership and its impact on advisees: A conceptual analysis. *Journal of Higher Education Theory and Practice, 20*(14), 156–169. https://doi.org/10.33423/jhetp.v20i14.3858

Pan, D., Valliant, M., & Reed, B. (2009). Creative collaboration: Developing a partnership with an academic advisor to promote information literacy and student success. *College & Undergraduate Libraries, 16*(2–3), 138–152. https://doi.org/10.1080/10691310902993191

Pargett, K. K. (2011). *The effects of academic advising on college student development in higher education* [Master's thesis, University of Nebraska-Lincoln]. https://digitalcommons.unl.edu/cehsedaddiss/81/

Paul, W. K., & Fitzpatrick, C. (2015). Advising as servant leadership: Investigating student satisfaction. *NACADA Journal, 35*(2), 28–35. https://doi.org/10.12930/NACADA-14-019

Shaw, M. (2018). Unplanned change and crisis management. In A. Farazmand (Ed.), *Global encyclopedia of public administration, public policy, and governance* (pp. 6058–6063). Springer. https://doi.org/10.1007/978-3-319-20928-9_748

Spears, L. C. (2010). Character and servant leadership: Ten characteristics of effective, caring leaders. *The Journal of Virtues & Leadership, 1*(1), 25–30.

Tsai, M. C.-H. (2012). *An empirical study of the conceptualization of overall organizational justice and its relationship with psychological empowerment, organizational commitment and turnover intention in higher education* [Doctoral dissertation, University of Washington]. https://digital.lib.washington.edu/researchworks/bitstream/handle/1773/20840/Tsai_washington_0250E_10683.pdf?sequence=1

Tushman, M. L., Newman, W. H., & Romanelli, E. (1986). Convergence and upheaval: Managing the unsteady pace of organizational evolution. *California Management Review, 29*(1), 29–44. https://doi.org/10.2307/41165225

van Dierendonck, D. (2011). Servant leadership: A review and synthesis. *Journal of Management, 37*(4), 1228–1261. https://doi.org/10.1177/0149206310380462

Waterman Jr., R. H., Peters, T. J., & Phillips, J. R. (1980). Structure is not organization. *Business Horizons, 23*(3), 14–26. https://doi.org/10.1016/0007-6813(80)90027-0

White, E. R. (2015). Academic advising in higher education: A place at the core. *The Journal of General Education, 64*(4), 263–277. https://doi.org/10.1353/jge.2015.0024

Xie, L. (2020). The impact of servant leadership and transformational leadership on learning organization: A comparative analysis. *Leadership & Organization Development Journal, 41*(2), 220–236. https://doi.org/10.1108/LODJ-04-2019-0148

Yammarino, F. J., & Bass, B. M. (1990). Transformational leadership and multiple levels of analysis. *Human Relations, 43*(10), 975–995. https://doi.org/10.1177/001872679004301003

5

LEGAL AND ETHICAL IMPLICATIONS FOR ADVISING ADMINISTRATORS

Susan M. Taffe Reed and John Wesley Lowery

Note: No part of this chapter should be interpreted as legal advice. Advising administrators should consult their institution's general counsel or seek personal counsel for appropriate legal guidance within their respective countries.

Legal and ethical issues contribute to some of the most challenging and complex professional experiences that advising administrators encounter. The terrain that academic advisors navigate is ever-shifting: Laws pertaining to higher education change; ethical norms in society evolve; and institutional policies are updated. Therefore, advising administrators must engage in consistent professional development, as they are charged with synthesizing legal and ethical considerations with institutional policies and procedures. This chapter reviews the current landscape of legal and ethical affairs in academic advising programs to provide advising administrators with the tools necessary to ensure ethical practices for themselves and those they supervise. It also aims to protect personnel and institutions from legal risk and addresses how advising administrators can position ethical and legal issues front and center through their leadership.

Robinson (2004) warned, "As we live in a litigious society, it is always possible that well-intentioned advisors can find themselves facing situations that could have been avoided" (para. 1). Knowing common legal issues in higher education can help advising administrators avoid pitfalls and identify liabilities. Despite conducting careful, high-quality work, they may nevertheless encounter situations where a student takes legal action based in theories such as "educational malpractice, negligence, breach of a fiduciary relationship, estoppel, and breach of contract" (Latourette, 2011, p. 216). Advising administrators should help prepare personnel and their

DOI: 10.4324/9781003437598-9

institution by including education on these issues through new advisor training and ongoing development for all advisors. As leaders of advising programs, administrators can strengthen their institution's response to legal and ethical issues by conducting regular audits of policy design/redesign, technology use, program management, and student advocacy.

In addition to decisions that have complex legal ramifications, advising administrators will encounter decisions with associated ethical dilemmas. The most common "ethical issues that affect helpers are competence, dual relationships, confidentiality, and duty to warn" (Reynolds, 2016, p. 461). Whereas legal decisions generally have clear-cut "right" answers, ethical decisions can present a multitude of possible choices and outcomes, all of which may seem "right," and yet, none of which are ideal. Ethical considerations have a layered relationship with academic advising theoretical foundations, practice, and praxis, because academic advisors must be "strong student advocates, neutral mediators, moral role models, and conscientious staff representatives" (Fisher, 2005, para. 16). Advising administrators should develop departmental cultures where advisors can talk about challenging ethical decisions, work to align processes and policies with their unit's philosophies and practices, and build more socially just systems that promote equity and inclusion.

Consulting the Pillars of Academic Advising

NACADA: The Global Community for Academic Advising (NACADA) endorses four documents to guide the profession that, collectively, constitute the Pillars of Academic Advising: The Concept of Academic Advising (NACADA, 2006), Academic Advising Core Competencies Model (2017a; hereafter referred to as Core Competencies), Core Values of Academic Advising (2017b; hereafter referred to as Core Values), and the Council for the Advancement of Standards in Higher Education: Standards and Guidelines for Academic Advising (CAS, 2015). Advising professionals can reference these pillars to steer professional work, inform advisor training topics, and shepherd student interactions.

The Concept of Academic Advising

The Concept of Academic Advising (NACADA, 2006) contains three parts: Curriculum, Pedagogy, and Student Learning Outcomes. The Pedagogy section explains that "although the specific methods, strategies, and techniques may vary, the relationship between advisors and students is fundamental and is characterized by mutual respect, trust, and ethical behavior" (NACADA, 2006, para. 7).

Academic Advising Core Competencies

In relation to "advising supervisors, managers, and mentors," NACADA's Core Competencies are intended to "identify strengths and areas for staff development, and to guide hiring, training, and evaluation" (NACADA, 2017a, para. 1). The three components of the Core Competencies— Conceptual, Informational, and Relational—all relate to legal and ethical issues. For example, the Conceptual component discusses "how equitable and inclusive environments are created and maintained" (NACADA, 2017a, para. 3), which is a significant ethical consideration. The Informational component includes "legal guidelines of advising practice, including privacy regulations and confidentiality" (NACADA, 2017a, para. 4). And the Relational component recommends that professionals "articulate a personal philosophy of academic advising" (NACADA, 2017a, para. 5), for which it is wise to consider ethics.

Core Values of Academic Advising

All seven of NACADA's (2017b) Core Values engage with ethics: Respect, Inclusivity, Commitment, Professionalism, Empowerment, Integrity, and Caring. Saunders and Wilson (2016) described the relationship between the Core Values and ethics, "It is easy to confuse values and ethics. Values describe what a person believes is important in life, whereas ethical principles and standards prescribe what is considered good or bad and right or wrong behavior" (p. 90). Professionalism and Inclusivity also relate to legal issues.

CAS Shared Ethical Standards

The seven basic principles outlined by CAS in the "Statement of Shared Ethical Principles" (2015) is one of the most readily used professional resources on ethical foundations in higher education. These principles include "autonomy, non-malfeasance, beneficence, justice, fidelity, veracity, and affiliation" (CAS, 2015, p. 22). Kitchener (1985) laid the groundwork for these concepts, which have been developed and expanded over time.

Making Ethical Decisions

Making ethical decisions is essential in the practice of academic advising (CAS, 2015). As supervisors, advising administrators are obligated to identify and resolve ethical issues while mentoring staff (Damminger, 2015) and providing regular opportunities for consultation with colleagues.

When considering an ethical decision, "professionals should be conversant with the professional association standards or frameworks with which their office or functional area aligns" (Saunders & Wilson, 2016, p. 96). Additionally, institutional policies and legal direction should be considered when making decisions. Put simply, ethics are the standards for what is deemed right and wrong, and, "Right and wrong are subjective concepts that vary according to culture, moral climate, and individual circumstance" (Fisher, 2005, para. 4).

> Ethical behavior overlaps, but should not be confused with legal behavior, which…is right and wrong behavior determined by others. Moral behavior is also about right verses wrong and affects the way people live their lives and make decisions. Ethics covers the former areas but extends beyond *right verses wrong* to *right verses right* decisions. Ethics is inclusive of the basic principles of right action.
>
> *(Damminger, 2011, p. 208)*

Some ethical decisions are clear, especially when options are on the extreme ends of the ethical spectrum. The work of advising administrators, however, inhabits gray areas. It can be challenging to identify the best path forward when dealing with ambiguity. There are usually many factors to consider, multiple answers, and differing approaches to solving problems. As Damminger (2015) explained, "The difficulty in determining the best course of action stems from the basic principles of right verses [sic] right behaviors; that is, more than one possible action may effectively resolve a dilemma" (p. 55).

Personal Values and Philosophy of Advising

Advising administrators bring their own set of values to professional work. Sometimes, personal values can conflict with those of others and with institutional policies and procedures (Chmielewski, 2004). Sometimes ethics is associated with a personal moral belief system; Compton (2014) provided analogies to explain this relationship:

> If morals are the traits that one aspires to, then ethics are the guiding philosophy behind them. Ethics are not static and may adapt and change over time … If an individual were driving a car, morals would be the components of the car and ethics would be the actual thinking about the choices that come along on the road … to go left, to go right, how to maneuver, and so on.
>
> *(Compton, 2014, para. 9–10)*

Keep in mind, "as advisors, we are institutional representatives and as such, must demonstrate loyalty and support for institutional policies" (Fisher, 2005, para. 13) while practicing "emotional objectivity" in making ethical decisions (Landon, 2007, para. 20).

Advising administrators should prioritize support and engagement with diversity and inclusion as part of ethical practices within their department. It is critical to ensure that all students are treated with respect and equality (Landon, 2007) free of discrimination (Damminger, 2011). Damminger (2015) explained that "equitable does not necessarily mean that individuals receive identical treatment or reap similar outcomes; it means that any differences in the treatment of others do not create inequalities" (p. 58). Furthermore, training that assists academic advising administrators in fostering an inclusive work environment is valuable. Cultural differences should also be considered (Landon, 2007). Advising administrators should ensure that all advisors know the process for students to report biases at their institution.

Advising administrators should consider encouraging personnel to write personal philosophies of advising as part of ongoing professional development. Additionally, advising administrators can ensure a collective interpretation of their unit's work by centering work around the advising office's mission, vision, and objectives. After composing their advising philosophy, advisors can reflect on it when weighing complicated decisions. Advising offices are only prepared to navigate legal and ethical issues when all personnel—especially student-facing personnel—are trained to identify potential issues and raise them at meetings and conversations. Addressing these performance issues with personnel can be challenging. Nevertheless, clear information, feedback, and support are crucial opportunities for growth and development.

While the advising administrator role necessitates quick thinking and action, there is also value in taking the necessary time to fully consider each situation. Damminger's (2015) advice to new advisors holds true for new advising administrators: "Avoid haphazard or rushed decisions, consider all perspectives, consult with more experienced colleagues, ensure thoroughness in the deliberations, consider consequences in both the short and long term, and follow up with everyone involved" (p. 64).

Ethics Committee

Development of an ethics committee, a specific group of colleagues who meet to discuss ethical questions regarding advising, can be beneficial. This group can come together swiftly as needed to discuss current student issues and periodically to review policies and procedures. As Compton (2014) queried, "How do we know when to do the *right* thing, versus just doing things *right*?" (para. 15). A sounding board, whether in the form of a trusted colleague, supervisor, ombudsperson, or committee, can expand the professional's perspective (Saunders & Wilson, 2016) and ensure a consistent institutional response. As a best practice, Damminger (2015) recommended: "Meet with other advisors in the unit and draft a check-list for solving ethical dilemmas. Share these ideas with administrators for final approval and store with other advising guidelines for easy reference and consistent utilization within the department" (p. 65).

Determining which standards and values should influence decisions is a critical aspect of ethical decision-making (Landon, 2007) and should be discussed at the outset of formulating an ethics committee. The group may wish to draw on the mission and vision of their institution and advising office, as well as a related professional organization for guidance.

The following steps and considerations may be useful in examining possible solutions for ethical decision-making by identifying the best possible solution that does the least harm:

- Collect relevant information about the problem and define the issue at hand (Damminger, 2011). Consider the various possible paths forward. What harm might come from each option, and to whom? What good might come from each option, and to whom? Map the ideas out on paper to create a visual representation. Can a specific approach be identified? If not, which of the seemingly equal decisions is the best course of action (Damminger, 2015)?
- Review your office and institution's mission and vision statements. What meaning can you glean to inform your decision? Is there relevant guidance from a professional organization or academic publication that speaks to the issue? How does this issue intersect with equity and inclusion?
- Identify and follow any applicable legal guidelines (Damminger, 2011; it may be necessary to consult general counsel).
- Imagine reflecting on the possible decisions one week, one month, and one year from now. Will the decision stand the test of time?
- Have a planned process in place for those who disagree with a decision to express their grievance and seek appeal (Landon, 2007).

Legal Issues to Consider

Regarding the legal issues present in advising administration, the issue of institutional control should first be considered. Public colleges and universities are agents of the state and therefore must comply with the requirements of both federal and state constitutions (Kaplin et al., 2020). Miller (2016) observed that "the fundamental area of law that governs the relationships between private colleges and universities and their students is contract law" (p. 114). At public institutions, these contracts are also important as institutions often make contractual promises beyond those required by the federal and state constitutions (Kaplin et al., 2020). Both public and private colleges are generally required to comply with other federal laws governing nondiscrimination, campus safety, and student privacy, which are all tied to receipt of federal financial assistance, including students receiving federal financial aid (Lowery, 2016).

Advising administrators should also be aware of general differences between public and private institutions, such as potential differences in beliefs, attitudes, communities, and ethical principles. For example, a private religiously affiliated college community may hold different values than a nearby nonreligiously affiliated state institution. An institution's mission and vision statements provide key insights into what the community prioritizes and holds dear.

Institutional Policies and Educational Malpractice

Advising administrators often find themselves involved in the communication and interpretation of institutional academic policies. Students expect that advisors will provide them with accurate and clear interpretations of academic policies, even as those policies change. Students have challenged institutions that had changed policies and program offerings after their admission (Kaplin et al., 2020). For example, in *Mahavongsanan v. Hall* (1976), a student sued after a comprehensive examination was added to their program's graduation requirements post admission; they were unable to pass it, resulting in the university's refusal to grant their master's degree. In ruling for the university, the court noted that institutions have "wide latitude and discretion ... in framing their academic degree requirements.... [T]he university clearly is entitled to modify [its requirements] so as to properly exercise its educational responsibility" (*Mahavongsanan v. Hall*, 1976, p. 449). The courts are even more unwilling to rule for students solely on the basis of oral promises. However, the failure to follow how policies are written or applying them to students in ways that are arbitrary or capricious has resulted in rulings against the institution (Kaplin et al., 2020). Students have also sought to challenge institutional action by claiming educational malpractice, largely without success, including cases where the heart of the student's complaint related to academic advising (for example, *Hendricks v. Clemson University*, 2003). Advising administrators can mitigate such scenarios by verifying that their office is updated on all policy changes, working closely with faculty members to avoid siloing, and training advisors specifically to addresses the institution's authority to modify academic policies.

Federal Laws and Academic Advising

With federal laws impacting higher education, the majority of these requirements are placed upon higher education institutions as a condition of the receipt of federal funds. The receipt of federal financial assistance in this context includes direct federal funding to the institution and students' participation in the federal financial aid system (Kaplin et al., 2020; Lowery, 2016). Commonly discussed federal laws directly impacting higher education include those related to nondiscrimination: Title VI of the Civil Rights Act of 1964, Title IX of the Education Amendments of 1972, Section 504 of the Rehabilitation Act of 1973, and the Americans with Disabilities Act of 1990; the Family Educational Rights and Privacy Act (FERPA) of 1974; and The Jeanne Clery Disclosure of Campus Security Policy and Campus Crime Statistics Act (1990). However, there are almost 200 federal laws that impact higher education practice (Hunter & Gehring, 2005), but only a handful of U.S. higher education institutions need to fully appreciate these laws as so many do not participate in the federal financial aid system.

Family Educational Rights and Privacy Act (FERPA)

Any discussion of federal laws and academic advising must begin with a consideration of student privacy. As Rust (2015) noted, "The confidential and trust-based nature of the advising relationship requires that advisors remain current on the policies and procedures in place to protect students' legal rights and to fulfill institutions' legal obligations" (p. 159). The primary federal law impacting student privacy in higher education is FERPA of 1974, which governs how colleges and universities handle students' education records. Under these regulations, education records are defined as "records, files, documents, and other materials which contain information directly related to a student; and are maintained by an educational agency or institution, or by a person acting for such agency or institution" (34 CFR § 99.1). FERPA provides college students three primary rights related to their education records:

- Right to inspect and review education records,
- Right to challenge the content of education records, and
- Right to consent to the disclosure of education records.

FERPA is best understood as a privacy law given the number of exceptions that allow the release of information about a student without their consent. For example, regulations allow the sharing of information with other school officials who have a "legitimate educational interest" (34 CFR § 99.31(a)(1)). The U.S. Department of Education places the obligation for defining legitimate educational interest with institutions but has offered a simple definition—information that is necessary for a school official to carry out their job responsibilities.

When students seek to transfer or continue their studies, FERPA allows institutions to share information with institutions where the student "seeks or intends to enroll" (34 CFR § 99.31(a)(2)). Institutions are also able to share information with the parents of a dependent student as defined by the IRS. Beyond these exceptions, FERPA allows for the release of information with the student's written consent; many institutions have developed online systems for students to collect releases. However, regulations do not require these disclosures, so advising administrators need to consider carefully any institutional policies in the development of their office's processes regarding sharing information with parents. Advising administrators should also ensure that all personnel have a working knowledge of both FERPA and their institution's individual policies.

Privacy Holds. Students must be given the opportunity to request a FERPA privacy block (i.e., a confidential hold) on their account to prevent third parties from accessing their directory information. Individual institutions set forth what constitutes directory information (Robinson, 2011), such as: student name, identification number (unless the number alone could allow access to the educational record), address, email, telephone number, academic major, date of birth, dates of attendance, activities, sports, awards, class standing, degree (Robinson, 2011; Rust, 2014, 2015).

Reporting

There are multiple state and federal laws that create reporting responsibilities for large numbers of university employees that may apply to advising administrators and their personnel. At the federal level, both Title IX of the Education Amendments of 1972 and the Clery Act create reporting obligations. Under Title IX, "responsible employees" must report incidents of sexual harassment to the Title IX Coordinator. Under the Trump administration, new regulations (Nondiscrimination on the Basis of Sex in Education Programs or Activities Receiving Federal Financial Assistance, 2020) were issued for Title IX, which afforded institutions the ability to more narrowly define responsible employees than previously permissible. Advising office personnel are often defined in institutional policies as responsible employees and as such they have reporting obligations to the Title IX Coordinator. Advising administrators are encouraged to familiarize personnel with the Title IX office and process for reporting.

With the Clery Act, institutions are required to collect crime statistics from "campus security authorities" (20 U.S.C. §1092(f)(4)(B)(i)) and report those statistics annually. In 2020, the U.S. Department of Education withdrew *The Handbook for Campus Safety and Security Reporting* (2016), which was replaced with a brief Clery Act Appendix for the FSA Handbook (2020). With this change, colleges and universities were given greater discretion to narrowly define campus security authorities. Still, while the guidance for both Title IX and the Clery Act has changed, many institutions have not changed their policies to narrow the institutional definition; it is incumbent upon advising administrators to understand how their institutions define these terms and comply with institutional policies. These issues are further unsettled as the Biden Administrator has begun the process of reviewing the 2020 Title IX regulations and has proposed regulatory changes.

There are also state laws requiring the reporting of child abuse cases (both physical and sexual). In meeting with advisors, students may disclose their experiences with abuse. Often state laws are far more inclusive in their reporting requirements than federal laws and require reporting directly to the state, so advising administrators need to have a clear understanding of these laws and state policy.

Constitutional Rights

Often, advising administrators are included among the institution's senior personnel. As such, they may be asked to join a range of committees and to collaborate with colleagues across campus on issues indirectly related to academic advising, such as joining a behavior intervention team (BIT) or campus assessment, response, and evaluation (CARE) team to address student health, behavior, and safety concerns, or joining a bias response team to review student-submitted reports. The personnel they oversee may also be connected with this work and encounter these issues during student advising appointments. Advising administrators will benefit from background on constitutional rights that may come up in their work. In fact, because of their extensive experience supporting students, familiarity with student issues, and skills regarding policies and procedures, advising administrators make highly valued members of institutional conversations surrounding these issues. Public colleges and universities are also required to comply with U.S. and state constitutions. The aspects of the U.S. Constitution that most commonly impact higher education are the First Amendment; the Second Amendment; the Fourth Amendment, particularly search and seizure; and the Fifth and Fourteenth Amendments' guarantees of due process.

Over the past 60 years, the courts have considered a number of issues in the context of the First Amendment, which have established, expanded, or clarified student rights in higher education. In *Tinker v. Des Moines* (1968), the Supreme Court observed, "It can hardly be argued that either students or teachers shed their constitutional rights to freedom of speech or expression at the schoolhouse gate" (p. 506). Colleges and universities have struggled to balance competing rights to create more inclusive campus environments. Justice Samuel Alito noted while serving on the U.S. Court of Appeals for the Third Circuit, that the free speech clause protected a "wide variety of speech that listeners may consider deeply offensive, including statements that impugn another's race or national origin or that denigrate religious beliefs" (*Saxe v. State College Area School District*, 2000, p. 206). As a result, many public colleges and universities have had their harassment policies overturned by the courts as unconstitutional because they prohibited some speech protected by the First Amendment (e.g., *McCauley v. Univ. of the Virgin Islands*, 2010). The law remains relatively unsettled regarding disciplining students for speech on social media platforms, despite the Supreme Court's ruling in *Mahanoy Area School Dist. v. B. L.* (2021). In cases where the courts have sided with institutions (*Tatro v. University of Minnesota*, 2012; *Yoder v. University of Louisville*, 2013), the student's online speech was directly related to their academic program and the program or institution had clearly defined, content-neutral policies. Academic advising administrators should understand the relationship between student's First Amendment rights and their academic endeavors. The issues that students might raise with academic advisors include concerns about freedom of expression in the classroom, experiences with racist and bigoted speech, and concerns about the intersections of social media and professional standards.

Potentially most significant in the context of academic advising offices are the Fifth and Fourteen Amendments. Advisors at public institutions are regarded as agents of the state whose actions must afford students due process under these amendments. However, the process required is different than other decisions within higher education institutions (Kaplin et al., 2020). For example, when considering the dismissal of a student from an academic program, the Supreme Court ruled that due process required only that a student be a "fully informed respondent of the faculty's dissatisfaction... [and that] the ultimate decision to dismiss respondent was careful and deliberate" (*Board of Curators, Univ. of Mo. v. Horowitz*, 1978, p. 85). Building upon this decision, the Supreme Court deferred to the decisions of administrators and faculty members regarding academic questions unless the decision is "a substantial departure from accepted academic norms as to demonstrate that the person or committee responsible did not actually exercise professional judgment" (*Regents of University of Michigan v. Ewing*, 1985, p. 226).

In both cases, the Supreme Court avoided answering the question as to whether students had either a liberty or property interest in their continued enrollment, even while assuming the requirements of the Fourteenth Amendment (Kaplin et al., 2020). Robinson (2004) identified two potential areas within the work of academic advisors where due process concerns are most significant, noting that "certainly an academic advisor involved in decisions or appeals of aid should offer due process to a student about to lose eligibility for future funding …. Admission to selective professional degree programs could also require due process" (p. 2). Academic advising administrators also influence considerations of cases involving students who are on probation or who do not meet academic requirements.

Risk Management and Legal Protection

Within the increasingly litigious context of society and higher education, advising administrators need to be prepared to regularly manage and address legal issues in advising practices. Simultaneously, they must build sensitivity toward identifying ethical issues. Saunders and Wilson (2016) pointed out that ethical issues in student affairs have always been complex, "but with increasing complexity in higher education administration and the intricacy of challenges faced by students, enhancing our ethical integrity requires even more diligence and careful considerations of morally ambiguous situations" (p. 103). While litigation may be impossible to avoid entirely, advising administrators have many opportunities to reduce potential issues. Obviously, activities that jeopardize student well-being and safety should not be practiced (Miller, 2016). All advisors should minimize the possibility of malpractice liability by only promoting "experiential learning opportunities (e.g., internships, service-learning, study abroad) that have been vetted by institution officials for appropriate educational quality and student safety" (Rust, 2015, p. 166), sharing only confirmed institutional information, promoting only institutionally endorsed programs, and avoiding promises of course availability, except in the case of having documented confirmation from the academic department offering the course (Rust, 2015).

Consulting General Counsel

In addition to developing knowledgeable and conscientious personnel, perhaps the greatest resource that advising administrators have at their disposal is general counsel. However, access to this resource varies considerably depending on one's institution. Some advising administrators meet regularly with one or more members of the general counsel team to discuss emergent student situations at some colleges and universities; at others, they may not have direct access. While large institutions might have several attorneys dedicated to student-related situations, small institutions might only have one lawyer on staff or might contract with a firm who serves a group or consortium of institutions, and approval may be required to reach out to legal counsel. Some institutions hire attorneys with specialization in certain areas of law (Moneta, 2021).

Advising administrators should prepare themselves to work with available legal resources to effectively guide their department's work. Whenever possible, advising administrators should develop a relationship with the lawyer in the Office of General Counsel with whom they work most often; at institutions where access to counsel is limited and a specific individual is the conduit to communicating with the firm, advising administrators should get to know this individual and carefully prioritize and organize potential questions. Advisors too should know the protocol for relaying their questions to the advising administrator or consulting with general counsel (Damminger, 2015). There may be times when legal services will be needed for small matters, such as signing student internship letters, entering into agreements with outside entities that could have legal implications for the institution, and establishing who is the appropriate contact person for students' and families' attorneys to contact. When more significant matters arise, advising administrators must understand how best to obtain legal advice. Damminger (2015) advised, "Do not wait until counsel is needed to research recommended procedures" (p. 66).

Insurance

Because students can sue advisors personally, advising administrators and academic advisors should consider personal liability insurance to augment legal support provided by their institution (Moneta, 2021). Justice (2019) noted that the institution's lawyers work for the board, who oversee responsibility for the college; they are not you or your supervisor's attorney. Moneta (2021) suggested, "Understand what support the college or university will provide and whether personal legal representation or coverage should be obtained" (p. 109).

Partnering with Faculty Members and Student Affairs Colleagues

Advising administrators have a great resource in their colleagues, especially those who have years of experience or expertise. Because of their familiarity with policies and procedures at the institution, faculty and staff members often consult advising office personnel with questions. There may be instances where faculty members look to advising administrators and academic advisors to understand institutional policies and protocol, despite these policies originating outside the advising office. In some cases, the advising administrator may be able to provide helpful information; in other situations, it is prudent to refer the faculty member to their department chair or another appropriate academic affairs administrator.

It is key that all colleagues work from and provide students with accurate information. Advising information can take many forms, such as official faculty and student handbooks, written documents, handouts, websites, and catalogs. In situations where the advising office is not the only resource for the student to utilize, or not the appropriate resource, making referrals is critical. Advising administrators should make sure that personnel are adequately trained to identify when students with whom they meet may need additional expertise and referral to other campus offices.

Advising administrators should forge relationships between their personnel and other colleagues on campus to assist in familiarizing advisors with available resources. Keeping the ethical guideline to do no harm top of mind, advising personnel should understand that "when practitioners work outside their areas of competence, it is possible to do more harm than good" (Reynolds, 2016, p. 461). It is essential that advisors "make a conscious effort to avoid speaking for areas outside our scopes," such as with regulations pertaining to international students or student athletes. Students may take an advisor's "vague assurance on a matter as official" (Robinson, 2004, para. 8). This ill-advised guidance may also lead to lawsuits.

Conclusion

There are broad opportunities for advising administrators to develop ethically and legally informed practices that prioritize student-centered education, safety, well-being, and socially-just policies and procedures. This chapter has identified a number of key areas to consider for the training and professional development of academic advisors.

Global conversations on ethical issues in advising administration are valuable within the profession. Legal issues in different national contexts may or may not be similar to the examples provided from the United States. Regardless of locale, because of the complexity and gravity of legal and ethical decisions, consultation with colleagues and legal counsel is recommended in the establishment of new policies and procedures and when specific questions arise.

This chapter has provided recommendations for ways that advising administrators can remain current with the changing landscape of legal and ethical issues in the field through reading newly published literature, seeking professional development, and consulting the guidance of general counsel and professional organizations. Advising administrators are encouraged to utilize these strategies in the management of advising offices, leadership of personnel, and support of students.

Reflection Questions

1 How would you design a training on privacy and student records with special attention to communication with parents?
2 What ethical issues in your professional practice have you frequently encountered?
3 What resources and processes would you utilize when you encounter an ethical dilemma?
4 How might legal issues be regularly incorporated into professional development for advisors?
5 Which colleagues could you collaborate with as you make legal and ethical decisions?

References

Board of Curators, University of Missouri v. Horowitz, 435 U.S. 78 (1978). https://supreme.justia.com/cases/federal/us/435/78/

Chmielewski, C. (2004). *The importance of values and culture in ethical decision making*. NACADA Clearinghouse of Academic Advising Resources. https://nacada.ksu.edu/Resources/Clearinghouse/View-Articles/Values-and-culture-in-ethical-decision-making.aspx

Clery Act Appendix for FSA Handbook (2020). U.S. Department of Education, Office of Postsecondary Education. https://ifap.ed.gov/sites/default/files/attachments/2020-10/CleryAppendixFinal.pdf

Compton, E. R. (2014, March). Doing the right thing: Integrity in advising. *Academic Advising Today*, 37(1). https://nacada.ksu.edu/Resources/Academic-Advising-Today/View-Articles/Doing-the-Right-Thing-Integrity-in-Advising.aspx

Council for the Advancement of Standards in Higher Education (2015). CAS statement of shared ethical principles. In J. B. Wells (Ed.), *CAS professional standards for higher education* (9th ed., pp. 22–23). Council for the Advancement of Standards in Higher Education.

Damminger, J. (2011). Ethical decision making in academic advising. In J. Joslin & N. Markee (Eds.), *Academic advising administration: Essential knowledge and skills for the 21st century* (Monograph No. 22; pp. 207–213). NACADA.

Damminger, J. (2015). Ethical issues in advising. In P. Folsom, F. Yoder, & J. E. Joslin. (Eds.), *The new advisor guidebook: Mastering the art of academic advising* (2nd ed., pp. 55–66). Jossey-Bass.

Family Educational Rights and Privacy Act, 20 U.S.C. §1232g (1974).

Family Educational Rights and Privacy Act, 34 C.F.R. §99 (2011).

Fisher, K. (2005). *Ethical decision making in academic advising.* NACADA Clearinghouse of Academic Advising Resources. https://nacada.ksu.edu/Resources/Clearinghouse/View-Articles/Ethical-decision-making.aspx

Hendricks v. Clemson Univ., 353 S.C. 449 (2003).

Hunter, B., & Gehring, D. G. (2005). The cost of federal legislation on higher education: The hidden tax on tuition. *NASPA Journal, 42*(4), 478–497.

Jeanne Clery Disclosure of Campus Security Policy and Campus Crime Statistics Act, 20 U.S.C. §1092 (1990).

Justice, G. (2019). *How to be a dean.* Johns Hopkins University Press.

Kaplin, W. A., Lee, B. A., Hutchens, N. H., & Rooksby, J. H. (2020). *The law of higher education* (6th ed., student version). Jossey-Bass.

Kitchener, K. (1985). Ethical principles and ethical decisions in student affairs. In H. J. Canon & R. D. Brown (Eds.), *Applied ethics in student services* (New Directions for Student Services, No. 30, pp. 17–30). Jossey-Bass.

Landon, P. A. (2007). *Advising ethics and decisions.* NACADA Clearinghouse of Academic Advising Resources. https://nacada.ksu.edu/Resources/Clearinghouse/View-Articles/Ethics-and-decisions.aspx

Latourette, A. W. (2011). Legal implications of academic advising. In J. Joslin & N. Markee (Eds.), *Academic Advising Administration: Essential Knowledge and Skills for the 21st Century* (Monograph No. 22; pp. 215–224). NACADA.

Lowery, J. W. (2016). Addressing legal and risk management issues. In G. S. McClellan & J. Stringer (Eds.), *The handbook of student affairs administration* (4th ed., pp. 535–560). Jossey-Bass.

Mahanoy Area School Dist. v. B. L., 141 S. Ct. 2038 (2021).

Mahavongsanan v. Hall, 529 F.2d 448 (5th Cir. 1976).

McCauley v. Univ. of the Virgin Islands, 618 F.3d 232 (3d Cir. 2010).

Miller, T. (2016). Legal foundations and issues. In J. H. Schuh, S. R. Jones, & V. Torres (Eds.), *Student services: A handbook for the profession* (6th ed., pp. 107–120). Jossey-Bass.

Moneta, L. (2021). *The business of student affairs: Fundamental skills for student affairs professionals.* NASPA–Student Affairs Administrators in Higher Education.

NACADA: The Global Community for Academic Advising. (2006). NACADA concept of academic advising. https://nacada.ksu.edu/Resources/Pillars/Concept.aspx

NACADA: The Global Community for Academic Advising. (2017a). NACADA academic advising core competencies model. https://www.nacada.ksu.edu/Resources/Pillars/CoreCompetencies.aspx

NACADA: The Global Community for Academic Advising. (2017b). NACADA core values of academic advising. https://www.nacada.ksu.edu/Resources/Pillars/CoreValues.aspx

Nondiscrimination on the Basis of Sex in Education Programs or Activities Receiving Federal Financial Assistance, 34 C.F.R. §106 (2020).

Regents of University of Michigan v. Ewing, 474 U.S. 214 (1985).

Reynolds, A. L. (2016). Counseling and helping skills. In J. H. Schuh, S. R. Jones, & V. Torres (Eds.), *Student services: A handbook for the profession* (6th ed., pp. 452–465). Jossey-Bass.

Robinson, S. E. (2004). *Legal issues for advisors: A primer.* NACADA Clear-inghouse of Academic Advising Resources. https://nacada.ksu.edu/Resources/Clearinghouse/View-Articles/Legal-issues-primer.aspx

Robinson, S. (2011). Voices from the Field, FERPA: Federal Educational Rights and Privacy Act. In J. Joslin & N. Markee (Eds.), *Academic Advising Adminis-tration: Essential Knowledge and Skills for the 21st Century* (Monograph No 22; pp. 225–228). NACADA.

Rust, M. M. (2014). *FERPA and its implications for academic advising practice.* NACADA Clearinghouse of Academic Advising Resources. https://nacada.ksu.edu/Resources/Clearinghouse/View-Articles/FERPA-overview.aspx

Rust, M. M. (2015). Legal issues in academic advising. In P. Folsom, F. Yoder, & J. E. Joslin (Eds.), *The new advisor guidebook: Mastering the art of academic advising* (2nd ed., pp. 159–173). Jossey-Bass.

Saunders, S. A., & Wilson, C. M. (2016). What is ethical professional practice? In J. H. Schuh, S. R. Jones, & V. Torres (Eds.), *Student services: A handbook for the profession* (6th ed., pp. 89–106). Jossey-Bass.

Saxe v. State College Area School District, 240 F.3d 200 (3d Cir. 2000).

Section 504 of the Rehabilitation Act of 1973, 29 USC § 794.

Tatro v. University of Minnesota, 816 N.W.2d 509 (Minn. 2012).

Tinker v. Des Moines Independent Community School District, 393 U.S. 503 (1968).

Title VI of the Civil Rights Act of 1964, 41 USC § 2000d.

Title IX of the Education Amendments of 1972, 20 U.S.C. § 1681 et seq.

U.S. Department of Education, Office of Postsecondary Education. (2020). *Rescission of and Replacement for the 2016 Handbook for Campus Safety and Security Reporting.* https://fsapartners.ed.gov/knowledge-center/library/electronic-announcements/2020-10-09/rescission-and-replacement-2016-handbook-campus-safety-and-security-reporting-updated-jan-19-2021

Yoder v. University of Louisville, 526 Fed. Appx. 537 (6th Cir. 2013).

VOICES FROM THE FIELD

Legal and Compliance Issues in Working with International Students

Rosanna J. Cabatic

International students have been, and continue to be, an important student population in many U.S. universities and colleges. The needs and experiences of this student population may differ from the traditional college-aged student with whom advising administrators and academic advisors work. For example, advising administrators may need to ensure the institution maintains specific certifications to enroll international students while also monitoring student visa requirements, which may be unique to the visa holder. This Voices from the Field (VFF) piece explores examples that may help advising administrators understand legal and compliance issues when working with international students and provide guidance and leadership to academic advisors who support this specific student population during their academic programs and careers.

Administrators can support students by equipping themselves and their advisors with the knowledge and tools needed to comply with visa regulations, developing an open and organized communication plan between advisors, faculty members, and students, and maintaining consistency in policy implementation to ensure all parties are following academic policies and government guidelines. This VFF shows these practices at a small private college; however, other administrators and advisors who work with multiple visa holders may already utilize these applications or find them helpful when working with a specific visa-holder population. Even if the academic advising administrator is not responsible for compliance issues, awareness of these matters and navigating them is vital when working with international students.

DOI: 10.4324/9781003437598-10

Understanding and Complying with Visa Regulations

Serving in the Office of International Student Services (ISS) at a small private college, I have had to navigate the intricacies of visa documentation and maintenance for the college's international student population. The primary focus of my work with international students is to ensure they follow the regulations specific to their visa and that the college complies with the rules specific to its visa certification, whether through the Student and Exchange Visitor Program (SEVP) or another visa program. The SEVP certification is assigned to schools and serves as "a legally binding commitment to comply with applicable federal laws, regulations and DHS [Department of Homeland Security] requirements" (Department of Homeland Security, n.d., para.9). The DHS recommends that school officials and administrators carefully consider the commitments and implications when applying for SEVP certification and how the responsibilities of following, reporting, and maintaining guidelines impact the school's strategic plans and long-term ability to act in accordance with regulatory laws and requirements.

Schools must have, at minimum, a primary designated school official (PDSO) and/or one designated school official (DSO) whose responsibility is to maintain SEVP certification and comply with regulations. Advising administrators and advisors may serve as PDSOs and/or DSOs to interpret various visa regulations. While it is not expected of PDSOs and DSOs to memorize the various intricacies and regulations of visas, I have utilized the information on the DHS website (e.g., Study in the States) to provide visa support to students and faculty. The website also includes publications on changes to current guidance and a list of tools and available resources. PDSOs, DSOs, and administrators may find this website immensely helpful, especially with maintaining student documentation and navigating the portal system that houses students' non-immigration paperwork. The DHS also offers webinars for administrators new to working with international students and those who would like to brush up on their knowledge of new guidance and documentation maintenance. To support administrators and advisors involved in international student services, a field representative is designated to a school or geographic area and serves as a one-on-one resource guide. The field representative I have worked with has served as a link to understanding federal regulations and compliance and has been one of my first lines of communication.

Open Communication Plan

To fully comply with the responsibilities attached to a SEVP certification and work with international students, administrators must establish and maintain an open channel of communication among critical campus stakeholders. Many individuals and offices may have some level of involvement with international students, including PDSOs and DSOs, an International Student Services office, academic and faculty advisors, the Registrar's office, Financial Services, and students' faculty members. These offices and individuals are important to a student's academic success and career. Still, they are equally important in ensuring that international students and school administrators conform to the requirements established in the visa certification.

International students, specifically F1 visa holders, are required to be enrolled in a full-time course load to enjoy the benefits of their visas. Students work with their academic advisors to create a full-time course load while following and completing necessary academic requirements. They must communicate with their immigration and academic advisors about any changes to their academic plan or progress that may impact visa compliance. Students are also advised to speak with their PDSO or DSO so that those individuals can accurately report and update visa documentation. It is federally required for administrators to maintain and update student records appropriately within the Student and Exchange Visitor Information System (SEVIS). This maintenance allows government agencies to collect data and monitor students' legal status regarding national security.

Administrators must consider the audience when setting up a communication plan. Who needs to know specific visa information, and how will that information be communicated? Faculty and primary-role advisors working with international students may not need to know the intricacies of visa requirements and law. Still, they should know what constitutes full-time status for international students at their respective institutions. Administrators may organize all communication through their offices or the International Student Services office and have one location responsible for collecting and disseminating information to students and the campus offices. However, organized communication, transparency, and consistency are vital to accurately supporting international students and campus stakeholders working with visa holders.

Consistency in Policies

When multiple advisors work with a single student, open communication between the student and their administrators and academic/immigration advisors is important in understanding the student's academic interests and providing consistent advice. This type of communication has allowed for a unified voice in my advising and ensured that no individuals/offices are providing conflicting advice to the student that would negatively impact their immigration, scholarship program, and/or academic responsibilities.

A lack of consistency or conformity in interpreting immigration requirements can cause major confusion for the student and campus stakeholders. Said confusion can even result in a student losing visa benefits (also known as a termination) and being required to return home regardless of whether they have completed their academic program. In addition, schools may be subject to review by the DHS and/or a withdrawal of their visa certification. Financial implications can also arise in an institution's failure to maintain consistent review and communication of policies and expectations. These implications can impact students and their ability to remain enrolled. Institutions may also face financial penalties resulting from loss of certification due to a failure to communicate accurate and timely information.

Ensuring international students have a successful college experience involves working with them on academic and educational planning. It also requires being cognizant of the legal compliance issues and concerns surrounding their enrollment. International students have much to consider outside of academics that do not affect domestic students. First and foremost, they must manage their immigration requirements and, if applicable, any financial assistance they may receive through an agency in their home country. Advising administrators and academic advisors must consider the legal implications of maintaining visa certifications and the ramifications of noncompliance. Administrators must establish and maintain open communication with campus stakeholders and students and decide what information should be delivered to whom and how. Finally, the development and interpretation of policy consistency are critically important when working with international students.

Advising administrators, academic advisors, and immigration advisors can all serve as international students' biggest support systems as they study in the United States. With academic and immigration support from the international student services office staff, international students and other visa holders studying at a U.S. college or university can successfully complete their program and earn their degree. In the ISS office where I work, the director, myself, and the coaching and tutoring staff created a "360-degree model," which involved academic advising, coaching, tutoring, and visa support for every international student enrolled. Although not all students took advantage of the comprehensive support offered, our staff was readily available for each student when needed.

Reference

Department of Homeland Security. (n.d.). *Getting started with SEVP certification.* https://studyinthestates.dhs.gov/schools/apply/getting-started-with-sevp-certification

6

THE ROLE OF THE ADMINISTRATOR IN SCHOLARLY ADVISING AND THE SCHOLARSHIP OF ADVISING

Wendy G. Troxel and Marian H. Gabra

Institutions that commit to nurturing a culture of curiosity inspire primary-role advisors, faculty advisors, and advising administrators to engage with advising-related literature; they also support those who seek to contribute to the field. Advising administrators and academic department chairs have two primary obligations: to understand the short- and long-term benefits of modeling *scholarly advising* through active engagement with the literature, and to support the professional growth of others through focused, intentional professional development that is embedded into the culture of their unit/department. Doing so has the potential to cultivate more meaningful advising interactions and to elevate the field of academic advising at every higher education institution, regardless of size, type, or location.

Scholarly advisors view their work from a position of professional curiosity and commitment. They consult relevant literature to inform their work, and many contribute to the literature. Advisors form their scholarly identity by intentionally connecting their current role, their professional aspirations, and their level of confidence related to research skills (Troxel, 2019). Too often advising administrators, primary-role advisors, and faculty advisors who seek to engage in scholarly inquiry related to advising are faced with inconsistent support and unclear expectations relative to the climates and cultures within their institutions. Through a shared understanding of and commitment to the complex literature base that informs their work, advising administrators are the key to advancing the place and role of advising in higher education. Through intentional support, advising administrators lead their staff and faculty members toward active professional engagement.

DOI: 10.4324/9781003437598-11

The notion of research may be intimidating for some primary-role advisors who may be less experienced or who may believe that research is not under their professional purview. The administrator plays a critical role in demystifying research so that it is both more accessible and a part of the advising culture. Framing research as a way to explore areas of curiosity will enable advisors to be more intentional about their practice. As professional educators, advisors should engage *with* practitioner research, even if they do not wish to engage *in* formal research studies.

If *advising is teaching* (Lowenstein, 2020), then there is a pedagogy to it and it brings student learning and developmental outcomes that can be documented, assessed, and studied. The *context* of advising provides the framework through which instructional strategies are intentionally developed and implemented. If advisors see themselves as professional educators, they not only engage more deeply with students; they also operate more purposefully with the teaching mission of the institution. Higher educators cannot operate in a vacuum, however. They must be supported and nurtured toward intentional application through the integration of theory and practice (Boyer, 1990). All the while, student learning should be the focus of the work and professionalization of advising the goal.

Creating a Climate of Scholarly Advising

Higher education operates within a hierarchical employment system, delineated by separate spaces of privilege, priority, and power (Whitchurch, 2015). Involvement in disciplinary-focused research is typically reserved for tenure track or tenured faculty members. Faculty advisors who wish to engage in pedagogical research (i.e., Scholarship of Teaching and Learning [SoTL]) are often challenged by limitations of what "counts" for promotion and tenure. Regardless, the expectation to be productive in the scholarly arena offers legitimate agency and professional identity for faculty members.

Primary-role advisors, alternatively, are increasingly encouraged to read scholarly and practical literature, but they are rarely expected to formally contribute to the literature on academic advising. This often results in a paradoxical dilemma for practitioners who have professional goals related to engaging in scholarly activities (Troxel, 2021). Advisors make informed, intuitive decisions within complex elements of student learning and development. Those reflective about such decisions and actions are both wiser and potentially more effective in practice. These practice-focused scholars have much to share with others in the field but many are often insecure in their research-related abilities and unsure of the extent to which such work would be supported by their supervisor.

Advising administrators can, and should, encourage and nurture a climate of *scholarly advising* within their units. Additionally, they should model scholarly behaviors and interests. Advising's unique lens on student learning and development is ripe for scholarly inquiry. Decisions about engagement with the Scholarship of Advising (SoA) are often individually determined, yet they are influenced by the professional environment where the work takes place.

An institution's level of commitment to grounding advising within the literature can be revealed by several processes and policies for those advising-related positions without academic rank, including:

- hiring documents (required and preferred qualifications and expectations),
- position descriptions (position role and scope),
- workload and assignments (specific responsibilities),
- performance review policies and processes (areas under review and evaluation),
- professional advancement and rewards (opportunities for professional goal setting and promotion parameters), and
- professional development and training activities offered by the institution (required/optional).

Quite often, however, there is little mention of expectations to engage with the literature base in official personnel documents, even for advising administrators, except at those institutions that offer intentional promotion and advancement opportunities. But the work of advising includes complex, contextual evidence regarding student learning and development.

While advising administrators may have limited authority to challenge institutional policies and infrastructure, the climate of an advising program is directly related to modeled behaviors and values. Regarding advising's influence on student learning and development, knowing more, assuming less, and identifying and interrogating issues of equity and social justice requires not only research-related skills but also a culture of curiosity that is consistently intentional across the institution.

This chapter addresses the critical elements necessary to build and nurture a dynamic academic advising program that situates reflective practice within a culture of professionalism and inquiry. First, we argue that advising administrators must reflect on their own approach to intentional leadership and the extent to which they value scholarly application in advising. Next, we explore common institutional policies and practices that may serve as barriers to this aspirational model. Finally, we propose several steps that advising administrators can take not only to examine their institution's structures and philosophical stances to this type of approach, but also map out intentional strategies and actions toward goals.

Philosophy of Scholarly Advising Administration

Fostering a culture of advising research and assessment at an institution is a process that requires *intentionality, curiosity and self-reflection, collaboration, and advocacy*. Before an advising administrator embarks upon this journey, it is critical to first look inward. Self-reflection and self-awareness are key in determining the path forward. This knowledge may lead them to take small steps in one direction or larger steps that have greater reach across the institution. Inspiring academic advisors to engage with advising research when they are already overworked with caseloads, administrative work, and programmatic "duties-as-assigned" will require leadership that intentionally models the value and impact of scholarly advising. It does not always have implications for budget adjustments but rather requires a purposeful philosophy of professional responsibility.

Intentionality

Given the conflicting demands of the profession, advisors must see firsthand how and why engagement with research is meaningful to students and to themselves, the institution, and the field. Fostering intentional engagement with advising research enables primary-role advisors, faculty advisors, and administrators to identify and express the value of advising in relation to student learning and development, to use evidence to inform their practices, and to create an intellectual learning community amongst professionals that thoughtfully considers the relationship between theory and practice.

Implementing research-driven strategies has the potential to increase resource investment in advising and for stakeholders to perceive advisors as experts within the field. Advisors have direct contact with students and are best positioned to analyze data and create impactful strategies. The acknowledgment of advisors as experts may grant advisors a seat at decision-making tables.

Curiosity and Self-reflection

Advising administrators must lead by example. Demonstrating curiosity and enthusiasm for advising, and rooting the practice in advising scholarship, will create an expectation and standard for quality advising. Administrators must ask themselves:

- Am I curious about advising and how it impacts students?
- What more can I learn about supporting diverse student populations?
- Am I invested in the professional development of advisors?
- Is continuous learning a core value for me and for the staff?
- How can I embed in the culture an enthusiasm for this engagement?

Once advising administrators determine that they are curious and invested in the development of both students and staff members, they can advance with intention into the collaborative phase.

Collaboration

One administrator cannot singlehandedly shift the culture of advising to be learning-centered and more scholarly; a cultural shift requires engagement and collaboration (not just "buy-in") from primary-role advisors, faculty members, campus partners, and higher-level administrators. At this point, it will be critical to consider:

- How do we operationalize the difference between program evaluation, assessment, and research?
- Which campus partners can provide technical support for advising assessment and research?
- How can I lead in a way that gets academic advisors invested and excited?
- How can advisors and other colleagues share knowledge and unique expertise?

Advocacy

In addition to curiosity and collaboration, *advocacy* is critical throughout this journey. The administrator is responsible for giving language to the value and impact of scholarly advising and for educating colleagues about the importance and application of advising-related assessment and research. Once the determination has been made to move toward a scholarly advising program, the administrator must turn to issues of infrastructure.

A Call to Action: Creating a Culture of Scholarly Advising

Creating a culture of scholarly advising is multifaceted. Critical elements of institutional infrastructure can be addressed at the unit or department level; others involve institution-level (and even system-level) decisions, policies, and practices. The areas of focus that follow mostly apply to different institutional types (private and public), sizes (small to large), and advising structures (centralized/decentralized, primary-role only/faculty only, or a combination) globally.

Each section includes scaffolded statements that can be used to assess and reflect on each key element at the foundational, emerging, and exceptional levels. They are intentionally aspirational and serve as elements for reflection, discussion, and collaborative decision-making.

- *Foundational* levels represent fundamental principles and practices that are likely evident in advising programs new to this approach.
- The *emerging* level acknowledges intentional actions that foster a culture of scholarly advising.
- An academic advising program that is *exceptional* reveals evidence of extraordinary effort. These programs have the best chance for sustained growth and impact.

The following critical elements—from overarching mission and vision statements to the specifics of human resource documents and professional development plans—can be modified to align with unit, institutional, or national contexts. They can also serve to inform the advising program's assessment plans and strategic benchmarks toward aspirational scholarly goals for all members of the advising community.

Critical Element #1: Mission and Vision Statements
Related to Scholarly Advising

Each advising program should consider the culture of the institution's mission and vision when crafting their explicit commitment to scholarly advising. A small liberal arts institution with a faculty advising structure may focus their statement differently than a research university with a large staff of primary-role advisors. Higher education institutions share a commitment to student learning, however, and advisors are positioned to contribute in ways that are intentional and documentable.

One institution added to their vision statement a claim that reflects the approach they value:

We stimulate scholarship: As higher education professionals, we use current advising theory to guide and enrich our everyday practice. In turn, we use what we learn from our practice to contribute back to the advising community and higher education more broadly.

(A. Mueller, personal communication, February 8, 2022)

Some advisors at the institution are actively involved in formal research projects while others are engaging more deeply with data analysis and assessment. As a unit they have publicly committed to approach their work in a scholarly way.

An increasing number of institutions purposely frame professional development programs that incorporate elements of scholarly inquiry. They partner with librarians, faculty members, and institutional research offices to provide comprehensive support and resources designed to build community, practice theory, and theorize practice.

Neither vision statements nor a purposeful framework for professional development events require major budget expenditures. Rather, they require a collaborative commitment to approach advising in a scholarly way and devote time, energy, and structure to bring the vision and framework to life. What emerges is a learning community that breaks down silos between departments and fosters intellectual engagement within the profession.

As a reminder, the rubric elements that follow are intentionally aspirational. Small steps can move an institution in a positive direction toward a culture of scholarly advising.

Rubric Elements: Mission & Vision Statements for Academic Advising

---

Foundational: The institution has a mission and vision statement for academic advising that is drafted collaboratively with advisors and key stakeholders but does not explicitly address commitment to or importance of grounding advising practice in the relevant literature. Intended outcomes of the advising program are articulated in a way that will lead to an advising syllabus.

Emerging: The institution has a mission and vision statement for academic advising. Some units, but not all, also explicitly address commitment to grounding advising practice in the relevant literature. Advising syllabi clearly articulate intended outcomes of the advising program.

Exceptional: The collaboratively-developed institutional mission and vision statement for advising explicitly addresses commitment to and importance of grounding advising practice in the relevant literature. Advising syllabi, documents, and materials are purposefully aligned, publicly available, and used regularly through professional development activities to inform the relationship between advising theory and practice.

Consultations with colleagues at other institutions and needs assessments within the advising community can inform the vision for scholarly advising toward a more collaborative, intentional culture of curiosity. To actively promote and advance professional development in this area, however, an institution must assign the responsibilities to one or more individuals.

Critical Element #2: Dedicated Administrative Oversight

A program that embraces scholarly initiatives requires consistent, intentional oversight by a staff or faculty member specifically assigned to it. Whether a new position or a reassignment of an existing position, this responsibility should be written into the individual's position description, with clearly defined expectations and performance goals. Individuals with these responsibilities should have the full support of their supervisors and colleagues and be included in ongoing conversations related to advising at the institution. The program may also benefit from clerical support, or at least another assigned staff member. Commitment to a succession plan is important, as is careful attention to increasing responsibilities often assigned to competent, dynamic, midlevel administrators.

Rubric Elements: Dedicated Administrative Oversight

> *Foundational*: At least one individual volunteers annually to coordinate and facilitate professional development that includes scholarly components.
>
> *Emerging*: At least 50% of one individual's duties are officially designated for coordinating and facilitating focused professional development. Staff members are aware of their formal role and how the unit or department vision relates to the activities and initiatives.
>
> *Exceptional*: At least one individual is directly and formally responsible for implementing and nurturing the mission, visions, goals, and intended outcomes of a professional development program that is grounded in the literature and supports active involvement of advisors. They strategically recommend new programs and initiatives and demonstrate evidence of impact on all stakeholders.

An advising unit that dedicates oversight to professional development related to the study of advising also links outcomes to practice. There is evidence of impact of the program—influence on students, advisors, institutional metrics, and institutional reputation—as well as a broader impact on the profession through presentations and publications. Institutions strengthen their commitment to scholarly advising through inclusion in official employment documents as well.

Critical Element #3: Explicit Language in Human Resource Documents

It is important to take inventory of policies and practices related to employment through the lens of this type of professional goal. The optional nature of involvement in scholarly activities is rarely documented in human resource documents (such as job descriptions, performance review processes, and advancement opportunities). As budgets tighten and staffing changes or shortages increase work responsibilities, areas not explicitly indicated in legal, formal documents are often the first to be put aside or made a lesser priority. This increases the *scholarly dilemma* (Troxel, 2021) for those desiring to engage in deeper inquiry. Advising administrators should advocate for changes to the institutional infrastructures that act as barriers to scholarly involvement.

Rubric Elements: Explicit Language in Human Resource Documents

> *Foundational*: Position announcements refer explicitly to the importance of continuous learning. Position descriptions include expectations related to continuous learning through engagement in advising-related literature and are explicitly stated in some unit-specific documents but are not adopted formally by the institution.
>
> *Emerging*: Expectations regarding contributions to advising literature (presenting and/or publishing) are explicitly stated in one or more "levels" within a progression of positions (i.e., career ladders) in some unit-specific documents.
>
> *Exceptional*: Expectations regarding contributions to advising literature (presenting or publishing) are explicitly stated in one or more "levels" within a progression of positions for primary-role advisors and advising administrators in both institution-level documents and unit-specific documents. Department-level faculty promotion and tenure documents include reference and clear guidelines to SoTL and/or SoA as acceptable for publication/presentation.

Structural opportunities and challenges should be intentionally and reflectively explored. Employment policies and structures often reveal unavoidable issues that limit flexible innovation, such as restrictions related to union status, university system requirements, and conflicts with institutional decisions about the nature of the role. But articulating aspirational goals for such changes increases the opportunities for serious consideration.

Critical Element #4: Workload, Assignments, and the Performance Review Process

Certain tasks and responsibilities must be addressed in an advising unit. Full-time advisors must meet with students and participate in administrative tasks and committee work. Some advisors excel at committee work and enjoy helping to articulate researchable questions. Others excel at conducting literature reviews, leading common reading activities, and writing for presentations and publications. Through transparent, intentional planning, the members of an advising unit could be engaged in a purposeful negotiation to distribute collective expertise and professional goals.

Rubric Elements: Workload, Assignments, and the Performance Review Process

> *Foundational*: Elements of the importance of continuous learning are addressed in the performance review process at least annually; engagement in scholarship is optional.
>
> *Emerging*: Commitment to continuous learning, including scholarly literature, is addressed in the performance review process at least annually. Engagement in scholarly endeavors is encouraged, but individuals are not necessarily held accountable for specific outcomes and outputs.
>
> *Exceptional*: Staff and faculty members negotiate their areas of growth and goals within the parameters of their position and the needs of the unit/ department. Engagement in scholarly inquiry can be documented and is directly connected to their articulated goals and negotiated assignments through conversations with supervisors.

Managing and leading a staff with differentiated responsibilities requires careful attention to institutional policies, transparent hiring practices, and a meaningful and documentable performance review process. Academic deans, directors, and department chairs support the overall culture of pedagogically focused scholarship at an institution by including it in the promotion and tenure process. Regardless of role or position, all staff and faculty members should engage regularly and openly to ensure they understand how they contribute to the overall responsibilities of the unit or academic department. This kind of professional goal setting can also be connected to a strong professional development program.

Critical Element #5: Purposeful Professional Development

Episodic and isolated professional development lacks influence. Advising administrators must commit explicitly and actively to create and sustain a culture of scholarly engagement and consider where this type of initiative fits into their overall professional development and training program. This type of training leads to documented competencies that involve operational skills and abilities often unique to the institution. It also relates to the deeper literature on learning and academic growth.

A scholarly professional development program should be ongoing (i.e., not episodic), publicly announced, open to all, and strategically constructed to include relevant literature examined through active engagement.

Rubric Elements: Purposeful Professional Development

Foundational: Professional development opportunities are optionally available at the unit or department level that include purposeful programming and initiatives grounded in the literature. A formal process for documenting involvement exists.

Emerging: Professional development opportunities including programming and initiatives grounded in the literature are available across the institution. There is active engagement by some staff or faculty members. Involvement, completion, and self-reported evidence of intellectual and professional growth are formally documented.

Exceptional: Professional development opportunities that include purposeful programming and initiatives grounded in the literature are mapped intentionally across the institution. Many staff and faculty members are actively engaged. Involvement, completion, and self-reported evidence of intellectual and professional growth are linked to the annual performance review and goal-setting process.

Effective professional development is strategic. Active engagement and synergy with aspirational elements of the advising profession, such as opportunities to explore NACADA's Core Competencies through the framework of NACADA's Research Agenda (Troxel & Dotterer, 2021), broadens the extent to which advisors reflect upon their role and engage in purposeful pedagogy (Givans Voller, 2016). Scholarly advisors also view the literature critically, interrogating both sources and lenses. They seek out literature written by scholars of color and encourage advisors' expertise and experiences that challenge normative, privileged assumptions.

While decisions to engage in scholarly arenas bring intrinsic satisfaction, ultimately the extent to which individual and collaborative energy is sustained can be influenced by public, tangible recognition at the institution.

Critical Element #6: Rewards and Recognition

Responsibilities for research and assessment are rarely found in job descriptions of primary-role advisors. Given that advisors manage heavy workloads and juggle competing responsibilities, it is critical to imagine how advisors can be compensated or acknowledged for this work. For example, it is important to highlight advisors who engage in research via newsletters, social media, and institutional ceremonies. This reinforces the value of the initiative and encourages participation. Administrators may consider offering incentives, such as release time, for advisors to engage in research. The value of advising research should be shared with academic leaders and others across the institution.

Rubric Elements: Rewards and Recognition

Foundational: Rewards and recognition for advisors exist at the unit or department level but are not publicly shared or celebrated.

Emerging: Rewards and recognition are granted consistently based on advisor growth, learning, and engagement, and are shared publicly.

Exceptional: Rewards and recognition directly impact advisor promotion and merit increases and are celebrated publicly alongside the institution's top awards for teaching, research, and service.

Nourishing a culture of inquiry across an institution does not necessarily require large financial investments. Most institutions support and reward expert faculty researchers and teachers in public ceremonies and spotlights. Advisors should be included in institutional award programs to recognize professional engagement, including effective practice and scholarly involvement. Staff members should be eligible for institutional grants that address critical issues related to learning and the contextual nature of advising. They should be encouraged to collaborate with colleagues to apply for external support, such as NACADA grants.

Advisors and administrators who have an interest in graduate education should be encouraged and supported, as well as given the opportunity to engage in writing groups, present at conferences, and mentored toward publication. Scholarly confidence is increased as individuals are supported and rewarded for commitment to their role as professional educators.

Critical Element #7: Opportunities for Involvement in Scholarly Inquiry

Advising programs aspiring to be *exceptional* in multiple areas of scholarly growth must provide an infrastructure through which advising administrators can model scholarly activities and nurture professional growth and identity for advisors.

Quite often, however, such endeavors are fragile. As of this writing, the world is still experiencing the effects of the COVID-19 pandemic, which affected every aspect of higher education and everyday life for students, staff, and faculty members. The shift to virtual modalities required creativity and new ways of communicating and interacting. Maintaining momentum for an existing professional development program related to scholarly involvement or launching a new program may seem by some to be an opportunity for critical issues to be explored, and by others to be a commitment to be sidelined for a while. Moving forward requires consistent, purposeful institutional commitment.

In most cases, the activities provide advising staff and faculty members a creative option toward their professional development goals, including opportunities for leadership to help maintain momentum and engagement. However, most activities are run by volunteers. Involvement in these areas should be discussed with supervisors to ensure that they fit into their formal work assignments and additional professional activities.

Rubric Elements: Opportunities for Involvement in Scholarly Inquiry

Foundational: Opportunities such as reading groups, writing groups, and workshops focused on advising scholarship exist at the unit level. Involvement is encouraged and supported by advising administrators.

Emerging: A designated administrator creates consistent and thoughtful opportunities for involvement in scholarly inquiry in collaboration with campus partners. There is evidence of active engagement from some members of the campus community.

Exceptional: The institution creates an infrastructure of support for advisors to engage in scholarly inquiry through purposeful leadership. Active involvement is recognized and celebrated publicly by the institution at least annually.

Previously we presented reflective questions related to administrators' individual philosophies and commitments to scholarly advising. The same is true for staff and faculty members who aspire to build a culture of curiosity together. Here we further underscore the importance of reflective awareness, which leads to deeper collaborative opportunities across an advising team. This provides a solid, sustainable foundation on which to build a culture of scholarly inquiry through purposeful advocacy.

Reflective Practice. Self-reflective activities are practiced by administrators, staff, and faculty members, and thereby inform advising practice and the engagement with advising scholarship. Administrators and team members consistently evaluate the relationship between advising theory and practice through intellectual dialogue. Intellectual learning communities are fostered throughout the institution.

Collaboration. Collaboration is embedded in structure and practice to create a shared language about the value and impact of scholarly inquiry to support students, faculty members, and staff. Collaboration is woven into the culture of the institution and cultivates an infrastructure of support for all interested parties.

Advocacy. Administrators secure consistent, predictable funding to engage in scholarly inquiry. Administrators demonstrate the value and impact of advising through assessment. The institution is aware of the value and impact of advising; advisors are respected as experts.

Conclusion

An institution that commits to an infrastructure that supports the short- and long-term goals of scholarly advising has the best opportunity for sustainable outcomes. Advising administrators should oversee systems that encourage evidence of engagement and growth and institutionalizes critical initiatives. Administrators must advocate for intentional fiscal and human resources (such as assessment specialists, professional development directors, and data analysts) to provide infrastructure that strengthens sustained commitment to scholarly goals. Short-term actions can lead to long-term benefits, such as:

- better morale and engagement, which increases advisor retention toward a more stable and loyal workforce;
- a better understanding of the pedagogies of advising, which increases effective and impactful influence on students and their learning;
- shared knowledge of and increased contribution to the literature related to advising, which enhances institutional and individual reputation; and

- a better understanding of role of advising, which leads to more consistent approaches to working with students within the institution, as well as continued growth of the advising profession.

We define *practitioner research* as workplace research that is rooted in curiosity. It provides professionals with the opportunity to evaluate their practices, to seek innovative solutions to challenges and questions, and to interrogate systemic inequities. It is also critical to continually reimagine individual and collective advising philosophies and practices within the evolving contexts of higher education both locally and globally. Advisors are best positioned to engage in practitioner research because they directly interact with students during challenging and transformative experiences. Administrators play a key role in nurturing and promoting scholarly advising and the SoA.

Advising administrators globally can build and promote a supportive climate for staff members to engage in activities that benefit students, the institution, and the profession of advising. Administrators should lead by example and commit time for scholarly activities that serve the institution and their professional goals. The role of the advising administrator is key in shepherding initiatives that cultivate curiosity and embrace advising research and assessment. Having a grasp of their own intentions, investments, and priorities, in addition to resources both within and outside of the department or unit, reveals the path forward. Steps in this direction foster a culture of scholarly advising.

Reflection Questions

Ask of myself:

1 To what extent do I **intentionally** consult the literature related to advising in my own work?
2 What am I **curious** about regarding the impact, context, and theories of advising?
3 To what extent do I **collaborate** with others to discuss scholarly literature?
4 How can I **advocate** for the advisors I oversee to be more engaged in the literature?

Ask of others:

1 With whom do I need to partner? Who are our advocates?
2 How does the institution help or hinder our goals?

3 How can we further educate, inform, and engage upper administration of the benefits of this approach?

References

Boyer, E. L. (1990). *Scholarship reconsidered: Priorities of the professoriate.* Jossey-Bass.

Givans Voller, J. (2016). Professional development. In T. J. Grites, M. A. Miller, & J. Givans Voller (Eds.), *Beyond foundations: Developing as a master advisor* (pp. 251–274). Jossey-Bass.

Lowenstein, M. (2020). If advising is teaching, what do advisors teach? *NACADA Journal, 40*(2), 5–14. https://doi.org/10.12930/NACADA-20-90

Troxel, W. G. (2019). Scholarly advising and the scholarship of advising. *NACADA Journal, 39*(2), 52–59. https://doi.org/10.12930/NACADA-19-203

Troxel, W. G. (2021, October 7). *The scholarly dilemma: Academic advisors as "Third Space Professionals"* [Paper]. NACADA Annual Conference, Cincinnati, OH.

Troxel, W. G., & Dotterer, D. A. (2021, September 14). *Scholarly advising and the NACADA Core Competencies: Practical frameworks for discussion, implementation, and inquiry* [Webinar]. NACADA.

Whitchurch, C. (2015). The rise of third space professionals: Paradoxes and dilemmas. In U. Teichler & W. K. Cummings (Eds.), *Forming, recruiting and managing the academic profession* (pp. 79–99). Springer.

7

SOCIALLY JUST ADVISING ADMINISTRATION

Mary Carmel Etienne

The 2020 protests for racial justice that arose in response to the murder of George Floyd (Taylor, 2021) once again brought the systemic inequalities embedded in American life into public consciousness. Higher education institutions were among the many organizations and companies that issued statements of solidarity for racial justice and committed, in varying degrees, to addressing institutional inequalities (Whitford, 2021).

Creating committees, making public declarations, and organizing cultural events are all ways to bring awareness to issues of equity that have existed since the beginning of higher education in this country. However, if we fail to make social justice an everyday part of our work as higher education administrators, these new programs will just become part of the status quo. To promote equity in advising and make positive changes in the lives of their students and colleagues, advising administrators must move beyond a cursory understanding of social justice and develop a commitment to social justice in their day-to-day practices.

There is not necessarily one static definition of social justice. Rather, the concept is informed by various theories and definitions. Davis and Harrison (2013) defined social justice as "essentially bridging the gap between mission statement and action" (p. 48). Another definition of social justice is the "full and equal participation of all groups in a society that is mutually shaped to meet their needs" (Bell, 2007, as cited in Davis & Harrison, 2013, p. 22).

In their introductory article to their special issue of *Equity and Excellence in Education*, Patton et al. (2010) provided an overview of how social justice and equity might be conceptualized in higher education. They start

DOI: 10.4324/9781003437598-12

first by expanding the definition of social justice beyond the conception of distributive justice (Rawls, 1971, as cited in Patton et al., 2010) to include other dimensions of justice, citing Young (1990, as cited in Patton et al., 2010) and Gewirtz (1998, as cited in Patton et al., 2010). They further stated: "To effectively understand and work toward social justice in higher education, we need to understand and evaluate the institutional processes, the patterns of distribution, social relations, and cultural/societal norms" (Patton et al., 2010, p. 269). Finally, they illuminated the distinctions between equality and equity, the importance of intersectionality, and the need to redefine diversity (Patton et al., 2010).

In the conclusion of their article, Patton et al. (2010) asked: "how do those within the academic field of higher education make it one where social justice is not simply a curricular issue, but is a philosophy that permeates how faculty, administrators, policymakers, students, and staff engage in everyday practices?" (p. 275). This chapter attempts to provide advising administrators with tools to bring social justice practice into their everyday lives.

A Framework for Socially Just Advising Administration: Kezar and Posselt (2020)

In *Higher Education Administration for Social Justice and Equity,* Kezar and Posselt (2020) proposed a framework that administrators can use as they work to advance the social justice goals of their institutions. The framework's seven components are: "1. Clear definitions of equity and justice, 2. Mindful administrative practice, 3. Wisdom in judgment, 4. Critical consciousness about power, 5. Knowledge of self and positionality, 6. Student centeredness, and 7. Routinizing mindfulness and wisdom" (p. 6). Using Kezar and Posselt's framework as a guide, this chapter will explore how advising administrators can promote and support socially just advising at their institutions. While this is not the only framework that administrators might use to situate their social justice practice, it was chosen as the basis for this chapter because it was designed specifically for the higher education administration context.

The chapter is organized into four sections. The first section details how to create a shared language for discussing social justice, situating practice within a theoretical framework, and developing a critical consciousness about power. The first section is framed by the first (clear definitions of equity and justice) and fourth (critical consciousness about power) components of Kezar and Posselt's (2020) framework. The "Framing an Understanding of Socially Just Administration" section defines the second, third, and fifth components of Kezar and Posselt's framework and discusses how administrators can use critical reflection to develop "knowledge of self and positionality," mindful administrative practice, and wisdom in judgment. The "Developing a Mindful Practice with Critical Reflection" section discusses how advising administrators can routinize mindfulness and wisdom using team meetings as a space for reflection, trust-building, and conflict. Finally, the conclusion of this chapter outlines how developing social justice practices will aid in putting students at the center (the sixth component of the framework).

Framing an Understanding of Socially Just Administration

Framing an understanding of *what socially just advising administration means* is foundational to the work of administrators who want to incorporate social justice into their units' advising practices. An understanding of socially just advising is based on developing a shared language for analyzing and discussing social justice practices in everyday life, situating practice in theoretical frameworks that guide advising work, and creating a critical consciousness about power.

Developing Shared Language: Definitions and Key Concepts

A common language for discussing social justice issues in everyday life is essential (Kezar & Posselt, 2020; McNair et al., 2020). Advising administrators should start by defining what social justice and equity mean in the context of their work. This definition must be inclusive of all populations. Developing shared definitions is essential to developing a shared understanding, as there are many ways one might define these concepts. Kezar and Posselt (2020) defined social justice as a concept that:

> is multifaceted and multi-dimensional, encompassing race, gender and gender identity, social class, sexual orientation, religion, and others as the needs of specific contexts demand. We also recognize that forms of justice may be interrelated, such as environmental and social justice. We strive for a capacious approach, one that accommodates multiple dimensions of equity and justice, and which is inclusive to the diverse population of students and other stakeholders in higher education today.
>
> *(p. 6)*

When discussing equity in social justice, Davis and Harrison (2013) made a clear distinction between equity and equality. Equality refers to the idea that everyone is treated the same, regardless of background;

equity considers the historical marginalization and difference in human experience.

One definition, advanced by the University of Southern California's Center for Urban Education (2022), stated:

> Equity refers to achieving parity in student educational outcomes, regardless of race and ethnicity. It moves beyond issues of access and places success outcomes for students of color at center focus. We at the Center for Urban Education focus our equity efforts specifically on race and ethnicity in light of the historical marginalization of some racial and ethnic groups in American education.
>
> *(What is Equity section)*

This definition calls for an understanding of the "historical and political understandings of [racial] stratification" (Bensimon et al., 2016, as cited in McNair et al., 2020, p. 5). McNair et al. (2020) elaborated:

> To examine equity effectively, practitioners must understand how racism and a pervasive belief in the hierarchy of human value have shaped our systems, policies, and practices. To ignore how structures were designed is to ignore the necessary processes for eliminating inequities.
>
> *(p. 5)*

In addition to defining social justice and equity, administrators also need to know key concepts to understand social justice issues (Davis & Harrison, 2013; Sensoy & DiAngelo, 2017). Concepts such as racism, White supremacy, power, privilege, and oppression should become part of the lexicon of administrators who wish to work toward social justice. To be able to do the work, advising administrators need to be willing to speak about it. Advising administrators can develop their understanding of these concepts by making them part of their personal or departmental professional development goals. Several chapters in this volume discuss some of these concepts.

Situating Practice in Theoretical Frameworks

Champlin-Scharff (2010) asserted that advisors should understand the epistemological frameworks that inform their work because beliefs about knowledge inform everyday practices. It is essential to understand the theories that guide advising practice if administrators plan to incorporate social justice into their advising practices. Epistemology, that is, how we know what we know, will also inform how we engage with social justice.

As Davis and Harrison (2013) suggested, "[d]iffering ways of knowing are deeply connected to our capacity to effect change" (p. 1).

Theories that challenge the status quo usually guide social justice practice. Critical theories are normative theories that seek to interrogate and disrupt the status quo to achieve emancipatory practice (Collins, 2009; Collins & Bilge, 2020; Delgado & Stefancic, 2017; Freire, 2018). For example, Collins (2009), in describing Black Feminist Theory, stated, "social theories emerging from and/or on behalf of U.S. Black women and other historically oppressed groups aim to find ways to escape from, survive in, and/or oppose prevailing social and economic injustice" (p. 11).

There is recent interest in using critical theories to inform the work of advising (Lee, 2018; Puroway, 2016). Lee (2018) proposed the use of critical race theory (CRT) to analyze and understand the experience of Black students at predominately White institutions (PWIs). She argued that for advisors to meet the social justice and cultural competency skills stipulated by professional organizations, self-reflection and introspection are required, as well as "an interest and commitment to exploring the experiences of others" (p. 79). Similarly, Puroway (2016) argued that advising is not a neutral activity and advocated for the use of advising approaches that promote social justice, in the vein of Paulo Freire's (2018) *Pedagogy of the Oppressed*. He articulated that "transformation in the direction of social justice can only come through critical reflection, which advising should foster" (p. 4). Regardless of the critical theory that administrators use to analyze and approach the work of advising, they will have to deal with the idea of advising as a neutral or political act, as authors have recently done in the *NACADA Journal* (Puroway, 2018; Winham, 2017). If advising administrators are committed to infusing social justice into their advising approaches and practices, they must be flexible with their theoretical frameworks to consider what supports change from the status quo. For this, academic advising administrators need an understanding of power.

Developing a Critical Consciousness About Power

"Socially just leadership means being aware of the way that power shapes administrative structure and culture—and working to dismantle these structures when power operates oppressively" (Kezar & Posselt, 2020, p. 12). "Power is the ability to influence circumstances toward desired outcomes. Power is positional and relational, making it a spatial human reality, one defined by the interaction between structure and agency" (Kuecker, 2009, pp. 50–51). While it is important to recognize that power dynamics often perpetuate the status quo, it is also important to recognize that power is relational and can be used to create more inclusive environments.

Collins (2017) used intersectionality to conceptualize power in four domains (interpersonal, disciplinary, cultural, and structural) and discussed how power operates to either perpetuate inequality or challenge it. For example, she stated, "When people use the rules and regulations of everyday life and public policy to uphold social hierarchy or challenge it, their agency and actions shape the *disciplinary domain of power*" (p. 26). This conceptualization of power may help advising administrators consider how power operates and impacts their work at various levels. For example, they may want to consider the policies governing students on probation (*structural*), but they will also want to consider the power dynamics at play during committee meetings (*interpersonal*).

It is vital for advising administrators to understand the power asymmetries that exist at their institutions because those asymmetries will influence the work they do and how well-positioned they are to influence change (Kezar & Posselt, 2020). For example, if an advising center exists in Academic Affairs, it may garner more power than a center housed in Student Affairs because of potentially uneven power dynamics between these two areas (Kezar & Posselt, 2020; Pusser, 2015). Alternatively, that same center may have diminished influence (*power*) within Academic Affairs because institutional priorities have shifted to valuing tuition-generating enterprises while undervaluing the work of instruction and advising (Kezar & Posselt, 2020). This shift may be evidenced by the perceived lack of recognition that faculty advisors receive for good advising from upper administration (Dillon & Fisher, 2000; Harrison, 2009).

Kezar and Posselt (2020) made the point that in the interrogation of power, administrators must consider the legacy and influence that racism has had, particularly in the history of higher education. Situating higher education within that history of racism that continues today, and the current economic-political landscape that veers toward neoliberalism will help give advising administrators a better understanding and awareness of how power operates within the institution (Davis & Harrison, 2013).

Developing a Mindful Practice with Critical Reflection

In addition to developing their knowledge of social justice, advising administrators must incorporate some practices in their daily work to make an impact. This section defines knowledge of self and positionality, mindful administrative practice, and wisdom of judgment (Kezar & Posselt, 2020). Then it introduces critical reflection as a tool that administrators can use to develop a mindful practice that positively impacts their students.

Knowledge of Self and Positionally

Kezar and Posselt (2020) argued that "knowledge of self and positionality" is necessary to practice social justice. Our positionality is our relationship to power based on our social identities (Collins & Bilge, 2020). Our backgrounds, family histories, and social identities shape our perspectives and experiences, and we need to understand how they shape our experiences to work toward justice. For example, as a first-generation college student, who was Pell-eligible, I have a perspective of the college experience that may be different from a colleague whose parents went to college. This self-knowledge will help us understand our views and consider others' perspectives. Advisors and advising administrators need to understand who they are and how their social identities have shaped their experiences.

Mindfulness

Mindful administrative practice is a way of approaching the decision-making process with deliberation. Mindfulness entails slowing down the process of thinking about how decisions are being made and learning from past decisions, instead of making quick decisions for expediency (Kezar & Posselt, 2020). A mindful administrator questions the process of making decisions. Kezar and Posselt advocated for using data as a reference point when making decisions instead of relying on instinct. For an advising administrator, mindfulness may look like not being overly reactive to pressures from upper administrators. Instead of basing decisions on a few anecdotes, a mindful administrator may choose to make data-informed decisions using the assessment of advising. Finally, Kezar and Posselt argued that wise leaders routinely consider and take in the perspectives of many different viewpoints and perspectives of stakeholders.

Wisdom of Judgment

Wisdom is the ability to use one's knowledge, creativity, intelligence, and ethics to make decisions for the common good, considering broader interests (Kezar & Posselt, 2020). "At its core, wisdom is about balancing many interests that exist, even when we are not aware of how many interests are at stake, part of wisdom is pushing oneself to see broader interests that should be weighed" (p. 10). Developing wisdom in judgment entails asking questions.

Advising administrators who want to exercise wisdom of judgment would question decision-making processes and consider more than personal or departmental interests (Kezar & Posselt, 2020). In the interest of social justice, they would consider power, collective good, and the justice of marginalized people and groups. For example, mindful administrators, exercising wisdom of judgment, may want to reflect on the decision to apply registration holds to the records of students with financial balances. They may consider that this decision could help streamline their department's administrative process. However, they should also consider how this decision could impact students. Which students will it affect most? How does this decision impact other units on campus? In addition to helping administrators make wise decisions, self-reflection is one essential habit that administrators can use to gain self-knowledge and develop mindful administrative practice.

Critical Reflection: A Tool for Mindful Practice

In Brookfield's (2017) view, "critical reflection is, quite simply, the sustained and intentional process of identifying and checking the accuracy and validity of our teaching assumptions" (p. 3). Although he described critical reflection in the context of teaching, it has been suggested that critical reflection is a concept that is relevant to advising (Etienne, 2020; Puroway, 2016). Critical reflection is poised to help advising practice because it asks administrators to challenge their assumptions and interrogate their relationship to power. Brookfield (2017) suggested that teachers use critical reflection to investigate their assumptions, illuminate power, and uncover hegemony. And they do this by using four lenses from which to gain perspective: "students' eyes, colleagues' perceptions, personal experiences, and theory and research" (p. 7).

Brookfield (2017) outlined several exercises that administrators can adopt to critically reflect on how their leadership perpetuates the status quo or helps move toward social justice. He suggested that teachers can reflect on their own experiences as learners to illuminate the assumptions they might be making about the learning process. In the context of advising, administrators may want to reflect on their experiences and their beliefs about the advising process. Administrators could also use critical reflection to deepen their understanding of the foundational concepts discussed in the first section of this chapter. For example, an administrator might want to reflect on how their relationship to power and privilege shapes their assumptions about the students they advise. By reflecting on advising using the concepts discussed earlier in this chapter, such as power and privilege, administrators may glean insights into how advising may help or hinder progress toward social justice goals.

When discussing critical reflection through the lens of theory, Brookfield (2017) stated that reading theory "provides us with a coherent and comprehensive explanation of a piece of the world" (p. 173). In addition to reading theory, he offers narrative theorizing, a process by which an author could write their personal story and weave theory into the text as a way of making meaning and challenging that narrative. These examples (and others) could help advising administrators gain knowledge of themselves and develop a mindful practice that can lead to wise decision-making. Equally important is the ability of advising administrators to reflect collectively with their team and other colleagues.

Tools for Routinizing Mindful Administrative Practice

In addition to developing an internally driven mindful administrative practice, advising administrators need to make mindful practice part of their daily work with their teams and make the process collective and collaborative. Routinizing mindfulness is the last component of Kezar and Posselt's (2020) social justice framework for administrative practice. They argued that administrators need to create "habits of the mind" that will help them continue the practice of being mindful and making wise decisions (p. 15). They argued that routinizing mindfulness is a way to continually build consciousness about power, build awareness of the structural and cultural Influences on our work in higher education, and develop the ability to make wise decisions. The collective input of a team will help administrators answer the questions related to equity and justice, and they will help gain new insights and reflect on new perspectives.

Staff meetings are where advising leaders discuss projects, brainstorm ideas, and make decisions about advising policies; as such, they are the prime locations for externalizing and routinizing mindful administrative practice. Critical reflection, building trust, and getting comfortable with conflict are three practices that can help prepare advising teams to engage fully in implementing equity and justice in the daily work of advising.

Building trust is necessary for advising administrators who want to work toward social justice goals. Challenging the status quo is not risk-free. Brookfield (2017) discussed the personal and professional risks someone takes when they make their reflections known in spaces where trust is absent. For this reason, teams must build trust so that people can share their honest feedback with the group. Trust is built by taking risks, being vulnerable, and collaborating (Barnett, 2011, 2018; Cook et al., 2005), and trust is a habit that develops over time (Brown, 2018; Head, 2012). Social justice advising will inherently mean advocating for change. Staff meetings are a place to practice being courageous in an environment where trust has been developed and nurtured.

Staff meetings also provide an opportunity to practice having meaningful conflict. Conflict is an inevitable part of social justice practice because using wisdom of judgment will require consideration of multiple, sometimes competing, viewpoints. Furthermore, change will often be met with resistance from colleagues who may not share social justice goals or understand the rationale for change. Conflict will arise as different people share their perspectives and advocate for what they feel is best. While these disagreements are inevitable and necessary to develop solutions that meet the needs of a group, having conflict will sometimes feel uncomfortable. The following three exercises, while not explicitly focused on social justice, would help advising teams reflect, build trust, and engage in conflict and thus prepare teams to engage in the often-difficult daily work of changing the status quo.

Collective Critical Reflection with Circle of Voices

Circle of voices (Brookfield, 2017) is an activity conducted with small groups of people (about four to six) where the facilitator poses a question or issue to the group. This prompt is followed by two rounds of discussion with the group. In the first round of discussion, each person is asked to give their reflections or ideas related to the problem posed. During this round, other group members remain silent. During the second round of discussion, group members are open to less structured conversation. Still, they must focus their responses on something said during the first round of discussion.

Circle of voices could be used in various ways in an advising office. Administrators might use the activity to brainstorm advocating for a change to an advising (or university) policy. For example, perhaps the advising team wants to address the problem of students with financial holds not being able to register for classes. The team leader might ask, "What are the consequences of financial holds on our student population?" and use circle of voices to elicit the perspectives of their team. Another way this activity could be used is during a professional development session focused on developing an advising team's knowledge of social justice practices. The group facilitator might use the activity to elicit early participation in the session by posing a reflective question (such as those included at the end of this chapter) to the group. Alternatively, it could be used to debrief a professional development session. Circle of voices will develop a team's capacity to listen and highlight the various perspectives in the room without the views of the strongest personalities taking over.

Building Trust with Hopes and Fears

Engaging in discussions about social justice and encouraging colleagues to reflect openly and honestly about it may inspire fear. There is a real risk of being vulnerable in spaces where sufficient trust has not been built. Hopes and fears (Barnett, 2011, 2018) is a trust-building exercise that goes beyond simple (but important) team icebreaker activities to develop a space of open dialogue. Barnett (2018) used the activity to build trust in a class in which race would be a topic of discussion and stated, "the Articulating Hopes and Fears exercise escalates the risk by asking students to reflect on, and potentially express, the hope and vulnerability they feel as they anticipate discussing race in a particular class, with particular people" (p. 116). The goal of the activity is to help build trust by having everyone in the group share one hope and one fear about a particular topic or session. While it is often used during discussions about race and other diversity topics, it could also be used to start a conversation about changing a particular campus policy that is not in students' best interests. While recently reflecting on a particularly difficult situation in my work, I considered the interpersonal power dynamics that might have been at play with my colleagues, who are White women, and me as a Black woman. As I reflected, I wondered if starting a meeting with our hopes and fears about the proposed changes might have brought to the surface some of the issues that could have been addressed to enable them to fully understand my perspective. Davis and Harrison (2013) contended that while most people will agree that social justice matters, taking social justice action is often controversial because of fear of changing the status quo. Giving people space to consider why they want to or don't want to do something may illuminate obstacles not previously considered.

Learning to Rumble as an entry into Conflict

The last activity, rumbling, comes from popular literature. In her research, Brené Brown (2018) found that senior leaders thought bravery and courage were missing from leadership. She identified ten behaviors that hindered leaders from developing courageous leadership. Two of the ten barriers she identified were: "tough conversations, including giving honest, productive feedback" (p. 7) and "People are opting out of vital conversations about diversity and inclusivity because they fear looking wrong, saying something wrong, or being wrong" (p. 9). *In Dare to Lead*, Brown (2018) makes the case that courageous leaders need to be able to have conversations with vulnerability. They must learn to "rumble." Brown (2018) defined the rumble as:

> a discussion, conversation, or meeting defined by a commitment to lean into vulnerability, to stay curious and generous, to stick with the messy

middle of problem identification and solving, to take a break and circle back when necessary, to be fearless in owning our parts.

(p. 10)

In *Dare to Lead,* Brown (2018) shared several resources that leaders could use to have conversations with vulnerability. One such activity is "permission slips," where a leader or facilitator invites the group to write down something they give themselves permission to think or feel during a meeting. These statements do not need to be shared with the larger group, but the act of writing them down provides space for a person to consciously reflect on how they want to show up in a meeting. For example, one might give permission to ask questions when something is unclear. This is a simple activity that teams could do at the start of staff meetings that, over time, may help them get more comfortable engaging in conversations with conflict.

Conclusion

The conclusion of this chapter focuses on a discussion of Kezar and Posselt's (2020) sixth component in their social justice framework: student centeredness. They suggested putting students at the center of the administrative decisions administrators make. They cited the work of McNair et al. (2016) in *Becoming a Student-Ready College* to argue that instead of assuming that students aren't ready, administrators should reflect on "how colleges can serve the students who come to college and, as institutions, become student-ready" (Kezar & Posselt, 2020, p. 14).

Student-centeredness is at the heart of good advising and advising administrators can use what has been discussed in this chapter to inform their practice. For example, developing a mission, vision, and student learning outcomes are critical components of an effective advising program (Campbell, 2008; NACADA, 2006). Explicitly articulating a commitment to social justice in these foundational texts will help put social justice and student-centeredness at the forefront of advising practice and serve as a basis for creating equitable programs that meet the needs of diverse student populations.

Changing systems, processes, and procedures will inevitably involve the collaboration of people in various departments or across the university. Additionally, advocating for change to the status quo will likely lead to conflicting perspectives and priorities that may produce fear in some colleagues. Making wise decisions may mean challenging a colleague's insistence that "this is how it has always been done." Administrators can use the tools discussed in these chapters to build trust across departments to interrogate and change policies that perpetuate inequities.

Reflection Questions

Advising administrators can use these questions as prompts for reflection, discussion, and action:

1 Who speaks up during meetings? Whose ideas are championed?
2 How can we prepare to meet students' needs?
3 Have I considered the populations/departments that will be affected by this change?
4 How have my social identities shaped my experience as a student? As a leader?
5 How do I know that I've built trust on my team?

References

Barnett, P. E. (2011). Discussions across difference: Addressing the affective dimensions of teaching diverse students about diversity. *Teaching in Higher Education, 16*(6), 669–679.

Barnett, P. E. (2018). Building trust and negotiating conflict when teaching race. In S. D. Brookfield (Ed.), *Teaching race: How to help students unmask and challenge racism* (pp. 109–130). Jossey-Bass.

Brookfield, S. D. (2017). *Becoming a critically reflective teacher*. Jossey-Bass.

Brown, B. (2018). *Dare to lead: Brave work. Tough conversations. Whole hearts.* Random House.

Campbell, S. M. (2008). Vision, mission, goals, and program objectives for academic advising programs. In V. N. Gordon, W. R. Habley, & T. J. Grites (Eds.), *Academic advising: A comprehensive handbook* (2nd ed., pp. 229–241). Jossey-Bass.

Center for Urban Education. (2022, April 18). *Equity and student success*. https://cue.usc.edu/equity/

Champlin-Scharff, S. (2010). A field guide to epistemology in academic advising research. In P. Hagen, T. L. Kuhn, & G. M. Padak (Eds.), *Scholarly inquiry in academic advising* (pp. 29–35). NACADA.

Collins, P. H. (2009). *Black feminist thought*. Routledge.

Collins, P. H. (2017). The difference that power makes: Intersectionality and participatory democracy. *Investigaciones Feministas, 8*(1), 19–39.

Collins, P. H., & Bilge, S. (2020). *Intersectionality*. Polity.

Cook, K. S., Yamagashi, T., Cheshire, C., Cooper, R., Matsuda, M., & Mashima, R. (2005). Trust building via risk taking: A cross-societal experiment. *Social Psychology Quarterly, 68*(2), 121–142.

Davis, T., & Harrison, L. M. (2013). *Advancing social justice: Tools, pedagogies, and strategies to transform your campus*. Jossey-Bass.

Delgado, R., & Stefancic, J. (2017). *Critical race theory*. New York University Press.

Dillon, R. K., & Fisher, B. J. (2000). Faculty as part of the advising equation: An inquiry into faculty viewpoints on advising. *NACADA Journal, 20*(1), 16–23.

Etienne, M. (2020, June). Review of the book *Becoming Critically Reflective Teacher*, by S. D. Brookfield. https://nacada.ksu.edu/Resources/Book-Reviews/ Current-Past-Book-Reviews/Becoming-a-Critically-Reflective-Teacher.aspx

Freire, P. (2018). *Pedagogy of the oppressed*. Bloomsbury Publishing.

Harrison, E. (2009). Faculty perceptions of academic advising: "I don't get no respect." *Nursing Education Perspectives, 30*(4), 229–233.

Head, N. (2012). Transforming conflict: Trust, empathy, and dialogue. *International Journal of Peace Studies, 17*(2), 33–55.

Kezar, A., & Posselt, J. (2020). Introduction: A call to just and equitable administrative practice. In A. Kezar & J. Posselt (Eds.), *Higher education administration for social justice and equity* (pp. 1–18). Routledge.

Kuecker, G. D. (2009) Academic activism and the socially just academy. In K. Skubikowski, C. Wright, & R. Graf (Eds.), *Social justice education: Inviting faculty to transform their institutions* (pp. 42–55). Stylus.

Lee, J. A. (2018). Affirmation, support, and advocacy: Critical race theory and academic advising. *NACADA Journal, 38*(1), 77–87.

McNair, T. B., Bensimon, E. M., & Malcom-Piqueux, L. (2020). *From equity talk to equity walk: Expanding practitioner knowledge for racial justice in higher education*. Jossey-Bass.

NACADA: The Global Community for Academic Advising. (2006). *NACADA concept of academic advising*. https://www.nacada.ksu.edu/Resources/Pillars/ Concept.aspx

Patton, L. D., Shahjahan, R. A., & Osei-Kofi, N. (2010). Introduction to the emergent approaches to diversity and social justice in higher education special issue. *Equity & Excellence in Education, 43*(3), 265–278.

Puroway, A. W. (2016). Critical advising: A Freirian-inspired approach. *NACADA Journal, 36*(2), 4–10.

Puroway, A. (2018). Letter to the editor: Response to "Is advising a political activity?" *NACADA Journal, 38*(1), 9–11.

Pusser, B. (2015). A critical approach to power in higher education. In A. M. Martinez-Alemán, B. Pusser, & E. M. Bensimon (Eds.), *Critical approaches to the study of higher education: A practical introduction* (pp. 59–79). Johns Hopkins University Press.

Sensoy, O., & DiAngelo, R. (2017). *Is everyone really equal?: An introduction to key concepts in social justice education*. Teachers College Press.

Taylor, D. B. (2021, November 5). George Floyd protests: A timeline. *The New York Times*. https://www.nytimes.com/article/george-floyd-protests-timeline. html

Whitford, E. (2021, August 5). *Going behind the rhetoric*. Inside Higher Ed. https://www.insidehighered.com/news/2021/08/05/naspa-report-examines-statements-wake-george-floyds-murder

Winham, I. (2017). Letter to the editor: Is advising a political activity? *NACADA Journal, 37*(2), 7–8.

VOICES FROM THE FIELD

Socially Just Advising Administration in Action

Keely S. Latopolski

Perhaps the most essential role of an advising administrator is to lead teams of academic advisors—those who are on the front lines of service to students in need of academic and personal support, mentorship, and guidance. Leading with socially just principles and purpose provides academic advisors with a supportive framework to guide their daily practice and interactions with students. Socially just advising administrators hold an equity mindset and leverage resources to support their team and create inclusive policies.

Advising administrators have a professional responsibility to model mindfulness, act as ethical and authentic leaders, and anchor their work with students at the center. Socially just advising administrators can transform students' experiences by empowering academic advisors to uphold equitable and inclusive advising policies. Administrators empower academic advisors through their active support, wisdom in judgment, critical consciousness about power, and knowledge of self and positionality. The purpose of socially just advising administrators is to support, educate, and inspire academic advisors to generate equity in academic advising and advance justice (Kezar & Posselt, 2019).

Mindfulness as Social Justice Administration

Mindfulness is at the heart of the socially just advising administrator's practice. Being mindful involves thinking thoughtfully about the implications and effects of decisions and policies. When making decisions and creating policies for students, being mindful involves posing questions such

DOI: 10.4324/9781003437598-13

as, "What barriers does this policy create for students?" or "How can we reduce barriers and increase to access advising resources for all students?" Empathy is activated when equity and mindfulness are at the forefront of policy development and decisions. Empathic advising administrators can take another perspective when evaluating students' academic progress and the support they need to be successful. Behaviors of empathetic administrators may include a willingness to listen and being open to hearing student and advisor experiences with which they do not identify.

Especially when students are academically at risk of academic probation, advising administrators should ask open-ended questions about their lives outside of class, such as, "How do you spend your time outside of class?" "What are you passionate about?" "How can I support you academically?" "What would help you be most successful academically?" Although academic advisors are not professional counselors and should not assume that role, such questions create space for students to feel valued, at which point, they can be directed to the appropriate resources and, in turn, be held accountable. While meeting with a student at risk of academic probation and asking them, "What's going on outside of class?" the student disclosed an alcohol addiction for which they were seeking help at the time. In our subsequent meetings over the years, the student proudly showed me the chips they had collected and their academic, personal, and professional successes. This student later revealed that one of the initial reasons they stayed committed to sobriety was to remain accountable during our meetings.

Creating a practice of mindfulness as an advising administrator requires reflection and reflexive considerations. Reflecting on successful programs and policies, while recognizing what can be improved, is an essential trait of mindfulness for the advising administrator. Having the awareness to think through what can be improved and leaning into the positive aspects of an event or policy underscore the consideration and understanding of an advising administrator. A practice of mindfulness and being aware also allows for increased creativity and an entrepreneurial mindset. Administrators, who are adaptable and willing to support their advisors' ideas, have the agility to navigate away from what does not work which permits fearless creativity to be released. Fearless creativity makes new forms of advising possible. Reflecting on the need to engage with commuter students, one institution launched a program where academic advisors met with commuter students taking evening classes in parking garages outside of traditional office hours. Unique approaches such as this can expand access for students who may only be on campus when the advising office is closed. This innovative initiative demonstrated mindfulness in advising administration by reflecting on and anticipating how to meet the needs of a specialized population of commuter students in a dynamic new way. Being courageous to try new things and adopting a fearlessly creative mindset opens new possibilities to meet students' needs and challenges administrators to be professionally agile. This was made possible through mindfulness, when advisors considered intentional thought, reflection, and the anticipation of needs.

Commitment to Inclusive Action

Employing the framework developed by Kezar and Posselt (2019), advising administrators can demonstrate their commitment to socially just practices through inclusive action and transparent, ethical leadership. As advising administrators communicate their commitment through inclusive actions and drive transformational change not only in the daily practices of their advising teams but also in the students' lives, their advisors meet daily. When working with students, this approach looks like providing support, doing intentional outreach, and connecting students with resources and offices across campus. This strategy can be especially meaningful to students experiencing mental health crises if advisors are trained by advising administrators to refer them, or even walk them, to campus resources dedicated to mental health support. Socially just advising administrators actively challenge students to believe in themselves and provide support and advocacy.

Commitment to inclusive action provides professional development opportunities for the advisors an administrator supports. Socially just administrators demonstrate ethical and transparent leadership by openly communicating with their staff. Through one-on-one meetings, administrators learn the strengths and opportunities each member of their advising team brings to the office and the professional goals they have for themselves. One of the best questions a former supervisor asked me was, "What are you looking for in your next professional position?" As a young professional in my first position, this question conveyed her support of my professional growth, and she offered opportunities to develop skills in the area I wanted to pursue.

The opportunity for advancement in the academic advising profession is fairly flat, so the more advising administrators can be transparent and illuminate administrative insights to their staff, the more prepared they will be for an upward career trajectory (see Chapter 18). Advising administrators can create exposure for their staff to learn about building a department budget and the factors that go into the financial oversight of a unit. Academic advisors often lack supervisory responsibilities, which can be an important experience for career advancement. Administrators can develop

TABLE VFF 7.1 Recommendations for Advising Administration in Action

Recommendations	What This Looks Like in Practice	Reasoning
Mindfulness as Social Justice	• End-of-year debrief with the advising team to reflect, learn, and evaluate from past semesters and advising practices • Reflect on office and advising policies to promote equity and inclusivity	• Recognizing actions or behaviors that were inequitable and preventing them from reoccurring • Anticipate the needs of the office and advising policies will require updating to be more inclusive
Ethical and Authentic Leadership	• Involving the advising team in administrative processes such as budgeting and strategic planning • Asking advisors/supervisees how they want to grow professionally	• Transparent leadership practice to advance professional development • Communicates and encourages support of professional growth
Fearless Creativity	• Holding brainstorming sessions with advisors to generate ideas for how to meet the needs of students in unique ways • Willingness to support unconventional initiatives and adopt a "try anything once" mentality to meet the needs of students	• Proactively creating ways to reduce barriers for students to engage with academic advising and increase access to advising services • Opens new possibilities of how to meet the increased demands of academic advisors
Inclusive Action	• Walking students to support services (e.g., counseling center) in times of need • Evaluate documents yearly to reflect inclusive language	• Puts student-centeredness into action and ensures the safety and security of students • Promotes inclusivity

unique ways for staff members to oversee student workers and graduate assistants or take a supervisor preparation course through their human resources department to gain exposure in this area.

Administrators must operate from a socially just framework as they lead academic advisors. Doing so engenders equity and supports justice among academic advisors who work daily in front-facing roles with students. Socially just advising administrators are leaders who enact mindfulness and foresight in their strategic decision-making. Advising administrators act socially just by committing to inclusive action by advocating for equitable policies and amplifying opportunities for their advising team. Socially just advising administrators are responsible for integrating and embedding these principles in their daily practices to promote equity and inspire justice. Table VFF 7.1 offers some examples for consideration.

Reference

Kezar, A., & Posselt, J. (2019). *Higher education administration for social justice and equity: Critical perspectives for leadership*. Routledge.

PART II

Advising Program Structures, Planning, Design, and Implementation

8

STRATEGIC PARTNERSHIPS

Cultivating Advising Leaders across the University

Richie Gebauer and Jennifer Tharp

Advising is part of an increasingly complex landscape of programs, services, and resources that support student success. Many higher education practitioners may attribute student success to retention, persistence, and graduation. For our purposes, student success also includes the development of productive mindsets, the ability to effectively cope with life experiences extraneous to college, and the successful navigation of relationships in light of the world around us (Lane et al., 2019). To effectively lead advising programs and to advocate for the value of advising and its contributions to student success, advising administrators must foster and sustain both internal partnerships with those on their teams and external strategic partnerships with others across campus. Advising cannot occur in a vacuum and must involve a variety of campus actors, each contributing to a process that seeks to help students thread together their curricular, cocurricular, and residential experiences. To move academic advising beyond its technical elements—supporting course selection and managing degree requirements—advising leaders must identify campus partners and build strategic and sustainable partnerships that will amplify the value of academic advising on a college or university campus. The cultivation of strategic partnerships will require advance planning, timely communication, an entrepreneurial spirit, and patience. The steps outlined in this chapter can take time and may prove difficult, depending on campus size and culture. Yet these are the strategic steps that effective administrators take to advance the student experience.

DOI: 10.4324/9781003437598-15

Clear Advising Philosophy

Advising, like all teaching and learning initiatives, "is a series of intentional interactions with a curriculum, a pedagogy, and a set of student learning outcomes" (NACADA, 2006, para. 9). Before cultivating internal and external strategic partnerships, academic advising administrators are encouraged to consider a theoretical advising framework—an advising pedagogy—that serves as the foundation for the university or academic school's advising curriculum. Just as a salesperson cannot sell a product that has yet to be created, advising administrators cannot secure campus partners until they clearly define what it is they are seeking to partner on. McGill (2018) said the role of academic advising in the larger context of both the student experience and institutional structures is often misunderstood by university stakeholders. It is the responsibility of advising administrators to design this pedagogy and curriculum and to educate colleagues across the institution about how this philosophy of advising developmentally "assists students in the clarification of their life/career goals and in the development of educational plans for realization of these goals" (Crockett, 1985, p. 248).

Effective advising permeates nuances of a student's experience; therefore, this work cannot live solely within an academic advising unit. Though retention in higher education is discussed as everyone's responsibility, creating a successful advising infrastructure is critical to retention. However, the shifting demographic of students—particularly increased enrollment of students of color (Espinosa et al., 2018) and students experiencing underpreparedness (Butrymowicz, 2017)—reinforces the argument that all must communicate the value and importance of advising. We recognize that not all advising partners are trained to advise students regarding curriculum, nor should they be. However, the current landscape of higher education requires a culture shift that moves advising away from course-focused academic advising toward advising the holistic student both in face-to-face and virtual contexts, regardless of time or place. Advising administrators must ensure their team establishes learning outcomes rooted in its advising philosophy, shifting the view of advising from solely the technical aspects of academic advising to the much larger lens of student success. They also must decide what strategic partners are needed to achieve these outcomes and carry out this pedagogical approach.

Creating a Network of Strategic Partners

Creating a network of strategic partners essentially means developing a community of practice (Wenger et al., 2002). As strategic partners are recruited, it is critical that a common advising language is shared and spoken by both advisors and strategic partners. This language must evolve as institutions learn more about their students and their needs. It is the responsibility of advising administrators to establish this common language across this community of practice, to train campus partners to understand how this language intersects with the strategic agenda surrounding advising at the institution, and to truly integrate advising around the student experience. This common language should be unique to the institution and connect directly to and support the university's mission and values. It should also place the student at the center of a transformative learning experience, moving students out of isolation and "connecting [them] with [their] fellow students and the broad world of experience and knowledge" (Soliday & Lombardi, 2018, p. 62).

When students ask about or seek out advising, this common language will reinforce how advising threads through their institutional experience. There must be a shared clarity among campus partners that supports institutional integrity, promoting student persistence and a cohesive campus culture (Braxton et al., 2013). It is through a common language that advising administrators can train and prepare strategic campus partners to support students from varied backgrounds with a vast array of needs.

Partnerships should be strategic. It is strongly recommended that advising administrators are fully transparent when outlining clear, intentional expectations for strategic partners. How does each strategic partner play a unique and critical role to advance advising? As advising administrators consider their advising learning outcomes and outline annual goals, it is their responsibility to engage in ongoing dialogue with all strategic partners to clearly articulate, in writing, the role of each partner versus the role of the advising office. These expectations should be developed via a joint process that includes leaders from all involved teams. How do both entities of the partnership support one another? This relationship must exist in writing to ensure sustainability. An explicit shared responsibility for developing common goals can serve as a succession plan, such as if strategic partners leave the university or transition roles. When clear processes, short- and long-term partnership needs, growth opportunities, and assessment measurements are outlined (Cavanaugh, 2017), and the effectiveness of the partnership is revisited annually, strategic partnerships can thrive. This approach to intentional strategic partnerships supports the advancement and evolution of the field of academic advising in ways that promote scholarship and result in the recognition of unique approaches to modeling advising through collaboration.

Partners in this advising process will want to view the results of their work and better understand the value-added impact advising has on student success. Therefore, establishing a research culture is important. Sriram (2017) defined a higher education division that has a research culture as one that "nudges everyone to be a scholar practitioner ... to put research skills to use to demonstrate the effects of their practice" (pp. 4–5). Sriram (2017) also wrote that "research is the search for truth" (p. 20). To identify strategic partnerships, advising administrators must discover this truth by evaluating data that will drive decision-making. Regardless of the advising structure/model (e.g., centralized, decentralized, supplementary, and split), evaluating data to understand student needs, to identify obstacles preventing student success, and to determine program effectiveness is essential to identifying which campus partnerships ensure students receive effective advising and the advising philosophy is being lived out.

Change can be difficult for campus stakeholders; however, it is required to strengthen advising and to build a larger advising network that threads through campus. When attempting this, it is critical to utilize scholarship of academic advising as the foundation for change. Advising administrators must educate stakeholders—potential strategic partners—about the current advising trends in higher education, about the literature that informs this field, and about advising best practices including the technological tools that provide students with clarity about their academic pathways and support as they navigate the learning experience. When academic advising administrators provide strategic partners with clear rationale for why they are being recruited to join a larger culture of change, administrators promote student success through advising.

Potential Strategic Partners

As advising administrators consider potential partnerships, they should strongly evaluate the roles that career services; first-year experience (FYE) stakeholders; faculty members; residence life; athletic coaches and departments; student activities; diversity, equity, and inclusion personnel; academic support; and counseling services (to name a few) play in advancing advising goals. Admittedly, these potential partners are U.S.-centric; thus, readers are encouraged to consider the transferability of the strategies presented here in light of their institutional structures.

Career Service Partners

When considering how advising is positioned on campus, career services is a natural partner given the relationship between academic and career exploration. Intentionally integrating career development into the advising process during the first year creates an opportunity for a scaffolded career development plan that spans four academic years and is promoted through effective advising that connects college to career. Tudor (2018) argued that academic advising is typically passive and encourages higher education professionals to instead consider how embedding career advising into the academic advising structure of the student experience will allow students to plan for a successful career from their first day on campus. It shifts advising to a transformational experience, with advising pedagogy driving students to consider how all aspects of their college experience intersect and to identify the transferable connections between these experiences and their life and career goals. Lowenstein (2015) identified this as a "locus of learning" (p. 121), helping students to derive value from the integration of their learning experiences across learning contexts.

First-Year Experience Stakeholders

Regardless of whether a student's career development begins in the first year as an intentional piece of the advising process, FYE stakeholders are important partners. Academic advising administrators, alongside FYE colleagues, must consider how advising is positioned in the FYE. Institutions must consider an infrastructure that embeds advising into the FYE to promote student success. Advising administrators must determine advising expectations in the first year that are guided by the advising pedagogy and curriculum, and they should require periodic advising meetings that are efficiently recorded and tracked (Fosnacht et al., 2017). These ongoing advising conversations introduce students early to what effective, transformational advising looks like, increasing student perception of the value of advising across four years. Intentional advising, from the FYE through graduation, helps students think critically about how in-class and out-of-class experiences interconnect and support each other instead of existing in isolation.

Faculty Member Partners

Involving faculty members in these conversations as either faculty advisors or advising advocates is critical. Faculty members design and deliver curriculum and cocurriculum both in the institution's general education programs and in academic departments. Partnering with faculty members to institutionalize advising in their departments; aiding in preparing students to connect core to major curriculum; and teaching students how academic, advising, and student engagement learning outcomes intersect and support each other is essential to student success. However, as critical as faculty members are to the advising process, many do not feel prepared to engage in advising that moves beyond traditional advising activities such as course selection (Vespia et al., 2018). While NACADA uses academic advising and holistic advising interchangeably, in reality, academic advising at many institutions remains a purely prescriptive and transactional process. It is the responsibility of advising administrators to engage faculty members in ongoing professional development opportunities that provide them with the tools to advise beyond the curriculum, given their central role in the life of students. This educational opportunity includes teaching faculty members about university life beyond the classroom so they can effectively situate students to consider those intersections between in-class and out-of-class experiences.

Out-of-Classroom Experience Partners

It is important that advising administrators have a thorough understanding of the operations of other campus units to best leverage those areas as partners. Key out-of-classroom experiences include residential and athletic experiences. Dedicating time to understand the learning outcomes that residence life staff have established for students living on campus and that athletic staff are working to achieve through athletic programs will help influence how advising brings these experiences to light in the advising process. These partnerships must also be driven by institutional data. If a campus is 80% residential, then residence life must be a strategic partner in the advising process. However, if only 10% of students live on campus, advising administrators may more effectively devote their time to better understanding the commuter experience and how advising supports the commuter. It is here that student activities or a student engagement and leadership unit that serves the institution's commuter population may act as strong advising advocates.

Diversity, Equity, and Inclusion Partners

To best serve Black, Indigenous, and people of color (BIPOC) students, establishing clear partnerships with diversity, equity, inclusion, and belonging units on campus is essential. As colleges and universities evolve to create paths to improving college access and completion for BIPOC students—many of whom are also first-generation students—it is critical for academic advising professionals to acknowledge and develop an understanding of the unique challenges and experiences these students carry with them because of their "racially minoritized identity" (Koo, 2021, p. 198). Partnering with colleagues leading diversity, equity, inclusion, and belonging (DEIB) offices and initiatives on campus will create space where advisors can learn to best serve students of color on their campus.

Academic Support Partners

In addition to identifying the populations of students enrolled at their institution, advising administrators must consider which populations are both academically underprepared or underserved. Doing so will clarify where to establish strategic partnerships with academic support services and/or accessibility resource centers to best support these students. What is the nature of student needs as they access counseling services? Can these needs—particularly those that focus on the development of coping mechanisms and action-oriented solutions to overcome barriers to student success—be supported through a strengthened relationship between counseling services and academic advising and potentially inform advising curriculum? These questions are important because data illuminates the nature of these partnerships: How much time and energy should be devoted to securing specific strategic partners? Where do opportunities for a range of interventions exist? How are socially just practices and partnerships critical to serving underprepared and underserved students through advising?

Other Potential Partnerships

The list of potential strategic partners we identified is not exhaustive. Personnel from admissions, financial aid, civic engagement, registrar, billing, student activities, veteran affairs, international student services, and Federal TRIO Programs—including Upward Bound, Talent Search, and Student Support Service—are viable partners who will play key roles in the advising process. Habley's Hub, as described in Chapter 1, offers additional opportunities to identify potential partners. Academic administrators are charged with considering how these areas can assist in advisors living out the university's advising philosophy.

Sustaining Strategic Partnerships

Once strategic partnerships for academic advising are established on campus, the advising administrator needs to lead the overall partnership project so it becomes a sustainable aspect of the campus environment. Such sustainability is aided by an active understanding of the norms that characterize partners' roles, clear communication to fuel partnerships, prioritization of shared spaces—technological and practical—that facilitate collaboration with campus partners, and steady vision for maintaining shared purpose in these partnerships. These markers of the advising administrator's task reflect the description of effective academic leadership given by Bolman and Gallos (2011). They argued that successful academic leaders:

1 Create campus arrangements and reporting relationships that offer clarity and facilitate work
2 Create caring and productive campus environments that channel talent and encourage cooperation
3 Respect differences, manage them productively, and respond ethically and responsibly to the needs of multiple constituencies
4 Infuse everyday efforts with energy and soul (p. 11).

To cultivate sustainable strategic partnerships for advising, administrators benefit from incorporating each of the following leadership tasks into their annual or semesterly reflection and prioritization.

Leadership Tasks to Advance Strategic Partnerships

The first leadership task involved in creating sustainable strategic partnerships is learning about campus partners' roles and what realities and contexts influence the nature of their partnership. Like academic advising, other long-established roles in higher education are rooted in philosophical contexts that inform professional norms, such as methods of communication and approaches to collaboration (Wilson et al., 2020). For example, faculty norms can often be observed in the use of parliamentary procedure (e.g., Robert's Rules of Order) to guide faculty senate proceedings and in the use of faculty committees to carry out academic business. Similarly, student support teams often utilize a variety of meeting types to facilitate campus business—some of which are guided by agendas linked to departmental goals; other meetings' proceedings are determined by the needs of the day. Understanding the philosophical underpinnings of such norms that contextualize strategic partners supports advising administrators in conceptualizing plans that honor and advance the underlying goals of each role.

Clear communication with strategic partners is the second essential component of developing sustainable partnerships. Effective communication will include reminders about the shared vision and goals of the overall partnership project, as well as about the distinct objectives of each stakeholder. Such communication can be facilitated semesterly or quarterly through meetings or monthly through email updates on the project and progress. The goal of effective communication is to fuel focus and energy around the project. Administrators can know they are effective in this way when campus partners understand the shared goals of collaborative projects, the roles of all involved, where to find answers to questions, and how the project will be assessed. In a sense, advising administrators can apply student-coaching approaches to strengthen strategic partnerships through clarity, resourcing, and a shared sense of vision to support engagement.

Considering the changing landscape of higher education, the third leadership task of advising administrators is to create spaces, both technological (e.g., use of the same software solution) and within the academic year (e.g., in-person meetings), for active collaboration and celebration with strategic partners. The primary features that support strategic partnerships in academic advising include streamlined data governance, comprehensive and real-time awareness around student needs and interventions, and ongoing insights reflected to primary users to improve the depth and breadth of support. Technology solutions can take many forms and will vary by campus. They can facilitate assessment of cross-departmental advising efforts and can provide the reports needed to sustain effective partnerships. Campus-wide planning can also support strategic partnerships around advising by ensuring key partners have regular time to collaborate and physical spaces to connect. Both technology and campus-wide planning require advance planning and partnership at the highest levels of the institution.

The fourth leadership task of the advising administrator is sustaining a steady vision for advising. For many college students, university life occurs at the nexus of financial pressures, mental health concerns, family responsibilities, and pressure to excel academically (Karaman et al., 2019; Watson & Watson, 2016). Amidst these challenges, academic advisors have the unique opportunity to know students and support them, creating chances for advising to move beyond course planning. In some institutional models—and depending on student engagement—the academic advisor may be the only person who knows a student personally and can speak into matters of concern. Advisors' knowledge of students beyond the classroom, as well as the curriculum, makes advisors critical decision-making partners throughout campus. Strategic partnerships enable informed conversations with students and prepare them for intentional referrals to other services on campus when needed.

Clear examples of strategic partnerships were offered to aid advising administrators in considering what academic and nonacademic units may contribute to a campus' culture shift that transforms advising into a sustainable aspect of the campus environment. These partnerships will result in the development or retooling of programs and services designed to support learners from diverse backgrounds. For example, coordinated cross-training at a basic level, with strategic partners representing academic and nonacademic units on campus, reflects institutional integrity (Braxton et al., 2013) and supports the goals of academic advisors, counselors, and strategic partners. Advising is critical in setting the tone for students' academic engagement the first year. Therefore, it is important to challenge students to consider what it means to thrive in college, which Schreiner (2020) defined as maintaining a sense of well-being through transitions. Additionally, linking college to career can support students' academic belonging at the institution, their resilience, and their confidence in their pathway to graduation. While many additional cohort-specific aspects of student success can be supported through academic advising, it is most critical that advisors are trained in *who* their students are and *how* to flex between advising styles. Thorough advisor training will involve collaboration with strategic partners across campus to ensure that effective referral systems are in place and that there are shared mindsets about what it means to thrive at the institution. It is the role of the advising administrator to guarantee that this training is prioritized in annual planning, budget, and assessment cycles. It subsequently requires participation and investment from other leaders on campus to successfully execute.

Advising Advocates

Earlier, we discussed using scholarship to create a culture of change that occurs through effective partnerships. When recruiting strategic partners, it is not abnormal to encounter roadblocks. It is not unusual that our colleagues will exhibit hesitancy surrounding change and that they may not view higher education advising as critical to student success. Advising administrators should anticipate this response and proactively educate colleagues about the true value of advising. Administrators must engage in a thorough review of the literature to provide evidence for a shifting advising culture to move advising from transactional to transformational. Advising administrators may need to teach potential partners the value of their role in the larger strategic advising agenda and how it promotes student advocacy.

For advising to continuously shift from transactional to transformational, institutional partners and the entirety of the institution must begin to recognize that true advising, not just academic advising, is advocacy. Nguyen (2015) discussed how academic advising is reactive and prescriptive in nature, providing students with answers and guidance only when they solicit that information. However, shifting culture to promote intentional strategic partnerships—to truly create a community of practice (Wenger et al., 2002) that threads across departments, divisions, and the university—can lead to systemic change. It is here that this community of practice, led by an advising administrator, interacts with institutional data to identify the recurring patterns among student issues (Nguyen, 2015) and begins to proactively identify pathways to progress that seek to prevent these issues. This type of effort responds to a charge that was made almost two decades ago. Campbell (2002) challenged all advising administrators and advocates to seek out the identification of patterns, to investigate in ways that will uncover the truth (Sriram, 2017), and to invest in furthering the academic advising agenda by "revitalizing or structuring, as the case may be, our roles as campus change agents" (Campbell, 2002). This moves advising from simply academic to a more intrusive process: advocacy. Advocacy embeds equity and justice into an advising model that promotes race, gender and gender identity, social class, sexual orientation, and religion. This ensures the faces, voices, and experiences of all students are reflected, valued, and validated throughout the advising experience. As such, this shift in the advising approach positions advisors to not only strengthen partnerships with DEIB-related offices at the institution, but it also serves to further develop advisors as advocates.

When students enter higher education institutions, they engage in the learning experience in pursuit of personal and professional goals. Yet challenges—those embedded in the transition and the learning experience and those that are unexpected and out of a student's control—can threaten a student's persistence toward their goals (Schreiner, 2020). Academic advising that goes beyond course selection to advocate for student success helps close the gap between students and their goal attainment. This subsequently benefits their future, their family, and society. When led by an advising pedagogy built for all students, and when operationalized by institutional culture and practices, advising can function as a source for meaning making (Wallace & Wallace, 2016) and wayfinding (Burnett & Evans, 2016). Advising administrators play a critical role in cultivating the strategic partnerships that characterize smooth academic experiences that support this holistic approach. When students' needs and unique experiences are considered at the institutional level, they will encounter opportunities to engage with timely support throughout the arc of their student experience.

Conclusion

For academic advising administrators hoping to develop or enhance integrated advising experiences, strategic partnerships are essential. Strategic partnerships involve a variety of leaders and departments throughout the institution and are best cultivated through a continual focus on the value of holistic advising as is revealed through campus data and relevant literature. Campus partnerships are sustained by clear and vision-directed communication, based on a shared philosophy of advising that is unique to individual campuses. When academic advising leaders are sensitive to the realities of institutional culture, the needs of specific student cohorts, and the norms that characterize various roles among their partners, they create an environment where academic advising can support student success. Intentionality in navigating these dynamics can also aid in smooth and sustainable collaboration, as can the strategic use of technology to support shared initiatives.

Advising leaders seeking new or strengthened strategic partnerships on their campus should consider which areas discussed present the greatest opportunities and challenges. Student-based focus groups can provide insight, direct data collection, and highlight aspects of advising that could be enhanced for students. Similarly, speaking with existing partners about the aspects of their participation that are perennially stressful or need improvement will reveal opportunities for exploration and clarification.

As advising leaders proceed, remember the value of holistic academic advising experiences. The strategic partnerships cultivated on individual campuses will enhance students' clarity about their academic pathways, their sense of belonging through integrated care, and their commitment to the institution resulting from the excellent support they receive. Advising is more critical to the student experience than ever before. An advising office's effort to create strategic partnerships will ultimately reap the benefits of student success, which is the goal of academic advising professionals, leaders, and institutions.

Reflection Questions

1 What do your executive and midlevel colleagues know about academic advising based on what you share at cross-departmental meetings?
2 To what extent are campus stakeholders aware of (and able to articulate) the purpose of academic advising on campus and how students can successfully engage?
3 In what ways does the advising philosophy and advising culture on campus promote and establish pathways for advocacy and change?
4 How do strategic partnerships for advising reflect the mission, values, and strategic plan of the institution? How can these be further highlighted?

References

Bolman, L. G., & Gallos, J. V. (2011). *Reframing academic leadership*. Jossey-Bass.
Braxton, J. M., Doyle, W. R., Hartley, H. V., III, Hirschy, A. S., Jones, W. A., & McLendon, M. K. (2013). *Rethinking college student retention*. Jossey-Bass.
Burnett, B., & Evans, D. (2016). *Designing your life: How to build a well-lived, joyful life*. Knopf.

Butrymowicz, S. (2017, January). Most colleges enroll many students who aren't prepared for higher education. *The Hechinger Report.* https://hechingerreport. org/colleges-enroll-students-arent-prepared-high-education/.

Campbell, S. (2002, June). Advancing academic advising through leadership. *Academic Advising Today, 25*(2). https://nacada.ksu.edu/Resources/Academic-Advising-Today/View-Articles/Advancing-Academic-Advising-Through-Leadership.aspx.

Cavanaugh, J. C. (2017). Who will lead? The success of succession planning. *Journal of Management Policy and Practice, 18*(2), 22–27. http://www.na-businesspress.com/JMPP/CavanaughJC_Web18_2_.pdf.

Crockett, D. S. (1985). Academic advising. In L. Noel, R. Levitz, & D. Saluri (Eds.), *Increasing student retention* (pp. 224–263). Jossey-Bass.

Espinosa, L. E., Kelchen, R., & Taylor, M. (2018). *Minority serving institutions as engines of upward mobility.* American Council on Education: Center for Policy Research and Strategy.

Fosnacht, K., McCormick, A. C., Nailos, J. N., & Ribera, A. K. (2017). Frequency of first-year student interactions with advisors. *NACADA Journal, 37*(1), 74–86. https://doi.org/10.12930/NACADA-15-048.

Karaman, M. E., Lerma, E., Cavazos Vela, J., & Watson, J. C. (2019). Predictors of academic stress among college students. *Journal of College Counseling, 22*(1), 41–55. https://doi.org/10.1002/jocc.12113.

Koo, K. K. (2021). Am I welcome here? Campus climate and psychological well-being among students of color. *Journal of Student Affairs Research and Practice, 58*(2), 196–213. https://doi.org/10.1080/19496591.2020.1853557.

Lane, M., Moore, A., Hooper, L., Menzies, V., Cooper, B., Shaw, N., & Rueckert, C. (2019). Dimensions of student success: A framework for defining and evaluating support for learning in higher education. *Higher Education Research & Development, 38*(5), 954–968. https://doi.org/10.1080/07294360.2019.1615418.

Lowenstein, M. (2015). General education, advising, and integrative learning. *The Journal of General Education, 64*(2), 117–130. https://doi.org/10.1353/jge.2015.0010.

McGill, C. M. (2018). Leaders' perceptions of the professionalization of academic advising: A phenomenology. *NACADA Journal, 38*(1), 88–102. https://doi.org/10.12930/NACADA-17-041.

NACADA: The Global Community for Academic Advising. (2006). *NACADA concept of academic advising.* https://www.nacada.ksu.edu/Resources/Pillars/Concept.aspx.

Nguyen, F. (2015). Academic advising or advocacy? *Academic Advising Today, 38*(2). https://nacada.ksu.edu/Resources/Academic-Advising-Today/View-Articles/Academic-Advising-or-Advocacy.aspx.

Schreiner, L. A. (2020). From surviving to thriving during transitions. In L. A. Schreiner, M. C. Louis, & D. D. Nelson (Eds.), *Thriving in transitions: A research-based approach to college student success* (pp. 17–32). National Resource Center for the First-Year Experience and Students in Transition.

Soliday, J., & Lombardi, M. (2018). *Pivot: A vision for the new university.* Advantage.

Sriram, R. (2017). *Student affairs by the numbers: Quantitative research and statistics for professionals.* Stylus.

Tudor, T. R. (2018). Fully integrating academic advising with career coaching to increase student retention, graduation rates, and future job satisfaction: An industry approach. *Industry and Higher Education, 32*(2), 73–79. https://doi.org/10.1177/0950422218759928.

Vespia, K. M., Freis, S. D., & Arrowood, R. M. (2018). Faculty and career advising: challenges, opportunities, and outcome assessment. *Teaching of Psychology, 45*(1), 24–31. https://doi.org/10.1177/0098628317744962.

Wallace, S. O., & Wallace, B. A. (2016). Defining student success. In T. J. Grites, M. A. Miller, & J. Givans Voller (Eds.), *Beyond foundations: Developing as a master academic advisor* (pp. 83–106). Jossey-Bass.

Watson, J. C., & Watson, A. A. (2016). Coping self-efficacy and academic stress among Hispanic first-year college students: The moderating role of emotional intelligence. *Journal of College Counseling, 19*(3), 218–230. https://doi.org/10.1002/jocc.12045.

Wenger, E., McDermott, R. A., & Snyder, W. (2002). *Cultivating communities of practice: A guide to managing knowledge.* Harvard Business School Press.

Wilson, M. E., Hirschy, A. S., Braxton, J. M., & Dumas, T. N. (2020). Inviolable norms of primary role advisors. *NACADA Journal, 40*(2), 74–84. https://doi.org/10.12930/NACADA-19-23.

VOICES FROM THE FIELD

Working Together to Support Students in Crisis

Calley Stevens Taylor and Rebecca L. Hapes

Academic advisors are often in a position to notice when a student is experiencing a variety of stressors (Harper & Peterson, 2005), including academic issues, financial insecurity, family stress, medical issues, experiences falling under Title IX protection, and mental health challenges. Any of these stressors can lead to crisis. It is our experience that academic advisors play a unique role in supporting students navigating these situations in the context of higher education. Yet, despite their insight into the challenges students face, advisors are not often integrated into institutional structures designed to help identify and prevent these issues from reaching crisis level, and advisors may not have the training and information necessary to best support these students. As a result of our experiences supporting students in partnership with care teams and Title IX offices, in particular, we believe advising administrators play an essential role in identifying opportunities for collaboration with other institutional partners to support students nearing or experiencing crisis and in preparing advisors to engage in this crucial work.

To better support students nearing or in crisis, advising administrators should consider identifying partnership opportunities at their institution. Advising administrators can approach a variety of resources: care teams, Title IX offices, basic need resources (e.g., emergency aid programs, health and counseling offices, and women's centers), centers for diversity and inclusion, and specialized services like veterans' offices or TRIO programs. Working collaboratively with these offices offers opportunities to develop efficient and effective referral systems, to design collaborative training opportunities, and to provide mutual promotion of resources and services.

DOI: 10.4324/9781003437598-16

On many campuses, a care or behavioral intervention team (BIT) serves as a coordinating body to support students nearing or experiencing a crisis (Sokolow & Lewis, 2013). Here, we offer this as an example of how advising administrators can partner with another institutional resource to better support students nearing or experiencing crisis.

Care and BITs

Many colleges and universities in the United States established teams to identify and support students nearing or experiencing crisis (Sokolow & Lewis, 2013). Before partnering with these teams, advising administrators should understand the history, purpose, and structure of these teams, which varies between institutions. These teams have existed in higher education for some time, but the shootings at Columbine High School, Virginia Tech, and Northern Illinois University resulted in an increased emphasis on behavioral intervention as a tool to prevent violence (Sokolow & Lewis, 2013). The National Behavioral Intervention Team Association (NABITA) defines BITs as "multi-disciplinary group[s] whose purpose is to…help detect early indicators of the potential for disruptive conduct, self-harm, and the risk of violence to others" (NABITA, n.d.). Care teams or students-of-concern teams may operate with less formal structures than BITs and tend to use more holistic approaches to identifying and mitigating a wider range of risks (Sokolow et al., 2014). At institutions where the BIT and care teams are different groups, advising administrators may find it more appropriate to partner with the care team.

Early teams most often managed cases involving psychological challenges, conduct violations, alcohol and drug issues, and academic misconduct (Van Brunt et al., 2014). By 2018, however, NABITA members reported that top case types managed by their teams had shifted to psychological—suicide or depression; other psychological; and academic, financial, or social stress/needs (Schiemann & Van Brunt, 2018). In 2020, NABITA members reported that 61% of referrals to these teams were for reasons related to mental health, and 26% of referrals were for other concerns related to students' well-being (e.g., academic, financial, and social services needs; NABITA, 2020), any of which can have significant implications for a student's academic experience.

NABITA recommends a tiered approach to care team membership: core members (essential), middle tier (engage as needed), and outer tier (important but not usually invited to team meetings) (Van Brunt et al., 2015). In 2015, NABITA categorized academic advisors in the outer tier (Van Brunt et al., 2015). Still, by 2018, 35% of NABITA member institutions reported that academic advisors were members of these teams (Schiemann & Van Brunt, 2018), indicating an increased recognition of the value of advising representation. However, despite the value advisors bring to both identifying and supporting students nearing or experiencing crisis, advisors were still not among the top core members reported by NABITA members in 2020 (NABITA, 2020)

Advocating for Advising Representation on Care Teams

Advising administrators play a key role in advocating for advising representation on care teams. Administrators who wish to work with their institutional partners to incorporate advisors into care teams may find it helpful to focus on two benefits offered by advisors: their role in referring those in need to care teams and the knowledge they bring to supporting students as they navigate the academic implications of challenging circumstances.

Advisors can be a rich source of referrals and supplementary information for care teams. Academic advisors often develop strong personal relationships with students; if a student has or is going through a traumatic or otherwise stressful experience, their academic advisor—someone with whom they have strong relational ties—may be the person to whom they disclose this information. Alternatively, if a student's behavior is changing in a way that might indicate the student is experiencing a significant stressor, an advisor may be the first to notice these changes through early alerts, faculty reports, variation in academic performance, or failure to make academic progress. But, despite access to information essential to care teams' work, NABITA reported low referral rates from advisors to care teams (Schiemann & Van Brunt, 2018). By working with institutional partners to place advisors on care teams or streamline referrals from advisors to care teams, advising administrators can help ensure more students get the support these teams offer.

In addition, advising administrators should advocate for advising representation on these teams because of the skills, knowledge, and expertise advisors offer. Advising representatives on care teams can contribute by bringing referrals from other advisors; gathering information from other advisors regarding student cases; communicating with faculty members about student's circumstances; facilitating communication between faculty members and students; assisting students with academic decision-making and navigating academic policies; and supporting students' return after an extended absence or leave. In doing so, they can support a more holistic approach to supporting students in crisis and help mitigate the potential academic impacts of these challenges.

Advising Students in Crisis

While advocating for advising involvement with care teams and seeking partnership opportunities to engage advisors with other offices that support students in crisis is important, advising administrators should also seek partnership opportunities to support advisors individually in their work with such students. Advisors need opportunities to hone their relational skills and practice case studies to increase their confidence in supporting students in crisis situations (Hapes, 2017). Advising administrators should support advisors by reinforcing positive interpersonal behaviors in these interactions, bolstering the ability of academic advisors to serve as individuals to whom their students turn for help.

Training and development in informational and relational skills can be especially effective when offered in partnership with other offices and programs that work with students nearing or in crisis—services such as counseling centers, disability services, centers for diversity and inclusion, and deans of students offices. By partnering with other offices to provide joint training and development opportunities, or incorporating their expertise into advisor training and development, advising administrators can also strengthen relationships between their advising team and these other services. These relationships can contribute to the development of a more seamless and holistic support network for students in crisis. Additionally, advising administrators should consider partnering with Title IX officers, institutional counsel, legal advisors, or counseling offices to develop training for advisors on a range of topics such as reporting responsibilities and protocols, institutional and community support services and resources, effective referral skills, and strategies for identifying patterns in student behavior that might indicate that an intervention is warranted.

Finally, advising administrators should recognize that supporting students in crisis can be emotionally and mentally demanding. They must seek opportunities to support the well-being of their advisors. Again, collaborating with offices such as counseling centers, centers for diversity and inclusion, Title IX officers, or student conduct offices can help advising administrators identify resources and strategies their advisors can use to care for themselves, so they can continue to care for their students.

Conclusion

Academic advisors should play an important role in supporting students experiencing stressors that could lead to crises. By doing so in partnership with other offices and services, advising administrators can ensure this support is holistic and comprehensive. Advocating for advising representation on care teams is one partnership opportunity we offer as a suggestion, though other partnership opportunities should be explored. Advising administrators can also leverage partnerships to provide advisor training and development and support advisors' well-being while they work with students experiencing such challenges.

References

Hapes, R. (2017, June). Sexual violence: Preparing academic advisors to respond and advocate. *Academic Advising Today, 40*(2). https://nacada.ksu.edu/Resources/Academic-Advising-Today/View-Aarticles/Sexual-Violence-Preparing-Academic-Advisors-to-Respond-and-Advocate.aspx.

Harper, R., & Peterson, M. (2005). Mental health issues and college students: What advisors can do. *NACADA Clearinghouse of Academic Advising Resources.* http://www.nacada.ksu.edu/tabid/3318/articleType/ArticleView/articleId/141/article.aspx.

National Association for Behavioral Intervention and Threat Assessment (NABITA). (n.d.). NABITA. https://www.nabita.org/.

National Association for Behavioral Intervention and Threat Assessment (NABITA). (2020). *2020 NABITA survey data overview.* Retrieved August 31, 2021, from https://www.nabita.org/resources/nabita-2020-survey-data-infographic/.

Schiemann, M., & Van Brunt, B. (2018). 2018 NaBITA survey of summary of findings. *NaBITA Member Survey.* Retrieved August 1, 2021, from https://cdn.nabita.org/website-media/nabita.org/wordpress/wp-content/uploads/2018/10/2018-NaBITA-Survey-Summary-Final.pdf.

Sokolow, B. A., & Lewis, W. S. (2013). *Behavioral intervention v. threat assessment: Best practices for violence prevention.* Unpublished manuscript, available at http://www.ncherm.org.

Sokolow, B. A., Lewis, W. S., Van Brunt, B., Schuster, S., & Swinton, D. (2014). *The book on Behavioral Intervention Teams (BIT)* (2nd ed.). NaBITA.

Van Brunt, B., Reese, A., & Lewis, W. S. (2015). *Who's on the team? Mission, membership, and motivation* [white paper]. NaBITA.

Van Brunt, B., Sokolow, B., Lewis, W., Schuster, S., & Golston, A. (2014). *NaBITA team survey.* Retrieved August 24, 2021, from https://cdn.nabita.org/website-media/nabita.org/wordpress/wp-content/uploads/2012/04/2014-BIT-survey-summary.pdf.

9

ASSESSMENT OF ACADEMIC ADVISING

Rich Robbins and Isaiah Vance

Assessment of academic advising is one of an academic advising administrator's most important responsibilities. The effects of the advising curriculum, pedagogy, and advisor training and development are unknown without assessment to demonstrate what students have learned from their advising experiences. Moreover, advising is not exempt from external demands for accountability from parents, accreditation agencies, local, state, and federal governments, and others. The administrator's role in assessment of advising is broad. It includes establishing and sustaining a culture of assessment, leading the development of an assessment plan and implementation process, reporting results, and coordinating the implementation of any data-informed changes. This chapter addresses these responsibilities, beginning with understanding the assessment cycle and the key elements of an assessment plan.

The Assessment Cycle and Plan

To develop an effective plan, the advising administrator must first be familiar with the structure and foundational elements of the assessment cycle. Assessment in higher education is an ongoing, intentional, systematic process in which information is collected, analyzed, interpreted, and acted upon to determine what students know, do, and value as a result of their curricular and cocurricular experiences (Erwin, 1991; Huba & Freed, 2000).

Summarizing a 2002 article by Peggy L. Maki, Robbins delineated the basic steps in an assessment cycle as "the identification of desired outcomes, the accumulation of evidence, the interpretation of evidence, and

DOI: 10.4324/9781003437598-17

the implementation of change based on the evidence" (Robbins, 2016a, p. 278). Based on this definition, Robbins et al. (2018) initially developed the NACADA Assessment Cycle for Academic Advising, revised by Robbins et al. (2021) and presented in Figure 9.1.

A step-by-step representation of the assessment cycle for advising similar to the one developed by Robbins (2020) is shown in Table 9.1. This

THE ASSESSMENT CYCLE
Adapted from Maki (2002, 2004)

FIGURE 9.1 NACADA Assessment Cycle

Note. The NACADA Assessment Cycle, online at https://nacada.ksu.edu/Events/Assessment-Institute/The-Assessment-Cycle.aspx (NACADA, 2022; Robbins et al., 2021). Reprinted with permission from NACADA.

representation can also be used by advising administrators as a template for the development of an assessment plan for academic advising.

Central to the assessment cycle are the institutional and advising program's statements of values, vision, mission, and goals. These statements should guide the development of the academic advising program. Alignment between these statements is essential to establishing the legitimacy of academic advising as integral to teaching and learning.

The advising program's mission statement delineates its purpose and serves as the roadmap toward achieving their vision (Robbins, 2011; Robbins et al., 2021). Goals are precise, long-range, action-oriented statements that focus on the advising process. Individual, specific, and measurable outcomes are derived from these statements (Robbins, 2016a; Robbins & Zarges, 2011; Robbins et al., 2021). These components form the foundation of the assessment plan and influence the development of desired student learning outcomes (SLOs) for advising (Campbell, 2008; Robbins et al., 2021).

The assessment plan itself is more than a listing of these foundational elements. It should also convey the organizational context for the work, the specific SLOs, a curriculum map of the experiences designed to evoke learning, evidence to be gathered, and metrics against which to gauge outcome achievement. The assessment plan should be developed as a dynamic document that informs action and also serves as a communication tool for the academic advising administrator.

Developing Culture of Assessment

The very concept of an assessment cycle assumes *formative* assessment, meaning that the process is intended to create growth and ongoing improvement (CAS, 2019; NACADA, 2017a), in contrast to summative assessments, which are final in nature (Fiddler et al., 2006). Regular assessment of an advising program is formative; simple, sustainable, and iterative is the objective (Banta & Palomba, 2014). Grant-funded initiatives and some types of accrediting agencies sometimes seek summative assessments (Bresciani Ludvik, 2021). However, most institutions, accrediting bodies, and boards of trustees/regents are more concerned with seeing a *process* or culture of continuous improvement (CHEA, 2018).

Over time (i.e., multiple assessment cycles), performance targets should evolve so the advising program is challenged to achieve the target level. The administrator ensures that targets are achievable but challenging. A practical piece of advice here is to not set target levels at 100%. The first cycle of assessment for any SLO should be considered a baseline for comparison for later assessment cycles; later targets may be set at values such that most, but not all, are likely to be met. However, if assessment has not

TABLE 9.1 Academic Advising Assessment Table

Institutional Mission Statement	Local Mission Statement	Specific Programmatic Goal or Objective	Specific Student Learning Outcome	Opportunities for Student Learning	Date by When You Want Student Learning to Occur	Outcome Measures	Data Instruments	Minimum Performance Criterial Threshold for Success	Action(s) Based on Data

← Mapping of Outcomes →

Note. Adapted from Robbins (2009, 2011, 2016a, 2020); Robbins and Zarges (2011); Robbins and Adams (2013).

been part of the culture or established as a regular activity, administrators may find it challenging to begin (Kramer & Swing, 2010). Getting buy-in for the assessment of advising may not be difficult if assessment is a mandated activity at the institution; where it is not a mandated activity, there may be resistance. Thus, it is essential that advising administrators take the lead in establishing the importance of assessment within the advising team, while also engaging other institutional partners to build buy-in. Strategies to gain buy-in have been offered by Robbins et al. (2022):

- Start with assessment of an outcome you anecdotally know is being met.
- Present literature that supports your assessment plan.
- Communicate how the assessment will benefit students.
- Include naysayers on the assessment team from the beginning, using aspects of their ideas and acknowledging their contributions.
- Strategically communicate how your assessment plan can benefit those you want to buy in (i.e., cost-benefit analysis).
- Identify key strategies to use your assessment plan as a marketing piece (p. 38).

The Assessment Team and Stakeholders

Developing and implementing an effective assessment plan, while a valuable activity, is time-consuming. Thus, the administrator may find it useful to identify an assessment team (Robbins et al., 2021). The responsibilities of the assessment team, preferably overseen by the administrator, include identifying SLOs, mapping SLOs, identifying data collection strategies, interpreting assessment results, and making decisions based on those results. In addition to academic advisors, assessment team membership should be drawn from a core group of stakeholders in a variety of roles who offer the most expert knowledge and skills to contribute to the assessment process.

Stakeholders are those who interact with or are affected by the advising program. Messia (2010) classified types of stakeholders for advising as: core stakeholders (para. 3), or those who are directly involved with the advising program such as the administrator, advisers, and students; internal but indirect stakeholders (para. 4) who are affected by the advising program, such as retention offices, admissions offices, and marketing entities; and external and indirect stakeholders (para. 5), those who influence but are not directly involved with the advising program, such as those who hold the "purse strings" for the advising program and accreditation agencies.

Students are the primary stakeholders. Therefore, mapping the student experience, including programs, services, and offices with which students interact, is a useful way to identify stakeholders for advising assessment. Stakeholders may also be determined by the institutional mission and organizational structure, as anyone with direct or indirect involvement with the advising program is considered a stakeholder to some degree. Administrators must also consider diversity and the characteristics of the students served when identifying stakeholders to ensure equitable representation. Equity in representation is more than what appears on the surface (e.g., is the student an athlete, an honors student, or an adult student), and extends to consideration of race, ethnicity, and identity. For example, if the advising program serves a student population with large numbers of LGBTQ students and veterans, the administrator is obligated to consider how best to ensure that the assessment process does not exclude them or their interests.

Types of Outcomes for Academic Advising

Once stakeholders have been identified and an assessment team has been convened, the next step in plan development is the identification of assessable outcomes. The administrator must be familiar with all relevant internal and external expectations and influences on the advising program to be able to guide the assessment team in the identification of desired outcomes. In this process, important internal sources include institutional values, vision and mission statements, and goals, as well as those of programs that impact the advising activities, including First-Year Experience programs or the expectations of specific academic departments or colleges. Other desired outcomes for advising may be drawn from institutional outcomes, such as student persistence and completion rates.

External sources of expected outcomes are also important. They include Boards of Regents or Boards of Trustees, requirements and expectations of regional accreditation bodies, specialized accreditation bodies for specific professional programs, state, regional, or provincial governments (Ratcliff et al., 2001), and performance-based funding outcomes (Miller, 2016). Other external sources include the NACADA Pillar Documents: the NACADA Concept of Academic Advising (NACADA, 2006), the NACADA Core Competencies of Academic Advising (NACADA, 2017a), the NACADA Core Values of Academic Advising (NACADA, 2017b), and the Council for the Advancement of Standards in Higher Education: Standards and Guidelines for Academic Advising (CAS, 2019). The information included in these recognized professional standards for academic advising, incorporated individually or in various combinations, will include some attributes of desired outcomes for any advising program.

SLOs address the knowledge (cognitive SLOs), behaviors (behavioral SLOs), and values (affective SLOs) that result from students' advising experiences (Robbins, 2009, 2011; Robbins & Adams, 2013). Paralleling SLOs are advisor outcomes (AOs) which include the knowledge (cognitive AOs), behaviors (behavioral AOs), and values (affective AOs) advisors must possess to effectively advise students (Robbins et al., 2022). Process delivery outcomes (PDOs) are processes that must be in place, and what/how information must be delivered, to support students' achievement of desired SLOs (Robbins & Adams, 2013; Robbins & Zarges, 2011). Backward design (Wiggins & McTighe, 2006) informs the relationship between these three different types of outcomes: knowing the desired SLOs identifies the AOs for advisors as well as the PDOs that must occur for students to achieve the desired SLOs (Robbins et al., 2021).

Student Learning Outcomes

While AOs, PDOs, institutional, and externally driven outcomes are assessable, SLOs remain the primary basis for assessment in higher education (Ewell, 2009; Suskie, 2009). Development of correct, individual, and measurable SLOs are the primary basis for assessment of academic advising. As the development of the vision, mission, and goals for advising is deliberate (Banta & Palomba, 2014), SLOs are likewise intentionally developed and must be measurable (Upcraft & Schuh, 2007). A well-formed SLO makes measurement a relatively smooth process. Details regarding the development of SLOs can be found in Robbins, 2011, 2016a, Robbins et al., 2022.

Cross-Departmental Collaboration

In some cases, sharing SLOs across multiple offices is appropriate, such as student success, registrar/records, and student financial aid (CAS, 2019; Smith & Vance, 2019). Collaborative opportunities with faculty to achieve advising-related SLOs may also be possible (Finley, 2019). Coordinated, holistic student support systems are critical for student success, particularly for those students deemed more at-risk of stopping out (Suskie, 2018), and collaborative coordination in assessment creates a shared culture of assessment and responsibility for addressing SLOs. The administrator plays a key role in establishing and cultivating relationships with outside offices and exploring opportunities to collaboratively support students (see Chapter 8).

Mapping SLOs for Academic Advising

Once SLOs have been identified, the advising administrator will want to lead a process of SLO mapping. Mapping SLOs is the process of determining by when a specific SLO should be achieved and the learning opportunities and experiences available for students to achieve the SLO (Aiken-Wisniewski et al., 2010; Robbins, 2011; Robbins & Zarges, 2011). The timing determines the advising curriculum and pedagogy scaffolding, including (a) student learning opportunities relative to the SLO, (b) timing these opportunities, (c) types of measures, and (d) when data will be collected for each SLO. The fifth and sixth columns of Table 9.1 represent the mapping process. In addition to guiding assessment strategies, mapping contributes to program evaluation by helping to identify desired SLOs that are not part of the advising curriculum or academic advisor training and development (Robbins et al., 2021).

Gathering and Measuring Data

The purpose of measurement is to determine the extent to which an SLO has been achieved (Robbins, 2016b; Robbins et al., 2022). In leading the implementation of data collection and analysis, the administrator ensures that the measurement of outcomes is achievable (Volkwein, 2011). Common barriers are lack of data, invalid measures, and insufficient numbers or mix of measures. To overcome these obstacles, the advising administrator, with the support of the assessment team, is responsible for establishing what evidence will be collected, confirming that the evidence validly measures outcomes, ensuring that multiple measures are employed, and identifying assessment cycle performance targets which should be planned at the beginning of the assessment cycle.

Identifying Data Sources and Measures

As noted earlier, the nature of the SLOs will determine the kind of data needed in the assessment process. A critical responsibility of the advising administrator is to work with the assessment team to identify measures and data that address the goals and outcomes the team has crafted. Some of the more common data collection approaches for assessment of SLOs are:

- Focus groups – useful for student perception, opinion, or awareness
- Surveys – generally associated with indirect measures (National Institute for Learning Outcomes Assessment, 2022) due to the nature of the student perception questions that are commonly asked
- Student information – includes student information systems, degree audit programs (Vance, 2021), retention software, and advisor notes
- Rubrics and Portfolios – direct measures (National Institute for Learning Outcomes Assessment, 2022), if there is expert rating and review included (Suskie, 2018)
- This list is comprehensive neither in respect to types of measures nor variations of those measures. See Robbins (2016b) and Robbins et al. (2022) for more a more detailed discussion of this topic.

Post Measurement Activities

After collecting data, the advising administrator leads the process of analysis and interpretation, making decisions on the basis of results and reviewing the assessment process to ensure its integrity.

Reviewing and Interpreting Outcome Data

If the assessment team has collected raw data, the first step is data cleanup. In the context of assessment, data cleanup generally means the process of ensuring that data fits definitions, is not corrupted, and can be deduplicated. Essentially, it is converting data into meaningful information. Administrators without expertise in this process may find it beneficial to include a colleague with this expertise for the assessment team (see Chapter 10).

Data should also be reviewed to ensure it is reliable. In the context of advising assessment, reliability is commonly related to the extent to which data may replicate in other contexts, which in turn addresses representation (Banta & Palomba, 2014). This is a point where questions of inclusivity must be addressed (CAS, 2019). As Suskie (2018) suggested, assessment must be unbiased, appropriate, and fair to all relevant student groups and subgroups, and must be conducted in a balanced, representative manner. If data are not representative (i.e., reliable), it does not mean they are useless; rather it will mean that action planning based on that information should be undertaken with an appropriate understanding of possible shortcomings and awareness that certain programming changes may inadvertently increase inequity gaps (Suskie, 2018). Scaling inequitable programming or initiatives (consciously or otherwise) will increase inequities. Administrators should ensure that reliability is taken into consideration throughout the assessment cycle. Consider asking: Does the sampling, whether by definition or practice, exclude/include or over/underrepresent any groups? Another way of asking this question is: Who might be missing from our data? Answers to such questions can help to better understand the population demographics of the sample, particularly if various underrepresented groups have been absent or represent a disproportionate minority within the current population (Suskie, 2018).

Interpretation of Outcome Data

While there is an empirically demonstrated positive relationship between students' satisfaction levels with their college experiences and retention (Bean, 1983; Noel et al., 1985; Roberts & Styron, 2010), there is no empirical research identifying a direct causal link between effective advising and student retention or persistence. Effective advising is just one of the multitude of factors involved in retention (Nutt, 2003), and retention efforts must focus on all campus components to build strong and effective connections between the advising program and the rest of campus (Kuh et al., 2005). Measuring SLOs for advising therefore serves as proxy indicators for such broader desired outcomes related to retention. It is imperative for the administrator to know this and educate others who expect effective advising to directly result in student retention and persistence.

A review of the data, particularly when segmented by various demographic groups, may reveal the need for more targeted programming to create more equitable outcomes (Bresciani Ludvik, 2021; Vance, 2018). The administrator should be knowledgeable about types of data that are available or could be made available to ensure measures are not out of the bounds of what is reasonably possible to ascertain or discover. In particular, the advising administrator should ensure the data – particularly if used as a basis for predictive analytics – does not become a way of stereotyping certain students, which may perpetuate and exacerbate inequities. Generally, such data are useful in the aggregate but less helpful when working with individual students. Be aware of data limitations for certain demographic groups when evaluating the data and measuring the outcomes (Fiddler et al., 2006). Categories such as sex, race, ethnicity, major, student classification, and some socioeconomic markers are commonly collected; thus, populations can be compared. Other demographic markers, such as gender, sexual orientation, and veteran status are more difficult to ascertain as these are generally self-reported and may even be inappropriate to collect in certain contexts. The difficulty in gathering information about these latter categories is not an excuse to disregard these important components of a student's identity (NACADA, 2017b), but data will be absent for certain types of student populations simply because a tracking mechanism does not exist.

Acting upon Outcome Data

Once assessment data is gathered, deemed valid and reliable, and interpreted (Banta & Palomba, 2014), findings are reported to various stakeholder groups and used to inform decisions about the advising program (see Chapter 10). Disseminating assessment findings to diverse constituents, as well as soliciting feedback from them, is essential, as each group looks at findings through slightly different lenses (Bresciani Ludvik, 2021). During this assessment phase, the administrator should be clear with stakeholder groups about the weight of their input and feedback in the overall process (Messia, 2010). Responding to feedback not ultimately incorporated into the plan is also a good practice, as it encourages future engagement in the process and helps articulate the rationale to constituents.

Sustaining the Assessment Cycle

Assessment is an ongoing process, and the advising administrator is essential to ensuring the sustainability of assessment practices. To maintain a sustainable assessment culture, administrators should continually review the advising program's assessment practices and incorporate necessary assessment activities as part of the daily advising process (Robbins et al., 2022). Strategies such as sampling, using data collection methods that facilitate the ease of gathering and sharing the outcome data, being aware of data already collected by others, and placing SLO assessment cycles on two-, three-, or four-year cycles rather than attempting to assess every SLO every cycle (Robbins, 2016b; Robbins et al, 2022) are all administrative considerations regarding the sustainability of assessment.

Advising administrators should also regularly perform an assessment of the assessment (or a *meta*-assessment; Robbins, 2020) to ensure that the assessment plan was appropriately enacted and to identify changes that should be implemented during the next cycle. These steps can help confirm that assessment is continually meaningful. This includes examining such factors as whether or not stakeholders were included at each step, that SLOs were measured to align with the institutional and programmatic goals for advising, and that the frequency of the assessment cycle for any given SLO was appropriate (Robbins, 2020).

Assessment as Scholarly Inquiry

Those involved in the assessment process may communicate the results of advising assessment beyond internal audiences as one of two forms of scholarly inquiry: action research (Suskie, 2009; Troxel, 2008) and quasi-experimental or case control research. The processes of establishing SLOs, mapping SLOs, outcome measurement, and implementing results-based improvements all parallel the action research process of plan, act, observe, and reflect (Robbins, 2016b; Robbins et al., 2021). Presentation of such information at conferences, in publications, or via other venues of dissemination helps to build the literature base for advising and promotes professionalization of the field.

Conclusion

Leading assessment efforts is a complex process that takes a team of stakeholders to complete, but it is achievable, worthwhile, and necessary to promote continuous improvement of advising. The administrator is a champion for assessment of advising, ensuring that assessment is sustained, especially from one cycle to the next (Robbins et al., 2022). Administrators must empower their assessment teams and think critically about what occurs at each stage. With proper administrative leadership, assessment becomes a tool with which the advising program becomes more intentional, self-aware, and equipped to better serve and support students.

Reflection Questions

1 What institutional or divisional goals and outcomes does your academic advising program support? How can you demonstrate your program's alignment with and support of those larger efforts?
2 How might you ensure that your SLOs for academic advising are appropriate for your program and institution? How will assessment of these outcomes assist in promoting student success?
3 In what ways might you utilize your assessment process and the resulting information to create greater equity regarding the advising program you oversee? How can you and your staff work to ensure all students, regardless of background and demographics, are included?
4 Considering the context of your institution and/or division (i.e., organization, politics, and culture), how might you as a leader of academic advising utilize assessment to gain buy-in from the campus community?

References

Aiken-Wisniewski, S., Campbell, S., Nutt, C., Robbins, R., Kirk-Kuwaye, M., & Higa, L. (2010). *Guide to assessment in academic advising* (2nd ed.) (Monograph No. 23). NACADA.

Banta, T. W., & Palomba, C. A. (2014). *Assessment essentials: Planning, implementing, and improving assessment in higher education*. Jossey-Bass.

Bean, J. P. (1983). The application of a model of turnover in work organizations to the student attrition process. *Review of Higher Education, 6*(2), 129–148. https://doi.org/10.1353/rhe.1983.0026.

Bresciani Ludvik, M. (2021). *Equity-driven, high achievement: Assessment of student learning and development*. NASPA-Student Affairs Administrators in Higher Education.

Campbell, S. M. (2008). Vision, mission, goals, and program objectives for academic advising programs. In V. N. Gordon, W. R. Habley, & T. J. Grites (Eds.), *Academic advising: A comprehensive handbook* (2nd ed., pp. 229–241). Jossey-Bass.

Council for the Advancement of Standards (CAS). (2019). CAS standards for academic advising. https://nacada.ksu.edu/Resources/Pillars/CASstandards.aspx.

Council for Higher Education Accreditation (CHEA). (2018). *CHEA standards and procedures for recognition*. CHEA International Quality Group.

Erwin, T. D. (1991). *Assessing student learning and development: A guide to the principles, goals and methods of determining college outcomes.* Jossey-Bass.

Ewell, P. T. (2009). *Assessment, accountability, and improvement: Revisiting the tension.* National Institute for Learning Outcomes Assessment.

Fiddler, M., Marienau, C., & Whitaker, U. (2006). *Assessing learning: Standards, principles, & procedures* (2nd ed.). Kendall Hunt.

Finley, A. (2019). *A comprehensive approach to assessment of high-impact practices* (Occasional Paper No. 41). National Institute for Learning Outcomes Assessment.

Huba, M. E., & Freed, J. E. (2000). *Learner-centered assessment on college campuses: Shifting the focus from teaching to learning.* Pearson.

Kramer, G. L., & Swing, R. L. (Eds.). (2010). *Higher education assessments: Leadership matters.* Rowan & Littlefield.

Kuh, G. D., Kinzie, J., Schuh, J. H., White, E. J., & Associates. (2005). *Student success in college: Creating conditions that matter.* Jossey-Bass.

Maki, P. L. (2002). Developing an assessment plan to learn about student learning. *Journal of Academic Librarianship, 28*(1–2), 8–13. https://doi.org/10.1016/S0099-1333(01)00295-6.

Messia, J. (2010). *Defining advising stakeholder groups.* NACADA Clearinghouse. http://www.nacada.ksu.edu/Resources/Clearinghouse/View-Articles/Defining-Advising-Stakeholder-Groups.aspx.

Miller, T. (2016). *Higher education outcomes-based funding models and academic quality.* Lumina Foundation. https://eric.ed.gov/?q=source%3a%22lumina%22&ff1=subState+Policy&id=ED587409.

NACADA: The Global Community for Academic Advising. (2006). *Concept of academic advising.* https://www.nacada.ksu.edu/Resources/Pillars/Concept.aspx.

NACADA: The Global Community for Academic Advising. (2017a). *NACADA academic advising core competencies model.* https://nacada.ksu.edu/Resources/Pillars/Core%20Competencies.aspx.

NACADA: The Global Community for Academic Advising. (2017b). *NACADA core values of academic advising.* https://www.nacada.ksu.edu/Resources/Pillars/CoreValues.aspx.

NACADA: The Global Community for Academic Advising. (2022). *The assessment cycle.* https://nacada.ksu.edu/Events/Assessment-Institute/The-Assessment-Cycle.aspx.

National Institute for Learning Outcomes Assessment. (2022). *Evidence of student learning.* https://www.learningoutcomesassessment.org/ourwork/transparency-framework/components/evidence-student-learning/.

Noel, L., Levitz, R., & Saluri, D. (1985). *Increasing student retention: New challenges and potential.* Jossey-Bass.

Nutt, C. L. (2003*). Academic advising and student retention and persistence.* NACADA Clearinghouse. http://www.nacada.ksu.edu/tabid/3318/articleType/ArticleView/articleId/636/article.aspx.

Ratcliff, J. L., Lubinescu, E. S., & Gaffney, M. A. (Eds.). (2001). *How accreditation influences assessment.* Jossey-Bass.

Robbins, R. (2009). Assessment of career advising. In K. Hughey, D. Burton Nelson, J. Damminger, & E. McCalla-Wriggins (Eds.), *Handbook of career advising* (pp. 266–292). Jossey-Bass.

Robbins, R. (2011). Assessment and accountability of academic advising. In J. E. Joslin, & N. L. Markee (Eds.), *Academic advising administration: Essential knowledge and skills for the 21st century* (pp. 53–64). NACADA.

Robbins, R. (2016a). Assessment of academic advising: Overview and student learning outcomes. In T. J. Grites, M. A. Miller, & J. Givens Voller (Eds.), *Beyond foundations: Developing as a master advisor* (pp. 275–288). Jossey-Bass.

Robbins, R. (2016b). Assessment of academic advising: Gathering outcome evidence and making changes. In T. J. Grites, M. A. Miller, & J. Givens Voller (Eds.), *Beyond foundations: Developing as a master advisor* (pp. 289–304). Jossey-Bass.

Robbins, R. (2020). Meta-assessment and stakeholder learning: Proposed rubrics and relevance to academic advising. *The Mentor, 22.* https://doi.org/10.26209/mj2261870.

Robbins, R., & Adams, T. (2013). Assessment of peer advising. In H. Koring, & D. T. Zahorik (Eds.), *Peer advising and mentoring: A guide for advising practitioners* (2nd ed., pp. 129–140). NACADA.

Robbins, R., Andre, J., & Campbell, S. (2018). *The assessment cycle.* NACADA.

Robbins, R., Miller, M., & Zarges, K. M. (2021). *Breaking down assessment of academic advising: The assessment cycle and student learning outcomes.* NACADA.

Robbins, R., & Zarges, K. M. (2011). *Assessment of academic advising: A summary of the process.* NACADA Clearinghouse. http://www.nacada.ksu.edu/Resources/Clearinghouse/View-Articles/Assessment-of-academic-advising.aspx.

Robbins, R., Zarges, K. M., & Equivel, S. (2022). *Breaking down the assessment of academic advising: Gathering evidence, reporting and planning, change and sustainability.* NACADA.

Roberts, J., & Styron Jr., R. (2010). Student satisfaction and persistence: Factors vital to student retention. *Research in Higher Education Journal, 6*(1), 1–18.

Smith, J., & Vance, I. (2019, April 10). *Flipping course data to improve your institution* [Conference session]. Ellucian Live Annual Conference, New Orleans, LA, United States.

Suskie, L. (2009). *Assessing student learning: A common sense guide* (2nd ed.). Anker Publishing.

Suskie, L. (2018). *Assessing student learning: A common sense guide* (3rd ed.). Jossey-Bass.

Troxel, W. G. (2008). Assessing the effectiveness of the advising program. In V. N. Gordon, W. R. Habley, & T. J. Grites (Eds.), *Academic advising: A comprehensive handbook* (2nd ed., pp. 386–395). Jossey-Bass.

Upcraft, M. L., & Schuh, J. H. (2007). *Assessment in student affairs: A guide for practitioners* (2nd ed.). Wiley.

Vance, I. (2018, February 10). *Academic advising and high-impact practices* [Conference session]. American Association of State Colleges & Universities [AASCU] Academic Affairs Winter Meeting, San Antonio, TX, United States.

Vance, I. (2021, October 13). *Using degree audit reports to improve the form and function of curriculum* [Conference session]. Cohesion Annual Conference, Virtual.

Volkwein, J. F. (2011, September). *Gaining ground: The role of institutional research in accessing student outcomes and demonstrating institutional effectiveness* (Occasional Paper No. 11). National Institute for Learning Outcomes Assessment (NILOA).

Wiggins, G., & McTighe, J. (2006). *Understanding by design* (2nd ed.). Pearson.

VOICES FROM THE FIELD

Assessment in Action

Scott Byington and Cristy Holmes

Like many institutions, our institution began a thorough data review and introspective examination of the college's processes and procedures in anticipation of our decennial reaccreditation. Our regional accreditor requires an institution-wide, quality enhancement plan (QEP)—in other words, a significant initiative to improve student learning. At the same time, we were developing our five-year strategic plan and evaluating advising goals and initiatives to ensure they were consistent with the institution's mission and vision. This two-year comprehensive review identified opportunities for improvement and a need for additional, intentional advising assessment, which had been previously lacking.

While the college had already launched some advising initiatives a couple of years prior, for the QEP, we chose to target the student learning experience in advising by examining and assessing particular learning goals. Thus, we needed to implement an intentional advising assessment plan to produce the necessary data for accreditation, examine the student learning experience in our split advising model, and identify opportunities for improvement.

Strategy and Culture

The advising administrator should create a culture to engage more than just advising personnel in the advising assessment process. By including other stakeholders, advising administrators help increase institutional investment in assessment and can improve the likelihood that the results will influence meaningful change. We helped stakeholders see the relevance

DOI: 10.4324/9781003437598-18

of advising data, strengthened the assessment culture, and identified and empowered advising assessment champions across campus. One strategy was continually reinforcing the relationship between student success and advising initiatives in meetings, professional development opportunities, and internal publications. As advising administrators, we stressed that effective advising would produce positive student outcomes, such as better academic performance and more use of support resources. We also repeatedly reiterated the relationship between effective advising and traditional student success metrics, such as retention and program completion.

Assessment Teamwork

While our advising administrators championed the advising assessment initiative, assigning work to be done by intentionally selected teams at distinct phases was a key strategy for developing an assessment culture. Three teams were formed, with advising administrators' input, not only to assist the organization of our initial advising assessment work but also to increase institutional buy-in and help more people see the relevance of advising assessment:

- One team, consisting of department chairs, primary role advisors, and admissions staff, developed and refined the academic advising mission statement, ensuring alignment with the institutional mission and vision. While external to the team but still important stakeholders, senior administrators offered support and feedback, which allowed us to link assessment work to institutional strategies and initiatives.
- A second team of primarily faculty advisors reviewed past advising-related data to identify potential student and advisor learning outcomes. Most institutional historical data was related to student and employee satisfaction with advising, but it still provided a launching point for other assessment conversations. Faculty advisors emerged as assessment proponents when they became more familiar with the purposes and processes of assessment.
- A third team, composed of administrators, faculty, and staff, attended a NACADA assessment institute. This group returned better prepared to refine learning outcomes, more deeply examine the level of learning and the advising strategies, map assessments, and determine how to share this information with additional stakeholders.

Assessment Tools

As we began to look at processes for collecting data on different parts of students' advising experiences, we explored the possibility of a paired "micro-survey," a tool both the advisor and advisee would take independently after an advising appointment. These short surveys, each doable in less than a minute, allowed us to collect information on the student's perceptions of the advising session and topics addressed by the advisor to identify specific student learning elements. For example, the survey asked the student and advisor if career goals were discussed in the appointment. If advisees indicate that this step is not happening (even though advisors believe it is), this indicates a need to address the discrepancy through dialogue and professional development.

While an indirect measure, this micro-survey enabled us to better understand the advising appointment experience and move beyond a student satisfaction survey with limited assessment value. We found the micro-survey yielded unique insights, allowing us to understand specific learning outcomes better and identify opportunities for advisor professional development. The role of the advising administrator in this phase was to ensure that processes were clear, confirm that data was reported ethically, communicate how the data would be used, and reassure advising stakeholders that such (potentially unflattering) data created opportunities for improvement and growth. Having such data allowed us to explore whether there are differences in advising experiences among student groups, including those related to diversity and equity.

Data-Informed Change

Advising administrators typically ensure that assessment results are properly generated, analyzed, and used to improve advising practices, whether it is student learning specifically or the performance of the advising program. Our institution's examples show that our assessment practices have improved student learning and advising and led us to establish a culture of advising assessment.

One student learning outcome identified for advising was that students would create, by the end of their first term, a complete and accurate academic plan to help them reach their academic goals. Faculty advisors have this responsibility at our institution, but our data indicated that this was not occurring systematically. This learning outcome, a direct measure of student learning, gives us important information about the student's ability to understand their academic program and create a plan that provides meaningful dialogue with their advisor. We subsequently developed an academic planning guide resource for faculty advisors, worked with our advising software vendor to improve the software's academic planning capability, and added academic planning as a topic of our shared micro-survey. As a result, we have seen significant increases in both completion and accuracy of academic planning since we measured this learning outcome.

Our data analysis led to another important learning outcome: helping students develop a financial plan for goal completion. Many non-returning students cited financial reasons for not continuing their education. Institutional data showed that a significant percentage of currently enrolled students identified one or more factors indicating personal financial instability. Advising champions at our institution felt advisors should make this an advising focus; thus, we established a student learning outcome for advising that read, "as a result of advising, students will be able to develop a financial plan for goal completion."

Data from the micro-survey showed that these conversations were not happening consistently in advising appointments and confirmed in subsequent focus groups. Our advisors determined that faculty advisors were not doing this because they felt uncomfortable with the topic and unclear on the basics of financial information and specific resources available to them. Through a coordinated effort among advising administrators and other campus professionals, targeted professional development and a faculty resource guide were developed, making advising conversations easier and more frequent.

To increase student learning and autonomy, we needed to identify key learning opportunities, collect evidence, and use that evidence to enhance our program. We wanted to use the data collected to document student learning, make identified improvements in our program, and offer contextualized professional development. As an added benefit, advising assessment has yielded data useful to other units on campus. Data collected by other departments, such as Institutional Research, has provided us with additional opportunities to understand better the role of advising for students. Advising assessment has enabled more stakeholders to see the value and relevance of this work.

One academic advising process that we have had to address is the availability of faculty advisors. Students have often indicated that they cannot reach a faculty advisor or are unsure who their advisor is. This trend undermines the student's ability to engage in advising. From this data, we launched an advising assistance form on our website. Several staff members monitor this form and respond quickly, usually within hours. Not only does this process help us connect students to advising, but student requests also offer the unexpected benefit of generating additional data that we have been able to analyze to target improvements. For example, when a significant number of students indicated they were having issues with one of our software applications, we were able to respond with some additional student-facing information and support. Using this information, we can determine where our advising process gaps are, how to refine our approaches, and if we need additional resources and professional development.

Conclusion

We have begun to examine our specific assessment measures critically and the data we are gathering to question program goals, student learning outcomes, and the resources we use to support our advising program. Yes, we still measure employee and student satisfaction with advising—after all, students will be less likely to use a service they do not like—but we use satisfaction results as additional data to help inform our next improvement steps. Advising administrators need to identify opportunities to improve through advising program assessment, recognizing that there is no objective way of measuring progress without assessment.

10

DATA-INFORMED PLANNING AND DECISION-MAKING

Stephanie D. Kraft-Terry and Jennifer Brown

Big data, or large complex data sets which require high amounts of processing capacity, have transformed higher education decision-making (Attaran et al., 2018; Daniel, 2015). With new platforms regularly becoming available and touted as the answer to university administrators' retention and student success challenges, advising administrators frequently have access to abundant data. It can be challenging to determine how to utilize the information to advocate for academic advising; therefore, intentional evidence-informed decision-making should be integral to advising operations. The Council for the Advancement of Standards in Higher Education (CAS) Standards for Academic Advising acknowledges the role that data plays in the decision-making process, highlighting that Academic Advising Programs must "incorporate data and information in decision making" (CAS, 2015, p. 13). Advising administrators should embrace forward-thinking approaches that seek to anticipate future needs and create a thoughtful plan to meet those goals. This evidence-informed planning process should occur at all institutional levels, with varying foci depending on the unit's purview (Kotler & Murphy, 1981).

Evidence-informed decision-making plays a key role in advising administrators' short- and long-term decisions, helping administrators advocate for advising at all institutional levels (Nutt, 2017). Data/evidence (referred to as "data" moving forward) is an objective tool. If employed thoughtfully, it can be used to justify practices, support resource requests, or catalyze change (Baepler & Murdoch, 2010). With many tools available, it can sometimes be overwhelming to determine where to start. Consequently, having a carefully constructed plan for data collection, analysis,

DOI: 10.4324/9781003437598-19

and dissemination of results aids advising administrators in being prepared whenever data-based decision-making is needed. Kraft-Terry and Kau (2016) suggest five steps to employ data in making evidence-based decisions: (1) identify the area of interest or proposed change, (2) identify the type of evidence (data) to examine, (3) identify who, where, and how, (4) identify when to collect and analyze evidence, and (5) draw conclusions and implement change. These steps are an excellent starting point for those new to data-informed decision-making and are broadly applicable across all institution sizes, types, and geographic locations across the globe.

Defining the Focus

To ensure focus, first designate a goal. Data-informed decision-making does not begin with data but with clear and agreed-upon goals (Mandinach & Schildkamp, 2021b). Defining the focus will appropriately guide data collection and the creation of an action plan. With endless amounts of data available, lacking focus can result in unnecessary data collection and analysis. As you review evidence, it is natural to adjust the goal to align with the information available; thus, defining the focus can be an adaptive process, informed by available data and evidence.

Goals can be simple, such as determining the number of appointment slots necessary for the upcoming term. In this example, appointment demand predictions can likely be extrapolated from current and previous semesters' enrollment counts, the historic appointment fill rate, and weekly advisor availability. If advisors in the unit have special populations assigned, then a more detailed segmenting of the data may be necessary to plan for the upcoming term appropriately. It may be tempting to begin separating the data to explore fill rates by advisor, number of appointments per student, or other permutations. Considering whether such details help achieve the goal is an important step.

When defining the focus, advising administrators should consider the various contextual factors at their institution. Are particular metrics used to evaluate campus units or the educational system? Are college or divisional leaders and other stakeholders interested in particular data or decisions? Administrative needs, such as advocating with the legislature for public institutions, reporting on student success to a Board of Regents or Directors, demonstrating programmatic success for regional accreditation processes, or applying for and reporting on grant funding outcomes, can all also influence the types of data available and needed to engage in evidence-based decision-making. Considering who the audience is will guide everything from data collection to the final presentation, as background knowledge and data needed to justify the request can vary vastly. Considering these factors can help you determine the type of data you need and how to analyze and present it to others, as there is no singular approach appropriate for all institutional contexts.

Identify and Collect Needed Data

Keeping the focus in mind, data collection should include all necessary elements but not be so expansive that the goal is lost. Each data type has its strengths and weaknesses as a tool for decision-making; therefore, employing multiple data types creates a comprehensive understanding of the issue and prevents accidentally missing an important concern. When collecting data, first determine the necessary access requirements. Whenever possible, collect data with corresponding demographic information, such as gender and ethnicity, to allow for later disaggregation. As universities work toward diversifying their student bodies, they must also ensure that students from all groups equitably achieve outcomes, which cannot be known without careful disaggregation and analysis (Bensimon, 2005; Teranishi et al., 2013). Depending on the type of evidence, this can include data security training, approvals from supervisors or upper administrators, or permissions from approving bodies to commence with data collection or access. The types of data are covered in more detail below.

Learning Evidence

Just as learning within the classroom is assessed to ensure the attainment of programmatic learning outcomes (Kuh et al., 2015), assessment of advising is essential to evaluate student learning within the advising setting (Robbins, 2016). As part of regular assessment cycles, collect learning evidence to evaluate the efficacy of current advising curricula in achieving stated student learning outcomes (see Chapter 9). The assessment process combines the collection of both direct and indirect learning evidence. Direct learning evidence requires students to demonstrate what they learned (Kraft-Terry & Kau, 2019), while indirect learning evidence typically involves reflecting on one's perception of what they learned, often through a survey (Robbins & Zarges, 2011). Use collected student learning samples for assessment purposes. Best practices in assessing student learning require that all student work be deidentified whenever possible (Ekowo & Palmer, 2016). Storage, both physical and virtual, should adhere to campus-level FERPA-protection rules. The outcomes of these assessment cycles may influence the vision and strategic plan for an advising unit by identifying areas needing attention or celebration, or by expanding the identified teaching approach that yielded successful learning outcome achievement (Aiken-Wisniewski et al., 2010; Robbins, 2016).

Institutional Data

Depending on an institution's resources, administrators may access a plethora of data from their institution's transaction systems. Institutions employ transaction systems for most functions, such as admissions, registration, appointment scheduling, early alert, and payment processing (Goldstein & Katz, 2005). Users with appropriate permissions to access desired data can typically run reports. Advising administrators may find it helpful to inquire about access and training for systems pertinent to the functions of their unit. Institutions frequently purchase third-party software or create homegrown applications to perform analytics on institutional data to predict student actions or behaviors. These systems are employed in an effort to improve student performance, retention, and graduation rates. Tools continue to enter the market, making complex analytical analysis accessible without needing advanced computational skills (Daniel, 2015). This means advising administrators and academic advisors have more tools available than ever.

Other data may be housed with the institutional research (IR) office. To access IR data, some institutions may have publicly available reports, internal database systems that allow for custom report generation, and custom query options that can be submitted directly to the IR office. Some institutions have basic metric information related to enrollment and graduation rates available openly on their websites, commonly maintained by the IR Office. IR offices support the campus in collecting and storing institutional data. They often create dashboards to access data to guide administrative decisions and assist in open communication of institutional metrics. In addition, they aid their campus in creating custom reports to meet campus data needs. However, while IR offices can provide large amounts of data, few are equipped to help with data analysis (Leimer, 2012). Advising administrators should familiarize themselves with their IR offices, including relevant data access portals or dashboards. For many administrators, these tools will meet all data needs when granted regular access. Should additional data be necessary, advising administrators should inquire with their IR office regarding opportunities for custom queries. Due to the sensitive nature of student data, some data requests may require advanced approval from the institution's data governance office or others involved in protecting student data. For this reason, planning is essential for timely data collection.

Advising administrator access to data varies by position and institutional policies. While the IR office may manage a majority of the data access, some data access may require assistance from the registrar, information technology office, or another unit on campus. Inquiring with these entities to ensure appropriate permissions are granted to access necessary data is an essential first step. These units will likely provide the necessary training to ensure the appropriate use of systems.

Predictive Analytics

Predictive analytics in academic advising are often used for targeted student advising. Predictive analytics may be found in systems such as early alert platforms or those that aid in course or program selection. Data used in these systems varies but often includes demographic data such as test scores, GPA, and class attendance, as well as aggregate data detailing past academic performance and learning analytics (Ekowo & Palmer, 2016). These technologies allow for intentional interventions with students considered at risk for attrition. Some institutions have deployed these systems to guide their advising teams with great success (Ekowo & Palmer, 2016; Pelletier & Hutt, 2021). Ideally, this technology can help target limited institutional resources to where they will most positively impact students and allow for earlier and faster interventions with the goal of student success (Pelletier & Hutt, 2021).

While the promise of predictive analytic systems is great, several reasons exist to employ them with caution. First, there is a risk of discriminating against or stigmatizing students because systems rely heavily on demographic information and may only target groups already identified as at risk of premature departure from the institution. When age, race, gender, and socioeconomic status are the primary factors in these systems, it can lead to entrenching disparities in access that are historical, steer students into or away from specific academic programs, or discourage them via messaging that implies they are not likely to succeed (Ekowo & Palmer, 2016). Using algorithms to intervene with students is a delicate task and requires training as well as an intentional focus on the system's design and how it is implemented on campus. The ethical use of predictive analytics requires intentional thought and effort to mitigate potential harm while increasing their positive impact (Ekowo & Palmer, 2017).

Other concerns include transparency, training needs, and the ability to secure the data. There is limited ability to evaluate the efficacy of these products because they are proprietary and often owned by private companies (Bird et al., 2021). Data security and privacy are also noteworthy concerns, along with transparency in data usage by the company and institution. Training on predictive analytics is needed and should include understanding that this type of data does not predict the future but highlights probabilities (Ekowo & Palmer, 2016). Gaining access to predictive analytics tools will depend on what is available at the institution. Security and functional training, as with other data types, will likely be required.

Surveys and Focus Groups

In addition to metrics available through transactional systems and predictive analytic software, many administrators have access to survey data at their unit, campus, or institution level, such as the National Survey on Student Engagement (NSSE; Robbins, 2009). The survey data can combine with other metrics to create a holistic picture of the student experience, institutional health, or other factors affecting student success. Units can also collect indirect student feedback via surveys or focus groups. Qualitative evidence collection can require extensive planning and approvals to ensure valid results. Attaining a meaningful response rate will require careful timing, advertising, and potentially incentives (Fossey et al., 2002). Advising administrators should consider what they may be able to achieve with student surveys and focus group data and if it is a necessity when other sources of students' voices exist in NSSE results and other institutional surveys.

Evidence collection through surveys or focus groups may require Institutional Review Board (IRB) approval. The IRB serves to protect human subjects, which the Office of Human Research Protections defines as "a living individual about whom an investigator (whether professional or student) conducting research…obtains information…through intervention or interaction with the individual, and uses, studies, or analyzes the information…[or] obtains, uses, studies, analyzes, or generates identifiable private information" (HHS, 2018). The type of information collected and the intended use will determine whether IRB approval is necessary. When information is collected and reviewed for internal assessment and improvement in an academic setting, IRB approval is not typically required. However, if the intent is to share the information outside the unit or institution, including in presentations or publications, IRB approval or documentation of obtaining IRB exempt status is required. Before collecting data through surveys or focus groups, advising administrators should contact their office overseeing human studies research activities if they are uncertain whether their activities fall under the purview of the IRB. Ultimately, advising administrators must ensure their practices limit any negative impacts on participants; therefore, IRB policies should always guide their decisions.

Process Mapping

When gathering data to inform evidence-based decisions, advising administrators should pay careful attention to learning evidence and institutional metrics as well as the procedures and activities of the advising unit and institution. Sometimes evidence-informed improvement requires evaluating the efficacy of current policies or procedures and proposing changes after identifying deficiencies. Process mapping was initially designed to maximize efficiency in manufacturing but has proven to be a useful tool in reviewing and analyzing organizational processes in other settings such as libraries, facilities management, and health care (Antonacci et al., 2021; Ornat & Moorefield, 2018). Process mapping is a visual way to explain the workflow of a current process and then review and analyze it for possible improvements. For advising activities, process mapping helps highlight potential institutional barriers for students; it can also bring together multiple stakeholders to "understand complex processes, as well as to find common solutions and enhance team engagement" when appropriately used (Antonacci et al., 2021, p. 10). For example, a process map for an academic petition workflow may highlight missing steps or unnecessary actions that can be rectified by revising the process. This can also be useful when reviewing academic advising campus-wide in decentralized settings. It is not uncommon for each institution, college, or school to manage its processes differently, which may affect overall student success.

Considerations for Collection of Other Data

Information outside the above categories may be essential to advising administrator decision-making. When planning to collect data on institutional policies or practices at the campus or unit level, administrators should consider all data elements needed from a single source and work to make a single ask for all data needs. If multiple advising administrators require the same information, creating a coordinated request with a plan to share collected information will ensure a greater likelihood of participation from requested offices. This limits the time each person or office is asked to provide information and helps eliminate redundant data requests. When utilizing process mapping, it is common to find that advising activities will touch many different units on campus; engaging those partner offices in process mapping can be helpful throughout, and engagement in the process may lead to increased support for any recommended revisions.

Data Collection Timeline

The source of data and intended use will govern the data collection timeline. For example, an institution usually does not have formal enrollment data until after the census date. Collecting enrollment information before this date can still be useful if the purpose is to explore timely issues informally, such as summer melt or early major changes. Still, such data may never align with formally published institutional data. When seeking data from intermediate time points throughout the semester, ensure careful collection of data at the same time point in future semesters if you desire accurate longitudinal comparisons. If you can request customized data reports from your IR office, you may be able to indicate a desire to acquire data from time points not typically reported in standard IR data.

When collecting data, such as survey information, directly from students, it is important to consider what point in the term will provide the highest response rates. For example, surveying students during midterms or for finals may negatively affect feedback levels. In addition, it is helpful to coordinate with the IR office or any other major office that may make similar requests of students to ensure that they do not experience unintended survey fatigue, which could harm response rates for all inquiries. Incentives for student participation can increase response rates, but the institution may limit this type of reward. Inquiring in advance and during the planning process can allow time to adjust the data collection and timeline as needed.

Planning for Data Needs

Once the focus is established, it is important to define future data needs carefully. Preparing in advance for how data will be collected and employed to assess efforts will save time and lead to clearly defined outcomes with measurable methods of evaluation. Advising administrators should consider gauging success and ensuring that unit goals can be evaluated consistently and thoughtfully. Having regularly needed data easily accessible aids advising administrators in making timely evidence-informed decisions and allows them to respond to external requests quickly and decisively.

Analyzing the Data

As technology advances, many institutions have purchased or created homegrown software that process and visualize large amounts of institutional data for use by various individuals (Daniel, 2015; McCoy & Rosenbaum, 2019). These decision support systems (DSSs), sometimes known as dashboards, are fed with real-time data to support just-in-time decision-making, including interventions to support student success (Bresfelean & Ghisoiu, 2009).

Even without a DSS, quantitative data can be powerful when employed appropriately. Sometimes people shy away from embracing quantitative data to make data-informed decisions because of discomfort working with numbers. It is important to understand that quantitative data review often requires nothing more than the ability to summarize descriptive statistics. An understanding of basic spreadsheet software skills can help tremendously, and there are several free resources available online that can easily acquaint users with the key features necessary to summarize large data tables. It is highly recommended that such skills be included in the position description of one or more advising positions in an advising unit. Intentionally including assessment and data responsibilities in advising positions emphasizes the importance of evaluating advising's effectiveness and requires the unit to prioritize time for these activities. In addition, involving the entire advising team in assessment and evaluation projects can serve as an excellent form of professional development.

Making Evidence-Based Decisions

Now that data has been collected and analyzed, what happens next? How can it be translated into actionable items? The answer will vary depending on the initial goal for data collection and overall institutional goals. Throughout this chapter, we have encouraged advising administrators to consider the context of their institution and who must approve data requests. One should also consider who will need to approve or support recommended changes if preparing for adjustments beyond the purview of advising alone. Clarity on how academic advising supports the institution's goals is important and will strengthen administrator decisions.

Data is often considered only in terms of accountability, and while it does serve this purpose, it also serves the goal of facilitating continuous improvement (Ewell, 2009; Mandinach & Schildkamp, 2021a). Decision-making occurs within the context of advising units and higher education institutions and is often limited by constraints beyond our control. As Voltaire said, do not let the perfect become the enemy of the good. If data can be employed to make small improvements in advising, students and advisors will all benefit. Focusing on the best interests of the student population will help determine how to move forward in decision-making and will most often be the strongest argument in favor of a change.

Common Pitfalls in the Use of Data

For those new to employing data to support decision-making, it is important to avoid unintended errors or problems that commonly occur in data selection and interpretation. It can be challenging to select the right data when copious amounts of information are available. Using multiple data types will enrich the review of the task at hand. Administrators should also ensure that data sources are appropriate for project goals but not limited by personal preference or comfort with certain data types. As discussed earlier in this chapter, it may be possible to access years or even decades of institution-wide data. In that time, institutions of higher education and the student populations they serve have changed significantly. Consider how old is "too old" when selecting date ranges. Institutions of higher education are always changing, so comparing time points when the students or the institution were quite different may yield meaningless results.

Data should be reviewed with an open mind to avoid reinforcing expectations or ignoring uncommon or unexpected results. Collaboratively identifying and collecting data can help broaden interpretation and data analysis, thereby limiting the chance of drawing inaccurate or biased conclusions. Advising administrators cannot be experts in all areas. Seeking support for data analysis and interpretation is encouraged should data review require skills beyond one's knowledge or abilities.

Communicating Evidence-Based Decisions

Effective data representation to ensure a clear understanding of findings is key when preparing data to present or share. Selecting appropriate data visualization approaches can support audiences in easily understanding data summaries and conclusions (Evergreen, 2019). They are typically the most efficient way to explain complicated data sets in a quickly understandable way (Evergreen, 2019; Sahay, 2016). They can include graphs, charts, and infographics. Well-designed visualizations can elicit emotional responses that convey expertise and knowledge (Kennedy & Engebretsen, 2020). For this reason, data visualization must be approached thoughtfully to ensure clear, accurate data portrayal. Due to the sometimes-simplified nature of visualizations, it can be easy to misinterpret or misrepresent data; thus, it is the responsibility of those preparing the visualizations to ensure objectivity (Kemp, 2014).

Conclusion

Advising administrators must consider all data available beyond the immediate functions of advising to understand where advising can support students. Nutt (2017) highlighted the importance of this broad approach to data review, encouraging the review of institutional data to aid advisors in understanding roadblocks to success to help plan appropriate support and intervention. Collecting and analyzing data can aid in planning for both program and staffing needs in advising units. Trends in appointment bookings, participation in engagement activities, and types of inquiries from students can support requests to hire advisors to meet student needs. Data can objectively support advising administration and should be embraced as an asset in the toolbox of any advising administrator.

Guided Activity

In the example below, the reader is encouraged to consider the scenario in the context of their advising unit and institution and think about what evidence they could use to determine whether a change from the current practice is warranted. Learning assessment may also help guide this decision-making. Refer to Chapter 9 in this volume for further guidance.

The advising unit currently schedules 30-minute appointments for advising. Advisors prefer 60-minute appointments to allow for longer advising discussions with students.

- Examples of useful data to explore:
  - Appointment availability vs. utilization
  - If the system is capable: actual appointment length
  - Appointment feedback from students
  - Is a new question necessary? For example: Do you feel the length of your appointment allowed for enough time to addresses your needs today?
  - A rubric that advisors complete assesses how many appointments need additional time and why. The "why" is important because it allows the unit to assess whether more time is needed or whether other procedures are consuming appointment time. Example: Do advisors need prep time before or after the appointment to complete additional associated tasks, such as lifting holds, writing notes, and reviewing pre-surveys?
  - Is this issue only for new advisors? Should they have a special schedule for certain times of the year?
  - Is this a certain type of appointment that needs more time? Can the appointment system help to guide appointment length selection to ensure students can access the appropriate length? Will that be easy for students to understand?
- Possible stakeholders to engage:
  - Students
  - Advisors in office
  - Peer Advisors
  - Student workers
  - Advising office staff (non-advisors)

Reflection Questions

1 Name the key types of data and provide examples of each.
2 Consider your institution. Who would you contact with questions about possible human studies research (research that may require IRB approval)? Is there any training required before you can request IRB approval?
3 Select an academic advising process on your campus that you would like to review via process mapping. Who might you include in the activity and why?
4 Think about data you feel should be shared externally to support requesting additional resources for your advising unit. How would you visually present this information to ensure that key points are easily discernible?

References

Aiken-Wisniewski, S., Campbell, S., Nutt, C., Robbins, R., Kirk-Kuwaye, M., & Higa, L. (2010). *Guide to assessment in academic advising* (2nd ed.). National Academic Advising Association.

Antonacci, G., Lennox, L., Barlow, J., Evans, L., & Reed, J. (2021). Process mapping in healthcare: A systematic review. *BMC Health Services Research, 21*(1), 1–15. https://doi.org/10.1186/s12913-021-06254-1.

Attaran, M., Stark, J., & Stotler, D. (2018). Opportunities and challenges for big data analytics in American higher education: A conceptual model for implementation. *Industry and Higher Education, 32*(3), 169–182. https://doi.org/10.1177/0950422218770937.

Baepler, P., & Murdoch, C. J. (2010). Academic analytics and data mining in higher education. *International Journal for the Scholarship of Teaching & Learning, 4*(2). https://doi.org/10.20429/ijsotl.2010.040217.

Bensimon, E. M. (2005). Closing the achievement gap in higher education: An organizational learning perspective. *New Directions for Higher Education, 2005*(131), 99–111. https://doi.org/10.1002/he.190.

Bird, K. A., Castleman, B. L., Mabel, Z., & Song, Y. (2021). Bringing transparency to predictive analytics: A systematic comparison of predictive modeling methods in higher education. *AERA Open, 7.* https://doi.org/10.1177/23328584211037630.

Bresfelean, V. P., & Ghisoiu, N. (2009). Higher education decision making and decision support systems. *Transactions on Advances in Engineering Education, 7*(2), 43–52. https://mpra.ub.uni-muenchen.de/26698/.

Council for the Advancement of Standards. (2015). *Academic advising programs: CAS standards and guidelines.* http://standards.cas.edu/getpdf.cfm?PDF=E864D2C4-D655-8F74-2E647CDECD29B7D0.

Daniel, B. (2015). Big data and analytics in higher education: Opportunities and challenges. *British Journal of Educational Technology, 46*(5), 904–920. https://doi.org/10.1111/bjet.12230.

Ekowo, M., & Palmer, I. (2016, October). *The promise and peril of predictive analytics in higher education: A landscape analysis*. New America. https://na-production.s3.amazonaws.com/documents/Promise-and-Peril_4.pdf.

Ekowo, M., & Palmer, I. (2017, March). *Predictive analytics in higher education: Five guiding practices for ethical use*. New America. https://d1y8sb8igg2f8e.cloudfront.net/documents/Predictive-Analytics-GuidingPractices_fbsrc53.pdf.

Evergreen, S. D. H. (2019). *Effective data visualization: The right chart for the right data* (2nd ed.). Sage Publications, Inc.

Ewell, P. T. (2009, November). *Assessment, accountability, and improvement: Revisiting the tension*. National Institute for Learning Outcomes Assessment. https://www.learningoutcomeassessment.org/documents/PeterEwell_008.pdf.

Fossey, E., Harvey, C., McDermott, F., & Davidson, L. (2002). Understanding and evaluating qualitative research. *Australian & New Zealand Journal of Psychiatry, 36*(6), 717–732. https://doi.org/10.1046/j.1440-1614.2002.01100.x.

Goldstein, P. J., & Katz, R. N. (2005). *Academic analytics: The uses of management information and technology in higher education* (Vol. 8). Educause. https://library.educause.edu/resources/2005/12/academic-analytics-the-uses-of-management-information-and-technology-in-higher-education.

HHS, Basic Health and Human Services Policy for Protection of Human Research Subjects, Definitions for purposes of this policy, §46.102. (2018). https://www.hhs.gov/ohrp/regulations-and-policy/regulations/45-cfr-46/revised-common-rule-regulatory-text/index.html.

Kemp, M. (2014). A question of trust: Old issues and new technologies. In C. Coopmans, J. Vertesi, M. E. Lynch, & S. Woolgar (Eds.), *Representation in scientific practice revisited* (pp. 343–346). MIT Press. https://doi.org/10.7551/mitpress/9780262525381.003.0021.

Kennedy, H., & Engebretsen, M. (2020). Introduction: The relationships between graphs, charts, maps and meanings, feelings, engagements. In M. Engebretsen, & H. Kennedy (Eds.), *Data visualization in society* (pp. 19–32). Amsterdam University Press. https://library.oapen.org/handle/20.500.12657/22273.

Kotler, P., & Murphy, P. E. (1981). Strategic planning for higher education. *The Journal of Higher Education, 52*(5), 470–489. https://doi.org/10.2307/1981836.

Kraft-Terry, S., & Kau, C. (2016). *Manageable steps to implementing data-informed advising*. NACADA Clearinghouse. https://nacada.ksu.edu/Resources/Clearinghouse/View-Articles/Manageable-Steps-to-Implementing-Data-Informed-Advising.aspx.

Kraft-Terry, S., & Kau, C. (2019). Direct measure assessment of learning outcome–driven proactive advising for academically at-risk students. *NACADA Journal, 39*(1), 60–76. https://doi.org/10.12930/nacada-18-005.

Kuh, G. D., Ikenberry, S. O., Jankowski, N. A., Cain, T. R., Ewell, P. T., Hutchings, P., & Kinzie, J. (2015). *Using evidence of student learning to improve higher education*. Jossy-Bass.

Leimer, C. (2012). Organizing for evidence-based decision making and improvement. *Change: The Magazine of Higher Learning, 44*(4), 45–51. https://doi.org/10.1080/00091383.2012.691865.

Mandinach, E. B., & Schildkamp, K. (2021a). The complexity of data-based decision making: An introduction to the special issue. *Studies in Educational Evaluation, 69*(2021), 100906. https://doi.org/10.1016/j.stueduc.2020.100906.

Mandinach, E. B., & Schildkamp, K. (2021b). Misconceptions about data-based decision making in education: An exploration of the literature. *Studies in Educational Evaluation, 69*(2021), 100842. https://doi.org/10.1016/j.stueduc.2020. 100842.

McCoy, C., & Rosenbaum, H. (2019). Uncovering unintended and shadow practices of users of decision support system dashboards in higher education institutions. *Journal of the Association for Information Science and Technology, 70*(4), 370–384. https://doi.org/10.1002/asi.24131.

Nutt, C. (2017, March). Creating a data-driven advising culture: Overcoming three central roadblocks. *Academic Advising Today, 40*(1). https://nacada.ksu.edu/ Resources/Academic-Advising-Today/View-Articles/From-the-Executive-Director-Creating-a-Data-Driven-Advising-Culture-Overcoming-Three-Central-Roadblocks.aspx.

Ornat, N., & Moorefield, R. (2018). Process mapping as an academic library tool: Five steps to improve your workflow. *College & Research Libraries News, 79*(6), 302–305. https://doi.org/10.5860/crln.79.6.302.

Pelletier, K., & Hutt, C. (2021). Digital transformation: Equipping advisors for the journey, students for success. *Change: The Magazine of Higher Learning, 53*(3), 30–36. https://doi.org/10.1080/00091383.2021.1906142.

Robbins, R. (2009). *Utilizing institutional research in the assessment of academic advising*. National Academic Advising Association Clearinghouse. http://www. nacada.ksu.edu/Resources/Clearinghouse/View-Articles/Assessment-and-Institutional-Research.aspx.

Robbins, R. (2016). Assessment of academic advising: Overview and student learning outcomes. In T. J. Grites, M. A. Miller, & J. G. Voller (Eds.), *Beyond foundations: Developing as a master academic advisor* (pp. 275–288). Jossy-Bass.

Robbins, R., & Zarges, K. M. (2011). *Assessment of academic advising: A summary of the process*. NACADA Clearinghouse of Academic Advising Resources. http://www.nacada.ksu.edu/Resources/Clearinghouse/View-Articles/Assessment-of-academic-advising.aspx.

Sahay, A. (2016). *Data visualization, volume I: Recent trends and applications using conventional and big data*. Business Expert Press.

Teranishi, R., Lok, L., & Nguyen, B. M. D. (2013). *iCount: A data quality movement for Asian Americans and Pacific Islanders in higher education*. Educational Testing Service.

11

PROGRAM DESIGN/REDESIGN FOR ACADEMIC ADVISING ADMINISTRATION

Sharon A. Aiken-Wisniewski, Deborah J. Taub and Rich Whitney

Academic advising administrators produce events, programs, and campus-wide activities through their work in higher education. They create new units and divisions to address the institutional mission as they meet the needs of students. This chapter offers the Integrated Model for Program Development (IMPD; Aiken-Wisniewski et al., 2021) to the academic advising community as a tool for advancing a program from an idea to a reality. This model centers on a commitment to theory informing practice, comprehensive planning to create a sound program structure, and assessment embedded in program creation and continuation. The goal of this chapter is to share with academic advising administrators a model for comprehensive program design as well as examples that support use and understanding.

The chapter begins by defining program development and its history, followed by a brief review of the program development literature that has informed the development of practice for the past 50 years. Based on this review of models and actual experience in programming, the IMPD emerged as a 21st-century strategy that incorporates key components for the development of a comprehensive program that can be used across the campus or in one specific department or college.

IMPD is the model selected because it is an inclusive approach incorporating previous program design models as well as practical experience. Through a vast number of books, courses, and workshops available on program development and design, IMPD provides the academic advising administrator a comprehensive, one-stop model. An advising administrator following the IMPD process has direction to develop a thorough

DOI: 10.4324/9781003437598-20

program. At this time, the scope of this model has not been applied globally in advising but offers food for thought to the international advising community. Also, the reader is advised to reference other chapters in this book to dive deeper into a specific topic in an IMPD stage that complements the program under development.

Program Development: Definition and History

The words *program* and *programming* have a long and continuous affiliation with student services. They appear in the 1937 Student Personnel Point of View and continue to be associated with fields in higher education that support student success (American Council on Education, 1937). In more recent literature cited by academic advising administrators, the words program and programming are referenced 267 times in 100 pages in *Learning Reconsidered 2* (Keeling et al., 2006). In academic advising, a program might refer to a single activity, such as a major fair or departmental advising event, or a unit focused on delivering a variety of services that are common in academic advising and support student success. Clarity for the meaning of *program* and *programming* is important through definition.

Barr and Keating (1985) defined program as "a theoretically based plan under which action is taken toward a goal within the context of institutions of higher education" (p. 2). This definition offers context. A program has a plan, uses theory, and addresses a goal, which leads to programming. However, the myriad meanings of the single word *program* are significant when considering academic advising. Does it refer to the delivery of an advising program in a department, college, or institution? Is it a semester program for undeclared majors? Is there a program for preprofessional school students in college? Does the advising center or services have a program that coordinates with TRIO or identity-based resource centers? The program can be one *and* many at the same time.

Programming is also defined as "the planning, scheduling, or performing of a program" (Merriam Webster Online Dictionary, n.d.), which suggests a process. IMPD is a structured process for developing a program. Before describing IMPD, it is important to briefly review the history of program development models for programs that address the needs of students.

Program development is one of the ways in which institutional personnel and faculty members contribute to the overall institutional mission through cocurricular experiences (Barr & Keating, 1985; Cooper & Saunders, 2000; Styles, 1985). Schuh and Triponey (1993) wrote that "there is no best program development model, but we hold that those that do plan programs well normally use a program development model" (p. 430).

The development of the IMPD is a synthesis of all program development models that have been presented in student affairs literature since 1973 (Aiken-Wisniewski et al., 2021). Created by analyzing the 21 previous student affairs program development models and identifying the salient components of each, this model has integrated the work of many scholars and practitioners into one contemporary model (Aiken-Wisniewski et al., 2021). The underpinning of a theoretical framework within the context of the program, the department (e.g., academic advising), or the needs of the population is also present in the IMPD. Programs, whether interpreted as the department/functional area or events (one-time or within a series), are the translation of theory to practice (Saunders & Cooper, 2001; Styles, 1985). This is true whether an advising administrator functions as the active programmer applying this expertise directly to the target populations or while functioning as the mentor/program coordinator for a team organizing an advising event.

Integrated Model for Program Development

This model offers guidance to advising administrators through stages built on top of a theoretical framework. The model is cyclical to encourage reflection and assessment for improvement, redesign, or closure. Figure 11.1 provides a visual representation of the model and each stage.

As shown in Figure 11.1, a theoretical foundation is paramount to the program development process for IMPD. It leads to the program definition stage, which includes needs assessment, is tied to the campus mission, and is followed by identification of people to serve as leaders, planners, and implementers for the advising program. Next is the program planning stage, which begins to address the details such as budget, location, assessment plan, and actual personnel. A thoughtful planning stage is augmented by on-going program monitoring to the point of implementation. The program launch or roll-out offers immediate feedback on the quality of the program planning process through program assessment tools. For example, a short questionnaire given to students who engage with the program within the first hour can offer feedback on learning outcomes or ease in finding specific information. By evaluating goals, learning outcomes, and/or programmatic outcomes with appropriate assessment tools, information and data emerge for the program reflection stage. In the reflection stage, accountability and program enhancement result in cycling back to program definition as the program continues or identifying steps for program closure. Each stage has a specific purpose.

As advising administrators engage with each stage in the model to create or redesign a variety of programs, they find direction and structure. It is

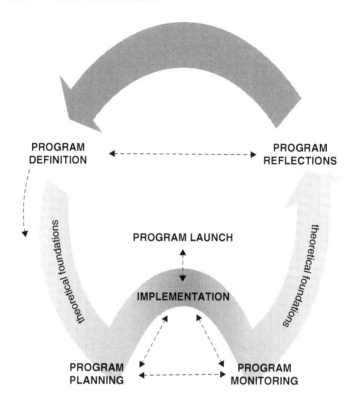

FIGURE 11.1   Integrated Model for Program Development.

Note. Figure republished with permission: Aiken-Wisniewski et al. (2021).

not uncommon for program development to include working on activities that are relevant to more than one stage in the model. The model offers flexibility and prompts to encourage a comprehensive product.

Theoretical Foundations—Basing a Practice on Relevant Theory

The professional identity of academic advising administrators includes identifying as scholar-practitioners. This affiliation suggests that advising personnel employ scholarly literature to inform their practice and programs (Kidder, 2010). This identity matches well with IMPD because any programming should be grounded in research. Engagement in a literature review will allow the program to emerge through documented knowledge from colleagues in the field, and possible theories will be identified for a conceptual framework. The identification of a theory is paramount to the entire model and significant within the first stage, program definition.

Theory can serve several purposes. The emphasis of the academic advising program should suggest appropriate theories based on the intent and context of the program being developed. For example, if the unit is focused on transitions (e.g., first-year students, transfer students, undecided students, returning adult learners, premajors), Schlossberg's Transition Theory (Schlossberg, 1981) can serve as a useful theoretical foundation. An advising program focused on retention might rely on theories related to engagement and belonging. Some examples are Astin's Involvement Theory (1984), Tinto's Theory of Attrition (1993), or Sense of Belonging as explained by Strayhorn (2019). Theories need not be used in isolation but can be combined to address a need.

The Practice-to-Theory-to-Practice Model

The Practice-to-Theory-to-Practice (PTP) model (Mueller, 2019) emphasizes the need to consider the context of one's student characteristics and one's environmental (campus, unit, etc.) characteristics from theoretical perspectives to determine how best to translate theory into practice. In doing so, one considers the challenges and supports (Sanford, 1966) facing one's students and the amount of challenges and supports in one's environment. Mueller (2019) offered:

> This is how we begin to assess the match between students and their environment. This *translation*—in which we analyze and describe both the students and the environment based on identifiable sources of challenge and support as indicated by each theory—gives us insight into the developmental needs of the students and what may be needed.
>
> *(p. 21)*

Theory Selection Supported by Literature Review

As the program coordinator or team members begin a literature review, there are many resources in books, journals, and websites they should consult for understanding current scholarship and practice in academic advising, including the *NACADA Journal* and *NACADA Review*. Both offer a literature source that addresses current advising practice. For example, Donaldson et al. (2020) explained a new model for an advising center at a community college called an *enhanced advising program*. The article highlights the characteristics of this model and offers advisors perspectives on adopting such a model to guide an advising center at a community college. By examining articles such as these, administrators developing new programs or redesigning programs in academic advising will engage with colleagues who have employed certain theories and models to frame a program.

Stage: Program Definition

After identifying a theoretical framework to guide the program, the next step is program definition. The work of advising administrators and leaders places them close to the student experience as well as campus colleagues. Through individual appointments and collaborative events, ideas for programs are generated continuously (Upcraft & Schuh, 1996). When the institution's mission is combined with ideas generated during daily practice, there is a need for a process that investigates the viability of any idea before it becomes part of a future advising program. This is the purpose of the program definition stage in IMPD.

Program definition asks administrators and advisors to take a step back to evaluate the idea. In this stage, the advising team should consider a variety of components from needs assessment to human capital. Table 11.1 identifies components and guiding questions for the administrator.

Through exploring each component in program definition, the viability of the program is established (Aiken-Wisniewski et al., 2021).

Upcraft and Schuh (1996) defined needs assessment as "the process of determining the presence or absence of the factors and conditions, resources, services, and learning opportunities that students need in order

TABLE 11.1 Program Components Advising Administrators Consider for Program Definition

Program Component	Guiding Questions to Ask
Needs Assessment: process to determine if the proposed program will contribute to meeting institutional mission	What is the current situation? How are campus data informing this initiative? How will this program improve the situation? How does this program contribute to the institutional mission (e.g., student success, faculty support, retention goals)?
Campus Setting: information on institutional type, location, student populations, and other relevant campus characteristics	What is the Carnegie classification? Describe the campus setting (e.g., physical space, campus housing availability, dining options, library). What are characteristics of the student population? Number of undergraduate and graduate students? How does this program idea enhance the campus setting?
Program Goals: broad, abstract, and general statements that a program would accomplish	What are the goals of this program? Why are these the goals? How will this program accomplish the goals?

(Continued)

TABLE 11.1 (Continued)

Program Component	Guiding Questions to Ask
Outcomes: programmatic or learning-based statements that describe specifically what will be accomplished by the program	What are the outcomes of this program? Are they programmatic or learning based? How will you measure the outcomes to evidence accomplishment? Describe how the outcomes fit into a program assessment plan.
Target Populations: who will be impacted by this program	Who needs this program and why? How do you know that this population would be positively impacted by this program? What data are available on this population? Local and national?
Theoretical Framework: the theory or model guiding this program	What are the basic principles of the theory? After conducting a literature review, what is known about this theory in relation to the target population and goal(s) of the program? How is the theory informing the development of the program?
Program Team: group of people who will champion, lead, develop, and launch the program	Who is the champion of this program? Who is the coordinator/leader/administrator to guide the development of the program? Is personnel needed? If so, what skills must they have? Do you need to hire new personnel? If current employees join the team, how are their other responsibilities accomplished (i.e., backfill)?

to meet their educational goals and objectives within the context of an institution's mission" (p. 128). Thus, it is important to assess the need before assigning resources to the project.

The needs assessment includes reviewing institutional data relevant to the project; identifying similar programs on other campuses for data and lessons learned; collecting input from the campus community through surveys, interviews, and focus groups to evaluate need and support; and developing a literature review that suggests best practices. This assessment will illuminate needs that can be matched to a theoretical framework. Other elements of the program definition are also addressed, such as the target population, campus setting, program goal, and learning outcomes. Based on the literature review and benchmarking, the working committee/program developer will match a theoretical foundation to needs for program structure. The needs assessment might also suggest either canceling or postponing the project or offer evidence and artifacts to justify resources to proceed to the next stage of the model, which is program planning.

Stage: Program Planning

The program planning stage reorients the program from a broad, comprehensive view to specific details. It is important that the program champion either assumes a role as program coordinator or assigns someone to lead the effort. In addition to the coordinator, a team of advisors and campus colleagues should comprise the working group that moves the program idea to a campus reality. Once the personnel are in place, an organizational tool called a *backdater* is employed to coordinate dates and details (Aiken-Wisniewski et al., 2021). This tool encourages the team to start planning by establishing a delivery date for every detail of the program and then identifying what needs to happen and when to meet the delivery goal. Figure 11.2 provides an example.

As the details emerge in the program planning stage, several program components will need to be addressed:

- a budget that addresses needs such as personnel
- an assessment plan for programmatic and learning outcomes
- a human resources plan for hiring and training
- a site location
- a marketing plan
- other components relevant to the institutional type (e.g., community college, private liberal arts college, or Historically Black College or University)

Back Dating Schedule

Tasks needed 6 to 12 months prior to event/program/program	Assigned To	Date Assigned	Date Needed	Date Completed
Define purpose of the program				
Choose event/program/program				
Is committee representative of students/participants				
Research/recruit chair				
Identify theoretical approach that supports the purpose of the program				
Draft Initial Learning Outcomes				
Determine Assessment and Evaluation plan				
Explore potential sites				
Determine if sites are fully accessible to all participants				
Determine rain plan possibilities for potential sites				
Determine entry and exit points for possible sites				

FIGURE 11.2 Example of Backdater Tool 6 to 12 Months Prior to Event.

Note. Reprinted with permission: Aiken-Wisniewski et al. (2021).

	Activity	Accomplish by	Assigned to	Cost	Note - Future	Complete
1	**Program: Academic Advisement Center**					
2	Team: Dayan (Chair), Luis, David, Kim, and Michelle					
4	Identify Venue	Jan. 1	Kim	Cost?	Is this a permanent location?	
5	Furniture	Jan. 15	Kim	Cost?	Is there any used options?	
6	Dayan visit Cliff Univ. to observe a major fair	Feb. 1	Dayan	$400	Airfare and hotel for one night.	
7	Coordinator meets with HR - Hiring	Feb. 1	Kim	$100	Team lunch to discuss HR Conversation	
8	Identify Technology needs	Feb. 15	Luis	Attend NACADA Regional – $400	Conversation at NACADA Regional Meeting w/Peers	
9	Meet w/online appointment provider	Feb. 1	Luis	Identify cost		
10	Update budget	Mar. 1	Dayan		Compare estimates to real	
11	Explore marketing tools	Jan. 15	Luis		Start with campus marketing	
12		Feb. 28	Luis			Yes
13		Sept. 1	Kim			

Planning | Monitoring | Implementing | Launching | Reflecting

FIGURE 11.3 Planning Worksheet for Academic Advisement Center.

The program planning stage is time intensive, filled with details, and often requires many meetings.

The program coordinator and team will need to develop meeting notes that are repurposed into checklists for specific components of the program (e.g., assessment, human resources, budget, marketing, and launch). Technology tools can be used by the committee to provide support, transparency, and opportunities to asynchronously work on developing the program with minimal cost; for instance, the team can utilize a shared-drive or cloud-based folder with documents such as the needs assignment and a project calendar, or a spreadsheet program with tabs to identify specific program components and assignments. Figure 11.3 offers an example of how a spreadsheet located in a shared virtual location is used in the planning stage of IMPD for an advising center.

The rich environment of the planning stage filled with dedicated people, deadlines, and details builds momentum for the program implementation stage of the academic advisement center.

Stage: Program Implementation and Launch

The implementation stage, which leads to a successful launch or roll-out, moves from planning to a structured checklist of specific assignments for the implementation team. This checklist of specific activities, responsible team members, vendor contacts, and campus collaborators drives the final preparation before the launch. In this stage, the program coordinator and planning team focus on:

- detailed time sequencing of activities
- specific team member assignments to activities
- signatures and filing of relevant paperwork (e.g., travel request for a guest speaker or request for student information not available via directory)
- permission for entry into physical or virtual spaces
- transportation-related details
- logistics on delivery
- marketing of the program including attention to social media platforms

The use of a detailed spreadsheet for implementation of the program in the weeks, days, and hours leading up to the launch is vital.

Months and weeks of planning culminate into the day the program will launch or roll-out. This point in the process is exciting as the program planning team and campus community continue to accomplish the institutional mission through initiation of this new or redesigned program. Before the launch, the program coordinator should remind the team of its accomplishment in developing this program, review small and big wins throughout the process, and share specific moments of success for each member. Be creative while conveying group and individual success. As the program unfolds, a checklist should develop to ensure that all program elements and products are in place.

Despite the best programming efforts, some details will be missed and will require quick action on the roll-out or launch day. For example, buildings might not be open, the accessibility ramps may be blocked, or event signage may misdirect students. Thus, the program coordinator needs to be agile in listening for immediate needs and addressing them. Also, it is important to take the time to make notes for future reference concerning later iterations of this program. It is also helpful to take notes on lessons learned for other programming activities.

Stage: Program Monitoring

The stages of planning and implementation are filled with activity and detail. Thus, it is important that the academic advising administrator focus on key components of the program to avoid an oversight due to the surge of activity generated in addressing program details. This stage is focused on counting, accounting, and recording (Aiken-Wisniewski et al., 2021).

Elements to concentrate on through this stage are budgets, data collection strategies and appropriate tools, communication with the campus community, risk management, and staffing (Aiken-Wisniewski et al., 2021). As programs are developed for 21st-century higher education, the monitoring stage is a good time to review details on these elements as well as technology and social justice.

Technology

Technology is one area that advising administrators need to engage with during the monitoring stage because of its significance to the advising process, campus-wide use, cost, security issues, and training needs. It is a significant component for a new or redesigned service unit for advising or other advising activities; therefore, the program coordinator and team members should create an inventory of tools and then understand their cost, implementation, and utilization.

Social Justice

The academic advising administrator needs to focus on creating programs that are inclusive and equitable for serving diverse college students (Museus, 2021). The fundamental characteristics of social justice are clearly identified in academic advising literature that guides the field, such as the NACADA Academic Advising Core Competencies Model (NACADA, 2017) and Academic Advising Program Guidelines from the Council for Advancement of Standards in Higher Education (CAS, 2018).

These guiding documents require the advising administrator to develop programs and personnel that advise and attend to the whole person (CAS, 2018; NACADA, 2017) and respect the student's identities. These identities might include but are not limited to race, ethnicity, ability, age, and gender. All distinctions of one's presenting and natural self is part of educational equity in higher education (Collins & Whitney, 2021).

Other details that the advising administrator must consider to advocate and advance academic advising efforts for inclusivity and mattering include aesthetics of space, language, and personnel. Table 11.2 offers a list of questions that serve as an inventory for the advising supervisor that focuses on social justice concepts.

As mentioned, theories and models are vital for program development. Advising administrators will find a wide variety of theories that offer strategies for designing programs that value students' needs based on identity. For example, the needs of all students can be met by considering Universal Design Language concepts in program development (Fornauf & Erickson,

TABLE 11.2 Questions for Advising Administrators to Explore for Adherence to Social Justice

Topic	Questions
Space	Is the advising program in a campus location that is welcoming to all student identities?
	Is the program accessible to all students?
	Does the physical space include art or décor that all students find welcoming?
Language	Do advisors introduce themselves to students by including their pronouns?
	Are materials available in multiple languages to signal inclusion of family members and student support systems?
	Are presentations, flyers, websites, and advising materials filled with jargon without adequate explanation?
	Are presentations, flyers, websites, and advising materials representative of a wide variety of identities or limited to traditional student identities?
Personnel	Do advisors and students share visible identities (e.g., race, ethnicity, gender, ability)?
	Is there representation of identities held by the student body across all levels of the advising personnel?
	What strategies are employed in the hiring process to identify a diverse applicant pool?
	What strategies are embraced to support diverse advising personnel?

2020; Rose & Meyer, 2000). The universal design model posits that if the innovative design of a program element or component will support a neurodivergent learner with access and understanding, it will probably support all learners with the same goal. By attending to all aspects of the delivery of advising, advising administrators improve the experience for all students (Schlossberg, 1989).

Stage: Program Reflection

The program reflection stage requires the administrator to look both backward and forward. As such, it closes the loop in the IMPD. It includes analyzing and interpreting assessment data, reporting, and using this information to inform future plans (see Chapters 9 and 10). This stage also includes recognition of the contributions made by personnel and students to the success of the program.

The academic advising administrator is often the leader in crafting the report for the program that includes assessment data, and often they identify who receives these reports (Aiken-Wisniewski et al., 2021). We specify the plural *reports* because different audiences require different reports (Schuh, 2009). Whereas the advising administrator's supervisor might want a detailed report, upper level administrators likely need an executive summary. Consider your audiences and what information they would desire about the new program. An important point to keep in mind is that some people respond to numbers, whereas others respond to stories. Therefore, where possible, it is best to include both in your reporting. In all cases, be sure to include how the program supports the institutional mission.

A review of the assessment results plays a critical role in the future of your program. Examine where the program fell short in terms of usage, satisfaction, program goals, and learning outcomes. Explore whether some groups of students responded more favorably than others. What data is missing that should be collected in the next cycle? Consider how assessment results can be used to improve the program.

Conclusion

The IMPD model is a tool for program design that is comprehensive and adaptable for a variety of programs, events, and projects in academic advising. This model draws from the robust history of program models used for designing programs to serve students during the past 50 years. Through this model, advising administrators engage with a process built on a theoretical framework and proceed through stages that offer guidance to plan, implement, monitor, and reflect on designing or redesigning a program. By employing this model, administrators and academic advisors reduce barriers and identify solutions as they design programs that impact student success in academic advising.

Reflection Questions

1 How is an understanding of program design/redesign important for academic advising administrators? Give examples of the kinds of programs designed and implemented by leaders in academic advising.
2 A theoretical foundation is an important part of the IMPD, and the chapter provides examples of potentially useful theories. What theories would be appropriate to serve as a foundation for an advising program for your students and in your unit?
3 In many cases, academic advising programs came to rely more on the use of technology to provide and support academic advising. In planning the implementation of a new technology platform, what questions would you ask in each phase of the IMPD process?

4 What do you think is important to assess in an academic advising program? How would you define and measure success? What stages include assessment and how are assessment strategies used in each stage?

5 In assessing your students' advising needs, how do you distinguish between what students need and what they want?

References

Aiken-Wisniewski, S. A., Whitney, R., & Taub, D. J. (2021). *The missing competency: An integrated model for program development for student affairs.* Stylus.

American Council on Education, Committee on Student Personnel Work. (1937). The student personnel point of view. *American Council on Education Studies, 1*(3), 37–50.

Astin, A. W. (1984). Student involvement: A developmental theory for higher education. *Journal of College Student Personnel, 25*(1), 297–308.

Barr, M. J., & Keating, L. A. (1985). *Developing effective student service programs: Systematic approaches for practitioners.* Jossey-Bass.

Collins, J. D., & Whitney, R. (2021). Critical approaches in leadership education: Making the case for racial equity via institutional type. *New Directions for Student Leadership: Advancing Racial Equity in Leadership Education: Centering Marginalized Institutional Contexts, 2021*(171), 15–22. https://doi.org/10.1002/yd.20451.

Cooper, D. L., & Saunders, S. A. (2000). Assessing programmatic needs. In D. L. Liddell, & J. P. Lund (Eds.), *Powerful programming for student learning* (pp. 5–20). Jossey-Bass.

Council for the Advancement of Standards in Higher Education (CAS). (2018). *Academic advising programs.* http://standards.cas.edu/getpdf.cfm?PDF=E864D2C4-D655-8F74-2E647CDECD29B7D0.

Donaldson, P., McKinney, L., Lee, M. M., Horn, C. L., Burridge, A., & Pino, D. (2020). Insider information: Advisors' perspectives on the effectiveness of enhanced advising programs for community college students. *NACADA Journal, 40*(2), 35–48. https://doi.org/10.12930/NACADA-18-26.

Fornauf, B. S., & Erickson J. D. (2020). Toward an inclusive pedagogy through Universal Design for Learning in higher education: A review of the literature. *Journal of Postsecondary Education and Disability, 33*(2), 183–199.

Keeling, R. P., American College Personnel Association, & National Association of Student Personnel Administrators (U.S.). (2006). *Learning reconsidered 2: Implementing a campus-wide focus on the student experience.* Human Kinetics.

Kidder, R. (2010). Administrators engaging the research process. *Developments, 8*(1). https://developments.myacpa.org/administrators-engaging-in-the-research-process/.

Merriam Webster. (n.d.). Programming. *Merriam-Webster.com Dictionary.* Retrieved November 1, 2019, from https://www.merriam-webster.com/dictionary/programming.

Mueller, J. A. (2019). *The PTP Model: A 35th anniversary re-introduction.* ACPA.

Museus, S. D. (2021). Revisiting the role of academic advising in equitably serving diverse college students. *NACADA Journal, 41*(1), 26–32. https://doi.org/10.12930/NACADA-21-06.

NACADA: The Global Community for Academic Advising. (2017). NACADA academic advising core competencies model. https://www.nacada.ksu.edu/Resources/Pillars/CoreCompetencies.aspx.

Rose, D., & Meyer, A. (2000). Universal design for individual differences. *Educational Leadership, 58*(3), 39–43.

Sanford, N. (1966). *Self and society: Social change and individual development.* Atherton.

Saunders, S. A., & Cooper, D. L. (2001). Programmatic interventions: Translating theory to practice. In R. B. Winston Jr., D. G. Creamer, T. K. Miller, & Associates (Eds.), *Professional student affairs administrator* (pp. 309–340). Routledge.

Schlossberg, N. K. (1981). A model for analyzing human adaptation to transition. *The Counseling Psychologist, 9*(2), 2–18. https://doi.org/10.1177/001100008100900202.

Schlossberg, N. K. (1989). Marginality and mattering: Key issues in building community. *New Directions for Student Services, 1989*(48), 5–15. https://doi.org/10.1002/ss.37119894803.

Schuh, J. H. (2009). Writing reports and conducting briefings. In J. H. Schuh, & Associates (Eds.), *Assessment methods for student affairs* (pp. 171–189). Jossey-Bass.

Schuh, J. H., & Triponey, V. L. (1993). Fundamentals of program design. In R. B. Winston Jr., S. Anchors, & Associates (Eds.), *Student housing and residential life: A handbook for professional committed to student development goals* (pp. 423–442). Jossey-Bass.

Strayhorn, T. L. (2019). *College students' sense of belonging: A key to educational success for all students* (2nd ed.). Routledge.

Styles, M. (1985). Effective models of systematic programming planning. In M. Barr, & L. Keating (Eds.), *Developing effective student service programs: Systematic approaches for practitioners* (pp. 181–202). Jossey-Bass.

Tinto, V. (1993). *Leaving college: Rethinking the causes and cures of student attrition* (2nd ed.). University of Chicago.

Upcraft, M. L., & Schuh, J. H. (1996). *Assessment in student affairs: A guide for practitioners.* Jossey-Bass.

VOICES FROM THE FIELD

Program Design/Redesign

Erica R. Compton

I came to work for one of the newest community colleges in the Pacific Northwest in 2010. At the time, the college was experiencing tremendous growth, growing from 1,200 to 8,000 students within two years. When I accepted a position in the advising department, we were a team of four professional advisors serving 8,000 students. We had a split advising model with faculty advisors serving 30–45 students in more of a mentor role. The professional advisors served all academic transfer and career technical students. I had an advising load of upwards of 800 students at one point. We operated chiefly on drop-ins where students could see whichever advisor was available at our One-Stop locations positioned at multiple campus buildings spanning two counties and several towns. Remembering those early years in the department, there was a shared feeling of being the "jack of all trades and master of none."

Program Definition

From its inception, the college operated under a siloed division, organizing students as either academic transfer or career and technical education (CTE). As the college continued to grow, more advisors were hired, and less demand was made for faculty advising. By 2016, the college no longer had faculty advisors and relied on three different divisions for advising:

- Professional advisors for academic transfer students (high caseloads of approximately 400–500; any student could see any advisor)

DOI: 10.4324/9781003437598-21

- Learning Community Coordinators (LCC advisor; low caseload of approximately 250 students)
- Career Center (sole advisor for all career-related advising)

Although the college's mission and values revolved around student success, that was not always the experience for a student. For example, a student interested in going into one of our CTE programs was initially assigned a professional advisor as they worked on General Education classes; however, once in the CTE program, they would switch to an LCC advisor. The professional advisor would not know all of the details of the CTE program, and the LCC advisors only worked with students in the program. Most poignantly, this interrupted the advising experience of the student. Once a student was ready to graduate, they would work with the Career Center advisor.

Student voices, not just our perceived experience, were a factor driving program change. These voices and experiences were shared in the 2017 Student Satisfaction Survey. Comments received on the survey included sentiments such as:

- "I would like a more personal and customizable relationship with an advisor,"
- "trying to schedule w/an advisor at times that is convenient for me is almost impossible,"
- "...don't know who my academic advisor is,"
- "Advisor could use a lot more improvement. I found myself winging it."

In short, it was clear that we could do better.

After the college received its initial accreditation from the Northwest Commission on Colleges and Universities (NWCCU) in 2017, it was reorganized under different schools. Instead of having siloed departments, schools combined both academic transfer and CTE programs. As the institution was reorganized, it was time to rethink and restructure advising.

The Director of Advising and the Director of the Learning Community Coordinators researched best practices and what resulted was a merger of the three advising areas of professional advisors, Learning Community Coordinators, and the career center into one department: Student Advising & Success (SAS). This integrated model relied heavily on the advising approaches of developmental, proactive advising, advising as coaching, and career advising. The centralized advising department would be responsible for all advising, including career and exploration advising; this design allowed advisors to model and support the newly redesigned instructional organization.

Program Planning and Implementation

From the research conducted by the Director of Advising and the Learning Community Coordinator Director, it was clear that the best advising model to support the college needed to be a caseload and centralized (although not physical) advising model. The concepts that guided the new advising department were intrusive, inclusive, holistic, appreciative, and collaborative.

- Intrusive – proactive, develop strong relationships early in students' academic journey
- Inclusive – from the point of admission through orientation and progression and degree/goal attainment, the assigned advisor would be there to support students
- Holistic – integrated career planning, exploration, and decision-making based on career development theories, assessments, and strategies
- Appreciative Advising – intentional advising practice of open-ended questions
- Collaborative – advisors and students co-create plans toward their educational goals

What resulted was the overarching mission: the mission of SAS is to foster student success by creating a resource-rich learning environment that will promote an academic, career, and personal growth. Student Success Advisors (SSAs) empower students through meaningful, intentional student interactions focused on completing the student's unique goals.

Combining multiple departments into one required the advising administration to decide what team structure would make the most sense. We first reviewed student enrollment by major and determined that some advisors would need to cover similar majors (e.g., history and sociology). In contrast, four or more advisors might be needed to cover one major (e.g., health science or business). We ended up with three squads of advisors listed under one assistant director and two managers.

One of our guiding philosophies within the department is "one student at a time" (initially utilized within the Enrollment and Student Services Division). Still, it is often used throughout the institution as the college's mantra. Metaphorically speaking, staff, faculty, and administration have been referred to as a three-legged stool; all of us are an essential leg of a student's successful journey. This would not have been possible without building intentional, collaborative relationships with faculty and the institutional administration. For example, the Director of Advising establishes these relationships at the dean level by working collaboratively and often between instruction and advising.

For example, before the integrated SAS merger, most advisors were located in and around One-Stop Student Services (a central location for financial aid, admission, registrar services, etc.). After the merger, when possible, the Director of Advising worked with the Deans of Instruction and Student Services leadership to advocate for the physical location change of the advisors. SSAs were then moved out of the One-Stop to in or near the departments and students they serve. Moving the office space near the faculty and student classes allowed advisors to fully integrate into the programs they served.

The relationships between the divisions of instruction and advising have further enabled the relationships of SSAs to become experts in a small number of majors and programs. They have allowed a mutual symbiotic relationship between the department faculty and administration with SSAs. SSAs are often involved in departmental meetings and give important curriculum feedback related to the student experience and transferability.

Since 2017, the SAS administrators have been key in the strategic development of the institution and advising department through leadership in the following critical areas:

- Leading and guiding the team from a split model with faculty and decentralized advising to centralized and caseload advising.
- Leading and guiding the team from generalist advisors with little depth and much breadth to specialized advisors that include knowledge in career advising.
- Decreasing the advisor loads from upwards of 800 to 300–350 advisees.
- Implemented and integrated a self-booking system allowing phone, in-person, and online (even before the COVID-19 pandemic) versus a purely drop-in appointment or 3rd party scheduler (staff).
- Ensured the team accommodated students' needs by expecting advisors to have appointments outside "normal business hours" (8–5 Monday through Friday).
- Established the framework in the advising department with policies and procedures for creating co-created plans that map the student's career or academic goals. Additionally, setting expectations on semesterly adjustments depends on the student's needs.
- Implemented mandatory first-semester advising. After a student has started their first semester with us, a hold is placed, preventing registration for the immediate subsequent semester. This allows advisors to engage with students early in the student life cycle.

Ongoing Operations

In leading a large team of advisors, the advising leadership must have clear policies, procedures, and expectations and an ongoing review of these items. Advising leadership has developed a standardized operating procedure manual for advisor responsibilities with procedures such as Satisfactory Academic Progress, but also has an expectations document to guide day-to-day operations. This separate document includes expectations regarding response times, minimum appointment expectations, etc. By providing a framework for advisors to operate within, we have allowed maximum flexibility to guide their days with continuity of services across the institution.

As enrollment trends have shifted, advising leadership has had to become agile in monitoring the enrollment trends of students. For instance, as new majors come on board, as others retire, or as enrollment fluctuates, the advising department must be ready to distribute advising loads based on the changes within enrollment. This is conducted by continuous monitoring, reviewing loads of currently enrolled advisees, and estimating incoming admits. Being agile and proactive in monitoring enrollment, we can adjust the number of advisees assigned to particular advisors.

An ongoing review of the Student Satisfaction Inventory (SSI) allows us to compare historical data and overall advisor effectiveness. Recent data indicates that the change to the advising model has been a positive experience for students, with areas of future development identified.

Future projects identified for the department include:

- A training program for the professional development of competencies that align with the standards of NACADA/NCDA.
- Additional leadership positions within our advising team allow the Assistant Director to focus more on strategic priorities and allow a clear professional development path for staff.
- More robust student persistence and retention data analysis to identify at-risk populations and initiatives and interventions to support these populations.
- Support concurrent enrollment through matriculation.
- Develop a robust undecided student framework.
- Ongoing needs for special populations, refugees, or multilingual student populations.

Overall Assessment

Overall, the current advising model has proved to be a positive change for both students and staff. Students, as shown in the SSI, have increased satisfaction with advising. SSAs feel empowered as professionals to become more involved with the programs they serve. With caseload advising, student relationships are built early. Advisors are often rewarded by seeing the accomplishments of their students as they graduate, enter professional programs, etc.

There is an ongoing need to be flexible, primarily as we adjust to the needs of the students. If the COVID-19 pandemic has taught us anything, an institution that is slow to change will find itself antiquated. We are poised to monitor the changing higher education landscape post-pandemic. We are prepared to implement new initiatives and adjust our department model. Most importantly, our intentions to advance student success have not changed, even if our model has.

12

FINANCIAL LEADERSHIP AND ADVISING ADVOCACY

Billie Streufert, Helena E. Cole, and Laurie B. Baker

Academic advisors and advising administrators know that "good advising may be the single most underestimated characteristic of a successful college experience" (Light, 2001, p. 81). Too often, such underestimation can come not just from students but from institutional leadership—even on campuses with relatively robust advising programs. This is particularly true regarding budget management. Advising leaders must effectively demonstrate the value of academic advising, perhaps most especially during times of relative economic scarcity. They must also make visible the essential contributions of advisors' work and successfully justify the allocation of resources to academic advising (Grites, 2003). If they are to achieve the profession's esteemed values and competencies (NACADA, 2017a, 2017b), advising leaders must keep both financial leadership and advising advocacy in mind when navigating institutional budgeting and resource allocation.

Perhaps not surprisingly, many faculty members and staff cannot answer basic questions about the financial status of their institution (Vaillancourt, 2020). To ensure appropriate resources are allocated to their units, advising leaders should understand the context of their institution, basic budget management, strategic planning, assessment, load analysis, and equity-based financial leadership. These fiduciary competencies are considered in this chapter to assist advising leaders in advancing the advising goals and outcomes on their campus and, more broadly, within higher education.

DOI: 10.4324/9781003437598-22

Institutional Context

Advising leaders should begin to build their case for resources by first analyzing the financial landscape of their institutions. If they have limited training in fiscal management, they should acquaint themselves with the financial terminology used by their institutions (Serna & Weiler, 2016). Although a detailed discussion of such terms is beyond the scope of this chapter, readers can refer to Smith (2019) for a primer on institutional to include community colleges budgeting.

There are fundamental differences between public and private institutional budgeting processes (Barr, 2016). At U.S. public colleges and universities, for example, legislative bodies exert greater influence on institutional budgets given their traditional (albeit diminishing) reliance on state appropriations (Gravely, 2021; Pew Research, 2019). Indeed, some states have moved to performance-based funding, where institutions receive state dollars based on students' progress toward graduation rather than merely student enrollment (Barr, 2016; Barrow & Rouse, 2018; Delaney, 2011; Kelchen, 2018; McKinney & Hagedorn, 2017). Alternatively, private institutions in the United States tend to be more tuition-dependent than public institutions and are more reliant on donations. Furthermore, while expenditures at private institutions are generally not made public, both public and private institutions must conduct audits and respond to changes within the external environment (Serna & Weiler, 2016).

Public and private institutions also vary in their governance structures, which impacts how budgets are requested, approved, and allocated. Private institutions often have more flexibility when it comes to determining how their funds are spent. Administrators at public institutions may need to navigate other complexities, such as published salaries, union contracts, the need to secure bids before purchasing specified items, and the return of unused funds (Barr, 2016; Smith, 2019).

There are, however, some budgetary questions that are common to both types of institutions. For example, are there procedures in place to request additional or increased funds once resources have been allocated? Are there sources of funds that may not come directly through the budgetary process, such as through grant writing or restricted donations (Smith, 2019)? Knowledge of all budgetary opportunities is essential when advocating for advising resources. For instance, student fees may be a revenue source for advising leaders at some institutions. Grants or specialized government-funded programs may also be secured and are common, especially for those who support underserved populations. Advising administrators must review such external funding opportunities carefully to identify whether their institutions qualify and whether there are sufficient financial resources available to sustain grant-funded initiatives long term (Licklider & the University of Missouri Grant Writer Network, 2012; Smith, 2019). Advising unit leaders might also consider strategies such as drafting a prospectus for their advancement and development offices to use to pitch gift ideas to donors.

Finally, administrators should consider how the advising structures of their institutions influence their financial leadership. Some institutions use an enterprise-wide approach to oversee advising and may have centralized funds allocated to advising (Joslin, 2018). Other universities may decentralize resources, such that funding is spread across multiple advising units. It is also possible that no funding exists. For instance, in faculty-only advising models, institutional leaders might not allocate financial resources specifically for academic advising. In these circumstances, administrators may need to request funds each year to support and advance advising objectives. If decentralized models or scarcity exist, collaboration and co-sponsored initiatives with other departments are paramount. For example, administrators can partner with other offices to invest in resources such as shared appointment booking systems, early alert tools, academic planning technology, major selection/career assessments, academic support, or student programming.

Budget Management and Strategic Planning

Once administrators understand the budgetary context of their institutions, they are ready to participate in budget management. Smith (2019) emphasized that administrators must perceive budgets as both a noun (i.e., records of financial transactions) and a verb (i.e., the act of financial planning, forecasting, and strategic spending). Some may find the second definition confusing or may shy away from tackling budgetary issues. However, if advising is to act as and remain a strategic priority, administrators must embrace the fiduciary aspect of their positions.

The *when* (timing) and *how* (organization) of the budgetary process are both essential elements of advising leadership. Typically, institutions call for budget proposals once per year. The process may also involve several steps, revisions, reviews, and approvals before it is finalized. As a result of being more tuition-driven, private institutions may need to wait to finalize the budget until they know enrollment or census numbers, while budget allocations at public institutions may be delayed until the state determines budget appropriations (Hossler et al., 2015; Marcy, 2020; Smith, 2019).

In terms of organization, institutional budgets can take many forms. For example, *incremental budgeting* occurs when advising administrators are awarded the same amount from the previous year, with an automatic small percentage increase included to account for inflation (Barr, 2016; Serna & Weiler, 2016). Alternatively, some advising leaders may encounter *zero-based budgeting* and need to reevaluate or justify existing funding structures annually (Barr, 2016; Smith, 2019). Other possible models include *formula-based funding*, which allocates resources based on predetermined criteria (e.g., enrollment), and *cost or responsibility-centers*, which treat advising offices as independent entities expected to generate their own revenue (Smith, 2019).

All advising leaders must navigate competing priorities and scarce resources, so they must engage in divergent thinking to identify alternatives, ground their budget plans in the institutions' strategic plans, and prioritize needs over wants (Barr, 2016; Mullin, 2020; Serna & Weiler, 2016). In most cases, the strategic plan will drive the budget (Smith, 2019). A careful examination of current revenue and expenses, as well as an analysis of average historical spending, may also enhance forecasting or decision-making. In more complex models, administrators can use correlations and linear models to predict the financial status of departments or institutions (Serna & Weiler, 2016). Additionally, advising leaders should incorporate institutional values such as student learning and diversity, equity, and inclusion in their advocacy for strategic financial investments in advising. They can support such arguments by including campus climate survey results and other assessment data. In so doing, administrators demonstrate excellent financial leadership while also advancing social justice and student learning outcomes.

Once their budgets have been approved, advising administrators must continue to monitor expenses and engage in "what-if" analyses (Serna & Weiler, 2016). Flexibility is often required, as even the best forecasting and planning cannot predict every need. As they revise the proposed or existing budget, administrators should invite input from the advisors they supervise to provide suggestions about cost savings or equity-advancement ideas and priorities (Mullin, 2020; Serna & Weiler, 2016). Participation in both the process and the outcome of budget management can positively impact personnel development and morale. As part of this conversation, advising leaders should be prepared to explain the budget process and why funding for certain areas may not be available or obtainable on the desired timeline; this ongoing and proactive approach can help minimize disappointment or frustration about resource allocation.

Assessment and Retention

Although academic advising has a clear role in supporting student persistence and graduation, advisors cannot and should not be viewed as solely responsible for those goals (Lowenstein, 2021; Menke et al., 2020; Thomas & McFarlane, 2018). Nonetheless, it is essential for academic advising administrators to understand and to articulate the substantial contributions of academic advising to student success (Drake, 2011; Habley, 1981; Klepfer & Hull, 2012; Zarges et al., 2018). Assessment plays an essential role in justifying the value of advising and directly connecting it to the educational mission of the institution (Aiken-Wisniewski et al., 2010; Council for the Advancement of Standards in Higher Education, 2018; McFarlane & Thomas, 2016; Robbins, 2016). Furthermore, with the advent of early alert systems, advising leaders can now analyze robust student data that can assist in predicting retention and graduation rates. Advisors can also use return-on-investment models to demonstrate the impact they have on retention and completion (Noel-Levitz, n.d.). They can pair such analyses with student narratives captured in interviews, surveys, or focus groups to humanize and support the institution's investment in academic advising.

Before submitting their budget proposals, Barr (2016) suggested that administrators carefully examine their calculations, cost savings, impact on other departments, and the clarity of the rationale they articulated. Brevity and direct requests are often the most effective. After advising leaders have aligned their budget objectives with institutional values, they are ready to present their budget proposal to senior leadership.

Personnel and Load Analysis

Pay and benefits to employees are often the largest line item in the institution's budget (Smith, 2019). Often as a part of the budget submission process, administrators may decide to advocate for additional personnel, which requires an analysis of advisors' loads and student utilization of advising services. Such analyses traditionally include frequency distributions showcasing the number of students assigned to each advisor. Defining what constitutes an advising load will vary by institution, department, or advising unit. In some instances, loads may be based on the number of students who need registration clearance. In other settings, administrators may calculate the number of students who have met with each specific advisor in the past or who have access to advisors' calendars.

In addition, issues of diversity, equity, and inclusion must also be considered in load analysis, as advisors from systemically nondominant groups often engage in informal, invisible advising with students who seek them out because those advisors share their background (McGee, 2020; Moss-Racusin et al., 2021). Finally, if advising administrators elect to compare the loads in their unit to loads at other institutions, they must account for other complexities such as whether advising is mandatory, the unique needs of the students they advise, the objectives of advising, and the extent to which faculty members and staff share responsibility for advising (Miller, 2012; NACADA, 2011; Robbins, 2013).

As they prepare to present staffing proposals, advising leaders must account for costs associated with new personnel such as benefits (e.g., health insurance, retirement), payroll taxes, additional equipment or technology licenses, and professional development (Steele, 2018; Zarges et al., 2018). Advising leaders can then compare these costs against the average net price (after discounts). This calculation can demonstrate that if the institutional employee retains a certain number of students per year, the position will pay for itself and avoid potential harm to students resulting

---

PRACTICAL APPLICATION

Advising administrators must understand how to advocate for advising resources and input. To practice this skill, formulate responses to each scenario below.

Situation #1: You are a member of the Provost's Administrative Council. When the provost shares the agenda for the first meeting of the spring semester, they announce that they have been asked to make budget reductions to the current semester's operating expenses because of low enrollment. They are expecting everyone to arrive at the meeting with ideas. How will you evaluate what constitutes a good recommendation? What are you trying to achieve, avoid, and maintain as the advising administrator? What information do you need to seek out to make informed statements?

Situation #2: You are the advising administrator at a large public university. When you were hired, the associate vice president articulated a clear commitment to an enterprise-wide approach to advising and transparency related to spending. You found it inspiring to hear that advising was central to the strategic plan and paired with dollars to achieve the vision. After serving in the position for three years, however, you now realize this vision has not been achieved or fully implemented. When you compare historical records, you observe little growth or change in allocated dollars, despite increased student enrollment and requests for resources. You have been asked to submit your budget proposal. How will you make a case to support advising?

from inadequate service. If advising administrators are unable to hire additional employees, they can reduce load impacts through group advising, peer advising, technology-enabled responses, cross-campus collaboration, or a flipped advising curriculum (McCaul, 2011; Pentecost, 2011; Spence, 2011; Steele, 2018; Workman et al., 2013; Zarges et al., 2018). It is important to document how these strategies improve service to students and make effective use of the institution's resources.

Financial Aid, Public Policy, and Social Justice

Advising leaders are increasingly called to make advising not only cost-efficient but also effective and equitable. Administrators must consider the ways funding decisions influence students in aggregate and across specific subgroups. An equity-based analysis prevents leaders from overlooking the unintended consequences of their budgetary decisions (Mullin, 2020). Advising leaders may not be at the table when public policy decisions are made. They can, however, take an interest in such legislation and how it affects their units. They also are typically on the front lines in terms of assessing the structural inequities that institutional funding practices can create and are thus positioned to frame equity-based initiatives as value-added investments (Mullin, 2020). Advising leaders should be equipped to evaluate the impact of these systems on advising and ready themselves to advocate for change when needed (Dowd & Elmore, 2020; Mullin, 2020).

When leaders collaborate to conduct an equity audit, they might evaluate the clarity of institutional cost of attendance calculations, current debt inequities among student subgroups, Free Application for Federal Student Aid (FAFSA) work penalties, barriers created by holds or fees (e.g., printing costs, cap/gown expenses, premier residence halls), and need-based aid reform (Ardoin, 2020; Atkinson, 2020; Chaplot et al., 2015; Cheslock et al., 2018; Davis et al., 2019; Draeger, 2013; Hornak et al., 2010; Kelchen et al., 2017; Kezar, 2011; Pasquerella & Oates, 2020; Pew Research, 2019; Walpole, 2011). They also may want to consider ways effective campus design can support students who must work to remain in school but who consequently encounter time constraints and are unable to access supportive resources (advising, tutoring, etc.) or educational components crucial to their learning, such as study away, internships, or faculty-mentored research (Ardoin, 2020; Engle & Lynch, 2011; Hornak et al., 2010; McClure & Ryder, 2018; Rowan-Kenyon et al., 2010). Community partnerships or resources related to food insecurities, housing, or professional interview clothing closets may also be needed (Ardoin, 2020). Identifying such equity concerns is an essential consideration when advocating for the advising resources necessary to address them.

Finally, financial advising leadership includes fostering partnerships (Spence, 2011) and collaborating with diverse stakeholders (Messia, 2010). Academic advising leaders are in a unique position to build bridges and break down institutional silos, as their work lives at "the intersection of academic affairs and student affairs" (Miller, 2016, p. 55). If advising administrators work on campuses with decentralized advising structures, they can begin by collaborating with other advising leaders across the academy to achieve unifying institutional goals or foster student learning (Joslin, 2018). Embracing the idea of a learning

---

PRACTICAL APPLICATION

Excellent advising administrators exhibit equity-based financial leadership. To situate the practices included in this section in your work as a leader, consider and respond to the scenarios below.

Situation #1: You are the advising administrator of an integrated academic and career advising office. Your supervisor reviews your budget and notices you have allocated funds for the administration of career assessments and career fairs. In an email to you two days before budgets are due, they suggest the costs for these inventories and events be forwarded to students, particularly because these initiatives are not named in the strategic plan. They also suggest the department begin to charge students exam proctoring fees for the CLEP exams it administers. They are excited about "the new dollars this would create and the programming we could finally launch to advance student success as the result of these funds." What are the ramifications of moving toward or away from such a model? Who is helped, and who might be harmed? Draft an email in response to their request.

Situation #2: You serve as the lead administrator of an advising office that serves exploratory students at a public institution. The university has elected to move to a competitive budget structure, such that academic departments will now receive funding based on the number of declared majors enrolled within these programs or the number of credits completed across schools within the institution (Smith, 2019). You have been asked by the provost to provide input on this budget structure proposal. What ethical dilemmas or unintended consequences may advisors encounter as a result of this model?

partnership model (Thomas & McFarlane, 2018) serves to communicate to other offices and stakeholders that advising is not simply a service function (Spence, 2011; Steele & White, 2019). Building and maintaining relationships with the core internal stakeholders of faculty members, student affairs staff, enrollment personnel, and campus administrators are key to the success of academic advising programs and will also assist advising administrators in their advocacy for equity or additional resources (Messia, 2010).

Conclusion

Nearly every decision in higher education is predicated on financial analysis (Serna & Weiler, 2016). Equity, efficiency, effectiveness, and ethical decision-making are guiding principles that inform financial advising excellence. All of higher education must respond to the external environment, allocate resources based on their strategic plans, and demonstrate fiduciary responsibility in audits.

Staffing is one of the largest investments institutions make in advising. As advising administrators advocate for more resources, they must use both quantitative and qualitative metrics to demonstrate the value of advising, emphasizing the ways advisors advance student learning. Advising leaders must also exhibit continuous humility and collaborate to design student-ready campus environments that remove barriers for both advisors and students. Through continuous reflection and thoughtful action, advising administrators can embody the values and core competencies of the field as they engage in financial decision-making and advising advocacy (NACADA, 2017a, 2017b).

Reflection Questions

1 Why should advising administrators engage more proactively in budgeting? What might be achieved as a result?

2 Examine the financial practices of an institution of your choosing. First, locate the mission, vision, and strategic plan of an institution. Then, retrieve its budget. Compare the institution's use of funds to its stated values and goals. To what degree do these documents align? What discrepancies exist between its espoused objectives and spending patterns?

3 To what degree should advising administrators be transparent or share the details about their budgets with the advisors they supervise? How

should frontline personnel be involved in budgetary processes? What are the benefits and consequences of wherever administrators fall on these continua? How might personnel participation advance equity (Mullin, 2020)?

4 Make a wish list for an advising department. Consider human, structural, and material resources. Prioritize the items. Then, compare your list to a colleague's. How are your responses alike and different? If professional development dollars are on your list, brainstorm creative funding sources or solutions that exist to ensure staff has access to ongoing training, trends, and renewal as advisors.

5 Review higher education news publications such as *The Chronicle of Higher Education* or *Inside Higher Education*. Locate a recent article about a financial topic. Examples of hot topics might include performance-based funding, alternative funding strategies, government appropriations, tuition increases, support for low-income students, and financial well-being approaches. After you have located and read the article, review it more critically. What dimensions of the issue does the author address in the article, and what are their recommendations? How does this issue directly or indirectly influence advising? React to and evaluate the author's claims. What do you agree or disagree with? Why?

References

Aiken-Wisniewski, S., Campbell, S., Nutt, C., Robbins, R., Kirk-Kuwaye, M., & Higa, L. (2010). *Guide to assessment in academic advising* (2nd ed.) (Monograph No. 23). NACADA.

Ardoin, S. (2020). Engaging poor and working-class students. In S. J. Quaye, S. R. Harper, & S. L. Pendakur (Eds.), *Student engagement in higher education: Theoretical perspectives and practical approaches for diverse populations* (3rd ed., pp. 307–324). Routledge.

Atkinson, A. (2020). Borrowing equality. *Columbia Law Review, 120*(6), 1403–1469. https://columbialawreview.org/content/borrowing-equality/.

Barr, M. J. (2016). Budgeting and fiscal management for student affairs. In G. S. McClellan, J. Stringer, & Associates (Eds.), *The handbook of student affairs administration* (4th ed., pp. 509–534). Jossey-Bass.

Barrow, L., & Rouse, C. E. (2018). Financial incentives and educational investment: The impact of performance-based scholarships on student time use. *Education Finance and Policy, 13*(4), 419–448. https://ideas.repec.org/a/tpr/edfpol/v13y2018i4p419-448.html.

Chaplot, P., Cooper, D., Johnstone, R., & Karandjeff, K. (2015). *Beyond financial aid: How colleges can strengthen the financial stability of low-income students and improve student outcomes*. Lumina Foundation. https://www.luminafoundation.org/files/resources/beyond-financial-aid.pdf.

Cheslock, J. J., Hughes, R. P, Cardelle, R. F., & Heller, D. E. (2018). Filling the gap: The use of intentional and incidental need-meeting financial aid. *The Review of Higher Education, 41*(4), 577–605. https://doi.org/10.1353/rhe.2018.0026.

Council for the Advancement of Standards in Higher Education (CAS). (2018). *CAS standards for academic advising programs.* http://standards.cas.edu/get-pdf.cfm?PDF=E864D2C4-D655-8F74-2E647CDECD29B7D0.

Davis, L. A., Wolniak, G. C., George, C. E., & Nelson, G. R. (2019). Demystifying tuition? A content analysis of the information quality of public college and university websites. *AERA Open, 5*(3). https://www.doi.org/10.1177/23328584 19867650.

Delaney, J. A. (2011). Earmarks and state appropriations for higher education. *Journal of Education Finance, 37*(1), 3–23.

Dowd, A. C., & Elmore, B. D. (2020). Leadership for equity-minded data use toward racial equity in higher education. In A. Kezar, & J. Posselt (Eds.), *Higher administration for social justice and equity: Critical perspectives for leadership* (pp. 159–176). Routledge.

Draeger, J. (2013). *Reimagining financial aid to improve student access and outcomes.* NASFAA: National Association of Student Financial Aid Administrators. http://www.nasfaa.org/uploads/documents/ektron/67439aeb-419d-4e9c-9035-4278d0bbed61/d19119911e864c39abb555e99f130d122.pdf.

Drake, J. K. (2011). The role of academic advising in student retention and persistence. *About Campus, 16*(3), 8–12. https://doi.org/10.1002/abc.20062.

Engle, J., & Lynch, M. G. (2011). Demography is not destiny: What colleges and universities can do to improve persistence among low-income students. In A. Kezar (Ed.), *Recognizing and serving low-income students in higher education: An examination of institutional policies, practices, and culture* (pp. 161–175). Routledge.

Gravely, A. (2021, October 29). Down to $40 billion. *Inside Higher Ed.* https://www.insidehighered.com/news/2021/10/29/higher-ed-funding-continues-shrink-social-spending-bill.

Grites, T. (2003). Determining the worth of an advising unit. *Academic Advising News, 26*(1). https://nacada.ksu.edu/Resources/Clearinghouse/View-Articles/Determining-the-Worth-of-an-Advising-Unit.aspx.

Habley, W. R. (1981). Academic advisement: The critical link in student retention. *NASPA Journal, 18*(4), 45–50. https://doi.org/10.1080/00220973.1981.11071797.

Hornak, A. M., Farrell, P. L., & Jackson, N. J. (2010). Making it (or not) on a dime in college: Implications for practice. *Journal of College Student Development, 51*(5), 481–495. https://doi.org/10.1353/csd.2010.0003.

Hossler, D., Kalsbeck, D. H., & Bontrager, B. (2015). Successful strategic enrollment management organizations. In D. Hossler, B. Bontrager, & Associates (Eds.), *Handbook of strategic enrollment management* (pp. 31–46). Jossey Bass.

Joslin, J. E. (2018). The case for strategic academic advising management. *New Directions for Higher Education, 2018*(184), 11–20. https://doi.org/10.1002/he.20299.

Kelchen, R. (2018). Do performance-based funding policies affect underrepresented student enrollment? *The Journal of Higher Education, 89*(5), 702–727. https://doi.org/10.1080/00221546.2018.1434282.

Kelchen, R., Goldrick-Rab, S., & Hosch, B. (2017). The costs of college attendance: Examining variation and consistency in institutional living cost allowances. *The Journal of Higher Education, 88*(6), 947–971. https://doi.org/10.1080/00221546.2016.1272092.

Kezar, A. (2011). Rethinking postsecondary institutions for low-income student success: The power of post-structural theory. In A. Kezar (Ed.), *Recognizing and serving low-income students in higher education: An examination of institutional policies, practices, and culture* (pp. 3–26). Routledge.

Klepfer, K., & Hull, J. (2012). *High school rigor and good advice: Setting up students to succeed.* Center for Public Education National School Boards Association. https://fordhaminstitute.org/ohio/commentary/high-school-rigor-and-good-advice-setting-students-succeed.

Licklider, M. M., & the University of Missouri Grant Writer Network. (2012). *Grant seeking in higher education: Strategies and tools for college faculty.* Jossey-Bass.

Light, R. J. (2001). *Making the most of college: Students speak their minds.* Harvard University Press.

Lowenstein, M. (2021). Learning and its tokens: A fallacy and its danger for advising. *The Mentor: Innovative scholarship on academic advising.* https://doi.org/10.26209/mj2362387.

Marcy, M. B. (2020). *The small college imperative: Models for sustainable futures.* Stylus.

McCaul, J. L. (2011). Key elements of strategic planning. In J. E. Joslin, & N. L. Markee (Eds.), *Academic advising administration: Essential knowledge and skills for the 21st century* (pp. 12–20). NACADA.

McClure, K., & Ryder, A. J. (2018). The costs of belonging: How spending money influences social relationships in college. *Journal of Student Affairs Research and Practice, 55*(2), 196–209. https://doi.org/10.1080/19496591.2017.1360190.

McFarlane, B., & Thomas, C. (2016). Advocating for academic advising. In T. J. Grites, M. A. Miller, & J. Givans Voller (Eds.), *Beyond foundations: Developing as a master academic advisor* (pp. 199–223). Jossey-Bass.

McGee, E. O. (2020). *Black, brown, bruised: How racialized STEM education stifles innovation.* Harvard Education Press.

McKinney, L., & Hagedorn, L. S. (2017). Performance-based funding for community colleges: Are colleges disadvantaged by serving the most disadvantaged students? *The Journal of Higher Education, 88*(2), 159–182. https://doi.org/10.1080/00221546.2016.1243948.

Menke, D. J., Duslak, M., & McGill, C. M. (2020). Administrator perceptions of academic advisor tasks. *NACADA Journal, 40*(2), 85–96. https://doi.org/10.12930/NACADA-20-12.

Messia, J. (2010). Defining advising stakeholder groups. *NACADA Clearinghouse.* http://www.nacada.ksu.edu/Resources/Clearinghouse/View-Articles/Defining-Advising-Stakeholder-Groups.aspx.

Miller, M. A. (2012). Structuring our conversations: Shifting to four dimensional advising models. In A. Carlstrom, & M. A. Miller (Eds.), *2011 national survey of academic advising*. (Monograph No. 25). NACADA. http://www.nacada. ksu.edu/Resources/Clearinghouse/View-Articles/Structuring-Our-Conversations-Shifting-to-Four-Dimensional-Advising-Models.aspx.

Miller, M. A. (2016). Building upon the components of academic advising to facilitate change. In T. J. Grites, M. A. Miller, & J. Givans Voller (Eds.), *Beyond foundations: Developing as a master advisor* (pp. 43–64). Jossey-Bass.

Moss-Racusin, C. A., Pietri, E. S., van der Toorn, J., & Ashburhn-Nardo, L. (2021). Boosting the sustainable representation of women in STEM with evidence-based policy initiatives. *Policy Insights from the Behavioral and Brain Sciences, 8*(1), 50–58. https://doi.org/10.1177/2372732220980092.

Mullin, M. (2020). Elevating equity through a strategic finance approach: Empowerment as the goal. In A. Kezar, & J. Posselt (Eds.), *Higher education administration for social justice and equity: Critical perspectives for leadership* (pp. 67–81). Routledge.

NACADA: The Global Community for Academic Advising. (2011). *Professional advisor load*. https://nacada.ksu.edu/Resources/Clearinghouse/View-Articles/2011-NACADA-National-Survey.aspx.

NACADA: The Global Community for Academic Advising. (2017a). *NACADA academic advising core competencies model*. https://www.nacada.ksu.edu/Resources/Pillars/CoreCompetencies.aspx.

NACADA: The Global Community for Academic Advising. (2017b). *NACADA core values of academic advising*. https://www.nacada.ksu.edu/Resources/Pillars/CoreValues.aspx.

Noel-Levitz. (n.d.). *Return on investment estimator*. https://www.ruffalonl.com/wp-content/uploads/pdf/ReturnonInvestmentEstimator.pdf.

Pasquerella, L., & Oates, J. (2020, April 6). The urgency of reforming federal student aid policy. *Inside Higher Education*. https://www.insidehighered.com/views/2020/04/06/federal-student-aid-policy-must-be-reformed-make-college-affordable-low-income.

Pentecost, M. W. (2011). Dealing with budget cuts. In J. E. Joslin, & N. L. Markee (Eds.), *Academic advising administration: Essential knowledge and skills for the 21st century* (pp. 191–197). NACADA.

Pew Research. (2019, October 15). *Two decades of change in federal and state higher education funding*. https://www.pewtrusts.org/en/research-and-analysis/issue-briefs/2019/10/two-decades-of-change-in-federal-and-state-higher-education-funding.

Robbins, R. (2013). *Advisor load*. NACADA Clearinghouse. http://www.nacada.ksu.edu/Resources/Clearinghouse/View-Articles/Advisor-Load.aspx.

Robbins, R. (2016). Assessment of academic advising: Overview and student learning outcomes. In T. J. Grites, M. A. Miller, & J. Givans Voller (Eds.), *Beyond foundations: Developing as a master academic advisor* (pp. 275–288). Jossey-Bass.

Rowan-Kenyon, H. T., Swan, A. K., Deutsch, N. L., & Gansneder, B. (2010). Academic success for working adult students. In L. W. Perna (Ed.), *Understanding the working college student: New research and its implications for policy and practice* (pp. 93–114). Stylus.

Serna, G. R., & Weiler, S. C. (2016). *Higher education, fiscal administration, and budgeting: An applied approach.* Rowman and Littlefield.

Smith, D. (2019). *How university budgets work.* John Hopkins University Press.

Spence, J. M. (2011). Developing strategic and effective partnerships with others on campus. In J. E. Joslin, & N. L. Markee (Eds.), *Academic advising administration: Essential knowledge and skills for the 21st century* (pp. 169–176). NACADA.

Steele, G. E. (2018). Student success: Academic advising, student learning data, and technology. *New Directions for Higher Education, 2018*(184), 59–68. https://doi.org/10.1002/he.20303.

Steele, G., & White, E. R. (2019). Leadership in higher education: Insights from academic advisors. *The Mentor: Innovative Scholarship on Academic Advising, 21*(2019), 1–10. https://doi.org/10.18113/P8mj2161110.

Thomas, C., & McFarlane, B. (2018). Playing the long game: Surviving fads and creating lasting student success through academic advising. *New Directions for Higher Education, 2018*(184), 97–106. https://doi.org/10.1002/he.20306.

Vaillancourt, A. M. (2020, September 11). What if everyone on campus understood the money? *The Chronicle of Higher Education.* https://www.chronicle.com/article/what-if-everyone-on-campus-understood-the-money?cid=gen_sign_in.

Walpole, M. (2011). Academics, campus administration, and social interaction: Examining campus structures using post-structural theory. In A. Kezar (Ed.), *Recognizing and serving low-income students in higher education* (pp. 99–120). Routledge.

Workman, T., Farr, T., Frobish, J., & Almeda, A. (2013, March). Creating a collaborative culture in academic advisement. *Academic Advising Today, 36*(1). https://nacada.ksu.edu/Resources/Academic-Advising-Today/View-Articles/Creating-a-Collaborative-Culture-in-Academic-Advisement.aspx.

Zarges, K. M., Adams, T. A., Higgins, E. M., & Muhovich, N. (2018). Assessing the impact of academic advising: Current issues and future trends. *New Directions for Higher Education, 2018*(184), 47–57. https://doi.org/10.1002/he.20302.

13

STRATEGIC COMMUNICATIONS

Culture Is Key

Katherine Schmidt and Karen Sullivan-Vance

While a healthy culture of communication is the heart of a well-functioning advising unit, one of an advising administrator's most difficult responsibilities is the development and management of strategic communications for students, families, faculty, staff, administrators, and outside constituents. Advising administrators are tasked with developing communication plans that are intentional, focused, and targeted for the range of populations who function in higher education. Communication strategies and consistent messaging do not only ensure that the purpose and role of academic advising becomes ingrained in campus culture; they also impact student intentionality, in both curricular and cocurricular decision-making, and uplift advising unit morale. This chapter serves as a starting point for advising administrators to reconceptualize and reprioritize strategic communications in advising.

Thorson (2013) described *strategic communication* as "a term used to denote the higher-level concerns behind communicative efforts by organizations to advance [an] organizational mission." These concerns include traditional elements, like purpose, audience, and medium, as well as less conspicuous elements like values and assumptions. In a comprehensive review of the terms *strategic* and *communication*, Hallahan et al. (2007) challenged the "rational model of strategic decision making that implies that strategic decisions are objective, and culture and gender free" (p. 13). They went on to note the following:

> The term *strategic* might offer one of the most inclusive, although conflicting and contradictory, descriptions of the field of communication

DOI: 10.4324/9781003437598-23

practice. Although it emphasizes the role of communication as a management practice, it does not necessarily imply power and control of management over other constituents. It also allows for the study of participatory communication practices that include stakeholder communication, change management, and complex analyses of organizational environments.

(p. 16)

Tufte and Mefalopulos (2009) described participatory communication as "dialogue, which allows the sharing of information, perceptions and opinions among the various stakeholders" (p. 17), a more inclusive approach empowering all parties involved.

For advising administrators who are juggling multiple demands, adding intentional strategic communications to their list of responsibilities may be daunting. While advising, budgeting processes, administrative policies, and leadership cultivation are explicit components of an administrator's wheelhouse, the area of communication often remains invisible.

Advising administrators know that interactions between students and advisors are built on communication. Ordinary interactions that may seem trivial, repetitive, or unimportant to an outsider are often moments that matter. Swecker et al. (2013) noted that for every meeting with an advisor, student retention increased 13%, meaning that communication is crucial to student success. Jordan (2015) identified *communication* as "an exchange of information and ideas between two or more people" including "verbal, nonverbal, written, and electronic interchanges" (p. 213); however, administrators know that *effective communication* is key. Jordan (2015) described an effective exchange as an active process of an advisor listening, helping the student to process information, setting goals, and possessing the ability to tend to a student's unspoken words. These basic tenets also apply to other one-to-one contexts. Thus, an administrator needs to develop a vision for effective communication.

When an advising administrator is intentional and inclusive in their communications, they are not only more responsive to diverse student populations—Black and Indigenous people of color (BIPOC), first-generation, international, veterans, the LGBTQ+ community—they also model intentional and inclusive communications for staff, faculty, and other administrators. Additionally, communication strategies should be positioned as explicit and integral foci in unit self-assessments, with the goal of gathering evidence on effectiveness and identifying areas for improvement.

Of course, no one-size-fits-all strategic communication strategy exists because advising models vary: there are decentralized, centralized, and shared models. A faculty member may approach communications differently than a first-year advising center administrator; furthermore, two- and four-year colleges may also differ in their approach to communications. Considering variability among programs can become challenging at large universities where one individual may be tasked with campus-wide advising initiatives while negotiating within multiple and well-established advising structures. A strategic communication plan is even more vital in this context to ensure that messaging is consistent across the institution.

Regardless of the institutional advising model, communication tends to be only one part of a larger strategic plan for an academic advising unit. Strategies are merely communication operations and movements. For instance, strategy enables advising administrators to finesse student communications, allowing for more personalized approaches and reducing the number of emails sent. Strategy can also include social media campaigns designed for specific student populations, proactive outreach via email to students with academic difficulty, and Learning Management Systems (LMS) communication embeds in courses with high D/F/W rates (i.e., the percentage of students who earn a grade of D or F or who withdraw from a course), alerting students to supplemental instruction and tutoring.

Too often, however, these communication operations and movements are viewed as the key to effective communication. In reality, they should be positioned as tools in service to something much larger. When vision becomes the driving force behind communication operations and movements, everything changes. A shared vision cultivates clarity, transparency, reflection, individual and collective growth, and strategic communications.

Internal Communications: Cultivating Culture through Habits of Mind

Building a culture of communication should be the starting point for advising administrators. This process starts inside the advising unit. Advising administrators who cultivate a culture of communication not only build credibility but also pivot easily as communication strategies change. To that end, advising administrators need to focus on people. In "Relationships: The Critical Ties That Bind Professionals" (2002), Roper stated the following:

> The challenge before us as student affairs professionals is to develop an approach that places relationships with others at the center of both our personal and professional life … As we develop a pattern of consistently successful interactions and demonstrate to those in our communities that we have the capacity to be engaged in the issues that matter to

others, we will construct a network of successful relationships and a reputation of caring about others.

(pp. 11–12)

Relationships matter, and communication is, first and foremost, relational. To decenter strategy and recenter on cultivating a culture of communication requires first establishing a set of priorities for exchanges. Advising administrators can think about these priorities as *habits of mind*. According to Costa (2008),

> A Habit of Mind is a composite of many skills, attitudes, cues, past experiences, and proclivities. It means that we value one pattern of intellectual behaviors over another; therefore, it implies making choices about which patterns we should use at a certain time.
>
> *(p. 17)*

Clearly, establishing a set of habits of mind for communication both within and outside of the advising unit helps advising administrators to cultivate the culture that Roper described.

There are many habits of mind that help to promote a common vision for responding to and engaging with people, especially when confronted with new or complex challenges. Lee (2004) urged units to imagine a ladder of priorities that are clearly defined and practiced in all exchanges, with an understanding that everyone is committed to valuing one pattern of thinking over others. For example, *courtesy* and *efficiency* (Lee, 2004), as well as *accuracy* (Costa, 2008) and *inclusion*, could serve as the core habits of mind for an advising unit. These habits guide the administrator and advisors in their in-person, virtual, and written communications. However, these four habits of mind are not horizontally situated, but hierarchically organized to eliminate confusion about the chain of priorities (Lee, 2004).

Courtesy and Inclusion

At the top of the hierarchy are courtesy and inclusion. Both place the relational human experience as the priority and help to "achieve full engagement with the other person" (Roper, 2002, p. 12). Courtesy is marked by actions and expressions that embody respect. Courteous advising administrators are active listeners who are responsive to others' needs and ensure that each individual with whom they interact feels worthy and valuable. Courtesy's companion is inclusion, marked by the leveraging of diversity to "create a fair, equitable, healthy, and high-performing organization or community where all individuals are respected, feel engaged and motivated, and their contributions toward meeting organizational and societal goals are valued" (O'Mara & Richter, 2014, p. 2). Inclusive advising administrators seek to dismantle the barriers that structural inequities impose; cultural competence and cultural humility are infused into the frameworks of their thinking, words, and actions. Courteous and inclusive advising administrators also address challenges quickly, kindly, and with honesty for the sake of both an employee's or student's personal and professional growth and overall unit morale. Courtesy and inclusion are prioritized over accuracy and efficiency in every interaction because perceptions matter first and foremost: "People will forget what you said, people will forget what you did, but people will never forget how you made them feel."[1]

Accuracy and Efficiency

Once courtesy and inclusion are prioritized, accuracy follows. Accuracy is the act of being precise and correct, of being free from carelessness. Advising administrators who position accuracy as a priority understand that excellence in this area requires a spirit of teachability and a willingness to engage in continuous learning:

> Embodied in the stamina, grace, and elegance of a ballerina, a writer, a shoemaker, or a street sweeper is the desire for craftsmanship, mastery, flawlessness, and economy of energy to produce exceptional results. People who value accuracy, precision, and craftsmanship ... review the high standards by which they abide; they review the models and visions they value; and they review the criteria that will confirm that their finished product matches and exceeds those criteria.
>
> *(Institute for Habits of Mind, 2022, para. 3)*

Advising administrators need to ensure equity of information, processes, and opportunities for all students, and without fail act as sources of accurate information for their students. Earning their trust is paramount, especially for students who have been marginalized. Accuracy also requires a protocol for when advisors are faced with questions they cannot answer, such as a standardized script that advisors commit to using in such situations (Lee, 2004). Imagine if every administrator and advisor in a unit agreed to never guess, pretend, or send a student to another office when confronted with a question they are unable to answer. That, instead, they committed to the following script: "I don't know, but let's find out together." This powerful phrase situates the advising staff and the advisee in shared responsibility (Crookston, 1972). The advisor thus builds trust by being open, honest, and transparent; by modeling how to find answers, they can develop student self-efficacy.

As advising staff members embrace courtesy, inclusion, and accuracy, they should feel empowered and equipped to explore ways to be more efficient, the final shared priority. Efficiency is the art of finding ways to maximize methods, materials, energy, efforts, and time in relational situations. Advising administrators understand that efficiencies are often developed in response to productivity challenges, and those efficiencies are evaluated, revised, replaced, and retired along a continuum. Administrators also know that increased efficiency requires time and experience. While staff who are new to an advising environment will benefit greatly from pre-established efficiencies, they will need ample room to develop individual professional efficiencies that match those of seasoned advisors.

The possibilities for unit-level and individual-level communication efficiencies are countless: when an advisor tracks questions they receive on a regular basis, they may notice patterns and design an infographic to serve as a visual guide in advising sessions with future students. When an advisor finds that they spend much of their time explaining the purpose of advising to students, they may design an LMS module that new advisees could complete prior to a first advising session. Or, when an advisor finds roadblocks to efficiencies, they may explore alternatives to system requirements that pose as a barrier, like paper processes as opposed to digital forms and signatures. What begins as one advisor's efficient solution to a challenge often becomes an efficiency shared by the team.

In sum, advising administrators should model and encourage habits of mind, like courtesy, inclusion, accuracy, and efficiency. Administrators cannot expect their teams to embrace a culture of communication if they themselves do not model these habits of mind in all interactions. When every employee commits to developing proficiency in choosing patterns that value particular ways of thinking and communicating, culture changes in profound ways.

Four Habits in Action

Advising administrators will find that strategies for cultivating a culture of communication abound. One example is to "create more empowered [advisors] by dismantling functional silos and pushing decision making and problem solving closer to the front lines" (Lee, 2004, p. 86). A second example is to encourage advisors to share their stories of unexpected memorable advising moments with the team. Lee (2004) explained that "it takes something memorable to turn an ordinary, satisfactory experience into something special" (p. 50). When advising administrators create spaces for the recognition of stories, they are more likely to see an increase in staff morale, student loyalty, and moments that matter. A third example is the infusion of habits of mind in the search process by creating position descriptions and interview questions that attract individuals who are predisposed to being courteous and inclusive, as accuracy and efficiency can be learned in the position.

A final example is the collaborative creation of maps that diagram the communications that will be sent out to students, campus partners, and/or outside constituents. This process is a good starting point for discussions about communication effectiveness and needs for improvement. Figure 13.1 illustrates a process for mapping communication through the lens of a topic, issue, and/or event. The initial step is to collaboratively consider the center of the circle; for example, if the topic were academic warning, it would serve as the central focus. Beginning with courtesy and inclusion, the advising administrator and advisors would brainstorm aspects of the topic. Generating ideas and exploring ways of thinking involves a non-linear—and some may even say *messy*—conversation: What do we know about the topic? What do we know about obstacles students are facing outside the classroom? What do we want students to know, beyond dates and policies?

Accuracy and efficiency then drive the group in the third step, an articulation of the target audience. Ask yourself: What needs to be included in the message? What is the appropriate medium to get the message out to our audience? What is our plan for evaluating the effectiveness of the communication? The next step in the wheel is assessing results, and a plan for changes for future communications regarding academic warning. The communication wheel serves as a template which flows from the center outward and then back into the center—with learning and evaluation happening at each level—to ensure that the culture of communication is deeply embedded in the process.

Informal exchanges are also opportunities. Conversations that advising staff have with colleagues in the hallway, on the campus sidewalk, or in line at the campus coffee shop, provide opportunities to be courteous, to connect, and to converse. These small moments afford the ongoing development of intentional skills while building relationships with colleagues.

Feedback loops guided by habits of mind should also play a central role in internal communications. Feedback loops are tools by which to evaluate communication strategies and how they impact the overall culture. According to Lee (2004), "People do not do what organizations expect. They do what their [supervisors] pay attention to" (p. 35), which means that supervisors need to make time to recognize moments that highlight the good work that team members do for others, especially in the areas of

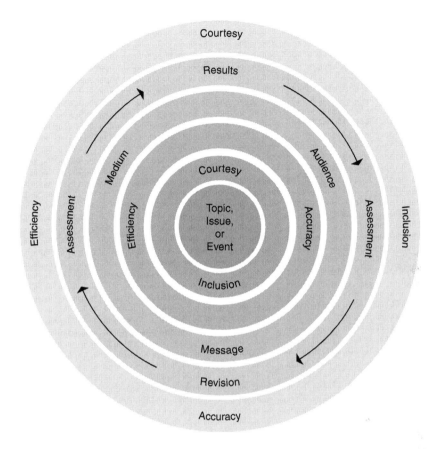

FIGURE 13.1   *Communication Wheel.*

Note. Adapted from Lee (2004), as well as Costa (2008).

courtesy, inclusivity, accuracy, and efficiency. Equally important, though, is the need to address employee challenges quickly, kindly, and honestly, which requires administrators to grow their courage while keeping empathy on the forefront of interventions. Developing the capacity to communicate challenges and solutions as soon as possible will improve unit morale in ways that are difficult to quantify but impossible to deny.

Annual evaluation processes are opportunities to invite advisors to reflect in writing, using strategic prompts, to help guide the trajectory and shape of written feedback that will be written by a supervisor (see Chapter 17). The participatory process is not only courteous and inclusive, it is empowering. Too often, however, communication is one way. While advising administrators routinely provide individual feedback for staff, institutional cultures rarely encourage processes for employees to offer feedback to supervisors. Safe and responsive feedback loops for staff to offer feedback to their supervisors can drastically improve the culture of communication within a unit, especially when advising administrators model an authentic commitment to communication by soliciting, listening, and adjusting to staff needs, concerns, and desires.

Communicating with Students

Today's students expect immediate information and the ability to have personalized conversations with their advisors. Advising administrators not only understand the tension between this immediacy and depth, they also know that students are able to quickly identify whether an office on campus is courteous, inclusive, accurate, and efficient as a cumulative result of their in-person and virtual communication experiences.

All student communications should be aligned with the institution's mission and guided by the advising unit's prioritized habits of mind. As Nutt (2000) stated, "Communication skills are perhaps the most important set of skills needed by advisors in building relationships with their advisees" (p. 221). While technology allows advising units to connect with all students in a timely, accurate, and cost-effective manner, technology will never replace the human need for interpersonal connection. One-to-one exchanges are the hallmark of advising. Habits of mind not only provide a hierarchy for ensuring that every student's needs are met during exchanges, they also help to move a student beyond feeling merely satisfied with advising by "capturing [a student's] loyalty" (Lee, 2004, p. 52). Their biological and/or family of choice and friends also expect courteous, inclusive, accurate, and efficient information, which may act as the deciding factor in a student selecting a particular college or helping a student and their support network to understand how they can recover from a difficult term. When possible, communicating with the student in their preferred language is one step on the journey of dismantling the barriers that structural inequities impose.

Additionally, communication technology can become overused (Ben-Jacob & Glazerman, 2021). Because students are often bombarded with generic institutional emails, many feel overwhelmed and leave messages unread. Advising administrators should collaborate with campus partners to align messaging at strategic times throughout the year, as reducing the number of messages students receive can increase the likelihood they will read them. When messages are sent to students directly from an advisor, there are opportunities to make connections that feel highly personal. Advising administrators can encourage advisors to check in with students in simple ways that mimic the immediacy of social media. For example, Hutt (EAB, 2017) sent a 34-word email to students who had not yet registered, offering his assistance. His email was courteous, inclusive, accurate, and notably efficient, and he was flooded with responses from students. Small but vision-driven efforts can produce outstanding yields that impact both student perceptions and the potential for interventions that may have otherwise been missed.

In nurturing the culture of communication, seeking feedback from diverse student populations is essential. This process includes determining when communications did and did not reach an intended audience; the effectiveness, appropriateness, and timing of the communication; and communicative weaknesses and omissions. Student focus groups are one way advising administrators can get immediate narrative data on how students receive and perceive various communications and learn how students would like to connect with advising. Click and open rates are another source of data and serve to triangulate responses. Using multiple data streams on an ongoing basis will provide robust feedback for evaluation and evidence-based improvements.

Partnering with Campus Constituents

While intra-institutional communications are vital in higher education, the overall communication culture of a campus dictates the degree to which an advising administrator must innovate in the area of communication. Some campuses have a range of channels in place, with clear form and function guidelines, along with easy-to-find, accessible support. In these situations, campus-wide efficiencies already exist, making an administrator's job easier. Other campuses, however, have less-developed cultures of communication, and advising administrators must adopt a 30,000-foot view when sharing information. Fortunately, when a communication culture has been well established within the advising unit itself, the unit-level paradigm is useful for engaging with campus constituents.

Within the framework of institutional and unit-level cultures of communication, external constituents need to possess a working understanding of what the advising unit does, who it serves, and how it operates. In sharing with campus partners, NACADA's Concept of Academic Advising (2006) is a good place to begin to show "what students will demonstrate, know, value, and do" through advising (para. 8). Conversely, the advising unit needs to know what campus partners do, who they serve, and how they operate (NACADA, 2017a).

To help dismantle silos that may exist across the campus, advising administrators can and should invite units, such as the registrar's office, financial aid, and enrollment management, into regular conversations about the messaging, timing, and coordination of communications. A first step in this partnership is to create an inventory that logs the subject matter and timing of information that is shared throughout the year. When units become cognizant of the sheer volume and redundancy of messages that may inadvertently overwhelm students, they can strategize to streamline their communications and build cohesive and holistic channels for sharing information. Part of this process needs to include conversations about perceptions versus the reality experienced in communications, with an evaluation of engagement tactics. By collaborating with campus constituents, trust and accountability are established among units, administrators gain new perspectives and insights, accuracy of information is heightened, and communication barriers and their solutions become more visible.

An additional opportunity for partnerships in communication is described by Thomas and McFarlane (2018):

> With the advisor/student relationship being one of the few on a campus that potentially spans all years of study, advisors are in a perfect position to serve the role as institutional early-alert partners. Advisors know when a process, structure, or policy is not working for students, and, if empowered, advisors can then connect with key colleagues on campus to learn from struggles that students are having and co-create productive systemic solutions.
>
> *(p. 102)*

Within an established culture of communication, advising administrators can work with advisors to build channels for communicating vital information about barriers to student success to campus constituents who possess the capacity to make change (i.e., faculty senate, budget committee, TRiO programs, disability services, residential life, public safety, student employment, the diversity, equity, and inclusion office). Ultimately, student success is not the purview of one office; rather, it is the result of combined work by everyone at the institution. Working together across college, division, department, and unit lines allows for the identification and removal of barriers to student success.

Back to the Basics: Writing Strategy

Within the context of a culture committed to communication, basic written communication strategies matter. Strategies, however, will always be in service to the culture itself. With this in mind, there are a few strategies that remain constant, regardless of ongoing technological changes.

On a practical level, advising administrators must recognize that all communication is persuasive, yet there are few opportunities for developing these communication muscles, aside from on-the-job practice. Colleagues early in their careers often lament the absence of explicit instruction, practice, and feedback in their graduate programs in strategically adjusting communications to suit a range of individuals and groups across a variety of situations. To complicate matters further, effective communication is expected in professional contexts and does not call attention to itself, while less-developed communication skills are difficult to ignore and have the potential to impact the credibility of both the individual and their unit. Advising administrators should model appropriate communications to help early career professionals learn.

Therefore, strategic communication requires a basic understanding of rhetoric. According to Aristotle, rhetoric is an ability to see, in any given situation, the available means of persuasion. This ranges from how new projects are introduced to colleagues during a staff meeting to how to make sense of data in a report to the provost; it includes the more pathos-driven strategies for responding to a student who has just learned that they are on academic suspension or an institutional colleague who is expressing dissatisfaction with advising services. Annual or regular feedback to employees is included. Each rhetorical situation dictates the length, logic, and tone of an advising administrator's message. Advising administrators can learn to effortlessly pivot from one rhetorical situation to the next in the form of repeated practice over time, the examination of authentic texts as models, and the courage to solicit feedback from trusted colleagues on drafts.

Additionally, an ongoing cultivation of unit-level critical language awareness supports inclusion as a habit of mind. Because written communications are not neutral, as they are not "divorced from social context, politics, culture, and power" (Street, 1993, as cited in Richardson, 2003, p. 9), the development of metalinguistic awareness is foundational in becoming anti-racist communicators. In a position statement of the Conference on College Composition and Communication (2021), White Language Supremacy (WLS) is exposed for its perpetuation of systemic and structural harms:

> Contextualized within present exigencies, antiracist educators must work alongside students, communities, and institutions to push for the dismantling of WLS because of its deleterious effects on Black, Indigenous, and people of color (BIPOC), domination and dehumanization of all people, and its detrimental effects to our environment and its resources.
>
> *(para. 1)*

Metalinguistic awareness is an "individual's ability to focus attention on language as an object in and of itself, to reflect upon language, and to evaluate it" (Thomas, 1988, as cited in Spellerberg, 2015, p. 21). Like teachers and tutors, advising staff should be encouraged to "develop a critical consciousness of the effects of their choices at an individual and institutional level, and—most importantly—[to cultivate] ... a sense of agency in combating, linguistically and otherwise, the injustices they encounter along the way" (Greenfield, 2011, p. 58). Additionally, the use of singular *they*, as opposed to binary pronouns (as affirmed in authoritative style guides), is another step toward more inclusive written communication.

Two other more basic considerations include the rule of three and the role of conventions. The rule of three is a strategic communication principle attributed to Aristotle, who observed that individuals are more likely to remember information in groups of three. This pattern can take the form of distinct words, phrases, or ideas. The human brain is wired to recognize patterns, and three being the smallest pattern promotes easy recall and greater retention. Thus, strategic communication—whether a presentation for prospective students and their support communities, an email message to campus, or a written professional development plan for a new advisor—is most effective and engaging when there are three main points.

The second consideration is conventions, which makes for clearer communication. Conventions include grammar, punctuation, and spelling, as well as organizing and formatting expectations of a particular genre. For example, a formal email message contains particular conventions that are specific to that genre; an annual report has particular conventions that must be followed, as does the section on advising in an accreditation report. Learning to recognize that professional documents vary in form according to rhetorical situations is key to effective written communication. An advising administrator is encouraged to tap into campus resources—like the Writing Center or writing and communications faculty—to assist in the development of professional learning opportunities for themselves and for advisors.

Conclusion

Academic advising is fundamentally relational. One of the most vital skills in building relationships with students and colleagues is communication. A communication vision that places courtesy and inclusion as its highest priorities, with its acute focus not on strategies but on people, can uplift unit morale. In such a context, the advising administrator and advisors will know that "they are judged not so much against the standard of other [advisors] in similar settings, but against the standards set by the nicest people giving services anywhere" (Lee, 2004, p. 24). Accuracy of and efficiencies in communications will follow, always in service to courtesy and inclusion. Advising administrators who remain intentional in their commitment to a culture of communication will soon find that they have established credibility in the area of service excellence that other units will emulate. Ultimately, a culture of communication is key to unlocking strategic communication and is essential to student success.

Reflection Questions

1 How would you describe the communication culture within your unit? Would you say that the culture is intentional or by accident? Why?
2 Courtesy, inclusion, accuracy, and efficiency are examples of habits of mind for cultivating a culture of communication, with courtesy and inclusion positioned at the top of the ladder. Working with the colleagues in your unit, determine the habits of mind that could guide your communications, along with their positions on the ladder of priorities. Make a unit-level commitment to infuse the habits of mind in all exchanges, both spoken and written, formal and informal.
3 What would students currently say about communications from academic advising? Do you have mechanisms in place to solicit feedback from students? If not, what are some possible avenues for gauging communication successes and challenges?
4 How can you ensure that advising communications are inclusive and equitable?

Note

1 Attributed to a variety of individuals, but most often Maya Angelou.

References

Ben-Jacob, M. G. & Glazerman, A. H. (2021). The ethical implications of the overuse of technology in education. *Journal of Educational Technology Systems*, *50*(1), 5–8. https://doi.org/10.1177/00472395211013049.

Conference on College Composition & Communication. (2021, June). *CCCC statement on white language supremacy.* https://cccc.ncte.org/cccc/white-language-supremacy.

Costa, A. L. (2008). Describing the habits of mind. In A. L. Costa, & B. Kallick (Eds.), *Learning and leading with habits of mind: 16 essential characteristics for success* (pp. 15–41). Association for Supervision and Curriculum Development.

Crookston, B. B. (1972). A developmental view of academic advising as teaching. *Journal of College Student Personnel*, *13*(1), 12–17.

EAB. (2017, October 27). *ConnectED: Dr. Chris Hutt, Kennesaw State University: How a three sentence email changed my advising* [Video]. Youtube. https://www.youtube.com/watch?v=lXo27ywJZ5U.

Greenfield, L. (2011). The "standard English" fairy tale: A rhetorical analysis of racist pedagogies and commonplace assumptions about language diversity. In L. Greenfield, & K. Rowan (Eds.), *Writing centers and the new racism: A call for sustainable dialogue and change* (pp. 33–60). Utah State University Press.

Hallahan, K., Holtzhausen, D., van Ruler, B., Vercic, D., & Sriramesh, K. (2007). Defining strategic communication. *International Journal of Strategic Communication, 1*(1), 3–35. https://doi.org/10.1080/15531180701285244.

Institute for Habits of Mind. (2022). *Striving for accuracy and precision.* https://www.habitsofmindinstitute.org/striving-for-accuracy-and-precision/.

Jordan, P. (2015). Effective communication skills. In P. Folsom, F. Yoder, & J. E. Joslin (Eds.), *The new advisor guidebook: Mastering the art of academic advising* (2nd ed., pp. 213–228). Jossey-Bass.

Lee, F. (2004). *If Disney ran your hospital: 9½ things you would do differently.* Second River Healthcare Press.

NACADA: The Global Community for Academic Advising. (2006). *Concept of academic advising.* https://nacada.ksu.edu/Resources/Pillars/Concept.aspx.

NACADA: The Global Community for Academic Advising. (2017a). *Academic advising core competencies model.* https://nacada.ksu.edu/Resources/Pillars/CoreCompetencies.aspx.

Nutt, C. L. (2000). One-on-one advising. In V. N. Gordon, & W. R. Habley (Eds.), *Academic advising: A comprehensive handbook* (pp. 220–227). Jossey-Bass.

O'Mara, J., & Richter, A. (2014). *Global diversity and inclusion benchmarks: Standards for organizations around the world.* The Diversity Collegium. https://ww.omaraassoc.com/pdf/GDIB_2014_Standard_A4_Version.pdf.

Richardson, E. (2003). *African American literacies.* Routledge.

Roper, L. (2002). Relationships: The critical ties that bind professionals. *New Directions for Student Services, 2002*(98), 11–26. https://doi.org/10.1002/ss.46.

Spellerberg, S. M. (2015). Metalinguistic awareness and academic achievement in a linguistically diverse school setting: A study of lower secondary pupils in Denmark. *International Journal of Multilingualism, 13*(1), 19–39. https://doi.org/10.1080/14790718.2015.1053891.

Swecker, H. K., Fifolt, M., & Searby, L. (2013). Academic advising and first-generation college students: A quantitative study on student retention. *NACADA Journal, 33*(1), 46–53. https://doi.org/10.12930/NACADA-13-192.

Thomas, C., & McFarlane, B. (2018). Playing the long game: Surviving fads and creating lasting student success through academic advising. *New Directions in Higher Education, 2018*(184), 97–106. https://doi.org/10.1002/he.20306.

Thorson, K. (2013). *Strategic communication.* Oxford Bibliographies. https://doi.org/10.1093/OBO/9780199756841-0007.

Tufte, T., & Mefalopulos, P. (2009). *Participatory communication: A practical guide.* World Bank. https://openknowledge.worldbank.org/handle/10986/5940.

VOICES FROM THE FIELD

Building Relationships for Successful Communication

Elaine Lewis

Often advisors are easily frustrated when students do not read our communications. I was recently in a meeting where an advisor joked about reading their email as closely as students. This remark struck me—if even our advisors are not reading our communication, it is time to think differently about our strategy. As advising administrators, we must set a strong example of good communication in all its varied forms for our advisors. Ultimately, through my work in first-year advising, I have learned that good communication is about creating strong relationships with students and partners.

Student Communication

Each semester, our advisors set a goal to have a live, meaningful interaction with every student on their caseloads. As a result of our institution's participation in NACADA's Excellence in Academic Advising program, we know live interactions (i.e., in-person, video, or phone meetings) significantly impact the student-advisor relationship, which positively impacts students' academic success and persistence. It is important to be proactive in communicating to students the value of their academic advisor throughout their educational experience.

To relay this value, we often rely on other forms of communication, most commonly written messaging through email. Now, this is the moment where every reader will collectively sigh, "but students don't read my emails." Your comment is accurate. At my institution, students identified as high-risk open our email messages at a rate of 7%–12%. We

DOI: 10.4324/9781003437598-24

cannot give up on our students, so we need to think differently about our communication strategy and efforts. For every item shared with students, we first consider what benefit the message brings students and the best method to share. To do this, our team considers personalization, integrity, and creativity in our communication.

Like many institutions, we use a predictive analytics tool to personalize communication to identify students who may need intervention. The communication component of this tool allows us to conduct large-scale communication in a way that appears personal. Student focus groups showed us that these messages must be short, direct, and action driven. Our message with the highest response rate asks students to rate the semester on a five-point scale. We also see success with flashy subject lines (such as "free money!") around FAFSA completion and "Registration isn't Tetris" related to using a pre-scheduling tool.

Next, we need to protect the integrity of our communication. Advisors have wide access to students. Other campus community members often try to take advantage of this by asking us to send students messages, most often announcements, on their behalf. As administrators, it is our role to act as gatekeepers for these types of requests. I created a set of guidelines to help determine what campus partner messages to send students, considering factors such as impact, relevance, connection to academic advising, and frequency and urgency of the request. Most items do not fall within the guidelines, so I send them to advisors as a general announcement instead. We have also succeeded in using a generic email address to send all announcements; this protects the integrity of the messages advisors send from their accounts, so students are more likely to prioritize opening their messages.

Last, we need to think creatively about how we communicate and consider how our students receive information. Many institutions have transitioned to text messaging for some communication. This is a great method to create brief, action-driven communication. In our roles as administrators, we should consider holistic communication with students, the varied ways we can communicate, and the format of communication most successful for various types of messages.

Texting is not the only way to improve our communication with students—we also need to consider what grabs a student's attention. For example, post-traditional students may be more receptive to a direct message through a social media platform. Additionally, the advisors on our team have learned incorporating "emojis" in a subject line of an email increases the open rate, and images or infographics can relay key points in new ways. Our advisors need not be social media stars, but we must learn to embrace new, creative ways to communicate with students.

Communicating with Families

In first-year advising, we frequently interact with parents and other student support team members. Up to this point, parents have had access to all their student's academic information, so losing this access can be an adjustment. It is important that families feel confident in their student's educational experience and understand how their place in the student's academic life shifts.

For many parents and key support individuals, especially those who did not attend college, having a conversation with their student about college can be challenging. Many colleges and universities have individuals on staff with the unique responsibility of supporting parents and families. Common strategies they use are newsletters or calendars to help guide support team members in student conversations. As administrators, we should collaborate with these family programs to share advising-related messages, like questions to ask a student considering course withdrawal, the date of next semester registration and the importance of registering early, or career trajectories for their major. Providing these conversation points to a student's support team gives families additional confidence as they show support for the student's academic success.

In advising, we often have direct interactions with families as well. Advisors should aim to develop constructive relationships with families that align with a student's desire. It is important to respect the role the student has created for their family in their education, even when it is no role at all. This can be challenging for parents and support team members when trying to assist their students. Family Educational Rights and Privacy Act (FERPA) educational privacy laws prevent us from sharing specific information. Our advisors help parents understand that they can view FERPA, which is in place to keep the student's information private and secure, as an ally to our students to help maintain their safety. When framed around protecting the safety of students, parents are more understanding of FERPA restrictions. We also spend time walking students through the process of allowing or disallowing access to FERPA-protected information and the varied types of information that can be shared through approved information releases. Ultimately, we must balance our critical responsibility to student privacy with the desire of parents and support team members to invest in their student's educational journey to ensure academic and personal success for students.

Creating Faculty Connections

Much like FERPA is an ally for advisors in the communication process, we need to make faculty our allies. This is even more critical when faculty have academic and career advising responsibilities. Faculty who provide academic advising need to be empowered to support students and recognize if they have any limitations to their advising knowledge. As administrators, we are often responsible for providing this education. I have seen various models to disseminate information to faculty members, and each of these successful models has three key elements. First, they show faculty members the value advising adds for themselves and their students. Second, they make resources on advising readily accessible and easy to understand. Finally, they convey to faculty members a foundational knowledge of advising strategies and express our willingness to help in difficult situations.

Communication and strong relationships with our faculty are critical to a successful student experience. If you are part of a community without faculty advising, like I am, it is still critical to communicate with faculty and involve them in the advising process. Faculty members need to understand the value of academic advising as a teaching and learning practice. Our team has found that a faculty advisory board is a great way to relay our value. Our faculty board members gain a deeper insight into the critical role of advising, help share our advising work with their colleagues, and advocate for advising when we face opposition. We have also found faculty recommendations very helpful because they meet with students daily and understand student needs holistically.

Collaborating with Campus Partners, Administrators, and Other Stakeholders

There are countless other individuals in our campus community and beyond interested in academic advising. We must actively engage with these individuals through various communication channels. Campus partners, like those in orientation and financial aid, are important for our students' success. The relationship we create with campus partners must be reciprocal. Advertising is a quick and easy way to show the value of advising to a campus partner. Many creative ways to advertise to students do not involve email. One method we have recently tried is leveraging virtual backgrounds in online appointments, and they often spark a conversation to provide further information. We have succeeded in advertising key financial aid and scholarship deadlines this way. In gratitude for our efforts, our financial aid team created a private chat channel for our advisors to ask key financial aid questions. Now we are not just advertising on behalf of another office, but we are also helping students get critical information.

When discussing academic advising, we frequently assume that everyone knows our work's value. While this might be the case for some, it is not for all. As we work with campus and community partners, it is important to have an "elevator pitch" to succinctly explain what we do, how we do it, and why we do it. Administrators, and even our advisors, need to be able to articulate these things. For our team, we have three key points: we are proactive, holistic, and data-informed in our practice. It is also important to have some key data metrics available to show the value and impact of our work in a more tangible way. We need to be well equipped with the knowledge to successfully communicate our work to those unfamiliar with our services and value, no matter the time or location.

Conclusions

Setting strong examples and building relationships are keys to the success of communication in academic advising. We are responsible for communicating successfully with multiple stakeholders—students, families, faculty, and campus partners. Administrators are influential in advising-related communication and using strategies, such as those discussed above, in helping us provide an example to those advisors we interact with daily. Ultimately, no matter what group we communicate with, we must recognize that all our efforts to communicate and build strong relationships positively benefit our students, their success, their graduation, and their futures.

14

SUCCESSION PLANNING AND DEVELOPMENT

Karen L. Archambault

Students benefit from advising that is comprehensive and consistent. Such advising requires that advising personnel be well trained and well guided with effective supervision, management, and administration. Planning for the future—supporting personnel growth and planning for retirements, promotions, and other vacancies—is essential to ensuring continuity of service. A future focus ensures that students receive effective support for reaching academic goals and advisors have positive experiences with their institutions.

In this chapter, readers are encouraged to consider a view of future planning that considers the concept of *succession development* rather than traditional *succession planning*. Traditionally, succession planning focuses on identifying the connection between individual members of the team and potential future positions. In contrast, succession development is departmental and institutional in scope, considering strengths and challenges of the advising unit, and differentiating between structural and human resource concerns (Stangl, 2021). This relatively new term, found more often in public and business writing than in traditional academic research, defines an organization as focused on the future. This comprehensive future focus begins with departmental awareness, further develops through positional and functional awareness, and is supported by knowledge and information held both individually and collectively. Far from suggesting that succession development ignores individuals, this chapter culminates in considering how individual roles and departmental needs align, how leaders can be identified, and how succession can and should consider diversity of thought and experience. In doing so, this chapter

DOI: 10.4324/9781003437598-25

emphasizes a view of future planning that highlights equity and diversity and encourages departments and leaders to recognize the value brought by those with varied lived experiences.

This text recognizes that traditional succession planning often limits advancement for those of diverse backgrounds, especially when racial, ethnic, or gender identities may diverge from the past advising leadership. It also considers how succession development can assist in overcoming these barriers. Succession development allows and even encourages greater equity among personnel by emphasizing varied skill sets rather than structuring succession around the existing hierarchy. A mindset toward succession development has the dual benefit of providing effective support for both the unit and the individual. Succession development, when teamed with employee performance, has been shown to create a more positive relationship with employees (Ali et al., 2019).

Distinctions between Succession Planning and Succession Development

While it may seem no more than a matter of semantics, there are in fact distinct differences between succession planning and succession development. Upon review of these distinctions, administrators will find organizational value in a new model.

Traditional Succession Planning

Both succession planning and succession development intend to ensure that an operating unit or organization has the people available to fill needed positions when they arise. As described above, succession planning is individualized in nature, focused on specific positions and identifying how critical roles and positions will continue to be filled in the future (Rothwell, 2010). This positional view has some merit. For example, if one assumes that a director of advising is essential to the smooth operation of an advising unit and a long-term director announces a pending retirement, it makes sense to plan ahead to ensure continuity. This approach, however, works best for expected changes and assumes that current skill sets of personnel match the future needs for positional openings.

Succession Development

Unlike traditional succession planning, succession development assumes that while change is inevitable, not all change can be anticipated (Stangl, 2021). As a result, succession development favors creating a wide and multifaceted "bench" of talent, in line with the current and potential needs of the department or division. Creating a pool of talented potential leaders through succession development focuses on professional development for future leadership, skill building, building connections with peers to advance shared knowledge, and continually evaluating the needs of the organization to ensure that the loss of any single member, anticipated or not, does not result in gaps in service to students (Stangl, 2021). Certainly, identifying a single person for a single promotion opportunity works well for that person and that position, but in the longer term, this approach does little to support or enhance the organization as a whole. Succession development provides an administrative strategy to prepare for a future in which the personnel, the institution, and the needs of students may fluctuate. This approach centers planning on departmental longevity rather than positional longevity.

The strategy, and the chapter, begins with thinking about why succession matters and then shifts to departmental awareness, encouraging evaluation of departmental strengths, challenges, structure, and processes. After ensuring a clear view of their department, leaders can shift to functional awareness. Only as a culminating step should leaders consider alignment between individuals and roles, affirming that the needs of students drive the organization, rather than defining the advising work by the skill sets of the current personnel. After guiding leaders through this thought process, this chapter presents a case study that presents these steps in action.

Beginning Succession Development

Successful succession development requires buy-in from the start. To garner that buy-in, administrators should identify and name the *why* both for their institution and for advising more broadly, and they should be able to demonstrate that steps toward succession development are in place.

Why Succession Matters

There is little literature about planning for succession in higher education (Washington, 2016). Much of the available research focuses exclusively on the presidency (see also Barden, 2010; Hearn, 2006; Martin & Samels, 2004). Some scholars suggest that higher education practices run counter to the demands of succession planning (Hoffman et al., 2014; Sanaghan, 2016). Sanaghan (2016), for example, suggested that, unlike in corporate structures, it is "easy to get trapped into a single career path" (p. 28) in higher education, which may limit options for growth. González (2010) stressed that higher education institutions have limited training and support for leadership development, especially for women and minoritized people, and often focus on prestige from external candidates rather than developing internal talent. As a consequence, administrators must translate practices from other fields into academic advising. First among these translations is in the *why* of succession planning—why does it matter and what benefit does it bring?

Advising units might be compared to small or family businesses, which often have limited employee numbers and need to focus on the immediate (Leonard, 2015). Much like many advising units, small businesses may offer limited chances for career growth or promotion. When promotions do exist, they may be performative or based upon longevity rather than providing new opportunities that support the future of the organization. As a result, small and family businesses may fail to plan for the future, considering financial rewards rather than long-term planning as their strategy for the retention of high-quality employees (Leonard, 2015). Similarly, many advising units develop career ladders that have, at their core, the completion of benchmarks: length of service, completion of training, or similar markers in an employee's development. Units may have several advisors moving up the career ladder but few if any identified as having the needed skills to serve as leaders of the unit. Like in small businesses, the potential benefit of a future focus goes beyond financial support for the individual or retaining high-quality employees but considers the preservation of the unit as a whole (Leonard, 2015). This outcome may be amplified when considering the larger institution into which the advising unit fits. Future planning of the advising unit within rather than outside of the institution improves the ability of the advising unit to support its students and personnel through a road map for budgeting, hiring, and resource allocation. To best prepare for the future, advising units of any size should consider their organizational needs and determine how potential personnel roles can be harnessed to support their students.

Career Ladders as a Start to Succession Development

As suggested, many advising departments have career ladders to support the development of advisors' skills and abilities. Both career advancement and guidance for administrators are positive outcomes to effective career ladders (Thomas & Cunningham, 2018). Career ladders also provide a foundation for future succession development through alignment of skills, knowledge, and abilities with each tier of the career ladder. When done well, as shown in Chapter 18, career ladders utilize NACADA's Core

Competencies to ensure that personnel have a clear view of what they need to develop to advance within their department. The required evaluation of skills and abilities can serve departments well in understanding their advising needs and in supporting future succession work. However, because career ladders are often envisioned from the individual perspective—as in, what does an advisor need to know or what skills do they need to master to advance—they provide a valuable but incomplete step toward comprehensive succession development. Such development requires a plan that incorporates the missions, vision, and goals of the unit, as well as a complete view of the future expectations for the needs of the unit and the students it serves (Kaufman, 2003).

Steps in Succession Development

To effectively match a plan to the mission, vision, goals, and needs of the future unit, advising leaders should consider several aspects in succession development, including considering the student, the department, the personnel, and knowledge sources. In each step, units must consider a wide range of departmental characteristics and data points to further understand and focus their planning.

Identifying Needs and Demographics of Students

Perhaps most crucial in considering the future of a department or unit is to first understand the students served and any future changes in the demographics or needs of the students. For example, higher education in the United States has witnessed shifts, not the least of which is in decreased enrollment for many institutions and higher education as a whole, particularly in public institutions (National Student Clearinghouse Research Center, 2022). However, how these broad shifts impact a particular advising department or approach depends on understanding the individual institution. Some of the knowledge about students comes from knowing the institution and unit (Archambault, 2015). More urgently, though, for the purposes of succession planning, the administrator must understand that the personal and changing demographics of students may shift what is needed in the future. Hermann (2021) argued that demographic changes on the horizon for college students dramatically shift how faculty members should prepare for and teach their classes, reflecting increases in low-income students, first-generation students, and students of a wide range of ethnic and racial backgrounds. Similarly, changing student demographics may shift how advising leaders prepare for the future of their departments, including how personnel represent and identify with their students.

Identifying Departmental Strengths and Challenges

Upon understanding the students served, advising leadership should consider departmental strengths and challenges. To be effective, leaders should consider and clearly establish what the *department's* strengths are, including what programs and services serve students well, rather than beginning with identifying the strengths and challenges of individual current personnel. Desarno et al. (2021) argued that effective planning begins with connections to the mission and future needs. Advising departments should consider whether they are equipped to manage challenges that may be on the horizon. Departmental strengths and challenges may include staffing, resources, training, and access to collaboration with other departments or outside agencies, as well as programming, services, and student support. Strengths in staffing may include the specific skills of the current workforce, long tenure at the institution, or unique dedication amongst team members. Challenges in staffing might include interpersonal conflict, limits in personnel numbers, or resistance to change. Resource strengths could be financial in nature or they could be internal partnerships that allow for professional development or trading of valued skills and time. Similarly, resource challenges might result from financial deficits or may be the result of poor planning and management.

Identifying the Sources of Challenges and Strengths

While in the prior step leaders find and name the challenges and strengths of the department or unit, this step identifies their source. Strong programming can result from years of development, from extensive external resources, from a strong commitment to professional development, or from a particularly skilled individual staff member. Weak resources might stem from institutional budget limitations, a lack of understanding amongst decision makers about the value of advising, or unfocused priorities. Each of these mandates a different response. In considering strengths and challenges, this step can firm up or call into question the ways in which strengths can be sustained into the future. Accordingly, any future planning should seek to resolve or address challenges, by developing new strengths, and planning to address gaps between needs and resources.

Consider the following example: An advising unit serving undecided students is planning for a stronger future. The unit identifies strength in leadership dedicated to student success and a professional development/ training program that is delivered effectively and engagingly. In addition, the unit benefits from long-term personnel retention and a director who has been recognized as a campus and community leader. However, all is not perfect; the unit struggles with its institutional position and has recently moved under a new organizational structure. The unit has also recently had its budget cut dramatically as the institution struggles with enrollment.

In this scenario, the unit has numerous strengths that benefit its students. However, these strengths are built primarily on individual personnel. A departure could create a significant loss as it is not only the loss of a person, but the loss of a source of organizational strength. Challenges such as budgeting and reporting relationships, on the other hand, are structural and may therefore be more entrenched. A flipped scenario, with strengths in organization and challenges in staffing, may be more easily overcome. This is not to say that personnel challenges are easy but that planning for overcoming entrenched organizational challenges are that much more difficult.

Identify Outdated or Underutilized Functionality

While many advising units are under-resourced, they may also find themselves overextended with numerous competing priorities. Priorities may be essential to the success of students and central to the departmental mission, or they may be the result of many years of operation without introspection. Such legacy operations might include programs in which students show little interest or that are better presented via technology. In planning for the future, advising units must review their functions; prioritize mission central components; and determine whether programs, services, and offerings have outlived their usefulness.

Student Perception and Experience of Structure, Processes, and Staffing

While general departmental awareness is necessary, even more essential is viewing these components through the lens of students. Even seemingly flawless structures or processes are meaningless if they do not serve students well. Similarly, personnel are not effective if they do not adjust to students' changing needs. To a great extent, this is the most crucial intersection for succession development in advising—ensuring that students are met by the structures, processes, and people to support their future success.

Positional and Functional Awareness

Once departmental knowledge and awareness are established, leaders should consider work that needs to be done as compared to the personnel roles that currently comprise their organizational structure. In other words, succession development should align the needs of the department (as understood through the investigation described above) with the staffing (Desarno et al., 2021). One department might have extensive needs for particular skills during peak times but entirely different needs at other times of the year, for example. A department with an extensive role in orientation has distinct needs from one whose focus is on living learning communities or one whose emphasis is on first-year programming. The approach that follows can guide a determination of personnel needed to serve students well.

Evaluating Staffing Needs for Programs and Services

First, programs and services should be evaluated for specific staffing needs. This includes the number of personnel and the specific and unique skill sets required to support student needs. For example, one program might require high levels of institutional knowledge while another may benefit more from extensive relational or counseling skills. Others might need to specifically understand the needs of particular students, such as first-generation college students, or underrepresented and minoritized students. Similarly, some programs and services require specific transferrable skills, such as extensive organization or planning skills or superior talent with presentations.

Current and Future Organizational Structures

In addition to understanding the staffing characteristics needed, leaders considering succession development should consider how skill development might fit into an organizational hierarchy. Hierarchical structures are inherent in most if not all organizational units; they may have negative connotations such as through imbalanced power or they may have positive impacts in creating what Bunderson et al. (2016) referred to as "cascading influence." They can also impact the ability to identify and cultivate effective succession development. For example, flat hierarchical structures may struggle with identifying future leaders, as gaps between leadership and other personnel are too wide; more expansive hierarchies may support more layers of leadership development (Goldman, 2020). In flat structures with homogenous job descriptions, advancement based on time of service may appear as the primary distinguishing factor between personnel, while in more complex hierarchies, there may be more differentiation between tasks and roles. Effective succession development should consider not only whether individuals fit into the current organizational structures but whether that structure serves students well. Hierarchy and organizational structures do not necessarily limit growth, but they may change the way that skills are evaluated.

Informational Knowledge

After examining the match between organizational needs and the structure, succession development should then examine how information will be shared and transferred. Oftentimes, information is held by a single expert or a limited group; while this approach holds the benefit of allowing for potential deep knowledge, it creates potential gaps in the ability to serve students. Should a departmental expert be absent, especially if this absence is unplanned, students may suffer. Sharing information is therefore an essential part of any succession development (Desarno et al., 2021). Advisor professional development and cross-training can assist with shared knowledge. In addition, departments should seek to establish clear and consistent standard operating procedures to ensure that consistency can be maintained where needed.

Methods for Sharing Information

To effectively develop a plan for disseminating information, leaders must understand both the knowledge and the extent to which information is held by individuals, rather than shared. Information is often viewed as power (Foucault, 1980). As a result, leaders benefit from determining how to incentivize sharing knowledge so that future planning does not suffer from a lack of information. Personnel reviews and written evaluations (discussed in greater depth in Chapter 17) should encourage and value training of peers, sharing of information, and collaboration.

In addition to valuing the sharing of knowledge on an individual level, succession should emphasize how the department will encourage the sharing of information. This might include formal professional development or less formal conversations with experts. Information sharing allows for skill development amongst those who may be newer to the institution or limited by their experience or access, further enhancing succession development. According to Vito (2018), satisfaction amongst personnel was enhanced by increasing the availability of knowledge sharing, which encourages personnel to be retained and consider future opportunities.

People Awareness

Effective succession development aligns people to departmental, positional, and informational awareness. This is not to suggest that people are ignored until this point; quite to the contrary, the best decisions of an advising unit are made with an understanding of both students and personnel in mind. However, people awareness goes beyond mindfulness of the impact of decisions on personnel, and instead connects roles and individuals in an intentional manner, strongly connecting the needs of the organization and the potential of personnel (Fuentes, 2020). People awareness stresses how leadership can be cultivated in roles outside of official leadership and how realistic expectations can be set for the development of leadership without a necessary expectation of promotion or positional leadership. In addition, people awareness recognized that, too often, those outside of the historical norms of a department are often not recognized as bringing value, especially those of racial, ethnic, or gender minorities whose diversity of thought and experience is seen as "different" instead of valuable. While identifying personnel with potential can certainly be positive, it can also result in overlooking potential in others (Charan et al., 2011).

Diversity, Inclusion, and Equity in Succession Development

Such a limited view may identify leadership potential only in personnel who share characteristics such as race, gender, and ethnicity with current leadership. For example, Giuliano et al. (2011) found that promotions in one industry were limited and discipline more frequent by White managers when paired with non-White personnel; furthermore, they found that this bias was unconscious, not intentional. Though they were not studying academia, their findings demonstrate the need to combat implicit bias of managers across workplaces, including advising. Similarly, Fernandez and Fernandez-Mateo (2006) identified that minoritized individuals may be excluded from good job opportunities through limited networks, suggesting that they may never reach opportunities to be promoted. Far from uniquely related to the racial history of the United States, Quillian and Midtbøen's (2021) review of more than 140 studies related to ethno-racial minorities globally similarly concluded that such discrimination is a significant global concern. Hekman et al. (2016) suggested that racial and ethnic minorities, as well as women, are often discouraged from supporting each other's success and may be judged as less effective for doing so. Workplace environments may therefore limit the ability for minoritized individuals to be seen in the model of traditional leaders. Quach (2018) argued that underlying trauma experienced by minoritized people, including the impact of implicit bias and microaggressions, influences adjustment to traditional workplace expectations, many of which have little to do with the ability of personnel to be successful. Those looking for new leaders must recognize potential beyond traditional expectations; as a result, advising units can support overcoming racial and social trauma, rather than limiting upward mobility.

Recognizing Personnel Interests

Not all strong employees want to move up in a hierarchy; for some personnel, the desire for recognition and appreciation is distinct from a desire to be promoted. Scott (2019) referred to those seeking growth as *superstars* and those seeking to be strong contributors without upward mobility as *rockstars*. Too often, leadership identifies only the superstars as contributors and fails to recognize the strengths of rockstars as part of the foundation of the organization (Scott, 2019). For an advising unit, a traditional succession plan might focus only on leadership positions and ignore the needs for strength across the unit. Failure to recognize the strengths that rockstars bring may also prevent identification of skills across the team and assume that leadership must account for all knowledge within the unit.

Using Succession to Advance Departmental and Individual Development

In centering departmental needs, succession moves beyond identification and into development. Hiring should focus on skill sets that are missing amongst current personnel rather than on a job description shared across multiple positions, thus encouraging diversity of thought and experience. This might be accomplished through differentiated job descriptions, specialized project assignments, or a search for specific prior experiences amongst new hires. Professional development can be provided specifically for the needs of the department's students and programs but with an eye toward skill development rather than simply absorbing information. In addition, individual skills can be cultivated and matched with needed roles, rather than asking one, or a few, leaders to be all things to all people. As described, organizational hierarchy may be necessary—someone needs to sign forms and process approvals—but this need not limit the potential of personnel to develop skills that serve their students well. An advising unit still needs supervisors, but in effective succession development, they serve as leaders of vision, rather than managers who need to be experts and authorities on all topics.

Conclusion

Moving away from "tapping" individual personnel is a clear benefit of succession development, founded in a comprehensive needs assessment rather than attempting only to identify leaders. Individual staff-based succession planning, in which one individual is connected to one leadership position, may lead others to feel unappreciated, undervalued, or limited.

A more comprehensive view encourages valuing the gifts and talents of each individual, allowing all to grow.

Even more urgently, though, succession development encourages advising units to be introspective and forward thinking. Rather than focusing only on top levels of leadership within the unit, succession development locates serving students as the primary goal, with effective oversight as an outcome rather than a goal. Departments seeking to plan for their future are encouraged to consider succession development to support their aims to serve students and advance toward equity. This chapter has emphasized moving from the very specific nature of choosing a next leader to considering succession as a holistic evaluation of advising needs. In doing so, leaders are encouraged to engage in succession development as a continual process rather than a one-time effort.

Case Study

This case study asks readers to consider how succession development might be implemented in an advising department in the following example.

An advising director is planning for the future of a centralized department with 10 full time advisors and two assistant directors. The team has benefited from longevity amongst personnel with most personnel having tenure for at least 15 years. However, several advisors and both assistant directors are slated to retire within the next two years. When their positions opened, each was approached individually with an emphasis on departmental fit. The department's work has focused on individual relationships with students; the institution served a largely homogenous student body, primarily drawn from suburbs surrounding the institution. The institution's population has changed in the past decade, but the department's services and approach have been slower to adjust. The director has been with the team for approximately five years—much shorter than many others in the team, but long enough to have made their mark as a leader.

In reviewing the department's changing work, the director has established that while the department continues to provide individual student appointments, it will need to continue a shift from providing general (and somewhat homogenous) advising services to a cohort-based programming and services specific to individual student groups. Services developed specifically target the needs of first-year students, honors students, first-generation students, undecided students, career/technical program students, transfer students, and seniors. The new approach shows great early promise, as shown in correlated retention increases and early signs of closing a gap in retention, grade point average, and graduation rates between BIPOC and first-generation students and the institution overall. In evaluating these programs, the director identifies that while individual appointments remain important, the new nature of the division requires an emphasis on planning and program delivery and greater support for collaborative work to solidify the early wins from the approach.

The director recognizes that there is a disconnect between the needs of the division and the skills and abilities of current personnel; job descriptions are outdated, emphasizing individual student meetings rather than the programming that will increasingly become the norm for the department. In addition, the director discovers that the current organizational structure—a director, two assistant directors, and a team of equals—fails to meet the needs of the department, which requires greater collaboration and timely information sharing. As a result, the director considers reorganization into teams, a redesign of job descriptions, and a rethinking of leadership for the department. The director seeks a future focus to ensure that the advising unit will serve its students well.

Case Study Questions

1 How could the director and team use a succession development framework to rethink job descriptions to create a better match to the needs of the department?
2 How might the director determine the skill sets of current personnel, beyond job descriptions, and match the needs of the changing department and student body?
3 How might the role of leadership be reconsidered to emphasize the team redesign?
4 Given what is known here about this team and department, what might a comprehensive succession development proposal look like?

Reflection Questions

1 How prepared is your advising unit for a shift in leadership?
2 How does your department evaluate or identify leadership as compared to the departmental needs?
3 If a position within your department were to unexpectedly become open, or if you were to be granted budget for a new position, how might you evaluate how to fill this role within a succession development framework?
4 How can your department better recognize diversity as a part of your succession development and planning?

References

Ali, Z., Mahmood, B., & Mehreen, A. (2019). Linking succession planning to employee performance: The mediating roles of career development and performance appraisal. *Australian Journal of Career Development, 28*(2), 112–121. https://doi.org/10.1177/1038416219830419.

Archambault, K. (2015). Developing self-knowledge as a first step toward cultural competence. In P. Folsom, F. Yoder, & J. Joslin (Eds.), *The new advisor guidebook: Mastering the art of advising* (pp. 185–201). Jossey-Bass.

Barden, D. M. (2010). Where will you find your future leaders? The time has come for colleges and universities to get serious about succession planning. *The Chronicle of Higher Education, 56*(17), D20–D21.

Bunderson, J. S., van der Vegt, G. S., Cantimur, Y., & Rink, F. (2016). Different views of hierarchy and why they matter: Hierarchy as inequality or as cascading influence. *The Academy of Management Journal, 59*(4), 1265–1289. http://doi.org/10.5465/amj.2014.0601.

Charan, R., Drotter, S., & Noel, J. (2011). *The leadership pipeline: How to build the leadership powered company* (2nd ed.). Jossey-Bass.

Desarno, J., Perez, M., Rivas, R., Sandate, I., Reed, C., & Fonseca, I. (2021). Succession planning within the health care organization: Human resources management and human capital management considerations. *Nurse Leader, 19*(4), 411–415. https://doi.org/10.1016/j.mnl.2020.08.010.

Fernandez, R. M., & Fernandez-Mateo, I. (2006). Networks, race, and hiring. *American Sociological Review, 71*(1), 42–71. https://doi.org/10.1177/000312240607100103.

Foucault, M. (1980). *Power/knowledge: Selected interviews and other writings, 1972–1977.* Pantheon Books.

Fuentes, D. G. (2020). Rethinking approaches to succession planning and developing a leadership pipeline in academic pharmacy. *American Journal of Pharmaceutical Education, 84*(12), 8335. https://doi.org/10.5688/ajpe8335.

Giuliano, L., Levine, D. I., & Leonard, J. (2011). Racial bias in the manager-employee relationship: An analysis of quits, dismissals, and promotions at a large retail firm. *Journal of Human Resources, 46*(1), 26–52. https://doi.org/10.1353/jhr.2011.0022.

Goldman, C. (2020). Structure, culture, and agency: Examining succession planning in California State University (CSU) libraries. *Journal of Library Administration, 60*(1), 1–21. https://doi.org/10.1080/01930826.2019.1671035.

González, C. (2010). *Leadership, diversity and succession planning in academia.* Center for Studies in Higher Education.

Hearn, T. K., Jr. (2006). Leadership and teaching in the American university. In D. G. Brown (Ed.), *University presidents as moral leaders* (pp. 159–176). Rowman & Littlefield.

Hekman, D. R., Johnson, S. K., Foo, M.-D., & Yang, W. (2016). Does diversity-valuing behavior result in diminished performance ratings for non-white and female leaders? *Academy of Management Journal, 60*(2), 771–797. https://doi.org/10.5465/amj.2014.0538.

Hermann, J. R. (2021). A demographic shift in college students: A preparatory guide for political scientists and the discipline. In L. Waller, & S. Waller (Eds.), *Higher education—New approaches to accreditation, digitalization, and globalization in the age of Covid.* IntechOpen. https://doi.org/10.5772/intechopen.98804.

Hoffman, R., Casnocha, B., & Yeh, C. (2014). *The alliance: Managing talent in the networked age.* Harvard Business Review Press.

Kaufman, B. (2003). Succession planning means planning ahead. *University Business, 6*(9), 52–53.

Leonard, B. (2015, March 17). *Creating a succession plan that works.* Society for Human Resource Management. https://www.shrm.org/resourcesandtools/hr-topics/organizational-and-employee-development/pages/succession-plans-that-work.aspx.

Martin, J., & Samels, J. E. (2004). *Presidential transition in higher education: Managing leadership change.* Johns Hopkins University Press.

National Student Clearinghouse Research Center. (2022). *Current term enrollment estimates: Spring 2022.* https://nscresearchcenter.org/wp-content/uploads/CTEE_Report_Spring_2022.pdf.

Quach, D. (2018). *Calm clarity: How to use science to rewire your brain for greater wisdom, fulfillment, and joy.* TarcherPerigee.

Quillian, L., & Midtbøen, A. H. (2021). Comparative perspectives on racial discrimination in hiring: The rise of field experiments. *Annual Review of Sociology, 47*(1), 391–415. https://doi.org/10.1146/annurev-soc-090420-035144.

Rothwell, W. J. (2010). *Effective succession planning: Ensuring leadership continuity and building talent from within* (4th ed.). AMACOM.

Sanaghan, P. (2016, January). *Building leadership resilience in higher education.* Academic Impressions. http://www.academicimpressions.com/sites/default/files/0116-leadership-resilience-md.pdf.

Scott, K. (2019). *Radical candor: How to get what you want by saying what you mean.* Pan Macmillan.

Stangl, J. (2021, March 29). Purposeful talent development: From "succession planning" to "succession development." *CU Management.* https://www.cumanagement.com/blogs/2021/03/29/purposeful-talent-development-succession-planning-succession-development.

Thomas, A., & Cunningham, B. (2018, June). Academic advising career ladder development based on NACADA core competencies. *Academic Advising Today, 41*(2). https://nacada.ksu.edu/Resources/Academic-Advising-Today/View-Articles/Academic-Advising-Career-Ladder-Development-Based-on-NACADA-Core-Competencies.aspx.

Vito, R. (2018). Leadership development in human services: Variations in agency training, organizational investment, participant satisfaction, and succession planning. *Human Service Organizations: Management, Leadership & Governance, 42*(3), 251–266. https://doi.org/10.1080/23303131.2017.1421284.

Washington, C. E. (2016, March). *Succession planning in higher education.* [Paper presentation] Closing the Gender Gap: Advancing Leadership and Organizations, West Lafayette, IN, United States. https://doi.org/10.5703/1288284316079.

PART III

Building and Retaining the Advising Team

15

ADVISOR RECRUITMENT, SELECTION, AND HIRING

Lisa M. Cardello

The positive impact of effective academic advising on institutional success is well-documented. Thomas (2017) argued that academic advisors provide an element of consistency and caring that positively impacts the student experience and supports students in making meaning of their experiences, which leads to self-awareness, the discovery of unique talents, and encourages degree completion.

The recruitment, hiring, and retention of such influential staff are core functions of an academic advising administrator's role. However, this is no easy task, and advising administrators often receive little, if any, training and guidance in this area. As Chamorro-Premuzic and Kirschner (2020) explained, managers are typically experts in their fields and demonstrate leadership capability, but the skills of talent management or the ability to see talent before others is an often-overlooked critical skill in effective management.

When done effectively, hiring can breathe new life into advising programs. Conversely, the impact of "hiring gone wrong" can catastrophically impact an advising program, cause supervision challenges for advising administrators, damage staff morale, and harm student rapport. Chalmers (2005) pointed out:

> The most important job duty of an advising administrator is to hire the right people, because no other function done improperly or poorly will so quickly damage the advising operation and the mission of providing quality advising services to students.
>
> *(para. 1)*

DOI: 10.4324/9781003437598-27

This chapter shares effective hiring practices for primary-role advisors in the areas of recruitment, candidate selection, and interviewing, particularly as administrators attempt to navigate modern challenges. Hiring is a vital, yet stressful task, especially considering the high frequency in which administrators are faced with navigating this process. Academic advising and other student-support roles are plagued by high turnover rates (Marshall et al., 2016). Hiring and recruitment, which were once considered periodic tasks, have become ongoing processes. This chapter can help advisors navigate hiring challenges.

Meeting the Needs of Diverse Institutional Communities

Institutional contexts and student needs are ever-changing. Thus, a job vacancy within an advising department marks an ideal time to reassess the overall needs of the larger campus community to ensure that the advising department is best equipped to support its student body.

NACADA's Core Values provide a useful lens through which to examine a department's effectiveness in meeting campus needs, particularly in the area of inclusivity. The value states: "Academic advisors respect, engage, and value a supportive culture for diverse populations. Advisors strive to create and support environments that consider the needs and perspectives of students, institutions, and colleagues through openness, acceptance, and equity" (NACADA, 2017b, para. 7). Shaping such an environment involves building an advising team that mirrors campus student demographics. Chow (2019) wrote:

> As advisors are on the front lines … universities must commit to ensure diversity within this part of its structure, service, and support. Having advisors who match students' racial background, sexual orientation, or disabilities allows students to establish trust and empathy through mutuality.
>
> *(para. 5)*

This chapter provides suggestions for recruiting and retaining a diverse applicant pool below.

Prerecruitment

Planning greatly influences recruiting success (Trost, 2020). When filling a vacancy, academic advising administrators may be eager to launch into the recruitment process immediately, perhaps by updating a recent job description and working with the human resources (HR) department to post the vacancy. This sense of urgency is understandable. Academic advising offices often operate within a tight budget and with limited staff, so a vacancy can strain other staff members. However, a lack of prerecruitment planning and a hasty hiring process can have a long-lasting negative impact on the office.

Building a Recruitment Pipeline

The prerecruitment process begins long before a vacancy arises. Talent pipelining, also known as relationship recruitment, refers to an administrator's ability to build a network of potential candidates for future opportunities (Parrot, 2013). In other words, administrators recruit for positions before such openings actually exist. This approach may be new for some administrators and can be difficult to accomplish, but when done well, administrators can shift recruitment efforts from reactive to proactive. Active engagement on social media and ongoing engagement within professional organizations such as NACADA provide opportunities to connect with qualified, passionate individuals.

Job Analysis and the Development of Recruitment Materials

An effective job search relies on a thorough job analysis which informs targeted and purposeful recruitment. That starts with a clear job description.

Job Analysis

The Society for Human Resource Management (SHRM) defined job analysis as "the process of studying a job to determine which activities and responsibilities it includes, its relative importance to other jobs, the qualifications necessary for performance of the job and the conditions under which the work is performed" (SHRM, n.d., para. 2). While advising administrators have specific expectations for staff members, advisors often take on duties beyond their original job description. To recruit and identify the best candidate for an open position, it is crucial to fully understand the day-to-day responsibilities of the role. This will allow the administrator to assess the full scope of responsibilities, delegate tasks if necessary, and craft an appropriate job description. The job analysis process may include structured surveys and/or interviews with current and departing staff, staff work logs, and direct observation.

The job analysis process should provide a clear, realistic, and holistic view of the position alongside clearly communicated expectations and duties. A well-written job description sets the foundation for recruiting—and ideally, retaining—strong candidates by clarifying responsibilities and expected performance. Components of an effective job description include:

- Job Title: The job title should be specific and clearly reflect the content, purpose, and scope of the job (Noe et al., 2021a). It should also be consistent with other job titles of similar roles within the department, the larger college/university, and at other institutions. Administrators may work with their HR department to explore alternative recruiting strategies such as the use of a "working job title" if they feel the assigned job title does not clearly describe the role.
- Job Summary/Purpose: The job summary should provide an overview of the department and expectations for the position (Noe et al., 2021a). This description helps applicants understand where this position fits in the organization as well as the overall mission of the institution. In other words, it answers the question of "Why does this position exist?"
- Responsibilities and Duties: This section should describe the core functions of the role that will account for the vast majority of the staff member's time. The description should be detailed enough that applicants understand day-to-day responsibilities, yet concise. A useful strategy in helping candidates develop a realistic picture of the role involves describing the importance and/or frequency of tasks. For example, each duty listed may include a "percentage of time," or the estimated time an employee will spend on selected tasks each week (Royer, 2010). Alternatively, tasks may be presented in numbered format according to importance and/or frequency.
- Qualifications and Skills: List the required education, experience, skills, certifications, and/or licensure that are critical to the position's success. Preferred skills and experience may be listed as well but should be differentiated from those that are required. NACADA's Core Competencies page offers a useful framework to identify skills and knowledge crucial for academic advisors (NACADA, 2017a).
- Diversity Statement: To recruit diverse candidate pools that closely reflect the students served, a statement that reflects the department's commitment to diversity is encouraged.
- Additional Information: Additional sections may be added, as appropriate, such as supervisory responsibilities, travel, and work hours. These sections should be included if the expectations in these categories differ from what a job-seeker may anticipate.
- Required Statements: Advising administrators should consult with their HR department for the most up-to-date information and required statements regarding laws, labor contract agreements, and instructional practices.

Essential Requirements vs. Preferred Qualifications

Differentiating between preferred and essential qualifications is arguably one of the most critical tasks as it relates to the hiring process. All too often, administrators conceptualize an ideal candidate for a particular position and consequently develop a list of essential qualifications that closely reflect this ideal. The problem with job descriptions which contain a lengthy list of must-have requirements is that candidates with otherwise high potential may be deterred from applying, particularly applicants from minority groups, such as applicants from underrepresented backgrounds (e.g., women, veterans, and candidates with disabilities). For example, a landmark internal Hewlett Packard report found that women tend to apply for a new job only when they meet 100% of the listed criteria, compared to men who usually apply when they meet about 60% (Zenger, 2018).

Candidates with alternative backgrounds may also face discrimination in the hiring process. The academic advising field has grappled with whether or not advising is actually a defined profession, largely due to the fact that academic advisors hail from a wide range of educational and experiential backgrounds (Larson et al., 2015). Despite this, many postings for advising roles require specific advising experience within higher education. Candidates with strong industry experience may bring new perspectives and unique strengths that are relevant to the role but may feel discouraged from applying if they perceive that prior advising experience is required.

When developing a job description, advising administrators must carefully consider education, skills, and experiences that are listed as required or essential. As Miller-Merrell (2020) discussed, there is a "delicate balance between 'must-have' and 'nice to have,' or on biases that may prevent overlooked pools of top talent from applying for your jobs" (para. 2) Instead, administrators should examine their current, effective advising staff and consider what makes them successful. They may find the answer is related more to a staff member's interpersonal skills, work ethic, and commitment instead of prior experience. It is also important to gauge aspects of a role which can develop through coaching and training, as opposed to requiring those specific skills upon entry. Finally, administrators may consider directly addressing their interest in interviewing candidates from diverse backgrounds by including a statement in the job posting such as "Applicants who feel that their experience and background are consistent with the goals of our department are encouraged to apply even if they don't meet 100% of the requirements."

Recruitment

Recruitment is a multi-faceted process. It is also a process that can cause stress for advising administrators. The fear of a bad hire, the pressure to fill a vacancy and alleviate the strain on current staff, and the responsibility to meet departmental and institutional goals are all challenges that hiring managers face. The keys to a successful recruitment process should reflect the characteristics of an effective advising administrator: organized, planful, and proactive.

Recruitment Strategy and Plan

An effective recruitment strategy leverages information gained from the job analysis to inform recruitment efforts. By this point in the process, the advising administrator should have a sense of the types of professionals they want and how to reach them.

A critical aspect of a recruitment plan is a timeline. Often, advising administrators have little control over hiring processes and institutional approvals during both the job posting phase as well as the on-boarding phase. However, for the time period in between, advising administrators should have clear, time-driven goals. For example, if a job posting expires on a Monday, the administrator and search committee members might set aside time on Tuesday and Wednesday to review applicants with the goal of interviewing first-round applicants by Friday.

Momentum in the hiring process is also important. A recent national survey revealed that candidates left waiting too long lose interest in the position and consider other opportunities. Specifically, the survey found that 62% of professionals move on if they do not hear back from the employer within two weeks after the initial interview; that number rises to 77% if there is no status update within three weeks (Half, 2021). Therefore, advising administrators must prioritize the hiring process and carve out the time necessary to ensure that the process is progressing in a timely manner.

Dissemination of Recruitment Materials

The development of robust and culturally sensitive recruitment materials, such as a job description, is essential but not sufficient when recruiting applicants. These efforts are essentially meaningless if those materials never reach the intended pool of potential applicants. Advising administrators must consider how these materials are made available and disseminated in order to get them into the hands of qualified applicants.

Online Recruitment

An advising department's online presence and recruitment efforts are key factors in recruiting applicants (Michelson, 2022). According to a survey conducted by Glassdoor.com, nearly 80% of job-seekers use social media in their job search and employer research practices (Skaggs, 2018). It is likely that this statistic will continue to increase, given the technological nature of today's job search. Advising administrators must consider the overall message that their department website and social media presence convey. Additionally, they must develop an understanding of modern recruitment methods, including the use of social media as well as appropriate job search sites.

Networking

The power of networking cannot be understated. Recent studies show that as many as 85% of job seekers located their current position through networking (Adler, 2016). Professional organizations, namely NACADA, provide important opportunities to engage with potential qualified candidates. Advising administrators should familiarize themselves with networking opportunities offered by professional organizations, not only to attend these events themselves but also to encourage current staff to participate in recruitment efforts and disseminate recruitment materials once a job is available.

Strategic Outreach

Advising administrators have the opportunity to be strategic in their outreach efforts by considering alternative ways to reach potential applicants. Rather than hoping qualified candidates find their job posting, administrators should target a variety of outlets to maximize recruiting (Noe et al., 2021b). This is particularly effective in recruiting qualified candidates who may not be actively engaged in a job search. As an example, disseminating recruitment materials through student and alumni listservs associated with local graduate programs is one way to recruit active and passive job-seekers. Additionally, other social media outlets offer opportunities to engage with potential candidates through informal interest-based groups (SHRM, 2017).

Internal Resources

Advising administrators can also leverage current employees' networks by encouraging employee referrals. If feasible within the administrator's employment setting, an employee referral program provides a mechanism for current staff to identify potential candidates and participate in the recruiting process, thereby increasing the network of qualified candidates exponentially.

Recruiting a Diverse Candidate Pool

Consideration of essential requirements in the job description is important, but there are many other strategies advising administrators can employ to remove barriers of entry for diverse candidates, such as:

- Build and maintain a pipeline of diverse potential candidates. This is often achieved through networking, which should begin before a job opens and remain ongoing.
- Reword gender-specific and "othered" language from job descriptions to remove subtle bias. For example, consider "a person must demonstrate maturity" instead of "mature candidate preferred," language which could deter young and/or less-experienced applicants (Miller-Merrell, 2020, para. 10).
- Describe an inclusive culture in the job description and share departmental goals and initiatives related to diversity, equity, and inclusion on the department's webpage.
- Reflect department and institution diversity.
- Encourage current employees to recommend and promote job openings to qualified applicants from underrepresented groups.
- Avoid the urge to "clone yourself." Managers who lack systematic screening measures and a clear hiring strategy tend to define merit in "their own image" and gravitate towards interviewing candidates who remind them of themselves (Johnson, 2018). Doing so may inhibit the recruitment of a diverse candidate pool.

Candidate Selection

Candidate selection refers to the process of identifying the applicant with the highest potential for success in the identified role. Advising administrators must ensure that this process is fair and equitable at all stages.

The Search Committee

Before or during the active job posting period, the advising administrator should assemble the search committee. The search committee should collectively represent a variety of backgrounds, experiences, and perspectives, and therefore may include advising staff and administrators, staff from other departments, faculty, and students.

Applicant Screening

An organized screening approach ensures a systematic, fair hiring process. Many advising departments utilize screening tools such as checklists or rubrics to identify candidates for a short list of interviews. A three-step screening approach for candidates (Ghosh, 2021) has relevance for advising departments as a way to further organize this process and narrow the candidate pool.

1 Confirm required qualifications. For any position, there may be certain experiences or qualifications necessary to do the job effectively. Nonnegotiable required qualifications should be clearly identified for screening purposes.
2 Scan for preferred qualifications. This step requires a deeper dive into a candidate's resume, cover letter, and other documents to identify needed skills or qualifications.
3 Match the holistic picture of the candidate to the role. This step, which is perhaps the most crucial, is when the search committee attempts to view the candidate beyond their resume and assess fit for the open position. This is when consideration may be given to candidates who appear to demonstrate strong potential and transferable skills but may lack preferred experience or qualifications.

Revisiting Required and Preferred Qualifications

An analysis of essential requirements and preferred qualifications for a particular position is important during the development of the job description, but this process should be revisited during candidate selection. The scenario of a candidate with an impressive resume but who ultimately does not fit in a role is all too familiar for many administrators. Perhaps the candidate's experience and background mirrored the job description, but their interpersonal skills leave much to be desired, or their teamwork abilities are lacking. If so, a hiring manager's desire to replicate past or current staff may be partially to blame. A recent article in the Harvard Business Review (2021) advocates that administrators hire for potential, not experience:

> Stop thinking about hiring as a matter of replacing specific employees... When looking to fill a vacancy, too often managers simply put together a profile mirroring that of the person who has left, perhaps tacking on a few new requirements... At best, this yields candidates who are prepared for yesterday's challenges but probably not ready for tomorrow's.
> *(para. 7)*

Instead, managers and search committees should look past current needs and consider what skills and traits their department needs for future success.

Selecting and Retaining a Diverse Candidate Pool

Approach prerecruitment and recruitment with diversity in mind. If done effectively, these efforts should yield a pool that is diverse in a variety of ways, including race and ethnicity, gender, sexual orientation, and (dis)ability status. If the candidate pool appears to lack diversity, consider extending the posting and engaging in additional recruitment efforts. Furthermore, search committee members should make a conscious effort to retain diversity among the pool throughout the lifespan of the recruitment cycle. Approaching the screening process in a manner to include rather than exclude candidates is key as to not overlook potential candidates.

Advising administrators may consider requiring committee members to complete implicit bias training or other related training to ensure a fair and equitable search process. They should also be familiar with HR and university policies, as well as federal laws, related to equitable hiring practices.

Interviewing

Preplanning is the key to a successful and efficient interview process. Interview questions should be solidified prior to the start of interviews; they may require review by HR depending on the institution. These questions may be presented in a variety of ways but should specifically focus on the advising skills and experience necessary to perform the job. A written outline of main discussion points about the position as well as interview questions can ensure that the process is organized, and that the same information is shared with all applicants. Clear and honest discussions about the role help to ensure a genuine fit for both the employer and candidate (Tarki & Weiss, 2019).

Advising administrators who build rapport with candidates during the interview process may improve candidate retention. Rapport often builds from small gestures, such as initiating small talk prior to the interview to alleviate nervousness or remaining attentive throughout the discussion. Following a candidate's cues and encouraging them to talk about what matters to them may reveal their values and motivation for pursuing the position (Frontline Recruitment, 2019). Additionally, consider the interview format, time length, and size of the search committee. Large panel interviews can provide an efficient means for interviewing but may intimidate candidates. By contrast, small group interviews with three to four interviewers can provide a more intimate, less stressful setting and lead candidates to share their thoughts and experiences more fully and honestly. Any initial round of interviews can span 30–45 minutes, and final round interviews should last roughly 60 minutes.

Crafting Powerful Interview Questions

Traditional interview approaches often focus largely on past experiences with questions such as "Can you talk about your experience doing _____?", "What is the typical size of your student caseload in your current role?", and "What types of programs have you run in your current position?" While a limited number of these questions may be necessary to glean a candidate's qualifications, the majority of interview questions should assess their potential and interest. Questions that uncover capabilities, not just experience, can ensure that a candidate is a good fit both for now and in the future.

Powerful and effective interview questions are critical to the hiring decision-making process, yet they can be difficult to develop. The following well-established interview approaches can offer strategies for developing such questions.

Behavioral Interviewing

Behavioral interviewing incorporates strategically composed questions aimed at predicting behavior (Yate, n.d.). This approach is popular among advising administrators since candidate responses may provide insight into how they navigate conversations with students and challenging advising scenarios. These responses also allow an administrator to determine if a candidate's skills, experience, and personality all meet the job's requirements as well as how they may function in the advising team (Yate, n.d.). Example questions include "Discuss a time when you faced a conflict while working on a team. How did you handle this situation?" and "Talk about a time when you worked to create a welcoming and inclusive campus community. How did you do so?"

Motivation-Based Interviewing

Motivation-based interviewing expands upon behavioral-based interviewing by assessing how a candidate tackles obstacles or challenges, a potential predictor of future success (Quinn, 2018). This type of interviewing adopts a three-part question approach that asks a candidate to talk about an obstacle or situation they encountered, discuss their action steps, and describe the end results. An example of a motivation-based interview question series might be:

- Tell me about a time when you lacked the time necessary to achieve a goal. (Obstacle)
- Tell me about the actions you took. (Action)
- What were the end results? (Results)

Case-Based Questions

Case-based interview questions aim to reveal to the search committee how a candidate might react to a variety of circumstances (Indeed Editorial Team, 2018). It also provides an opportunity to gain information about a candidate's experience, skills, and strengths. These questions resemble behavioral interview questions but are focused on scenarios specific to the role. Examples might be:

- You are assigned to work with a student who is failing the majority of their courses. Can you walk us through how you would work with this student?
- How would you deal with a student who does not return phone calls or emails?

Advising administrators should note that these questions are not to be approached as having one right or wrong answer. Candidates should also not be expected to be experts in institutional procedures when asked case-based questions. Rather, these interview techniques can be used to better understand aspects such as how candidates might attempt to build rapport with students, strategies for navigating challenging situations, and their decision-making process for deciding when to seek help from supervisors.

Documentation

The importance of documentation should be familiar to advising administrators, given the importance of thorough note-keeping in their work with students. Documentation is useful in maintaining notes on each candidate throughout the interview process; it also provides a reference when evaluating candidates. Advising administrators should work with their HR department to ensure that federal, state, and institutional record-keeping requirements are followed.

Evaluation of the Process

A best practice associated with the recruitment and selection process includes a retrospective evaluation (Jobvite, 2016). This process can be informal but should engage all members of the search committee. The goal is to identify successful aspects as well as opportunities for improvement in future recruitment cycles. Conducting this evaluation within a few weeks of candidate selection is ideal. Questions to guide this discussion include:

- Was our candidate pool sufficient? Or do recruitment efforts need to be enhanced in the future? If yes, how can these efforts be improved?

- Did the job description attract candidates with appropriate qualifications? Are there opportunities to describe the role and responsibilities more accurately?
- Did the candidate pool reflect the institution's diversity?
- Do required qualifications need to be further clarified?
- Did the interview questions solicit the information necessary for identifying highly qualified candidates? Or were search committee members left with additional unanswered questions?
- Is there an opportunity to solicit honest feedback from recent hires about the process from the applicant's perspective?

Conclusion

Departmental vacancies can pose challenges for staff and administrators alike. However, with a proactive approach to recruitment and careful planning—using the strategies and advice given above—advising administrators can minimize the impact on day-to-day operations during a vacancy. Perhaps more importantly, they can also help their departments evolve to meet changing and future needs of diverse campus communities.

Reflection Questions

1 Recruitment is an ongoing responsibility of advising administrators, regardless of whether a current opening exists. What strategies can advising administrators use to build and maintain a network of qualified applicants?

2 For professional staff working within advising programs, what skills, experiences, and characteristics should be considered essential? Which should be considered preferred but not required? As an advising administrator, how would you assess these attributes when reviewing resumes/applications and interviewing candidates?

3 As mentioned in the chapter, it is important that advising staff resemble the demographic characteristics of the student body they serve. As an advising administrator, what are some strategies you would use to promote a diverse pool of candidates? Furthermore, what strategies would you use to ensure that diversity is preserved among the pool of candidates throughout the lifespan of the hiring process?

References

Adler, L. (2016, February 29). *New survey reveals 85% of all jobs are filled via networking*. LinkedIn. https://www.linkedin.com/pulse/new-survey-reveals-85-all-jobs-filled-via-networking-lou-adler/.

Chalmers, L. C. (2005, September 1). *An advising administrator's duty*. NACADA Clearinghouse of Academic Advising Resources. https://nacada.ksu.edu/

Resources/Academic-Advising-Today/View-Articles/An-Advising-Administrators-Duty.aspx#:~:text=I%20profess%20that%20the%20most,   quality%20 advising%20services%20to%20students.

Chamorro-Premuzic, T., & Kirschner, J. (2020, January 9). *How the best managers identify and develop talent.* Harvard Business Review. https://hbr.org/2020/01/how-the-best-managers-identify-and-develop-talent.

Chow, Y.-H. A. (2019, March). What advising administrators can do to promote and support diversity in their colleges and units. *Academic Advising Today, 42*(1). https://nacada.ksu.edu/Resources/Academic-Advising-Today/View-Articles/What-Advising-Administrators-Can-Do-to-Promote-and-Support-Diversity-in-their-Colleges-and-Units.aspx.

Frontline Recruitment. (2019, January 8). *10 ways to put an interviewee at ease.* https://www.frontlinerecruitmentgroup.com/news/10-ways-to-put-an-interviewee-at-ease/44650/

Ghosh, P. (2021, March 11). *Candidate screening and selection process: The complete guide for 2021.* Spiceworks. https://www.toolbox.com/hr/recruitment-onboarding/articles/what-is-candidate-screening-and-selection.

Half, R. (2021, March 5). *The biggest mistake you're making when hiring.* Robert Half Talent Solutions. https://www.roberthalf.com/blog/evaluating-job-candidates/the-biggest-mistake-youre-making-when-hiring.

Harvard Business Review. (2021, March-April). *Reengineering the recruitment process.* https://hbr.org/2021/03/reengineering-the-recruitment-process.

Indeed Editorial Team. (2018, November 30). *5 situational interview questions.* https://www.indeed.com/career-advice/interviewing/situational-interview-questions-and-answers.

Jobvite. (2016, October 3). *Key factors to evaluate your recruitment process.* https://www.jobvite.com/blog/recruiting-process/key-factors-evaluate-recruitment-process/

Johnson, W. (2018, July 4). *3 common hiring mistakes new managers should avoid.* Harvard Business Review. https://hbr.org/2018/07/3-common-hiring-mistakes-new-managers-should-avoid.

Larson, J. M., Barkemeyer, J. P., & Johnson, A. C. (2015). Academic advising is not a profession: Who knew? *The Mentor: An Academic Advising Journal, 17.* https://journals.psu.edu/mentor/article/view/61259/60892.

Marshall, S. M., Gardner, M. M., Hughes, C., & Lowery, U. (2016). Attrition from student affairs: Perspectives from those who exited the progression. *Journal of Student Affairs Research and Practice, 53*(2), 146–159. https://doi.org/10.1080/19496591.2016.1147359.

Michelson, S. (2022, March 2). Recruiting great employees starts online. *Forbes.* https://www.forbes.com/sites/forbesagencycouncil/2022/03/02/recruiting-great-employees-starts-online/?sh=e670c0f1f1fd.

Miller-Merrell, J. (2020, September 23). Removing barriers of entry: Inclusive job postings will attract diverse talent. *The Society of Human Resource Management (SHRM) Blog.* https://blog.shrm.org/blog/how-to-attract-diverse-talent-with-inclusive-job-postings.

NACADA: The Global Community for Academic Advising. (2017a). *NACADA academic advising core competencies model.* https://www.nacada.ksu.edu/Resources/Pillars/CoreCompetencies.aspx.

NACADA: The Global Community for Academic Advising. (2017b). *NACADA core values of academic advising.* https://nacada.ksu.edu/Resources/Pillars/CoreValues.aspx.

Noe, R. A., Hollenbeck, J. R., Gerhart, B., & Wright, P. M. (2021a). *Human resource management: Gaining a competitive advantage* (12th ed.). McGraw Hill.

Noe, R. A., Hollenbeck, J. R., Gerhart, B., & Wright, P. M. (2021b). *Fundamentals of human resource management* (9th ed.). McGraw Hill.

Parrot, H. (2013, June 25). *5 reasons why talent pipelining is a win for you and your company.* LinkedIn. https://www.linkedin.com/business/talent/blog/talent-acquisition/ways-talent-pipelining-is-win-for-you-and-your-company.

Quinn, C. (2018). *Motivation-based interviewing.* Society for Human Resource Management.

Royer, K. P. (2010). *Job descriptions and job analyses in practice: How research and application differ.* [Doctoral dissertation, DePaul College of Liberal Arts and Social Sciences]. https://via.library.depaul.edu/etd/50.

Skaggs, C. (2018, April 2). *Going inbound for talent acquisition.* Glassdoor. https://www.glassdoor.com/employers/blog/going-inbound-talent-acquisition/.

Society for Human Resource Management (SHRM). (n.d.) *Performing job analysis toolkit.* https://www.shrm.org/resourcesandtools/tools-and-samples/toolkits/pages/performingjobanalysis.aspx.

Society for Human Resource Management (SHRM). (2017, September 20). *Using social media for talent acquisition: Recruitment and screening.* https://www.shrm.org/hr-today/trends-and-forecasting/research-and-surveys/pages/social-media-recruiting-screening-2015.aspx.

Tarki, A., & Weiss, J. (2019, July 1). *Viewpoint: Stop lying to candidates about the role.* Society of Human Resource Management (SHRM). https://www.shrm.org/resourcesandtools/hr-topics/talent-acquisition/pages/stop-lying-to-job-candidates.aspx.

Thomas, C. (2017, March). Academic advising and institutional success. *Academic Advising Today, 40*(1). https://nacada.ksu.edu/Resources/Academic-Advising-Today/View-Articles/Academic-Advising-and-Institutional-Success.aspx.

Trost, A. (2020). *Human resources strategies: Balancing stability and agility in times of digitization.* Springer.

Yate, M. (n.d.). *How to answer behavioral interview questions and get more job offers.* Society of Human Resource Management (SHRM). https://www.shrm.org/resourcesandtools/hr-topics/organizational-and-employee-development/career-advice/pages/how-to-answer-behavioral-interview-questions-and-get-more-job-offers.aspx.

Zenger, J. (2018, April 8). The confidence gap in men and women: Why it matters and how to overcome it. *Forbes.* https://www.forbes.com/sites/jackzenger/2018/04/08/the-confidence-gap-in-men-and-women-why-it-matters-and-how-to-overcome-it/?sh=204e6a183bfa.

16

ADVISOR TRAINING AND PROFESSIONAL DEVELOPMENT

Elizabeth M. Higgins, Helen Gorgas Goulding, and Mary Anne Peabody

Academic advising administrators often oversee the development of faculty and primary-role advisor knowledge and skills. Advising, once seen solely as a transactional exchange of information between advisors and students, has evolved into a robust field that plays a critical role in college student success (Klepfer & Hull, 2012). Data from the National Survey of Student Engagement (NSSE; Lemire, 2006) suggests academic advising is the single most powerful predictor of satisfaction within a four-year college campus environment. These data, coupled with higher education's emphasis on degree completion, have highlighted the importance of effective academic advising and emphasized the need to ensure that advisors can do their jobs effectively.

Institutions of higher education have the potential to increase student persistence and success by leveraging academic advising as an essential element of student support (Campbell & Nutt, 2008; Grawe, 2021). Despite literature highlighting advising's importance in student success, ongoing training and professional development efforts are falling short. Folsom et al. (2015) present data from two advising surveys revealing that only 40%–61% of responding advising administrators offered an onboarding for new advisors—and some offered no training at all. This was the case for both faculty advisors and primary-role advisors (Grites, 2012). This dearth of training and professional development lowers the potential for advising to strengthen the student educational experience. Arguably, planning and leading a robust training and development initiative is essential to realizing advising's potential.

DOI: 10.4324/9781003437598-28

This chapter addresses how advising administrators can lead, design, implement, assess, and sustain effective advising training and professional development at any institution. Designing these programs is not an individual activity; it is vital for a training and professional development team (i.e., a design team) to identify targeted learning goals over multiple modalities and structures. Given that institutional change is a constant challenge, advising administrators must assess the educational landscape and provide training and professional development that is timely, progressively dynamic, and learning-centered. Sustaining this ongoing advisor development initiative requires leadership, commitment, and persistence from the advising administrator.

Learning-Centered Advising

Theoretically grounding academic advising in the scholarship of teaching and learning serves as the primary foundation for a comprehensive training and professional development plan that advances both student and advisor experiences. Advising scholarship connects to the scholarship of teaching and learning. Lowenstein (2013) presented advising as a "locus of learning" where advisors guide students through a teaching and learning sense-making experience much like classroom instructors (p. 245). Understanding and practicing advising as a transformational learning activity aligns the profession with faculty teaching and learning interests (White, 2015). A study of teachers who later became advisors (i.e., teacher-advisors) showed that prior teaching experience can influence the practice of advising as teaching and previous teaching strategies and theories are often applied to the advising practice (Coleman et al., 2021).

Compelling the institution to view advising through a scholarly lens increases expectations for the systematic study of advising as a teaching and learning activity. The sharing of research and scholarship, in turn, raises the discourse around best practices for student success (Troxel, 2019). In addition, aligning academic advising with the institution's teaching and learning mission encourages advisor scholarship. Further, for primary-role advisors, applied research can help improve critical thinking, time management, transferable skills, and self-directed learning—all important outcomes for advisor growth and development (Desbrow et al., 2014).

An advising culture steeped in student learning and success provides a structured venue for academic advisors to learn collectively and discuss effective practices. A carefully structured training and professional development program can establish a collaborative learning culture and build mutual respect between faculty members and advisors. In this regard, advising administrators should design and offer training and development topics that celebrate the uniqueness of all advisor identities—especially those who are underrepresented. Advising administrators can use training and professional development opportunities to build collaborative and inclusive advising communities.

Investment and engagement in this type of community help individuals feel supported and valued. Individuals want to be a part of something meaningful and that directly relates to their own values (Steger et al., 2012). When employees see that the organization is investing in their individual learning and professional growth, they in turn feel valued (Ryan & Oestreich, 1998). This sense of value assists the institution in retaining talent and expertise that can influence both student and employee experiences. Both Creamer (1980) and Harrison (2009) identified advising relationships, accurate information, assistance with decision-making, and goal identification as advising needs shared by all students. Hence, advising administrators need to offer training and professional development skills far beyond course planning and scheduling.

Academic advising is relationship based. Advisor interactions with students build relationships and contribute to students' sense of belonging. Offering professional development opportunities in areas related to self-knowledge, authenticity, and communication prepares advisors to build trusting relationships with students more effectively. As Schreiner et al. (2011) pointed out, "students do not stay in or leave institutions as much as they stay in or leave relationships" (p. 333). Thus, the more self-knowledge advisors possess, the more genuine and authentic advisors can be in their interactions with students. Increasing advisors' ability to make positive connections with students (Palmer, 1997) benefits all parties; it is also particularly important when ensuring advising equity for all students.

One pressing issue in higher education continues to be retention and graduation rates of historically underrepresented populations, particularly racial and ethnic minorities (Seidman, 2019). Museus and Ravello (2010) suggested that advisors have a responsibility to address these issues by how they deliver services to students of color. Virginia Gordon (1984) has suggested that advising is multidimensional in terms of student diversity as well as in the ways student needs are met. This multidimensional reality "makes the need for comprehensive and ongoing staff development essential" (p. 440). Thus, advising administrators must prioritize training around diversity, equity, inclusion, and socially-just advising practices to ensure equity in the advising experience and to ensure a welcoming campus environment (Burton et al., 2017; Council for the Advancement of Standards in Higher Education [CAS], 2018). Effective and comprehensive advisor training and professional development benefits the institution, advisors' growth, and, most importantly, student development.

Continuum of Learning

Advising administrators are routinely responsible for leading the institution's vision, mission, and goals by fostering a continuous learning environment through training and professional development—so, advising administrators must differentiate between *training* and *development*. While both involve learning, *training* is sometimes associated with one-time or isolated events; *development* is more often considered a slower, longer-lasting process. As is true in so many professions, continual learning is vital; it is equally important for advising administrators to facilitate a "learning culture" to provide more than lip service to this important construct.

For any learning environment to thrive, advising administrators should design a learning continuum as a guidepost. By conceiving learning as continuous, forward-moving, and sequential, the continuum places onboarding at one end and moves to ongoing training and development at the other. While onboarding provides an essential grounding, it is in the ongoing learning phase where advisors will spend most of their time. Going deeper and broader into learning over time makes development an iterative, continuous process that prepares individuals for the inevitable changing advising needs of students. The design of this continuum begins by identifying a design team.

Developing a Design Team

Excellence in advisor training and development begins by forming a diverse cross-sectional design team to work in partnership and develop a robust academic advisor training and development program. To make this a comprehensive and responsive program, advising administrators should bring together individuals to identify the specific development needs of advisors by type (i.e., faculty or primary-role) to design an appropriate program. Administrators should also utilize the skills and talents of those within the advising community and its stakeholders to help develop a design that embraces continuous improvement and creates a path for achieving advising excellence (Wallace & Wallace, 2015).

The Multifaceted Audience

As academic advising intersects with many parts of an institution, identifying stakeholders and program audiences are essential first steps in the design phase. Stakeholders are individuals who have a vested interest in the purpose and results of a training and development program. These could vary depending on the structure of the advising program. To identify audiences, administrators should focus on the advising model and who is performing academic advising duties. Most institutions can quickly identify primary-role and faculty advisors, but there are other advisor types (i.e., athletic, career, disability, TRIO, veteran, academic coaches, etc.) that would also benefit from such opportunities and who should be considered.

Student voices must be prominent throughout the design and implementation process. As recipients of academic advising, student perspectives and experiences are critical inputs into any program design. Another voice to consider is that of forward-facing, administrative personnel who have numerous and important student interactions, even if not directly advising themselves. These individuals often teach students about policies and procedures, how to make appointments, how to read degree audits, and they often deescalate student situations—so obviously they would benefit from training and development opportunities. Finally, understanding the myriad, often competing roles and responsibilities of faculty advisors is vital to designing a program responsive to the needs of this particular audience.

Faculty Advising

Faculty members play an integral role in fulfilling the overall institutional teaching and learning mission that includes advising (Carlstrom & Miller, 2013). The distinct role of faculty members also calls upon administrators and design teams to understand the professional development needs of advisors. To that end, the administrator and the design team must ask some reflective questions to understand the faculty's role in advising. Is advising viewed as an important faculty member responsibility? How do we recognize and reward faculty advisors? What do faculty members need to understand about advising and the student experience regarding student persistence and retention?

Advanced Primary-Role Advisors

Administrators should also explore the needs of advanced advisors. The continuous building of skills, knowledge, and abilities is necessary to develop beginners into experts (Yoder & Joslin, 2015). Cultivating experts' knowledge and experiences helps to expand the overall excellence of the academic advising program. Advanced advisors can facilitate workshops, discussions, mentoring programs, or publishing opportunities. Administrators should remember, however, that even advanced advisors have needs for ongoing training and professional development.

Relational Coordination

Administrators and the design team must assess and understand the needs of each advisor audience. This understanding contributes to the design and offering of learning opportunities that foster advisors' professional growth and development, promote the growth and stability of the academic advising program, and, most importantly, ensure equitable advising experiences for all students. Engaging in robust conversations focused on student experiences, various advising roles, challenges, and questions can help the team build shared goals, knowledge, and trust to form a sense of *relational coordination* (Gittell, 2016). Relational coordination grounds the group in a common understanding and leads to a more effective training and development design. Relational coordination can also assist advising administrators as they align the academic program within institutional and broader field constructs.

Alignment with Institution, Field, and Higher Education Standards

Training and development programs should synergize with the institutional and academic advising program's vision, mission, and goals. Advisors should appreciate how their learning connects to these overall vision, mission, and goals of the institution and its direct correlation to the overall student and advisor learning experience (Ramos, 1994).

Additionally, global competencies, core values, and standards should inform the program's design. NACADA's Core Competencies and Core Values (NACADA, 2017) should be cornerstones of a comprehensive academic advising training and development program. These can guide effective advisor professional development efforts. As the foundational elements of academic advising, core competencies highlight the conceptual, informational, and relational knowledge and skills necessary to advise students successfully. The NACADA Core Values (NACADA, n.d.) provide guidance to the global community of advisors, regardless of role and title, on the professional practice of academic advising. The Council for the Advancement of Standards in Higher Education (i.e., CAS, 2018) also highlights the importance of training and development.

Together the competencies, values, and CAS academic advising standards help advisors and advising programs understand the global expectations of the field while allowing individuals to reflect on their personal practices and assess their professional growth. Use of these documents helps advising administrators and design teams identify key components of a comprehensive training and development program. These components, alongside institutional and program-level vision, mission, and goals, are essential elements of the design foundation.

Planning and Assessing the Program

One of the first steps in creating a learning-centered plan is to have focused discussions on key issues, current advising trends, challenges, barriers, and needs of students with the entire design team. This approach will generate an inclusive list of thoughts and biases. Next, advising administrators should lead their teams in understanding the current state of academic advising at their institution. Understanding data is essential. Developing a portrait of the institutional model, numbers of advisors with approximate advising loads, and any assessment results from surveys, focus groups, or institutional assessments (NSSE, advising reports, etc.) will provide a current read of the advising landscape and inform the team's next steps. Next, the design team can focus on student and advisor expectations and needs. This may involve initiating an advising program assessment to identify outcomes for student learning and advisor outcomes (see Chapter 9).

The identified outcomes should inform the training and professional development topics important for the advising program. Individual advisor self-assessments can also help advising administrators and the design team to identify both the topics and the timing of educational offerings (Yoder & Joslin, 2015).

The program assessment and institutional data, along with the NACADA Core Competencies, values, and CAS standards should be used by the team to agree upon the basic and advanced knowledge and skills advisors need to create an overall training and professional development plan. Key questions to guide the design might include:

- What are the desired learning outcomes for students? For advisors?
- Who is the audience (i.e., new, advanced, faculty, primary-role, etc.)?
- Where in the advising cycle should this learning take place?
- What will be the format of the learning opportunities (i.e., presentations, online learning modules, etc.)? Are the formats equitable for all learners?
- How do the topics connect to the academic advising vision, mission, and goals?
- How do the topics connect with the institutional vision, mission, and goals?

Time should also be spent discussing the overall goals of a long-term training and development plan. Mastering all foundational knowledge, skills, and abilities can take up to three years (Yoder & Joslin, 2015). Onboarding can provide the foundation of this information, knowledge, and behaviors while the future years in the practice can provide for continuous learning. Creating a year-at-a-glance advisor training and development calendar or map helps align the topics with the institution's advising cycle and the different phases of implementation.

Onboarding and Continuous Development

The training and professional development onboarding phase focuses on the individual and organization at typically a single point in time. This process assists individuals in building necessary knowledge, skills, and behaviors, while also culturally integrating them into the institution (Bannon & Brewer, 2019). During the onboarding phase, new advisors should begin to identify the different populations of students and colleagues found within the institution as well as their role in the overall advising community.

Regardless of role, Bannon and Brewer (2019) recommended that the onboarding program be balanced in manageable learning blocks, cover areas within the core competencies, include a time for shadowing and reflection, and have an online reference guide. Essential topics recommended by NACADA (2017) are divided in four areas: (a) Conceptual-Professional Practice (i.e., values, competencies, theories, approaches, etc.); (b) Informational-Institutionally Focused (i.e., degree components, policies, procedures, resources, etc.); (c) Relational-Creating and Sharing (i.e., rapport, community, learning outcomes, meaning-making, etc.); and (d) Additional Topics and Actions (see Appendix A). Onboarding of new advisors should be followed by ongoing educational opportunities throughout the first year of employment.

A design plan should provide flexibility for differing advising roles and phases of development. For example, faculty advisors whose primary role is classroom teaching may need more foundational training in core competency areas that were not covered during their time-limited onboarding period, whereas primary-role advisors who experience a more vigorous onboarding may require more complex or advanced training to develop greater expertise in certain core areas. Therefore, it is important to offer foundational and advanced levels of training in accordance with individual growth and institutional goals.

After the initial onboarding process, introduce ongoing topics to support continuous growth and development. Topics should be covered in a "just in time" approach to ensure that knowledge gained is used almost immediately. Potential learning opportunities could include student populations, self-assessment tools, advising approaches and strategies, as well as the challenges of balancing teaching, research, advising, and service (see Appendix B).

As advising practitioners grow within their roles, they are also gaining expertise to share with others. Identifying these areas of expertise allows advising administrators to engage internal experts to lead areas of training and development, which paves the way for participants to become a community of teachers, learners, and mentors.

Modalities and Structures

Utilizing different training modalities respects different learning styles and ensures equity. Offering group, one-on-one, and individual opportunities allows for individuals to learn from and with others, or at their own pace. Group training and development opportunities bring learners together in a professional learning community. Regardless of the group type, a collaborative learning environment that encourages sharing, reflecting, and taking risks necessary for change and growth will help improve the advising and teaching practice (Vescio et al., 2008).

One-on-one learning can be found in ongoing supervision, mentoring, or professional interactions. Each connection provides a formal touchpoint and opportunity to engage the expertise of a senior-level individual and foster learning for both. Having both individuals involved in a mentoring relationship often leads to growth, creative energy, and new ways of thinking and acting (Chacon Vance, 2016). Peer observation provides another collaborative learning opportunity. Advisors observing practices can spark powerful conversations for improvement and allow both parties to learn from each other and undertake individual reflection.

Individual learning could be outlined in job descriptions, a self-directed initiative, or opportunities that often arise within the advising cycle. To support learning, advising administrators must introduce all learning activities as an improvement strategy separate from any individual performance evaluation. Through ongoing supervision, administrators can include conversations about how these opportunities complement learning interests and goals, while challenging advisors to reach their full potential. Digital or paper templates for individualized professional development plans can act as catalysts for advisor reflection. The individualized plan typically reflects which phase(s) of training and development the advisor is in, specific learning outcomes, and potential learning opportunities.

Training and professional development can be offered either in person or online. Online options are often more flexible but individuals may learn better when in person. Ongoing knowledge sharing that enhances learning and development is often found on social media and provides an avenue for advisors to connect and contribute within a circle of professional support (Pasquini & Eaton, 2019). When deciding which option works best, advising administrators and design teams must think about the audience, learning outcomes, and the curriculum. Staying mindful of these three critical areas is vital when choosing the modality and structure that best complements desired learning outcomes.

There are multiple structural options for training and professional development including workshops, conference-style presentations, observations, scholarly discussion groups, electronic modules, panels, and social media (see Appendix B). When reviewing these options, consider these questions:

- Will this structure assist in meeting learning outcome(s)?
- Does the structure assist participants' learning styles?
- Does the program provide an environment for learning and growing?
- How will program assessment be administered?

Each of these questions can help the team solidify needs, learning expectations, and programmatic offerings.

For assessment purposes, remember to align the topics of each training and professional development opportunity with specific learning outcomes. At the end of each training and professional development opportunity, conduct an assessment to better understand the level of learning achieved during a specific offering. Assessment tools include surveys, self-assessments, reflections, focus groups, or interviews. Regardless of the assessment tool, ask participants to share how they will or plan to use their learning while advising. This question helps participants identify how their learning influences advising practices. Data generated from this question also informs the sustainability of the training and development plan.

Sustainability

Sustaining the design of a comprehensive training and development program directly relates to institutional and advisor commitment. Financial resources are a necessary aspect of professional development, yet many institutions struggle with fully funding comprehensive training and professional development programs. Advising administrators should prioritize professional development budgets in management discussions (see Chapter 12) including low or no cost options. Institutional collaboration as well as partnerships within the global advising community can help reduce expenses.

Given the complex nature of the advising cycle, time can also be a challenge. The advising administrator plays a key role in encouraging advisors to regularly block off time to participate in training and professional development and reflect on their learning and individual development needs. Allowing advisors to commit time to their development showcases the value the institution has for advisor professional development while assisting with program sustainability. To sustain ongoing training and development, advising administrators must create a culture of continuous learning. This is accomplished by providing vibrant offerings focused on learning outcomes, ensuring institutional commitments, and designing programs for ongoing advisor development in the ever-changing higher education landscape.

Conclusion

The advising administrator is an active agent of teaching and learning, the linchpin in facilitating professional development opportunities that generate a greater capacity for the advising community to thrive. Administrators can lead, design, implement, assess, and sustain effective professional development initiatives that meet the multifaceted needs and various roles of the broader academic advising community at their institution. They should also align specific learning outcomes of training and professional development experiences with assessment to ensure efficacious programming.

Training and professional development initiatives hold synergistic power. They can form connections between ongoing learning processes that meet the needs of students and the ever-changing demands of higher education. Advising administrators can harness this power by supporting and growing advisor leaders to help shape a broad and inclusive learning environment that maximizes the advising learning community throughout their professional careers.

Reflection Questions

1 Given the interdependence of diverse advisor roles, what strategies can you implement to cocreate and deepen relationships across the institutional advising community?
2 After reflection on the concepts in the chapter, what should an advising administrator have as their top three priorities when designing a training and professional development program?
3 How can professional development be encouraged while maintaining a balance between daily duties and reflective practice?
4 How does the advising administrator incorporate scholarship as a professional development opportunity?
5 How can "teaching and learning" be established as a foundational element of a training and development program?

References

Bannon, K., & Brewer, J. (2019, September). Setting the stage: Onboarding using NACADA's core competencies. *Academic Advising Today, 42*(3). https://nacada.ksu.edu/Resources/Academic-Advising-Today/View-Articles/Setting-the-Stage-Onboarding-Using-NACADAs-Core-Competencies.aspx.

Burton, S. L., Puroway, D., & Stevens, S. E. (2017). *Academic advising and social justice: An advocacy approach.* NACADA: The Global Community for Academic Advising.

Campbell, S. M., & Nutt, C. L. (2008). *Academic advising in the new global century: Supporting student engagement and learning outcomes achievement.* Association of American Colleges & Universities.

Carlstrom, A. H., & Miller, M. A. (Eds.). (2013). *2011 NACADA national survey of academic advising* (Monograph No. 25). National Academic Advising Association. https://nacada.ksu.edu/Resources/Clearinghouse/View-Articles/2011-NACADA-National-Survey.aspx.

Chacon Vance, M. (2016, October 27). *The importance of mentoring for higher ed leadership.* Higher Ed Jobs. https://www.higheredjobs.com/articles/articleDisplay.cfm?ID=1077.

Coleman, M., Charmatz, K., Cook, A., Brokloff, S. E., & Matthews, K. (2021). From the classroom to the advising office: Exploring narratives of advising as teaching. *NACADA Review, 2*(1), 36–46. https://meridian.allenpress.com/nacada-review/article/2/1/36/475632/From-the-Classroom-to-the-Advising-Office.

Council for the Advancement of Standards in Higher Education. (2018). *Academic advising programs.* http://standards.cas.edu/getpdf.cfm?PDF=E864D2C4-D655-8F74-2E647CDECD29B7D0.

Creamer, D. G. (1980). Educational advising for student retention: An institutional perspective. *Community College Review, 7*(4), 11–18.

Desbrow, B., Leveritt, M., Palmer, M., & Hughes, R. (2014). Evaluation of a curriculum initiative designed to enhance the research training of dietetics graduates. *Nutrition & Dietetics, 71*(1), 57–63.

Folsom, P., Yoder, F., & Joslin, J. E. (Eds.). (2015). *The new advisor guidebook: Mastering the art of academic advising.* Jossey-Bass.

Gittell, J. H. (2016). *Transforming relationships for high performance: The power of relational coordination.* Stanford University Press.

Gordon, V. N. (1984). Training professional and paraprofessional advisors. In R. B. Winston, Jr., T. K. Miller, S. C. Ender, & T. J. Grites (Eds.), *Developmental academic advising* (pp. 440–455). Jossey-Bass.

Grawe, N. D. (2021). *The agile college: How institutions successfully navigate demographic changes.* Johns Hopkins University Press.

Grites, T. (2012, July 6). *Improving faculty advising.* Academic Impressions. https://www.academicimpressions.com/news/improving-faculty-advising.

Harrison, E. (2009). What constitutes good academic advising? Nursing students' perceptions of academic advising. *Journal of Nursing Education, 48*(7), 361–366.

Klepfer, K., & Hull, J. (2012). *High school rigor and good advice: Setting up students to succeed.* Center for Public Education, National School Boards Association.

Lemire, S. (2006, March). *National survey of student engagement 2005: Overview and descriptive statistics.* Office of Educational Assessment. http://depts.washington.edu/assessmt/pdfs/reports/0602/OEAReport0602.pdf.

Lowenstein, M. (2013). Envisioning the future. In J. K. Drake, P. Jordan, & M. A. Miller (Eds.), *Academic advising approaches: Strategies that teach students to make the most of college* (pp. 243–258). Jossey-Bass.

Museus, S. D., & Ravello, J. N. (2010). Characteristics of academic advising that contribute to racial and ethnic minority student success at predominantly White institutions. *NACADA Journal, 30*(1), 47–58.

NACADA: The Global Community for Academic Advising. (n.d.). *NACADA core values of academic advising.* https://nacada.ksu.edu/Resources/Pillars/CoreValues.aspx.

NACADA: The Global Community for Academic Advising. (2017). *NACADA academic advising core competencies model.* https://nacada.ksu.edu/Resources/Pillars/CoreCompetencies.aspx.

Palmer, P. J. (1997). The heart of a teacher: Identity and integrity in teaching. *Change: The Magazine of Higher Learning, 29*(6), 14–21.

Pasquini, L. A., & Eaton, P. W. (2019). The #acadv community: Networked practices, professional development, and ongoing knowledge sharing in advising. *NACADA Journal, 39*(1), 101–115.

Ramos, B. (1994). O'Banion revisited: Now more than ever. *NACADA Journal, 14*(2), 89–91.

Ryan, K. D., & Oestreich, D. K. (1998). *Driving fear out of the workplace* (2nd ed.). Jossey-Bass.

Schreiner, L. A., Noel, P., Anderson, E., & Cantwell, L. (2011). The impact of faculty and staff on high-risk college student persistence. *Journal of College Student Development, 52*(3), 321–338. https://doi.org/10.1353/csd.2011.0044.

Seidman, A. (2019). *Minority student retention: The best of the "Journal of College Student Retention: Research, Theory & Practice."* Routledge.

Steger, M. F., Dik, B. J., & Duffy, R. D. (2012). Measuring meaningful work: The work and meaning inventory (WAMI). *Journal of Career Assessment, 20*(3), 322–337.

Troxel, W. G. (2019). Scholarly advising and the scholarship of advising. *NACADA Journal, 39*(2), 52–59. https://doi.org/10.12930/NACADA-19-203.

Vescio, V., Ross, D., & Adams, A. (2008). A review of research on the impact of professional learning communities on teaching practice and student learning. *Teaching and Teacher Education, 24*(1), 80–91.

Wallace, S. O., & Wallace, B. A. (2015). The faculty advisor: Institutional and external information and knowledge. In P. Folsom, F. Yoder, & J. E. Joslin (Eds.), *The new advisor guidebook: Mastering the art of academic advising* (2nd ed., pp. 125–141). Jossey-Bass.

White, E. R. (2015). Academic advising in higher education: A place at the core. *The Journal of General Education, 64*(4), 263–277. https://doi.org/10.1353/jge.2015.0024.

Yoder, F., & Joslin, J. E. (2015). Advisor growth and development: Building a foundation for mastery. In P. Folsom, F. Yoder, & J. E. Joslin (Eds.), *The new advisor guidebook: Mastering the art of academic advising* (2nd ed., pp. 301–315). Jossey-Bass.

APPENDIX 16A

Essential Topics recommended by NACADA (2017)

1 Conceptual—Professional Practice

   a NACADA's core values and competencies
   b Theories relevant to academic advising
   c Academic advising approaches and strategies
   d Diversity, equity, access, and inclusivity within the academic advising context

2 Informational—Institutionally focused

   a Components of the degree, curriculum, and academic requirements
   b Policies and procedures
   c Advising practice policies and guidelines (legal, confidentiality, privacy, etc.)
   d Student support resources
   e Student information system and other advising technology

3 Relational—creating relationships and sharing knowledge

   a Identifying personal advising philosophy
   b Rapport building and successful advising interactions
   c Integrating into the institutional and global advising community
   d Advising as teaching: student learning outcomes
   e Engaging in assessment for improvement and development
   f Facilitating student problem-solving, decision-making, meaning-making, planning, and goal setting

4 Additional First-Year Topics and Actions

   a Meetings with supervisor, mentor, and colleagues
   b Completing mandatory training (FERPA, Title IX, etc.)
   c Shadowing advising appointments
   d Understanding how to facilitate an advising session
   e Understanding specific academic advising approaches (motivational interviewing, strengths, coaching, etc.)
   f Engage in reflection and discuss with colleagues
   g Campus tours
   h Understanding the year-long cycle of advising, student populations, and specific appointment types
   i Meet with campus partners for understanding and networking

APPENDIX 16B

Teaching Topics and Structural Options

- Deeper dive on student populations (i.e., undecided, sophomores, international, adult learners, online, veterans, athletes, part-time, Generation Z, etc.)
- Assessment of advising
- Advising as teaching
- Creating an inclusive office environment
- Having inclusive conversations
- Varying approaches to academic advising
- Optimizing the student information system
- Online advising tools
- How to write a helpful advising note
- Understanding general education
- The mysteries of financial aid
- Supporting students with disabilities
- Student mental health
- Justice involved students
- Advisor challenges
- Student barriers to success
- Strategies for advising students in difficult situations
- Creating an advising plan
- Effective use of degree planning tools
- Advising for student persistence and retention
- Advising underrepresented populations

- Balancing teaching, advising, research, and service
- Creating an advisor professional development plan
- Research and writing about academic advising
- Advisor rejuvenation and self-care

Structural Options

- All or half-day retreat
- Certificate program
- Workshop
- Presentation
- Institute/Seminar
- Conference
- Webinar
- Panel
- Role play
- Case study
- Article/Book discussion group
- Podcast with discussion
- Video
- Self-assessment
- Journaling
- Mentoring
- Electronic reference guide
- Research project
- Writing/Publishing
- Shadowing

VOICES FROM THE FIELD

Making Academic Advising Work in Japanese Universities: The Case of Study Abroad Advising

Yoshinobu Onishi

It is extremely encouraging that NACADA has been expanding globally in recent years by putting "The Global Community for Academic Advising" in its name, but it remains that there continue to be few professional development opportunities and little information is available from non-English-speaking countries (such as in Asia and South America). This article offers insight into current practices in Japan, focusing on trainings for study abroad advisors in a changing era.

Differences between Japan and the United States

Japanese and U.S. higher education systems differ greatly, even though they often use the same terminology. As in U.S. contexts, Japanese-based academic advising has been regarded mostly as faculty members' voluntary job for a long time. Japanese universities do not have as many nonacademic staff as U.S. universities, nor do most nonacademic staff hold a master's or a doctoral degree. The role of nonacaemic staff is to simply support faculty or play a subordinate role in academic advising. In addition, nonacademic staff in Japan regularly transfer sections, typically every three to five years, making it difficult for those staff members to acquire expertise regarding specific tasks, such as admissions, institutional research, public relations, finance, and academic advising (Torii, 2013). Finally, in Japan, many students turn to for-profit advisors certified through the Japan Association of Certified Study Abroad Counselors (JACSAC) to navigate specialized areas such as global education programs.

DOI: 10.4324/9781003437598-29

Thus, in Japanese universities, faculty members play a central role in academic advising for students. Sometimes they even advocate, design, implement, and evaluate the training programs for faculty advisors in an effort to support faculty development. Similar to U.S. contexts, not every faculty member in Japan feels honored or embraces the advising role. Moreover, not every faculty member thinks that they should be responsible for academic advising because it is not one of the major roles at their university for which they are evaluated. As a result, like in the United States, many faculty members in Japan tend to focus more on teaching and research than academic advising.

Study Abroad Advising as Key

The situation is gradually changing. As in many other parts of the world, academic advising has recently received increasing attention in Japan. For example, there was no research done on academic advising in Japan until 2013, while there were 15 published articles on the topic in 2020 (Onishi, 2021). Additionally, the first graduate-level course on academic advising was launched in 2016, and by 2021 the Japan Association for Academic Advising was established in collaboration with NACADA.

Among the various areas of advising, study abroad advising has some priority; since 2010, the Japanese government has promoted overseas studies for students in cooperation with many universities to develop global human resources further (Onishi, 2017). As a result, the number of students who have studied abroad has rapidly increased, from 36,302 in Academic Year (AY) 2009–2010 to 107,346 in AY 2019–2020 (JASSO, 2020). Given that the number of students who study abroad has tripled in just ten years, quantitatively, it is no longer realistic for only faculty to be responsible for academic advising, particularly in the field of study abroad. Furthermore, even in terms of qualitative aspects, more active participation by nonacademic staff should be encouraged in study abroad advising if for no other reason than because many have studied abroad themselves and/or go abroad with students yearly. By updating knowledge and experience, these nonacademic staff could make valuable contributions to advising opportunities than faculty members who may have never studied abroad.

The significant increase in the number of Japanese students studying abroad today also means that fewer current primary-role advisors experienced studying abroad during their own higher education experiences. As more of today's students enter the field as nonacademic staff who have studied abroad, they will bring their own experiences to their advising practice and likely play a central role in that field.

Current Training Situation

Training today's advisors in Japan presents two types of difficulties. One concerns the number of training opportunities. Although the number of staff development programs has increased in Japanese universities, many tend to focus on general topics such as "Higher Education in the 21st Century" or "Work-Life Balance in Your Office," to reach a wide audience. Very few training opportunities focus on more specific topics, such as academic advising or study abroad advising. In fact, only 12% of the nonacademic staff in Japanese universities have pursued job-relevant trainings in the areas they cover, and only 5% of offices have work manuals for on-the-job trainings (Kato, 2017). While the learning environment for nonacademic staff exists, it is limited to specific topical areas.

The other difficulty concerns the quality and style of the training methods. Most trainings are conducted as seminars or simple lectures, in which participants or trainees are expected to sit and listen passively, which likely has less of an educational impact than workshops and group work, in which participants are encouraged to think deeply and discuss actively. For example, the *asagao* mailing list, provided by Kyoto University, was a popular higher education platform in Japan which allowed people to share information on academic events such as seminars, symposiums, lectures, workshops, and academic gatherings in a timely manner. In April 2022, *asagao* ("morning glory" in English) sent 111 emails to subscribers and approximately 80% of them offered opportunities to attend sit-and-listen seminars and lectures. Although *asagao* was suddenly closed at the end of summer in 2022, this statistic reflects demand and implies that other types of training and additional training resources should be developed. This is mainly due to the fact that other infrastructure is still in place to contact/reach out to advisors. Such methods could be used once trainings are more developed and sophisticated.

Student Satisfaction

Regrettably, most nonacademic staff perform their roles with few, if any, dedicated training opportunities. As a result, students often evaluate the study abroad counselors in the for-profit sector more favorably than they do study abroad advisors in universities (see Table VFF 16.1; Onishi, 2022). Arguably, both the for-profit sector and university advisors have staff who are equally kind and sincere with students; the difference between them is how well and deeply they know the target countries, universities, and institutions—information referenced as "expertise."

From where does this difference stem? It is from the difference between advisors who have undergone training and those who have not. In other

TABLE VFF 16.1 Student Satisfaction (on a 4-Point Scale)

	Attitude				Expertise		Knowledge of Process		
	Q1	Q2	Q3	A4	Q5	Q6	Q7	Q8	Q9
Advisors at University	3.28	3.16	3.09	2.83	2.86	2.98	3.16	3.12	3.18
Counselors in for-profit sector	3.11	3.04	3.12	3.07	3.04	3.13	3.15	3.11	N/A

Note. Onishi (2022).

words, the main difference between for-profit advisors and those in the non-profit sector is the number of training opportunities. As mentioned above, the former enjoys regular training opportunities while the latter has only limited opportunities. Students desire reliable and skilled study abroad advisors on campus. In a recent survey of students who actually studied abroad, out of 500 respondents, only 92 visited in-house study abroad advisors. Of the 408 respondents who did not visit advisors on campus, 106 did not expect much about the service and expertise that the advisors could provide (Onishi, 2022).

Advisors are admittedly frustrated because they want to help students, but they have few opportunities to attend trainings to improve their knowledge and skills. Most professional counselors in the for-profit sector regularly receive training either in-house or from professional organizations such as the JACSAC (Onishi, 2017). JACSAC trainings are facilitated monthly, with topics including legal issues related to studying abroad, the U.S. education system, several official English tests, and detailed and specific country reports. Historically, advisors employed by colleges and universities have not availed themselves of these resources or interacted with the private sector advisors who do. In addition, like their American counterparts, individual universities may struggle to solve this issue while facing financial constraints and juggling countless other priorities.

What Can Be Done?

There are two ways to provide trainings for study abroad advisors working at Japanese universities. In the short term, study abroad advisors working at universities can join trainings organized by study abroad counselors in the for-profit sector (Onishi, 2017). The most popular opportunity is a monthly JACSAC training. For many years, JACSAC has also implemented a more intensive and professional training program at a reasonable cost for prospective, certified study abroad counselors. This may require an administrator or committee of dedicated professionals to outline the specific knowledge and skillsets needed by advisors working with students who wish to study abroad. They then might curate the most appropriate (and affordable) training opportunities available outside of academia. Moreover, academic associations and professional organizations in Japan can provide their members such training opportunities, while most individual universities cannot.

In the longer term, administrators and advisors interested in their own and others' development can begin to answer the questions posed in Chapter 16. Answering these questions will help to guide development of no to low-cost institutional professional development opportunities for staff and faculty advisors. Further, administrators and advisors can internally partner with faculty and departments who feature high-quality educational workshops. As student interest in global education has increased in the last decade, professional development for the faculty and staff working with these students has not kept pace—but that does not mean that it cannot catch up. In the early stages of training development, administrators and advisors may need to lean into public-private partnerships for successful staff development. Over time, and through intentional dialog, goal setting, and program design, Japanese universities and their staffs may be able to offer training commensurate with those programs offered by professional organizations.

Acknowledgment

JSPS KAKENHI, grant number 21K02626, supported this work.

References

JASSO. (2020). *Survey result on study abroad by Japanese students*. https://www.studyinjapan.go.jp/ja/_mt/2022/03/date2020n.pdf.

Kato, T. (2017). Duties and working environment of college administrators in Japan. *Koto Kyoiku Kenkyu Sosho, 136*, 1–114.

Onishi, Y. (2017). Academic advisors and study abroad counselors in Japan: Implementing a new forum for both to learn from each other. *Academic Advising Today, 40*(4). https://nacada.ksu.edu/Resources/Academic-Advising-Today/View-Articles/Academic-Advisors-and-Study-Abroad-Counselors-in-Japan.aspx.

Onishi, Y. (2021). Review of the book *Learning support and quality assurance of higher education*, by K. Yamanouchi & H. Take (2016). *Journal of Studies on Humanities and Public Affairs, 42*, 145–151.

Onishi, Y. (2022). *Proceedings of JAILA annual conference: Challenges of study abroad counseling as academic advising*. Japan Association of International Liberal Arts (JAILA). https://jaila.org/activity/taikai20220319/proceedings20220319/jaila-proc-010-05-20220319.pdf.

Torii, T. (2013). How can institutional research (IR) contribute to the management of academic affairs for further quality assuarance?: Experience of academic IR at Ritsumeikan University. *University & College Management, 9*(3), 2–7.

17

ADVISOR PERFORMANCE MANAGEMENT

Katie Lackey, Ruthanna Spiers, and Beth Yarbrough

The value of academic advising to both individual students and institutional health is clear. Developing, supporting, and retaining professionals in the field of academic advising are some of the most important responsibilities of an advising administrator. Executed intentionally, performance management provides administrators with the structure to carry out these responsibilities and create spaces for both the administrator and advisor to focus on professional growth and fulfillment. When employees feel supported and engaged in their development, they are more likely to stay and develop in their roles (Mampane, 2020a; Pandita & Ray, 2018).

Performance evaluation is a standard practice across professions and a core function of human resources (Armstrong, 2006). To retain employment, employees must uphold their responsibilities. It is the supervisor's responsibility to ensure that this is happening and to take appropriate action if needed. Administrators also set the tone regarding performance evaluations for their team. Through their research, Weiherl and Frost (2016) found that performance evaluations with judgmental tones decrease an individual's organizational commitment. On the other hand, Darling-Hammond and Hyler (2013) discussed how well-executed performance evaluations can help people focus on what is being evaluated and positively change behavior by changing focus.

The practice of performance management has evolved to reflect a focus on employee development through ongoing formative and summative feedback (Mampane, 2020b). Before performance management, performance

DOI: 10.4324/9781003437598-30

appraisal systems focused on salary justification to motivate an employee to improve performance or continue to perform well (Das & Mukherjee, 2017). Performance appraisal consisted of a supervisor reporting on the employee's performance and provided minimal focus on supporting the employee's development. The practice of performance management has evolved from performance appraisal to better set the stage for supporting employee development and connecting individual performance to organizational success. "Performance management is a goal-oriented process" used to maximize "productivity of employees, teams, and ultimately" the organization (Mampane, 2020b, p. 205). It is a "continuous process of identifying, measuring, and developing the performance of individuals and teams and aligning performance with the strategic goals of the organization" (Aguinis & Pierce, 2008, pp. 139–140). "Performance management has become…more strategic [in its] approach to integrating HR activities and business policies" of job descriptions, professional development, and promotion (Fletcher, 2001, p. 473).

It is important to acknowledge that performance management also can be one of the most challenging responsibilities for an administrator, especially for those new to the role (Gyamfi et al., 2022). Participating in the performance management process as an employee offers valuable experience; however, transitioning to a supervisory role requires more than just engagement. Managing the process takes practice, learning, and time to master. Additionally, each advisor is unique not only in their development but also in their style of giving and receiving feedback. Much like adapting advising approaches to best support students, advising administrators must learn to be nimble and adaptive in their approach to performance management. Growing as a supervisor is a continuous process; advising administrators should give themselves grace and seek help from mentors as they develop in this important responsibility. Advising administrators must also remain open to learn from their advisors in the performance management process, especially from those who hold different lenses.

Helmold and Terry (2021) viewed performance management as a continuous cycle encompassing ensuring accuracy of position descriptions, creating measurement rubrics, involving personnel in self-appraisal, conducting review meetings with employees, and designing individual development plans along with the employee. This cycle takes place within a context of frequent and timely feedback. This chapter seeks to empower advising administrators to reframe performance management from an annual requirement to a continual developmental process. It also provides practical strategies for developing as a performance manager.

Position Descriptions

Performance management begins with clear and accurate position descriptions that allow employees to understand the expectations of the role at the point of hire and serve as continual guides for performance development planning. Gan and Kleiner (2005) compare a well-written job description to a blueprint for performance that creates transparency in expectations and serves as a guide for training needs and promotion pathways. This is a tall order for one document, but demonstrates the importance of taking the time to set a clear foundation for performance management. Cardello (see Chapter 15) provided a detailed description of the components of a quality position description. The essential responsibilities and duties listed on the position description will become the criteria contained in the advisor performance management tool upon which advisors are rated.

While a time-consuming process, confirming that position descriptions accurately reflect the day-to-day work of advisors ensures that they begin employment aware of their roles and goals. It is important to remember that an effective job description provides transparency in expectations, serves as a guide for development planning, is general enough to be applicable across units and withstand change, and connects to the mission of the institution.

Performance Rubrics

The position description identifies essential job functions and specific duties for academic advisors. However, both the administrator and advisor must define effective performance, as clear performance standards are needed for effective and fair performance management (Biron et al., 2011). Further clarity of standards requires providing descriptions and behavioral examples of effective as well as unsatisfactory and exemplary performance. Rubrics have long been used in education and other fields to clarify performance expectations (Stevens & Levi, 2005). They provide transparency and enable equity in assessment. Watland (2012) suggested that rubrics can play a parallel function in performance management as they "serve as an effective framework to communicate, plan, and discuss performance expectations" (p. 5). Additionally, rubrics can empower the advisor to reframe the performance appraisal experience of one-sided feedback to the performance management experience of evaluative judgment, where all involved learn to reflect on their own performance and intentionally engage in development opportunities that support self-directed growth (Gyamfi et al., 2022).

Infusing Core Values

Operationalizing essential job functions in a rubric should begin with a grounding in the core values of advising: caring, commitment, empowerment, inclusivity, integrity, professionalism, and respect (NACADA, 2017). These values lay a common ground for the creation of descriptions and behavioral examples of the essential functions.

Behavioral Examples

Behavioral examples operationalize the performance of essential job functions for the advisor and introduce objective measurables for supervisor rating (Arnăutu & Panc, 2015). Feedback can focus on the documentation of evidence through the sustained practice of these behaviors. In the case of maintaining accurate advising records, sample behaviors of effective performance include:

- compiling advising notes that are concise, relevant, consistent, and adhere to institutional policy;
- employing filing systems that ensure appropriate file storage;
- using advising technologies effectively to maintain records;
- upholding Family Educational Rights and Privacy Act (FERPA); and
- completing certifications accurately and on time.

It is also helpful to provide illustrations of unsatisfactory and exemplary performance. For example, using the case of record keeping, Table 17.1 identifies some sample behaviors. Both the advisor and supervisor can document performance of these behaviors throughout the performance cycle.

TABLE 17.1 Examples of Exemplary and Unsatisfactory Performance

Exemplary Performance	Unsatisfactory Performance
Communicates with program manager of degree audit software to report errors or needed updates	Does not complete advising notes in a timely fashion
Develops unit templates for advising notes to ensure necessary information is included	Keeps student folders unlocked or on desk regularly
Regularly creates workflows or quick flows to make advising record keeping more efficient	Does not utilize degree audit software
Creates tools (i.e., workflows, forms, etc.) to strengthen certification process	Makes repeated mistakes in certifications or fails to complete certifications
Proactively seeks appropriate course substitutions in the case of department change	Fails to secure course substitutions

Rubrics as Training Tools

The exercise of identifying essential job functions and creating performance rubrics takes time and should involve a broad representation of senior administrators, advising administrators, experienced advisors, and human resources personnel. The investment of time has a valuable return of much more than a written job description. Advisors gain a refreshed and expanded clarity of their role and its value, while advising administrators gain a clear matrix for professional development planning for their advising teams. Professionals outside of advising benefit from a clearer understanding of the broad role and impact of advising, which can aid human resources colleagues in supporting performance management for advising professionals.

Performance rubrics are invaluable parts of the performance management process. Rubrics can be introduced during onboarding to provide a roadmap for performance and lay the foundation for a performance culture where advisors are empowered to actively engage in conversations about their development on a regular basis (Mohapatra & Mishra, 2018). This ensures that advisors know exactly what behaviors are expected and that supervisors can objectively document observed behaviors over time to justify metrics. Supervisors can train on performance management using case studies and rubrics to garner interrater reliability if a campus is decentralized; this interrater reliability ensures that advisors are treated fairly, even with different supervisors. A performance culture grounded in fairness supports professional satisfaction at individual and institutional levels by creating an environment where advisors do not feel they need to change units for more development opportunities (Meng & Berger, 2019).

Self-Appraisal

Another important component of performance management is self-appraisal, which has been both praised and criticized. Heidemeier and Moser (2009) recounted pitfalls of self-appraisal, including rating inflation by employees. Dash and Mohanty (2019) linked self-appraisals to increased employee engagement. Geldermann (2000) argued that effective self-appraisal for employees demands that honesty and fairness be integral parts of the process. Employees must be willing to admit weakness or failure, while the institution must use that information as a starting point for additional support and training, not punishment. Geldermann's requirement of honesty and trust may appear so optimistic that self-appraisal is dismissed as impractical, unreliable, or irrelevant.

Campbell and Lee (1988) made an excellent and detailed case about the complexity of self-appraisals (SAs) and their misuse. They stated, "it seems highly unlikely that traditional SAs can function as purely evaluative tools" (p. 310). However, they were unwilling to dismiss them altogether. They argued that self-appraisal, in particular appraisal focused on future behaviors and development, has value for employees. The most critical role of self-appraisal is not providing evaluation in the moment but informing and creating the context in which performance and evaluation occur (Campbell & Lee, 1988).

Self-appraisal is a window into employees' understanding of the job and their relationship to it. Self-appraisals reveal areas of confidence and uncertainty, desires for growth, needs for support, and causes of joy and frustration. Strong supervisors use that information to align expectations, find avenues for professional development, reassign responsibilities to better reflect employees' passions or goals, and deepen relationships with employees.

Self-appraisal can be a significant tool in mitigating cultural, identity, and other social disparities that may arise within a diverse workplace. "Self-assessment and identity are inextricably linked, both occurring through lived experiences and interactions with others within multiple and different socio-cultural contexts" (Bourke & Mentis, 2013, p. 854). The environment experienced by an administrator who supervises the majority may be very different from the workplace environment that someone from an underrepresented group experienced. Identifying and addressing barriers and other threats to identity in the workplace is a critical function of good supervision. Open discussion about identity in the workplace—within the context of performance evaluation—demonstrates a commitment to equity and inclusion.

Many institutions have self-appraisal methods built into evaluation processes, whether mandatory or optional. Some employees may find the process of self-appraisal uncomfortable or intimidating. Ways to help them approach this process include:

- encouraging employees to complete them if optional;
- allowing them time to self-reflect. Do not rush the deadline;
- keeping it simple and relevant;
- using open-ended questions;
- asking employees what should have been asked but was not;
- recommending that employees put time on their calendar to complete the self-appraisal and to keep that time reserved as they would any other appointment.

Supervisors interested in developing their own self-appraisal tools have numerous online examples of questions, rubrics, and goal-setting exercises.

They should emphasize the use of good survey construction guidelines in creating new tools. Ultimately, the exact format of the method is less important than the resulting conversation.

Performance Conversations

Performance management often conjures up anxiety for both supervisors and employees. "Evaluation" can carry connotations of judgment that may be hard for both parties to manage (Peccei et al., 2013). However, McClellan (2014) discussed the importance of trust building that occurs in personnel management interviews. To ensure open communication, establish and implement routines; create processes for collecting, analyzing, and monitoring data. These steps allow supervisors to provide advisors with timely feedback and suggestions for continuous improvement. By establishing deadlines, all participants can have conversations within an appropriate timeframe (Reform Support Network, 2013).

Preparation can help supervisors create effective conversations about performance that sustain and elevate job commitment. Preparedness by both parties can alleviate anxiety that surrounds the dialog. The conversation about evaluation should not and must not be the only conversation between employees and supervisors each year. "Attentive guidance and coaching, whether scheduled or spontaneous, should be an ongoing part of your working relationship throughout the year" (Harvard Business Review Press, 2015, p. 6). Advising administrators can draw parallels between advising conversations and performance management conversations. The same characteristics that make for positive interactions apply to both types of relationships. Table 17.2 demonstrates effective practices before, during, and after the performance review meeting.

Performance management should center on the needs and goals of the employee and should connect these to institutional success. Use this time to learn about individual employees' goals, dreams, and concerns. How do they view their role when working toward institutional goals? What changes would they make to their jobs? What needs do they have (i.e. physical, intellectual, social, or emotional) that a supervisor could help meet? What barriers—physical or emotional—do they perceive that hinder improving their performance? What would help them and their students thrive?

Performance management talks may be a continuation of difficult conversations. If an employee is not meeting expectations, the supervisor must address that immediately and often. While these conversations may be unpleasant, ignoring poor performance will undermine office morale and motivation (Plump, 2010). A rubric that outlines where the employee

TABLE 17.2 Effective Practices for Conducting Performance Reviews

Before the Performance Review Meeting	During the Performance Review Meeting	After the Performance Review Meeting
Gather information and relevant material ahead of the appointment	Provide the employee with a copy of the written review at the beginning of the meeting (or prior) and allow them to read over the document before beginning the conversation	Document the key points of conversation for future reference
Review notes on past interactions to refresh memory and comprehension	As much as possible, allow the employee to set the content and pace of the conversation	Follow up with the employee via email. Include topics discussed, next steps, deadlines, and relevant referrals
Schedule the performance review meeting. Allot ample, uninterrupted time in a quiet environment for the conversation	Ask open-ended questions and listen more than talk	File and appropriately store advisor information in a confidential, secure manner
Ensure a face-to-face modality, either in-person or over video conference for remote employees	Orient the conversation toward the future (specific behavioral changes, roles, and goals)	
	Avoid surprising the employee with new concerns about past performance	
	Refer the advisor to relevant resources for professional development or performance improvement	
	Ensure that the advisor is aware of relevant institutional and departmental policies	

Is deficient in the goals that were set can alleviate some of the tension surrounding this discussion. Comparing the rubric and the self-appraisal can help the employee and supervisor find misalignment. No greater responsibility exists for supervisors than to be willing to undertake difficult tasks on behalf of the office. Consistent intervention, clarification of expectations and goals, and documentation are all critical to this process.

Administrators should refer to institutional policies and human resource departments for specific local guidance regarding conducting corrective sessions with advisors.

Performance Development Plans

The final performance management component consists of performance development plans, which can be powerful tools in setting expectations and managing behavior. Strong developmental plans are written and goal-oriented to clearly outline how and when goals should be met (Zukof, 2021). Developmental plans may be corrective, functional, or aspirational. An employee's plan may have components in all three categories, making them valuable for employees at all performance levels.

Corrective Plans

Corrective developmental plans contain action items that must be accomplished to return an employee to satisfactory performance. Corrective plans must be carefully constructed and consistently monitored. Expectations for successful completion of the plan must be absolutely clear and measurable. For example, if accuracy is a concern, the stated goal of "improving accuracy on graduation checks" is unclear. A clearer goal may be "no more than one mistake per 50 completed graduation checks." Be sure to include timeframes for reevaluation and accomplishment of the goal as well. Rubrics and benchmarks can also illustrate acceptable performance.

Advising administrators need to ask about possible barriers to performance, what the employee believes are contributing factors and what can help mitigate the challenges. Below are suggested questions for conversation and action.

- Are personal concerns impacting work?
- Is the office environment conducive to work?
- How can any identified concerns be addressed?
- Can we be creative in finding support for employees that are struggling?
- Might we consider pairing them with people who excel in the specific area or task for mentoring or help?
- Are there professional development courses on campus that could help?
- Would learning more about available technology provide support?
- Are there NACADA resources on this subject? Credit courses on your campus that the employee could complete or audit? Books in the library?
- Do they need additional office equipment?

Like students, employees may have more than one reason for poor performance (Adin, 2021). Address as many as possible in any corrective plan.

Well-executed corrective plans take time. Consistent monitoring is key to the advisor's future success. Meet with the employee regularly to revisit the plan and discuss progress. Provide the employee written documentation of any progress or regression they have made in meeting goals. Clear documentation of an issue and how it should be resolved becomes increasingly important if the employee fails to meet expectations going forward and additional action is needed. At that point, human resources and the institution's disciplinary process may begin.

Functional Plans

Functional developmental plans contain short-term action items that target improvement in the function of the office or the employee. These can be accomplished in a single performance cycle. These goals are targeted to meet individual or unit goals, such as promotion, improved performance evaluations, or targeted intervention or programming for students.

The performance evaluation should include conversations about goals the employee may have and how the supervisor can help them reach those goals or create the interventions they see lacking. Ideally, functional plans are driven by the employee's individual goals and passions rather than mandated by the supervisor. Even if a mandate is given, allowing the employee flexibility in meeting that mandate can generate excitement, commitment, and trust with the employee.

An important part of a supervisor's role is to help facilitate the accomplishment of employees' professional goals. Find opportunities for employees to stretch their abilities. Allow them to create a program or workshop, improve an office process, or reconsider the approach to required advising. Create teams and task forces for people with similar or interconnected interests. Play to strengths and create growth opportunities. Provide professional development whenever and however possible to enable them to expand their knowledge and skillset. Set timelines for task completion and identify outcomes for assessment. Provide regular follow up but avoid micromanaging.

Aspirational Plans

Aspirational developmental plans include long-term goals, big dreams, and even crazy ideas. These plans may take multiple evaluation cycles or require resources that are unavailable. No negative action should be incurred if progress is not made. Aspirational goals may need more time and conversation to identify. Encourage employees to dream big; tell them when they have what it takes, as a push from a supervisor may be the spark they need. Find ways to support employee aspirational goals for as long as possible. Supervisors who provide cheerleading and scaffolding help ensure long-term advancement.

As tough as it may feel, actively give up control. The next generation of advising leaders are currently front-line advisors, and they need opportunities to thrive and grow into exceptional administrators (Zukof, 2021). As advisors express interest in administration, find administrative tasks that they can oversee, such as project management, supervision of administrative assistants or students, or leading search committees. Administrator-focused institutes, webinars, and other leadership opportunities are available through NACADA and likely the institution. All three developmental plan types must ensure transparency in expectations and allow advisors to feel valued and seen so they can become passionate about their work.

Conclusion

Effective performance management is similar to advising and teaching. Employees, like students, need challenge, support, and a clear understanding of expectations and evaluation metrics. They need motivation, trust, enthusiasm, and to know how to improve when they fall short. They need to find meaning in their efforts, know that their goals factor into their successes, and build strong relationships within the institution to achieve their dreams. Supervisors who foster this type of environment provide exceptional value to employees, students, units, and institutions.

Advising administrators also need challenge and support in developing as performance managers. This chapter provides a foundation. Seek out mentors and colleagues to learn with and from. Advising administrators must continuously seek feedback, grow more comfortable with radical candor, and remain open to self-learning through that feedback. Administrators who embrace performance management as an opportunity for their entire team to grow can create a sustainable culture of innovation and excellence in the practice of academic advising and, hopefully, create a place that their advisors desire to show up for every day and for days to come.

Guiding Questions and Considerations

1 Does your academic advisor job description effectively define the position? Are essential job functions identified? Is it written to be sustainable across advising units and across change?

2 Translate the essential job functions on your campus into performance rubrics that provide not only descriptions but also behavioral examples.

3 What is your process when creating a self-appraisal plan? What are your strengths and opportunities for growth?

4 What are some ways to handle a difficult conversation with an advisor? Consider an employee who has a situation outside of their control that is affecting their work. How does a supervisor balance compassion, professionalism, and the needs of others who depend on the advisor?

5 Compose a plan in each of the three categories—corrective, functional, and aspirational—for yourself or for an advisor in your office.

References

Adin, C. A. (2021). Addressing unsatisfactory performance in employees. *Veterinary Clinics of North America: Small Animal Practice, 51*(5), 1061–1069. https://doi.org/10.1016/j.cvsm.2021.04.022.

Aguinis, H., & Pierce, C. A. (2008). Enhancing the relevance of organizational behavior by embracing performance management research. *Journal of Organizational Behavior, 29*(1), 139–145.

Armstrong, M. (2006). *Performance management: Key strategies and practical guidelines* (3rd ed.). Kogan Page Business Books.

Arnăutu, E., & Panc, I. (2015). Evaluation criteria for performance appraisal of faculty members. *Procedia—Social and Behavioral Sciences, 203*, 386–392. https://doi.org/10.1016/j.sbspro.2015.08.313.

Biron, M., Farndale, E., & Paauwe, J. (2011). Performance management effectiveness: Lessons from world-leading firms. *The International Journal of Human Resource Management, 22*(6), 1294–1311.

Bourke, R., & Mentis, M. (2013). Self-assessment as a process for inclusion. *International Journal of Inclusive Education, 17*(8), 854–867. https://doi.org/10.10 80/13603116.2011.602288.

Campbell, D. J., & Lee, C. (1988). Self-appraisal in performance evaluation: Development versus evaluation. *Academy of Management Review, 13*(2), 302–314. https://doi.org/10.5465/amr.1988.4306896.

Darling-Hammond, L., & Hyler, M. E. (2013). The role of performance assessment in developing teaching as profession. *Rethinking Schools, 27*(4), 10–15.

Das, P., & Mukherjee, S. (2017). Designing a fuzzy approach for modelling the performance evaluation of education service providers. *International Journal of Services and Operations Management, 26*(1), 49–67.

Dash, B., & Mohanty, P. K. (2019). The effects of work environment, self-evaluation at workplace and employee morale on employee engagement. *Srusti Management Review, 12*(1), 33–39.

Fletcher, C. (2001). Performance appraisal and management: The developing research agenda. *Journal of Occupational and Organizational Psychology, 74*(4), 473–487. https://doi.org/10.1348/096317901167488.

Gan, M., & Kleiner, B. H. (2005). How to write job descriptions effectively. *Management Research News, 28*(8), 48–54. https://doi.org/10.1108/014091705 10784959.

Geldermann, B. (2000). *Self-assessment and self-evaluation in new forms of training near the workplace.* https://eric.ed.gov/?id=ED468229.

Gyamfi, G., Hanna, B. E., & Khosravi, H. (2022). The effects of rubrics on evaluative judgement: A randomised controlled experiment. *Assessment and Evaluation in Higher Education, 47*(1), 126–143.

Heidemeier, H., & Moser, K. (2009). Self–other agreement in job performance ratings: A meta-analytic test of a process model. *Journal of Applied Psychology, 94*(2), 353–370. https://doi.org/10.1037/0021-9010.94.2.353.

Helmold, M., & Terry, B. (2021). Performance management cycle, KPI, and OKR. In M. Helmold, & B. Terry (Eds.), *Operations and supply management 4.0: Industry insights, case studies and best practices* (pp. 145–154). Springer. https://doi.org/10.1007/978-3-030-68696-3_12.

Mampane, S. T. (2020a). Exploring academic promotion practices within higher education institutions: Enablers and constraints in the physical space. In N. Popov, C. Wolhuter, L. de Beer, G. Hilton, J. Ogunleye, E. Achinewhu-Nworgu, & E. Niemczyk (Eds.), *Educational reforms worldwide* (pp. 184–190). Bulgarian Comparative Education Society.

Mampane, S. T. (2020b). Understanding and application of the institutional performance management system within higher education institution departments. In N. Popov, C. Wolhuter, L. de Beer, G. Hilton, J. Ogunleye, E. Achinewhu-Nworgu, & E. Niemczyk (Eds.), *Educational reforms worldwide* (pp. 205–211). Bulgarian Comparative Education Society.

McClellan, J. (2014). Promoting trust through effective advising administration. *The Mentor: An Academic Advising Journal, 16*(2014). https://journals.psu.edu/mentor/article/view/61261/60894.

Meng, J., & Berger, B. K. (2019). The impact of organizational culture and leadership performance on PR professionals' job satisfaction: Testing the joint mediating effects of engagement and trust. *Public Relations Review, 45*(1), 64–75. https://doi.org/10.1016/j.pubrev.2018.11.002.

Mohapatra, M., & Mishra, S. (2018). The employee empowerment as a key factor defining organizational performance in emerging market. *International Journal of Business Insights and Transformation, 12*(1), 48–52.

NACADA: The Global Community for Academic Advising. (2017). NACADA core values of academic advising. https://www.nacada.ksu.edu/Resources/Pillars/CoreValues.aspx.

Pandita, D., & Ray, S. (2018). Talent management and employee engagement—A meta-analysis of their impact on talent retention. *Industrial and Commercial Training, 50*(4), 185–199.

Peccei, R., van de Voorde, K., and van Veldhoven, M. (2013). HRM, well-being and performance: A theoretical and empirical review. In J. Paauwe, D. Guest, & P. M. Wright (Eds.), *HRM and performance: Achievements and challenges* (pp. 15–46). Wiley.

Harvard Business Review Press (2015). *Performance reviews: Evaluate performance, offer constructive feedback, discuss tough topics.* Harvard Business Review Press.

Plump, C. M. (2010). Dealing with problem employees: A legal guide for employers. *Business Horizons, 53*(6), 607–618. https://doi.org/10.1016/j.bushor.2010.07.003.

Reform Support Network. (2013, March). *Performance management.* [Brochure]. Reform Support Network.

Stevens, D. D., & Levi, A. (2005). Leveling the field: Using rubrics to achieve greater equity in teaching and grading. *Essays on Teaching Excellence: Toward the Best in the Academy, 17*(1). https://pdxscholar.library.pdx.edu/edu_fac/86/.

Watland, K. H. (2012). Just tell us what you want! Using rubrics to help MBA students become better performance managers. *Transformative Dialogues: Teaching & Learning Journal, 6*(1), 1–8.

Weiherl, J., & Frost, J. (2016). Professional and organizational commitment in universities: From judgmental to developmental performance management. In J. Frost, F. Hattke, & M. Reihlen (Eds.), *Multi-level governance in universities* (pp. 173–192). Springer.

Zukof, K. (2021, July 30). When it comes to change, get employees off the sidelines. *TD Magazine, 75*(8), 56–61. https://www.td.org/magazines/td-magazine/when-it-comes-to-change-get-employees-off-the-sidelines

18

ADVISOR RETENTION AND INTENTIONAL CAREER PATHS

Claire Robinson and Mike Dial

As noted in Chapter 1, academic advising is a core function of student success and the "hub of the wheel" for collaborative efforts. To support this core function in the collegiate experience, advising administrators must develop an advising program that is sustainable for both students and advisors. Perhaps the most important role of advisors is to develop meaningful, informed relationships with their student advisees. To create a sustainable advising infrastructure that promotes a consistent and meaningful student experience, colleges with primary-role advisors must develop creative ways to retain them. Arguably, high turnover and the "great resignation" have disrupted academic advising more profoundly than nearly any other student-facing staff position on campus. Why? Because when an advisor leaves their position, the student experience is automatically disrupted and students are in the position of needing to retell their stories to someone new. In addition, advisor assignments must be reconfigured, administrative duties transferred, and perhaps budgets need to be realigned. Administrators must post positions or fill vacancies, and new advisors must be onboarded and trained in complex curricula or university policies. All of these changes, and perhaps more, must be managed along with the day-to-day and programmatic demands such as registration, new student orientation, parent inquiries, policy changes, curriculum updates, degree audits, and technology utilization. In short, high turnover and advisor vacancies can negatively affect nearly every aspect of an advising program, making the retention of advisors an important administrative function.

When individuals begin to consider a professional career in higher education, two paths are typically considered: becoming a faculty member

DOI: 10.4324/9781003437598-31

or pursuing a role in student affairs. Academic advising may offer a third path that straddles both. Advising, through its connection with the curriculum, advances higher education's teaching and learning mission (i.e., academic affairs) and supports student engagement in curricular and cocurricular opportunities (i.e., student affairs) to facilitate goal achievement. In essence, academic advising is a unique and challenging profession that allows practitioners to engage in the work of both academic and student affairs.

Students benefit from advisors with extensive knowledge of student development and learning, career development, and institutional knowledge of policies and resources. Thus, it is in the best interests of and integral to the success of advising programs as well as the advising profession that high-potential, high-achieving advisors are retained in their student-facing positions. For academic advising to remain a sustainable field, administrators in advising leadership positions must be intentional about establishing programs aimed at developing and retaining academic advisors.

This chapter will explore the development and implementation of advising career ladders, mentorship programs, and other initiatives that offer frontline advisors a voice in organizational strategy and encourage long-term commitment to careers in advising. Several strategies, beginning with career ladders, will be shared to equip administrators with ideas to create an advising environment that supports the learning, well-being, and growth of advisors and, in turn, students.

Career Ladders

The quality of academic advising on any given campus is directly related to the interactions between advisors and students. The consistency of this interaction is important and academic advising administrators must attract and retain academic advisors from diverse backgrounds to promote a robust student experience. Career ladders support advisor retention by providing recognition and advancement opportunities, such as an increase in duties and responsibilities, an enhanced job title, and additional compensation for exceptionally high-performance. While poorly designed staffing support and recognition structures may lead to advisors leaving for other positions, effectively designed career ladders can support retention and advancement. As Dial et al. (2021) suggest, effective career ladders:

- Allow for professional advancement and signal value in academic advising.
- Tie promotion to knowledge, skill, and performance, not solely time on the job.

- Add additional duties and responsibilities to advisors' portfolios with each promotion.
- Make promotion feel attainable (generally every two to four years).

Nationally, a variety of advisor career ladders exist and an internet search will reveal several for you to consider. For example, a large research institution in the southeast offers a comprehensive three-tiered program outlining skills, competencies, and compensation bands tied to the NACADA core competencies model. Another institution in the northeast offers five levels of advisor experience, typical work duties, and advanced job responsibilities. The levels in a career ladder vary in terms of title. Several institutions signal advancement using Roman numerals (e.g., Advisor I, Advisor II, Advisor III), and/or other institutions mirror faculty promotion language (e.g., Assistant Advisor, Associate Advisor, Senior Advisor).

When designing a career ladder, it is important to remember that advisor roles at each level need to include responsibilities that focus primarily on student interaction. This ensures that advisors prioritize student interactions while approaching any additional administrative duties as complementary rather than reducing advising students to a secondary responsibility. That said, career ladders also need to accommodate those who wish to gain the experience to move into more senior-level management and administrative roles, which may include decreases in the amount of time spent advising students directly.

The career trajectory for these individuals will look different and, as noted later in this chapter, mentoring may be a more appropriate growth and development avenue for them.

Developing a Career Ladder

Developing an advising career ladder requires time, research, and institutional investment. One of the highest hurdles to navigate when establishing advising career ladders is securing adequate funding to ensure the sustainability of the effort. According to Taylor (2011), "salary considerations should be informed by the regional market, fiscal considerations on campus, and compensation levels for similar positions at benchmarks, including peer institutions and comparable advising operations, with cost-of-living adjustments" (p. 135). In times of decreasing higher education budgets, administrators may need to demonstrate a career ladder's institutional return on investment in order to secure future funding.

Much like the retention of students, retaining advisors in their positions saves the organization time, money, and resources by avoiding posting positions, screening, interviewing, conducting reference checks, and all the other logistics relevant to the hiring process. By retaining advisors, administrators can use employee retention and promotion to plan budgets and advocate for resources to ensure and maintain an appropriate level of full-time equivalent advisors in student-facing positions. Administrators should resist the urge to supplant primary-role advisors with students when advisors move into more administrative work. Prioritizing an advisor career ladder demonstrates a commitment to student-facing advisor positions.

Planning and budgeting for advisor career ladders is important. Advising administrators should identify the timing of promotion (i.e., every two to four years), establish a number or percentage of possible promotions during this time frame (e.g., 10%–15% of the staff roster), and budget for a realistic promotional amount (5%–15% of the staff salary). By projecting advisor promotion five or even ten years in advance, advising administrators can make a clear and formulaic request for additional funding as needed.

To promote equity among advisors and budget appropriately, advising career ladders are best positioned at an institutional level rather than within individual colleges. An institution-wide approach also allows maximum flexibility to develop and refine advising career ladders to position advisors where they are most needed. This equitable approach can benefit advisors and allow administrators to create promotional opportunities that are responsive to institutional needs with regard to special populations, such as first-generation, transfer students, veterans, etc. Building needed population expertise within academic advising career ladders contributes to a sustainable advising environment. In sum, good advising should not be left to chance. All students should have access to great advisors who are there to support them, have appropriate and adequate training on various student populations, and can implement key communication strategies that are culturally sensitive.

The best career ladders consider more than just an advisor's time on the job. Administrators can tie promotion opportunities to successful performance evaluation (see Chapter 17), direct work with students, service to the institution through committees and various projects, collaborations with campus partners, and professional development.

The use of promotion committees can help to ensure equity in the career ladder review process. These committees should include those who can "effectively contribute to the evaluation and garner buy-in from key colleagues and departments" (Taylor, 2011, p. 137). Ideally, committee member should include those from advising and academic leadership. Advisors should be asked to present a portfolio, including their curriculum vitae or resume, written reflection, and other documents demonstrating success in their current role as well as how their experiences meet the requirements of the promotion level there are seeking.

Establishing Levels

In developing a career ladder, administrators should map the desired experience across the career ladder levels, essentially creating a rubric to be used in the decision-making and review process. This process begins with identifying the responsibilities that often fall within an advisor's weekly work experience. While needing to be tailored to the particular institution, Table 18.1 offers a sample of responsibilities to consider.

Within the first 12–24 months in a new advising position, curriculum mastery and university policy are usually any new hire's focus. However, as advisors rise through the ranks of the career ladder, their roles

TABLE 18.1 Essential Functions of Academic Advising

- Accelerated study plans
- Admitted student days/outreach events
- AP/IB/transfer credit
- Attend training
- Availability and accessibility to students
- Career conversations
- Course needs monitoring
- Cross-training in multiple majors
- Degree audit
- Integration into department/college/school
- Interventions/proactive advising
- Knowledge of the curriculum
- Knowledge of university policy
- Manage exceptions/course substitutions
- Monitor progress reports/faculty referrals
- Monitoring caseloads, enrollment, registration
- Orientation
- Placement scores
- Predictive analytics
- Prioritizing the student
- Promotion of part term, winter term, summer term
- Referrals
- Regular communication with students
- Specialized advising/special student populations
- Student notes and record keeping
- Transfer advising
- Work with faculty
- Work with parents

become increasingly complex; they often take on additional duties and responsibilities and gain a deeper knowledge of the work. All of these responsibilities and components of advisor roles reveal a balance between the "science" of advising (i.e., curriculum, policies, procedures, knowledge of campus offices, technology usage, etc.) and the "art" of advising (i.e., communication skills, a variety of approaches to advising perhaps including appreciative advising, strengths-based advising, and information that points to a level of engagement with the scholarly literature of academic advising).

There are several key considerations when designing a career ladder for advisors. For example, administrators should design opportunities to tap into employee strengths by identifying their areas of interest and crafting opportunities to meet student needs. There is also an opportunity to design tiered career ladders to allow flexibility in a promotion to meet department needs. Additional duties may include population-specific (i.e. first-generation, transfer, underrepresented) student specialization, advisor and/or student worker supervision, project or program management, and more. Program management could include taking the lead on orientation practices for the advising unit, working on strategic assessment projects, or serving as an official liaison to partner offices such as the registrar, bursar, or financial aid. Advising administrators are encouraged to be intentional about the design of a career ladder, particularly with regard to how the levels are structured, titled, and sequenced. Administrators may decide to use both levels (e.g., Academic Advisor I, II, III) and titles (e.g., Coordinator, Program Manager, Assistant Director) to offer more specificity of responsibilities for the advancing advisor. For example, at an institution taking this approach, titles might include both advisor rank and secondary titles, such as:

Jane Doe, M. Ed.
Academic Advisor II
Coordinator of Orientation & First-Year Programming
Psychology, College of Arts and Sciences
John Doe, M.A.
Academic Advisor III
Program Manager, Advising Assessment and Outreach
College of Nursing

Titles are one way to signify advancement publicly. Supervisors and administrators can identify opportunities for leadership or management and place these under a specific advisor's job portfolio. Administrators can design advising programs that balance student and institutional needs by providing opportunities for advisors to remain in primarily student-facing positions while also developing expertise in programmatic or administrative duties; being responsible for orientation might be an example.

As advisors progress, they maintain their primary focus of supporting students' success in their academic pursuits while taking on significantly more administrative responsibilities. Advanced advisors can be considered in the pipeline for advising administration sustainability (see Chapter 14).

Finally, administrators should consider the long-term goals and plans for how advisor career ladders are implemented and executed with special consideration given to the advisor's developmental path upon reaching the highest tier of the career ladder. By this time, the advisor's position should have a clearly established, significant area of focus for them to exercise their expertise and offer leadership to the advising unit. Engagement in departmental decision-making and assuming supervisory responsibility might be additions to an advisor's portfolio that enhances their role. While perhaps not realistic, in an ideal situation, the majority of academic advisors would strive for the highest tier of the career ladder, have a high level of satisfaction with the work, and remain at the institution for a significant amount of time. However, administrators should also celebrate advancement of advisors even when it means leaving the unit or institution.

Additional Methods for Advisor Growth and Retention

In addition to developing advising career ladders, administrators may improve advisors' morale and retention by enacting one or more of several administrative-adjacent initiatives that create a shared culture around organizational mission and vision. Huggett (2000) points out that the decentralized nature of many advising operations can lead to professional silos and isolation. Administrators can create opportunities for advisors to engage with one another across departmental boundaries through the creation of committees, formal communities of practice, and mentorship opportunities. Each finds root in the work of Lave and Wenger (1991), who suggest that advisors "move toward full participation in the sociocultural practices of a community" as they develop "mastery of knowledge and skill[s]" (p. 29). By providing advisors with increasingly complex opportunities to engage in organizational development, administrators allow frontline staff to increase buy-in to advising operations.

Committees and Communities of Practice

Advising is an occupation that requires professionals to spend a significant portion of their time in meetings with students. Creating a space for advisors to serve on committees allows for a break in the routine and may provide opportunities for advisors to develop their skills in other interesting ways. Faculty advisors likely already have ample opportunities to engage in institutional and departmental governance through varying service levels to the university. For primary-role advisors, the opportunity to serve on various committees could further professional development and a sense of belonging to the department or institution by demonstrating value in advisors' thoughts and opinions.

Academic advisors can be integrated into committee and task force work at the department, college, or institutional levels. At the department level, advisors could be invited to serve on committees with departmental faculty. At a more central level, primary-role advisors could be invited to serve on a committee focused on advisor training and development. At one institution, the University Advising Center Training and Professional Development Committee helps to influence professional development opportunities, including ensuring that training and certification modules are accurate, relevant, and timely, planning monthly meetings, and suggesting in-person training opportunities. Another committee, the Advisor Consulting Group, provides non-binding strategic guidance to advising leadership. The Consulting Group is engaged when new initiatives may be rolled out that will significantly impact the advising community. Committees, then, also create a space for advisors to engage in departmental or advising community decision-making, taking some of the onus off the administrators' shoulders.

Administrators may establish internal committees and task forces to allow for input and feedback loops and in the process create a space for advisors to feel heard and valued by the advising program – thereby making advisors feel more invested in administrators' decision-making. Administrators could also advocate for advisor participation in existing campus committees. Advisors may benefit from working alongside faculty and staff with whom they have not previously interacted and bring curricular and student expertise to ongoing campus conversations.

According to Wenger et al. (2002), "Communities of practice are groups of people who share a concern, a set of problems, or a passion about a topic, and who deepen their knowledge and expertise in this area by interacting on an ongoing basis" (p. 4). Regarding this publication, we differentiate between formal communities of practice (i.e. those about to be described) and the natural communities of practice that occur and develop in shared work contexts. Communities of practice involve three key concepts: the domain, the community, and the practice. More than a social group, communities of practice share a common problem or interest, the domain, which guides questions that the group pursues and how knowledge is organized and shared. The community is the second key concept that makes communities of practice successful. A community of practice is a group of advisors who collaborate, learn together, develop personal connections, and develop a sense of belonging and mutual commitment. Members of a community of practice do not need to work in the same advising unit. Because of this social engagement, communities of practice can aid advisors in making connections across departments and silos. Finally, communities of practice share a set of frameworks, ideas, tools, information, language, and stories. They work to document and disseminate ideas, resources, and best practices. The practice is the specific knowledge that the community develops.

Communities of practice can be formed to help advisors solve day-to-day work problems or engage deeply in areas of interest. Through their work, communities of practice can develop and disseminate effective practices across the institutional advising community. They identify and steward the tools, insights, and approaches advisors need to perform their roles effectively.

Advisors can serve as "community coordinators" and lead a community of practice. This coordination creates a collaborative environment enabling the administrator to either step back or take a more participatory role allowing for peer-to-peer leadership among advisors. The coordinator's primary role is to facilitate dialog, not provide answers. Coordinators help identify important issues for the community to review, plan and facilitate meetings, and link members across unit silos. They facilitate dialog between the community, advising administrators, and campus leadership (Wenger et al., 2002).

Through membership and contribution to a community of practice, academic advisors connect their professional development to the institution's strategic direction and advising leadership. Significant contributions to communities of practices enhance the advisor's visibility and profile within the organization. Advisors in a community of practice can engage in literature review and intellectual dialog on academic intervention, advisor well-being, orientation advising, experiential learning, and flipped advising, to name a few. They bring their college/department experience to their community, discuss new solutions, document them, and integrate them into practice. Finally, they return to their college/department with expanded capabilities to test the application of their ideas against real-world problems.

Communities of practice can be invited to share their learning with the advising center or advising team at regular meetings. Through their dedication to specific topics, advisors in communities of practice can influence strategic direction and decision-making at the department and institutional

TABLE 18.2 Establishing Committees and Communities of Practice

	1 *Committee*	2 *Community of Practice*
Leadership	Often chaired by administrators with formal authority	Community "peer" coordinator
Purpose	Clearly defined; often delineated in a committee charge	Indeterminate; defined by the group
Duration	Set in committee charge; may be established as a permanent standing committee or ad hoc with a defined time to complete activities	Can exist indefinitely with a focus on continuous improvement
Membership	Formal; members are identified and take an active part in committee work	Informal; members may come and go from activities as their time and interest allow

levels. Opportunities for authentic and productive dialog should be encouraged to challenge, improve, and explore existing paradigms surrounding advising and advising administration (Thatchenkery & Metzker, 2006).

Participation in committees and communities of practice can provide advisors with unique opportunities to showcase their passions and talents outside of advising. Both can require significant investments of time and energy on the part of administrators to set these initiatives up for success. If done well, they also provide advisors an opportunity to engage deeply in organizational development. Table 18.2 provides a summary comparison of committees and communities of practice.

Mentorship

Advisor-to-advisor mentoring opportunities help establish a robust onboarding and training program for new advisors; they also help to establish a community. Seasoned advisors can be matched with new advisors to welcome and support new hires in their first year and beyond through formal and informal mentoring opportunities. Research suggests that formal mentoring programs increase staff retention and role satisfaction, develop leadership skills in mentors, and reduce the time needed for newcomers to develop skills and competence (Dominguez Garcia, 2013). This individualized support verifies essential on-the-job information and fosters essential relationships within and between advisors on staff. Mentoring is defined as:

a situation in which a more-experienced member of an organization maintains a relationship with a less-experienced, often new member to the organization and provides information, support, and guidance so as to enhance the less-experienced member's chances of success in the organization and beyond.

(Campbell & Campbell, 2000, para. 3)

Mentoring is often characterized as an informal process, one that requires a mutually agreed upon one-to-one relationship, develops a learning alliance, and is reciprocal. Defining characteristics of mentoring include establishing a longstanding relationship (quantified as six months to five years), expectation sharing, and guidance the mentor provides to the protégé. Reciprocity is also a primary function of mentoring, signifying that both the mentor and protégé believe they will benefit from the experience.

Established mentoring programs wherein more seasoned advisors welcome new advisors to the organization and the profession have reciprocal benefits for mentors, mentees, and the organization. Mentors guide and support mentees through their first year as advisors. Through this mentorship, mentors expand the capacity of administrators to support and develop new staff while developing a supportive relationship with their mentees from their first days. Advisors interested in supervising professional staff in the future may benefit from serving as a mentor by gaining supervisory experience and skills, including observations, onboarding, providing feedback, and handling difficult conversations. Through establishing mentoring programs, administrators can also encourage the development of their advising spaces as learning organizations. Senge (1990) defines the learning organization as:

> [a place] where people continually expand their capacity to create the results they truly desire, where new and expansive patterns of thinking are nurtured, where collective aspiration is set free, and where people are continually learning how to learn together.
>
> *(p. 3)*

Administrators should strive to pair mentors with mentees with intentionality. One way to approach this process intentionally is to have potential mentors and mentees fill out an intake form delineating what each is looking for in the mentoring experience. If funding allows, administrators could encourage individual meetings between mentors and mentees by purchasing and distributing coffee or meal vouchers to campus or community establishments. Finally, semi-formal mentoring contracts allow mentors and mentees to establish foundations for their time together, including setting mutual goals, agreeing to relationship duration, and meeting frequency.

Recognition Programs

Some advisors may be content in their current roles or lack interest in further service through committees, communities of practice, or mentorship. However, administrators can still seek ways to recognize employees with this perspective. Recognition opportunities and programs are often integral to an advisor retention initiative. Some advisors excel in a particular facet of their work (i.e. career advising, flipped advising, targeted population support) and can be identified as "gurus" or go-to experts on the topic (Scott, 2017). Formal awards programs modeled after the NACADA awards, which include award criteria, selection rubrics, and selection committees (to ensure equitable evaluation), could be instituted or refined. Additionally, administrators could create programs that allow students and other advisors to recognize advisors through a formal gratitude effort. Effective recognition and reward programs are "relevant, affordable, and timely" while representing "the values, mission, and culture of the institution" and engaging advisors in both design and execution (Drake, 2008, p. 410).

What kind of recognition and rewards do academic advisors most appreciate? According to Drake (2008), in a survey of 1,969 advisors and advising administrators, 74% of respondents indicated that support for professional development opportunities (NACADA membership, national and regional conference travel, etc.) was the most valuable reward an institution could offer (p. 405). While cost-effective for institutions, "certificates of appreciation, plaques, trophies, news releases, and preferential parking" carried little value for most academic advisors (p. 404).

Finally, administrators should not forget the power of saying "thank you." In addition to praising and formally recognizing advisors, administrators' expression of personal gratitude signifies authentic appreciation by sharing why the advisor's effort matters (Scott, 2017). Gratitude can be expressed in writing, in person, in public, or in private. Administrators should consider which medium and setting will impact the receiving advisor most.

Providing authentic recognition may be one of the single most impactful advisor retention efforts that administrators can enact. It is all too common for academic advisors to express feeling overworked and underappreciated. According to one recent study (Workhuman & Gallup 2022), employees who receive recognition from leaders only a few times a year or less are five times more likely to be disengaged. In addition, they are 74% more likely to indicate a desire to leave their organization within the year. Moreover, unmet recognition needs can lead to significantly higher burnout rates. Inversely, the same study found that employees who receive recognition from their leaders are three times as likely to express that their organization cares about them, making their well-being a critical factor in employees' intentions to stay with an organization.

Hybrid Work

As evidenced by the "great resignation," many advisors may leave their position to move into a more flexible career that offers remote work or more flexible schedules. This trend can be difficult to counter when the essence of great advising is meaningful student relationships that are mostly conducted in person on residential campuses. However, institutions can get creative by offering advisors hybrid work options. For example, advisors could come to campus during peak advising season and work remotely during times when student demand is lower. Administrative duties, student emails, technology utilization, and other tasks that can be done remotely enable advisors to work from home. In addition, virtual platforms such as Microsoft Teams or Zoom enable advisors to communicate with students virtually.

Conclusion

Like those in many professions, professionals in academic advising desire to progress in their chosen fields. Advisors need to see that advancement and progression in careers are attainable. It is possible to create an organizational culture that enables advisors to see professional growth and development opportunities within their existing roles. Through intentional practices that engage advisors in their career direction and organizational evolution, administrators endorse the idea of professional advising as a career. This may involve significant institutional investments in some contexts (i.e. career ladders, worthwhile pay, etc.). In these instances, advising administrators should be ready to demonstrate the return on investment that highly trained and retained academic advisors provide to students and the institution. In other contexts, additional opportunities to engage advisors as quasi or adjacent administrators (i.e. mentorship, committee work, organizational development, etc.) may involve significant administrator time.

Any advising initiative on campus is directly related to the quality of advisors. Administrators should strive to recruit, hire, train, and support high-performing advisors. If advising as a profession is to be sustained at our campuses, administrators must design programs that retain, support, and promote high-performing and student-centered advisors. Clear opportunities for career advancement, pay increases, and additional responsibilities are key to the new generation of employees; in turn, advisor retention is central to the student experience at our colleges and universities.

Reflection Questions

1 Considering primary-role academic advisor retention, what is in your locus of control? What can you influence? How can you advocate for resources (financial or otherwise) to create a sustainable advising system?

2　How can advising career ladders benefit your institution's retention and graduation goals and/or other metrics related to student success?

3　Picture someone who has mentored you. What made that relationship work? How did they assist you in your professional journey?

References

Campbell, D. E., & Campbell, T. A. (2000). The mentoring relationship: Differing perceptions of benefits. *College Student Journal, 34*(4), 516–516.

Dial, M., Bouknight, J., & McKeown, P. (2021). Appreciative onboarding and professional development of academic advisors. *Journal of Appreciative Education, 8*, 47–61.

Dominguez Garcia, N. (2013). *Mentoring unfolded: The evolution of an emerging discipline* (Publication No. 1315766986) [Doctoral dissertation, University of New Mexico]. UNM Digital Repository.

Drake, J. K. (2008). Recognition and reward for academic advising in theory and in practice. In V. N. Gordon, W. R. Habley, & T. J. Grites (Eds.), *Academic advising: A comprehensive handbook* (2nd ed., pp. 396–412). Jossey-Bass.

Huggett, K. D. (2000). Professional development in an uncertain profession: Finding a place for academic and career advisors. *NACADA Journal, 20*(2), 46–51.

Lave, J., & Wenger, E. (1991). *Situated learning: Legitimate peripheral participation*. Cambridge University Press.

Scott, K. (2017). *Radical candor: Be a kick-ass boss without losing your humanity*. St. Martin's Press.

Senge, P. M. (1990). *The fifth discipline: The art and practice of the learning organization*. Doubleday.

Taylor, M. A. (2011). Career ladders performance evaluations for academic advisors. In J. E. Joslin, & N. L. Markee (Eds.), *Academic advising administration: Essential knowledge and skills for the 21st century* (pp. 133–144). NACADA.

Thatchenkery, T., & Metzker, C. (2006). *Appreciative intelligence: Seeing the mighty oak in the acorn*. Berrett-Koehler.

Wenger, E., McDermott, R., & Snyder, W. (2002). *Cultivating communities of practice: A guide to managing knowledge*. Harvard Business Review Press.

Workhuman & Gallup. (2022, May 11). *Unleashing the human element at work: Transforming workplaces through recognition*. [Report]. Workhuman. com. https://www.workhuman.com/resources/reports-guides/unleashing-the-human-element-at-work-transforming-workplaces-through-recognition?utm_source=google&utm_medium=cpc&utm_campaign=2022q3_wh_sem_nb_awareness_primary_na_phr_rlsa&utm_content=recognition_in_workplace&campaignid=14425877748&adgroupid=129239523009&adid=601566-154691&network=g&gclid=CjwKCAjwwo-WBhAMEiwAV4dybTBTBss6eI raPJnZN-1jqMbmSW6CZfIqV0vTmwAkXspw298gMVweJBoCd4oQAvD_BwE&gclsrc=aw.ds.

19

MITIGATING BURNOUT AND PROMOTING PROFESSIONAL WELL-BEING IN ADVISORS

Amalauna Brock

Managing well-being is critical to advisor performance, student satisfaction, and the overall health of the advising unit. Prolonged exposure to stressful situations can result in ill health that impacts people throughout their lifespan (Hunt, 2021). Advisors are inundated with student needs, and most interactions with students are not simply a rote recitation of courses needed for degree completion. In many cases, advisors act as first responders to student crises. On any given day, an advisor might respond to a student facing an academic crisis, navigate a Title IX case, and learn about a grave family issue impacting a student's academic and personal success. As helping professionals, advisors are well equipped to help students navigate campus and community resources—but often are not licensed counselors. This lack of professional training coupled with large caseloads can wear advisors down. Further, an unstable working environment, uncaring administration, budgetary issues, an institution's political environment, and colleague interactions can all impact advisors and administrator well-being and contribute to mental health issues. Effective advising administrators are mindful of their team's challenges and create supports that allow them to thrive. This chapter gives administrators a basic framework for supporting the advising team's well-being.

Well-Being, Burnout, Empathy Fatigue, and the Stress Cycle

Well-being is an overall feeling of mental, emotional, and physical health. It includes dealing with setbacks, challenges, triumphs, and joys (Centers for Disease Control and Prevention, 2018; Hird, 2003; Selwyn & Wood,

DOI: 10.4324/9781003437598-32

2015). Burnout or empathy fatigue, used interchangeably in this chapter, is the opposite of well-being and can be a significant challenge for people in helping professions. The term "burnout" was first used by Herbert Fruedenberger (Dubois & Mistretta, 2020). The Mayo Clinic Staff (2021, para. 1) defined burnout as "a state of physical or emotional exhaustion that also involves a sense of reduced accomplishment and loss of personal identity" (para. 1). Stebnicki (2008) stated that advisors often experience anxiety and distress from interactions with students with negative life experiences. Advisors generally must manage student, departmental, and institutional expectations alongside demands of accrediting bodies and parents. Advisors often empathize, negotiate, encourage, and serve as a life coach for students. When students experience distressing, challenging, or traumatic experiences, so often it is their advisor in whom they confide. These are the same conditions that lead to burnout in traditional counseling professions (Stebnicki, 2008). In short, working with students, faculty members, and institutional personnel can be draining (Dubois & Mistretta, 2020).

Burnout manifests differently for everyone; however, there are common symptoms. These include exhaustion, anxiety, crankiness, sleep issues, reduced empathy for others' needs, less energy to complete basic tasks, negativity, getting sick more often, inability to concentrate, inability to achieve, and less satisfaction with work, family, and life. Descriptions of the stages and degrees of burnout range from not feeling burnout, to being unable to work effectively, to being completely incapacitated (Nagoski & Nagoski, 2020; Stebnicki, 2008). Burnout makes everyday tasks seem harder to accomplish. Empathy fatigue can also build up over time and contribute to fatigue (Stebnicki, 2008). Often, symptoms of burnout— no longer enjoying things you once enjoyed, hopelessness, seclusion, and disinterestedness—are confused with depression (Dubois & Mistretta, 2020).

Empathy fatigue and burnout are related but they may feel or manifest differently (Dubois & Mistretta, 2020). Dedicated advising professionals tend to engage in behaviors that contribute to burnout, such as taking on students' emotions, becoming overly involved in student trauma, and overcommitting to projects (Stebnicki, 2008). Furthermore, a host of factors add to the potential for empathy fatigue, including lack of counseling training, personal trauma, lack of supervisor/colleague/institutional support, lack of workload control, lack of options for professional development, dramatic changes in working conditions, little reward, and toxic working environments (Dubois & Mistretta, 2020). Additionally, supporting students who have high needs (i.e., academically underachieving, on academic probation/suspension, or who have trauma) can negatively impact advisor's well-being (Dubois & Mistretta, 2020).

Nagoski and Nagoski's (2020) book, *Burnout*, posited that the stress cycle (stressful responses, reactions, hormones, etc.) must be completed to eliminate stress from the body. They argued that there are many ways to do this (Nagoski & Nagoski, 2020), so advisors and administrators should look for ways to incorporate the activities that work for them into their daily routines. These include meditation, exercise, journaling, and other activities.

The value and impact of quality advising can be significant to students, alumni, and parents. Devoting time to maintaining and improving advisor well-being can result in a substantial return on investment in the form of advisor retention and improved student outcomes. When academic advisors feel their best and work at optimal levels, they can better support their students, who will be more likely to meet outcomes that the institution values (Dubois & Mistretta, 2020).

Managing Well-Being

There are as many ways to manage well-being as there are people. The following sections provide some tips and tricks for administrators to manage their own well-being while also finding solutions that might work for others as well. Remember, administrators are not required to have all the answers. It is okay to reach out for help from professionals, on or off campus. Professionals can help find solutions or provide resources. Rely on their expertise.

Administrator Self-Care

Any number of daily tasks and responsibilities can drain administrators' energy. They may supervise advisors and support personnel, manage student workers, maintain an advising caseload, engage in professional development, attend meetings, and serve on committees. Separately, each of these issues can be stressful; together, they can be overwhelming. Finding a way to juggle work and manage self-care can be daunting when this occurs.

Advisors unknowingly contribute to administrator stress. Administrators may lead a team of new advisors or advisors who struggle to work independently or who need extra support. Whatever the case may be—intentionally or not—the advising team can be a source of stress for administrators. Further, campus politics or lack of support from campus leadership can cause anxiety.

Administrators who are invested in creating an equitable work environment for their team may take on extra projects and work that needs to be done. However, this can do a disservice to the administrator and the team. Some advisors would be energized by taking on a new project and doing so could help them develop professionally. Delegation is an essential skill for effective advising administrators to learn and do. Allowing advisors and others on the team to take on tasks the administrator would otherwise oversee frees administrator time for tasks they cannot delegate and allows advisors to take on administrative responsibilities.

Importance of Administrator Self-Care

As with anything, the airline advice to put your own oxygen mask on first also holds true here. Administrators have to take care of themselves first if they are going to be genuinely productive and present for their team. The team needs administrators to be fully present and engaged. Modeling a healthy self-care routine and setting appropriate boundaries lets the team know that administrators are invested in everyone's well-being. Like students, advisors watch administrators' actions to learn how to be advisors. As leaders, administrators set the tone for their direct reports regarding self-care.

Self-Care Activities

Self-care refers to activities that benefit one's mental and physical well-being and can include many different types of pursuits depending on individual needs. Engaging in self-care is important to maintain mental and physical health (National Institute of Mental Health, 2021). The activities below provide a starting point for a personalized self-care routine.

Reconnecting With People. Spending time with family, friends, colleagues, and others who uplift is beneficial for completing the stress cycle. Any encouraging interaction with another human being can help. Try recruiting a close friend or family member for a long hug. Around half a minute (just 30 seconds) of hugging a special someone can shift a body into feelings of safety and security (Nagoski & Nagoski, 2020). "Loneliness is a form of starvation" (Nagoski & Nagoski, 2020, p. 134). Maybe lean on a partner for emotional support; consult professional caretakers to sort out basic needs (i.e., someone to clean house, a meal delivery service for food); find friends to have fun with; identify a book club to stimulate your intellectual side; or join a knitting club to be creative. The people in one's life who help support well-being are their support network. Having a strong support network allows everyone to deal with stress more effectively.

Journaling and Self-Reflection. Journaling or self-reflection can help alleviate the impacts of stress. Writing down frustrations and negative experiences can help to close the stress cycle. Further, starting a gratitude journal can help one realize the good things in life and gain a deeper appreciation for the world. Journaling does not have to be daily, nor does it need to be long. It can be one simple, stream-of-consciousness paragraph in the morning while having a cup of coffee or a wind-down practice before bed with a cup of chamomile tea. There is no right or wrong way to start a journaling practice. Make it unique.

Meditation and Breathing. Mindful meditation and breathing exercises are one way to bring the mind back to focus and to the present moment. Even a few deep breaths can help shift perspectives and begin to calm the nervous system. There are several free resources (i.e., videos, apps, etc.) that can aid users in developing mindful practices. Those unsure where to start can simply begin by getting comfortable (i.e., sitting, standing, lying, mindful movement) and taking a few deep breaths. Don't worry about doing it right or wrong. Just breathe deeply and allow the mind to wander.

Exercise. Physical activity can negate the effects of stress on the body. Simply removing the stressor—concluding a bad day or leaving a difficult conversation, for example—will not rid the body of the stress response. To get rid of stress, the stress loop needs to be closed. Exercise is one way to accomplish this closure. Exercise does not have to be strenuous to be effective at eliminating stress in the body; it can be as simple as tensing and releasing muscles or as strenuous as running a marathon. There are many guides online for finding ways to incorporate exercise to fit physical limitations and personal preferences (Nagoski & Nagoski, 2020).

Hobbies and Pleasurable Pastimes. Anything one enjoys doing can help end the stress cycle. But everyone should do whatever feels joyful to them. Maybe color a page in a coloring book, do pottery, or go bird-watching. Perhaps putting together puzzles or doing a crossword brings relief. Whatever helps the mind focus, allows a flow state, and recharges the creative/mental battery can be beneficial (Nagoski & Nagoski, 2020).

Downtime. Taking time to recharge is critical to overall well-being. This can take many forms. Getting adequate sleep is important, but so are other forms of rest, such as daydreaming, planning, taking a walk, watching funny videos, or playing an instrument. Any other favorite way to recharge is acceptable and needed (Nagoski & Nagoski, 2020).

Therapy. Therapy is not just for people with emotional trauma nor does it have to be long term. The stigma associated with therapy is thankfully losing traction (Drexler, 2019). Everyone can benefit from therapy at different times in their lives. Maybe one finds the need to talk through a bad day or month or work on ways to be kind to themselves because they are perfectionists. Maybe they have deeper trauma. Either way, therapy can help them cope, heal, and move on. It can be especially helpful for those experiencing burnout or empathy fatigue. Therapy works as a safety valve allowing the built-up pressure to escape. It can help close the stress loop and sometimes even provide closure.

Where to Begin

If one is too tired or does not know where to start, they should begin by slowly adding in healthier habits. Better sleep habits are a great place to start to improve or create a foundation for well-being. Next, focus on nutrition followed by exercise. Each habit should have a solid foundation before moving on to the next to avoid becoming overwhelmed (Saunders, 2022).

Supporting Advisors to Prevent Burnout

Advisors and administrators have a place in creating an environment to support advisor well-being. Advising administrative support is crucial to a successful advising team. The role of the administrator is to carefully monitor each advisor and the team's overall emotions, moods, and mental states. This can be done informally by paying attention to team members' energy levels, facial expressions, engagement in meetings, or other work activities. Checking in with team members regularly is an effective practice. Just like there is no singular way to practice self-care, there is no one right way to support an advisor (Hunt, 2021). Administrators need to have an arsenal of compassionate and supportive mechanisms to assist advisors. While unfortunately some advising administrators will not have the flexibility or authority to act on some of the opportunities to create a healthier working environment, there are recommendations that can work within every budget and constraint. Administrators should feel empowered to identify and enact activities that work best at the institution.

Encouraging Self-Care

In much the same way that administrators should engage in self-care, they should encourage their advisors to do the same. Advisors should be urged to employ self-care strategies that work for them. This will likely include several different strategies: movement, supportive relationships, and other activities. One important way to help prevent and alleviate burnout is by setting healthy boundaries with all the people in one's life—supervisors, students, family, friends, acquaintances, and strangers (Dubois & Mistretta, 2020).

Monitoring and Supporting Team Well-Being

Recognizing fatigue and burnout in the advising team is critical to keeping the whole team healthy. One burnt-out employee can dramatically change the mood, motivation, and composition of an advising team (Knight, 2019).

However, administrators should work with professionals who can assist with this process. No one has all the answers. Referrals to appropriate resources (such as human resources, counselors, and other experts) will be an important part of supporting the team. Burnout can also impact advisor performance and effectiveness with students. Maybe the administrator has noticed a normally outgoing advisor becoming more withdrawn or someone with a positive outlook needing to vent more. Is there an advisor who seems unhappy or unwilling to perform at expected levels? These could all be indicators of burnout or fatigue. Having a conversation with advisors about their emotional state is key to helping them navigate these feelings.

Additionally, administrators should hold one-on-one meetings with each advisor they supervise. Meeting individually with team members allows administrators and advisors get to know one another, talk through issues together, and generally just have time together. This time is not just another meeting, but valuable time spent with each other focusing on the needs of individual team members. Individual check-ins should be regular but do not need to be weekly. Research shows that being able to talk to someone—a friend or colleague even—can help mitigate stress (Hunt, 2021). Also, time together allows advisors to ask for help if they need it (Hunt, 2021). As leaders, administrators should feel comfortable talking with their teams about burnout. One-on-one planned or spontaneous meetings with advisors are beneficial and allow advisors and administrators to work together to debrief tough student situations, life challenges, and other emotional needs (Dubois & Mistretta, 2020).

An administrator will not always be able to "fix" the well-being of the team—individually or as a group. However, there are ways that administrators can help support advisors as they work through their self-care processes on their own. Not every institution will have the same flexibility to offer some of these suggestions. Sometimes budgets, staffing, student loads, and other institutional or departmental strengths can make this more difficult. By thinking outside the box and being flexible with resources, any administrator can make a huge impact. Creative administrators consider these problems as challenges to be solved and strive for workable solutions.

Setting the tone for how the team responds to challenges can make or break advising units. Sometimes there will be no perfect options (i.e., budget cuts, increased workloads, changing situations, new projects/goals/expectations), but putting a positive spin on the situation can help the team understand how to navigate the situation and set the mood for how this information is received (Dubois & Mistretta, 2020). Administrators often must carry the weight of difficult situations (i.e., angry parents, lack of institutional support) for the team so that advisors can thrive. This can be challenging and exemplifies why administrators should make sure that their self-care is also a priority.

Ideas for Supporting Advisors

There are many ways to support advisors. The ideas below are not the only options; they may not even be the best way to support every advisor at every institution. Administrators should evaluate what will work at their institution, with their team, and within the authority they have.

Time

Time is the most precious resource we all have. It is so easy to get caught up in the day-to-day that we forget that we have larger lives and missions. As individuals, academic advisors constantly juggle various competing priorities in both their personal and professional lives. Everyone's time needs are different. Allowing advisors flexible work times is the most appreciated assistance an administrator can offer (Chapman & White, 2019; Hunt, 2021). This may take the form of allowing advisors to shift their lunchtime to accommodate personal appointments (i.e., medical, financial, and even self-care) or allowing employees to use sick leave to take a mental health day.

People feel valued when their time and well-being become a priority to their supervisors. Research shows that time off and flexible schedules are preferred for employees (Chapman & White, 2019; Hunt, 2021). If institutional or department policies allow advisors to have a flexible schedule (be it always, on a case-by-case basis, or occasionally) to better balance their work and personal lives, research shows that this is the most preferred method of appreciation (Chapman & White, 2019; Hunt, 2021). Institutional policies may serve as constraints to administrators in providing time off to employees. If nothing else, focusing on respecting boundaries when advisors do take leave can make a huge impact.

In this fast-paced, instant-answer world, sometimes it feels like everyone should be constantly connected. Yet, respecting and setting firm boundaries regarding time away from work and contact is essential. After hours and time off (i.e., vacation, personal appointments, etc.), texts and calls should be infrequent or never happen. Intruding on the mental breaks that advisors have planned can often fill them with anxieties about work and what is going on when they are not there (Knight, 2019). This is counterproductive and not the point of their planned break.

Rebalancing Priorities

Advisors have many functions and responsibilities (i.e., student meetings, program events, documenting advisor notes, emails, scheduling, planning orientations, etc.), and managing so many daily tasks is somewhat of an art form. At times, balance can seem impossible to achieve, particularly if caseloads are high. Sometimes, simply sitting down and going over all the responsibilities of your advisors can help administrators balance the load of the whole team. Some advisors feel overwhelmed by anything extra added to their load while others will need more engagement in different areas to feel productive. Facilitating the equitable distribution of advising tasks can ensure that your entire team feels seen and supported while preventing fatigue and burnout. This will look different in every unit and with every advisor. Some advisors will want to focus on outside priorities such as NACADA participation; others will feel more comfortable working on specific projects at their institution or with students. Allowing people to shine in their assignments versus making everyone fit into ill-fitting boxes will allow everyone to feel more empowered and less burnt out (Chapman & White, 2019).

Professional Development

Being able to engage with other people and their ideas can be energizing. Professional development is an important component of advisor well-being. However, the types of development available to the team should be based on their interests and professional needs. Some development activities should target all advisors (i.e., advising technology and workflow recommendations, institutional policy updates, inclusivity training), but optional activities based on interests can help team members feel energized and allow for creativity and flexibility throughout the unit.

Retreats, Team-Based Downtime, and Team Building

Spending time together can make a world of difference to the overall well-being of individual advisors and the team (Dubois & Mistretta, 2020). Spending time together as a team is a great way to battle burnout. Retreats are a good way to recharge together. These can either be working retreats (focused on problem-solving or planning) or fun retreats. They do not have to be full-day events. Consider hosting a monthly get-together during work hours so that everyone can be included and no one is forced to forgo family time and do something fun. This can be a good way to connect differently and strengthen bonds within the group. Doing routine tasks together can also feel supportive. During busy periods when advisors are working on similar tasks, it can be enjoyable to all work in a conference room together while listening to calming music and sharing snacks. Team building helps keep the team strong so that when one or more person(s) or the whole team faces difficulties and burnout, people may rely on their team to help them (Knight, 2019).

Referrals to Resources

Just as students need referrals to campus resources, advisors may need to be referred to sources of support as well. Pointing advisors to mental health benefits and providers, support groups, or other support professionals can show care and concern. The same skills used for pointing these resources out to students can be used here. Administrators never want to impinge on their employee's freedom to make decisions for themselves but letting them know that they have support for their utilization of these resources can reduce stigma.

Recognition for Good Work

Recognizing the hard work of the advising team is an important part of helping manage the team's well-being. However, appreciation is not one size fits all, and understanding that reality will be important to target feedback individually and to understand what motivates each employee (Chapman & White, 2019). Appreciation does not have to come in the form of raises, bonuses, gifts, or other monetary compensations; additionally, recognition programs or awards that have little value can backfire (Chapman & White, 2019). How do you truly recognize the hard work that team members are completing? It depends on the person. In *The 5 Languages of Appreciation in the Workplace*, Chapman and White explore how everyone has differing appreciation preferences and how using the wrong methods of appreciation can thwart the support directors may be offering. Having every team member take a personality assessment would be an excellent way to learn each individual's different appreciation types so that the right approach can be targeted. If this cannot be done, pay attention to each report. Do they enjoy getting gifts? Getting positive feedback or help? Giving the right kind of support "communicates a sense of respect and value for the person and helps create healthy workplace relationships" (Chapman & White, 2019, p. 43).

Challenges Administrators May Face

The most common challenges an administrator faces in supporting advisor well-being are lack of funding, lack of institutional support, challenging leave policies, or too much work/responsibilities. There may be creative ways to work around these four challenges. Of course, advising administrators must work closely with their human resources department to ensure that any creative solution fits within accepted policies and practices.

For budgeting constraints that do not allow for travel to professional conferences, perhaps the administrator can provide access to digital resources for the entire team. This can be much more cost-effective and allow everyone the opportunity to participate. Or perhaps if there is a small travel budget, a rotating schedule dictates which team members travel each year. Regional conferences or drive-in events are other resource-friendly options. Consider creating team professional development experiences using the expertise within the team. Perhaps the team researches advising practices and hosts an in-office conference.

Maybe there is an adequate budget, but the institution is strict about time spent working in the office and there is not the ability to provide flex time for the team. While tricky, there are ways to work around this scenario, perhaps something as simple as allowing a person to substitute a lunch period for a personal appointment. Brainstorming with the team about the best ways to return valuable time can help form solutions that work at the institution.

Maybe the department has a healthy budget, a generous leave policy, and institutional support, but the amount of work that needs to be done each day feels too overwhelming to take a day off, or everyone feels like they need to take work home to get everything done. In this case, sit down with the team and list everything that needs to be done. Ask if there are outdated practices to jettison or new ways to be more efficient. Reflecting on what the team is doing can provide a big-picture view and maybe reveal small ways to carve out more time. If the institution is lucky enough to provide ample support and a budget, it might be time to create a proposal for additional support.

Conclusion

In an ever-changing higher education environment where advisors and administrators balance various negative and positive moments, taking care of oneself has never been more critical. Further, the impact of personal, global, and social justice issues adds to the strain professionals must navigate. Providing a safe space for holistic well-being for oneself and advising teams will benefit institutions in several ways: to retain great advising professionals at the institution and in the field, positively impact the work advising units do to support students, and create a culture that allows everyone to thrive. Well-being, burnout avoidance, and mental health are key. Below are some activities teams can do together to check in and reflect on their mental health.

Self-Care Activity Examples

1 *Five Finger Scale*: Ask advisors to hold up their hand and, on a scale of 1 to 5, show how they are feeling (with one being the lowest or worst and five being the highest or best). Some example questions include:

How are you doing? How stressed out are you? How tired are you? How much empathy/compassion fatigue are you experiencing? You can have advisors close their eyes if they would feel more comfortable. (This tactic also works for other questions you would like to gauge feelings about.)

2 *Thoughts Circle*: In this activity, ask the team to share anything they would like to know about what is going on in their lives so that the rest of the team can support them. This activity works best with a group that is already relatively close and connected.

Reflection Questions

1 What are you doing that gives you energy?
2 What drains your energy?
3 What is the most helpful thing I could do for myself?
4 What is the most compassionate thing I could do for myself?
5 What would make me feel content, peaceful, or joyful right now?
6 Do you need more training to do your job well?
7 Do you feel you have the support of your supervisor/institution? Why or why not?
8 What do you need to feel supported?
9 Do you make a list of every work task you have to do every semester? If so, what can you delegate (if possible), rethink, or streamline?
10 What types of students feel the most emotionally difficult for you and why?

References

Centers for Disease Control and Prevention. (2018, October 31). *Well-being concepts*. https://www.cdc.gov/hrqol/wellbeing.htm.

Chapman, G., & White, P. (2019). *The 5 languages of appreciation in the workplace: Empowering organizations by encouraging people*. Northfield Publishing.

Drexler, P. (2019, March 1). Millennials are the therapy generation. *Wall Street Journal*. https://www.wsj.com/articles/millennials-are-the-therapy-generation-11551452286.

Dubois, A. L., & Mistretta, M. A. (2020). *Overcoming burnout and compassion fatigue in schools: A guide for counselors, administrators, and educators*. Routledge.

Hird, S. (2003). *What is well-being? A brief review of current literature and concepts*. National Health Service - Scotland.

Hunt, E. (2021, September 1). *The chronic stress survival guide: How to live with the anxiety and grief you can't escape*. NewsBreak. https://www.newsbreak.com/news/2358042646865/the-chronic-stress-survival-guide-how-to-live-with-the-anxiety-and-grief-you-can-t-escape.

Knight, R. (2019, March 20). *How to help your team with burnout when you're burned out yourself*. Harvard Business Review. https://hbr.org/2019/03/how-to-help-your-team-with-burnout-when-youre-burned-out-yourself.

Mayo Clinic Staff. (2021, June 5). *Job burnout: How to spot it and take action*. MayoClinic.https://www.mayoclinic.org/healthy-lifestyle/adult-health/in-depth/burnout/art-20046642.

Nagoski, E., & Nagoski, A. (2020). *Burnout: The secret to unlocking the stress cycle*. Ballantine Books.

National Institute of Mental Health. (2021, April). *Caring for your mental health*. https://www.nimh.nih.gov/health/topics/caring-for-your-mental-health.

Saunders, E. G. (2022, April 1). *Building healthy habits when you're truly exhausted*. Harvard Business Review. https://hbr.org/2022/04/building-healthy-habits-when-youre-truly-exhausted?utm_source=pocket-newtab.

Selwyn, J., & Wood, M. (2015). *Measuring well-being: A literature review*. University of Bristol. https://research-information.bris.ac.uk/ws/portalfiles/portal/41278115/Measuring_Wellbeing_FINAL.pdf.

Stebnicki, M. A. (2008). *Empathy fatigue: Healing the mind, body, and spirit of professional counselors*. Springer Publishing Company.

20

LEADING AND CREATING A CULTURE OF AUTHENTICITY

Caleb Morris, Paige McKeown, and Mike Dial

The advising administrator is responsible for establishing an environment and culture that provides advisors with a psychologically safe space to develop and thrive as individual professionals and as a team (Delizonna, 2017). The advising administrator creates a space where high-potential advisors may become high-performing advisors by providing regular guidance, fostering relationships with and among the team, and authentically caring about team members. Many higher education positions require collaboration to achieve shared goals. Administrators must consider the advising team and how being a part of a team allows advisors to actively learn together, develop solutions to common problems, and meet institutional goals. In doing so, the skilled administrator creates a safe space for academic advisors to engage with one another and administrators.

Psychological Safety

"Psychological safety is defined as a shared belief that the team is safe for interpersonal risk taking" (Edmondson, 1999, p. 354). Psychological safety leads to a willingness to contribute ideas for improvement and take initiative. The concept is focused on minimizing risk involved in collaborating with others. When environments feature high levels of psychological safety, advisors are "free to focus on collective goals and problem prevention rather than on self-protection" (Edmondson & Lei, 2014, p. 25). Individuals on teams that exhibit high psychological safety have "confidence that the team will not embarrass, reject, or punish someone for speaking up" (Edmondson, 1999, p. 354). Creating an environment of

DOI: 10.4324/9781003437598-33

mutual respect and interpersonal trust is a prerequisite for organizational learning and advisor effectiveness. According to Bloom and McClellan (2016), administrators who wanted to establish trusting relationships could do so by "demonstrating integrity, competence, loyalty, openness, and consistency, with a particular emphasis on demonstrating honesty and competence" (p. 200). The supervisor's candidness benefits effectiveness and is not a detraction (Scott, 2017). When advisors trust administrators and believe that administrators care about them, they are more likely to receive and critically reflect on praise and criticism; to be open and honest about what they think of administrators' and organizational performance; to treat one another with honesty, respect, and humility; to accept their role in the organization; and to strive for results (Scott, 2017).

Building a Culture of Authenticity

A genuine culture of authenticity in the workplace refers to the employee's sense that leaders are honest about both the business and themselves. Organizational leaders who embody authenticity are transparent, solution-oriented, proactive, and fair—traits that, when held by those who manage, transmit to others. Extant research has shown correlations between environments of authenticity and overall psychological well-being, which naturally fosters workspaces where employees are happy, productive, and retained. Toor and Ofori (2008) report that there is a positive relationship between authentic spaces and people and autonomy, environmental mastery, personal growth, positive interpersonal relationships, and even purpose. Carl Rogers (1965), the preeminent psychologist of person-centered theory, summarized that one's subjective experience with authenticity is so important that it acts as an indicator of the level to which an individual might fulfill their real potential (van den Bosch & Taris, 2014, p. 2).

Authentic leadership must form a culture of authenticity, especially in a turbulent environment such as higher education. Authentic leadership is comprised of four key components: self-awareness, relational transparency, balanced processing, and internalized moral perspective (Riggio, 2014). Self-awareness will be discussed later in this chapter. Relational transparency is the ability to be straightforward in dealing with others and to operate without hidden motives (Kempster et al., 2019). Balanced processing requires that leaders operate from a fair-minded perspective, taking in and considering varying and often opposing viewpoints, especially during conflict management. This tenet is also important in terms of decision-making. Administrators engaging in balanced processing will make decisions only after weighing options; they avoid acting on impulse. Ideally, those affected by decisions will feel that the plans were openly discussed and that the process was transparent, even if they were not involved in the final decision. Finally, an internalized moral perspective speaks to a leader's ethical nature, how they demonstrate fairness in their leadership and decisions and their striving for an ideal solution (i.e. doing what is "right") even if it is not easy. Authenticity, then, entails accepting the good with the bad regarding maintaining transparency in an organization.

Eschewing negative events, thoughts, and feelings for the sake of maintaining the status quo is "toxic positivity," a phenomenon that cannot be permitted if the goal is authenticity (Gallaher, 2021). According to Gallaher (2021), toxic positivity "actively looks to suppress, minimize, or invalidate real, negative emotions" (para. 3). It can also entail downplaying negative events or gaslighting for the sake of positivity. It creates an environment that is directly counter to authenticity because it degrades trust in leadership to respect the reality of a situation and creates an atmosphere where employees feel the need to conceal all thoughts and emotions, not just negative ones. Toxic positivity also deteriorates individual employee well-being. Research has shown that when people feel that the expectation is to avoid negative emotions, their actual experience of these emotions is increased significantly (Bastian et al., 2012). In other words, social expectations of emotions (i.e. in the workplace) contribute more to actual felt emotions than do personal expectations. In sum, toxic positivity in the workplace, in place of authenticity or because of a lack of authenticity, has long-range negative ramifications on the lives of employees both in and out of the office.

Creating a Culture of Self-awareness

Self-awareness is key when cultivating authenticity. It is also critical for leadership as it is a component of authenticity that can be modeled for others. Self-awareness can be defined as an objective knowledge of one's own strengths, limitations, and values. It has been shown to affect well-being, mediated by practices for improvement such as mindfulness (Richards et al., 2010). Because self-awareness as a trait can be modeled and demonstrated, the administrator's engagement in examining their own self-awareness has both positive effects that carry over to their leadership style and sets a precedent for their team members.

Self-awareness is a component of emotional intelligence (EI)—another critical skill for ensuring a workplace and its members are operating with authenticity. Along with self-regulation, intrinsic motivation, empathy, and social skills, self-awareness is critical for demonstrating emotional EI. Arguably, it is the very foundation of this vital skill, upon which the other components depend (Harvard Professional Development, 2019). By cultivating an environment of self-awareness, leaders set the stage for employees to develop and demonstrate EI in their own lives and in interactions with others. Having EI also has a strong positive correlation with job satisfaction. This bidirectional relationship, if supported properly, can be incredibly beneficial for employees and leaders in the higher education space (Vrontis et al., 2021).

Critical Reflection

The advising profession has a diverse array of intersecting identities (Frey, 2018). Administrators are charged with including and supporting this diverse group, keeping in mind how advisors' race/ethnicity, gender, sexuality, socioeconomic status, and other identity factors influence how they view and navigate the world and the job at hand. The first step for an administrator seeking to support advisors adequately, especially those holding minoritized identities, is for the administrator to become more self-aware, particularly through reflection on their own identity and social location. Social location refers to the individual's relationship to a broader system of privilege, oppression, and power (Kendall & Wijeyesinghe, 2017). This process of reflection and consciousness-raising builds a greater understanding of how history and socialization shape our own experiences and values. Failure to engage advisors and experts from historically excluded backgrounds may lead to missing or misinterpreting important elements of a situation, applying inaccurate or uninformed assumptions, and perpetuating oppression and marginalization (Suarez et al., 2008).

We focus our attention on three models for this critical reflection: Edwards (2006), Fook (2007), and Rouse (2011). Each example has a unique focus that lends itself to critical reflection. Edward's (2006) framework begins with a question: Is the administrator engaging in reflection for self-interest, altruism, or social justice? Fook's (2007) process emphasizes "critical incidents," or naming a lived experience, deconstructing that experience through several lenses—beliefs, values, preconceptions, and actions—and then reconstructing the experience with an eye on any learning or change that came from the experience. Rouse's (2011) model centers the self in three phases—awareness, transformation, and action—in the search for continuous improvement and professional development. Advising administrators can use these frameworks to build their own awareness of the self and critically examine their own intentions, lived experiences, and plans for personal and professional development. In addition to harnessing the frameworks, critical questions advising administrators can ask of themselves to become more aware include:

- What are my personal and social identities?
- How do my identities shape how I perceive myself? How do I relate to others?

- How was I socialized into understanding my own identities? How was I socialized into understanding the identities of those different from me?
- How do my identities relate to broader systems of privilege and oppression?
- How do I work to dismantle oppression in my professional practice?

As advising administrators apply the frameworks and questions to critically reflect, they should seek to uncover potentially unrecognized biases. Harro's (2000b) *Cycle of Socialization* begins before people are even born and continues through childhood, adolescence, and on into adulthood. We as people are constantly bombarded with implicit and explicit messages about themselves and others, which are reinforced by families, teachers, mentors, institutions, and cultures. These influence our perception about our own identities and the identities of other people, creating biases, and fostering environments ripe for oppression. Critical reflection offers the opportunity to break this cycle of socialization, resulting in consciousness around bias and motivating changes in mindset and behavior.

Intrapersonal and Interpersonal Change

After carefully considering critical questions and incidents, administrators can evaluate and improve their practices, actualizing the process of critical reflection. Intrapersonal change refers to changes within an individual's mind or self. It is an ongoing process. Harro's *Cycle of Liberation* (2000a) takes the intrapersonal change fostered by critical reflection and uses it to fuel interpersonal change and, ultimately, systemic change. Once administrators have done their own self-work, they can work with advisors to further the advisor's own development and build a workforce set to influence the broader system in a more positive, culturally sustaining direction. However, while the goal of liberation is systemic change, the interpersonal change dimension, a process of community and coalition building, is important especially considering the administrators' positionality as supervisor. Administrators will be unable to influence their team members toward mutual goals without key touch points like trust, mutual commitment, and connection (Beinart, 2014). Given the diversity of identity in the advising profession, the administrator must establish an identity-conscious and culturally responsive supervisory practice as a basis for interpersonal change.

Identity-Conscious and Culturally Responsive Supervision

One goal of supervision is to maximize employees' potential, thereby enhancing motivation and ultimately increasing performance (Saunders et al., 2000).

Particularly for employees from marginalized identities, understanding potential can be directly tied into understanding identity and lived experiences (Brown et al., 2019). While some argue the virtue of a color-blind perspective—as applied to race and other marginalized backgrounds—literature suggests the harmful effects involved with denying systems of privilege and oppression (Neville et al., 2016). Gloria Ladson-Billings coined *culturally responsive pedagogy* as an equity approach for working with and celebrating the identity of African American students in the United States (1990). Since then, culturally responsive pedagogy has been shown to improve outcomes for students across identities (Ladson-Billings, 2014). While the relationship between a teacher and a student may be different than the relationship between an administrator and advisor, key tenets of cultural responsiveness can inspire advising administrators to build quality and identity-conscious relationships with their teams. Bowes (2017) emphasized the importance of safe spaces, high expectations, and servant leadership as defining practices of cultural responsivity; several approaches to supervision align with these practices, including synergistic supervision and appreciative administration (Bloom & McClellan, 2016; Winston & Creamer, 1997, 1998). Bloom and McClellan (2016) applied Bloom et al.'s (2013) concept of *Appreciative Education* into administrative and supervisory practice, with key practices to include building trust, cultivating positivity and strengths in leaders and followers, coauthoring powerful shared visions of the future, developing and implementing action plans, and constantly striving for improvement. Synergistic supervision is a collaboration between supervisors and supervisees, with an emphasis on professional development and characteristics of joint effort and two-way communication to focus on competence and goals (Winston & Creamer, 1997).

Advising administrators can take inspiration from both practices to tap into and utilize the unique potential of advisors of all identities. The early phases of appreciative administration call for building relationships and understanding individual and collective strengths. As strengths are identified, administrators can leverage synergistic supervision practices to coauthor dreams and action plans with advisors, connect them to broader organizational values and goals, and develop strengths for use to better the system overall. This liberatory practice of understanding identity-based strengths is especially critical for those holding targeted social identities, who must navigate tokenism, the myth of meritocracy, implicit bias, victim blaming, imposter syndrome, and marginalization (Harro, 2000b; Reed, 2021). Cumulatively, these deficit-based cognitive systems and exclusionary practices impact the ability of these diverse communities to thrive in the workplace. Administrators should work to change or dismantle historic systems of workplace oppression.

To counter this type of deficit thinking, Yosso (2005) revealed a model of cultural wealth as a framework for discovering all the capital and strengths a person of color can derive from their identities. Yosso identified various forms of cultural wealth—aspiration, family, social, navigational, resistant, and linguistic capital. Taking the time to discover the individual strengths of colleagues will extend and expand these categories. Supervisors are in a powerful position to support their supervisees by fostering belonging, reframing false narratives, and connecting cultural capital and strengths into high job performance.

Brown (2019) presented several inclusive leadership practices that can be incorporated into supervision:

- Finding your way into the conversation and tapping into your "why"
- Remaining humble
- Seeking to understand and interrupt bias
- Surrounding yourself with diverse perspectives and centering those voices
- Remaining open-minded
- Understanding agency
- Learning the context
- Practicing allyship
- Serving as a mentor and sponsor
- Maintaining a systems-based perspective

Brown's (2019) principle of mentorship and sponsorship as an inclusive leadership practice augments appreciative administration and synergistic supervision mindsets. As a supervisor, taking time to understand and appreciate the unique capital and strengths inclusive of and expanding beyond the social identities of supervisees will help them feel seen and cared for. Further, collaborating with supervisees on projects, mutually defined goals, and professional-development endeavors will help supervisees see the investment the supervisor has in them and their willingness to be a partner on a journey of development. With these approaches in mind, administrators can unlock or further the critical reflection of advisors, thereby continuing the cycle of liberation, building a more conscious advising body, and creating a culture that values identity, inclusion, and growth.

Yosso (2005) highlighted systemic societal deficit thinking that impacts the ability of communities of color to thrive and revealed a model of cultural wealth as a framework for discovering all the capital or strengths a person of color can derive from their identities. Given the pervasive deficit thinking regarding marginalized identities, supervisees may need support in reframing false narratives and connecting cultural capital and strengths into high job performance.

Practical Methods for Enacting Authenticity

So far, this chapter has focused on theoretical approaches useful in creating psychologically safe spaces for advisors. Now, it highlights practical strategies grounded in theory that administrators can use to model authenticity and create safe spaces in which academic advisors can thrive personally and professionally.

Self-assessments

Leaders can highlight self-awareness in the workplace by modeling associated behaviors and encouraging the use of assessment instruments. In the current professional landscape, many self-assessment instruments exist. Using a common instrument as a team can be a powerful tool to bring employees together in their pursuit of self-awareness. The Meyers-Briggs Type Indicator is one instrument that laid a foundation for self-assessment in the workplace. It is still widely utilized and understood today, but some have argued that it lacks specificity and applicability (Pittenger, 1993).

Clifton Strengths is another popular instrument that has gained momentum in the past decade. It seeks to answer what Meyers-Briggs leaves out—how awareness of one's traits can be best utilized to capitalize on individual strengths (Gallup, 2021). Specifically, self-awareness of strengths, modeled by leadership, allows employees to do what they are naturally good at, experience success, and utilize the strengths of others. They are then more engaged, experience greater authenticity in the workplace, and possess the language to talk about where they need support. Of course, no one instrument for developing self-awareness is a panacea. More data points are better and can serve to best set up leaders and employees to synthesize knowledge and awareness about themselves and how they interact with others.

One-on-One Meetings

Given the importance of relationship building and discovery to the work of authenticity, one-on-one meetings are important spaces for fostering dialogue. These individual meetings provide a time and space for administrators to understand advisors' personal and professional goals and challenges. Regarding one-on-one meetings, the most important thing an administrator can do is show up. Canceling or rescheduling these meetings signals to advisors that they are not important or not a priority.

The tenets of *Appreciative Administration* (Bloom & McClellan, 2016) present both strategy and structure for facilitating meaning in one-on-one meetings. Appreciative inquiry refers to asking questions that seek to uncover and bring out the best in a person, situation, or organization (Cooperrider & Whitney, 1999). Questions based in four areas—discover, dream, design, and deliver—help advisors and administrators further their own critical reflections and dream for a greater future for the organization (see Table 20.1). Appreciative inquiry puts into practice the antideficit thinking and inclusive leadership concepts presented earlier by focusing on the positive, centering a growth mindset, and ensuring problem-solving is a mutual and collaborative activity. As practitioners construct a vision for a greater future, Cockell and McArthur-Blair (2012) applied criticality to the appreciative inquiry process by centering reflection on biases and worldviews, uplifting all voices, recognizing systems that create edges to progress, and reframing challenges into opportunities. Individual conversations allow the administrator and advisor to explore ways to improve and recognize limitations while maximizing potential.

Asking appreciative inquiry-based questions is but one means of facilitating effective one-on-one meetings; motivational interviewing offers key skills and practices, such as open-ended questioning, affirmations,

TABLE 20.1 Appreciative Inquiry Questions

Discover	*Dream*	*Design*	*Deliver*
When have you felt like you were working toward liberation in your role?	If you were to wake up tomorrow and everything was just as you hoped it would be, what would be happening?	What are your next steps in achieving [x] goal?	How will you know you are successful?
What opportunities currently exist that support students from marginalized backgrounds?	What are your hopes for your or institutional growth during the next 6 months? The next year? 5 years?	What capital, either your own or others, will you engage with to enact your plan (i.e. social, cultural, etc.)?	What will you do when you hit a roadblock?
Who can we collaborate with ensure a more equitable campus experience?	How can we use our strengths to better the experience for students from all identities?	How can I support you?	What will you do to take your plan from good to great?

reflective listening, and summarizing, which helps to demonstrate care and support (Miller & Rollnick, 2002). In addition to questioning and dialogue, advisors and administrators should practice positive affirmations, recognize strengths, listen reflectively, clarify each other's narratives, and ensure that they are all in agreement. As there is a natural power imbalance between administrators and advisors, motivational interviewing skills can promote a more equitable space by tangibly showing how the person in a power position actively shares space with a subordinate. The administrator asking open-ended questions ensures the advisor has a voice and an opportunity to share their narrative. Affirming the advisor's experiences and strengths helps them feel seen; listening and summarizing shows that they have been heard.

Another interesting opportunity to consider is skip-level meetings (Detert & Treviño, 2010). Skip-level meetings allow administrators to meet with, identify challenges faced by, and brainstorm with advisors, or others, who are direct reports of the staff that administrators manage. A skip-level leader is technically any leader in the organization chart above one's own direct supervisor. Assuming administrators manage a team of supervisors, occasional skip-level meetings allow managers to better grasp the working environments for potentially front-line advisors or other personnel. They also model inclusivity and encourage candor in conversations with departmental leadership.

Team Meetings

Like one-on-one meetings, team meetings may be one of the most underestimated yet ubiquitous opportunities for building authentic workplace cultures. Effective meetings have three purposes: they can review past performance; share important updates; and when appropriate, encourage the team to illuminate important short-term decisions (Scott, 2017). Poorly planned and executed meetings can have significant negative "effects on general employee performance, job satisfaction, attendance at meetings, behavior during meetings, and the outcomes achieved in those meetings" (LeBlanc & Nosik, 2019, p. 696). More dramatically, a critical mass of ineffective meetings may have long-term consequences, such as advisors' inclination to leave their current roles.

For these reasons, good meetings are integral to creating positive team cultures but require significant investments of time and energy. Leach et al. (2009) identified several elements that influence meeting effectiveness. Meetings deemed more effective featured an agenda and record keeping, began on time, were held in the appropriate venues, and had a clear meeting leader. Administrators should ensure these elements are met and conditions are created that allow individual advisors the opportunity to prepare for and participate authentically in team meetings.

Agendas can be seen as planning tools that aid in the facilitation and time management of meetings. When agendas are shared before meetings, advisors can prepare and participate more fully in conversations. Agendas should include meeting goals, tasks or topics associated with the goals, and time estimates for each task or topic. It is also vital to ensure that diverse experiences and voices are represented in team activities.

Determining ideal meeting venues has been complicated with the increased use of online meetings. Online meetings have several advantages over in-person meetings. For example, the time cost of traveling to a meeting location can be reduced or eliminated, providing advisors more time to prioritize mission-critical aspects of their role. Further, participants in online meetings report greater feelings of inclusion when joining remotely because in-meeting chats allow more people to share their perspective (Spataro, 2020). However, online collaboration is more mentally challenging, and administrators need to be prepared for technical issues. Stress and feelings of overwork can both increase when collaborating remotely. Researchers found that stress begins to set in about two hours into a day filled with video meetings because of continued focus, reduced nonverbal cues, and limited views of colleagues while screens are shared (Spataro, 2020). In-person meeting, on the other hand, may require greater time costs in travel but allow for more personal connections and authentic culture development. Especially difficult to plan are hybrid meetings. This environment requires the meeting leader to have someone facilitating dialogue between online participants and sharing questions that come from those not in the room. Hybrid meetings also require rooms with adequate technology.

One of the most important things an administrator can do is start meetings on time. This sends the message that advisor time is respected and valued by leadership. When meetings start late to accommodate tardiness, those who arrived on time are forced to wait and give up important person-hours. Meetings should begin with stated purposes to introduce or review goals. Time must also be managed as delays and interruptions can limit meeting effectiveness and may cause issues important to individual advisors to be tabled for later meetings or dismissed entirely.

Conclusion

No workplace is perfect all the time. Administrators have a responsibility to create spaces that are physically and psychologically safe and are conducive to honesty, integrity, and individual creativity. By fostering spaces that are open and welcoming to advisors from diverse backgrounds, administrators create environments that provide fertile ground for individual advisors and teams to thrive. Intentionality is critically important for creating authentic spaces. From meaningful self-reflection to the ways in which administrators plan and facilitate interactions with and among the team, administrators have a vital opportunity to create spaces that allow individual advisors to thrive. Creating physical and psychologically safe spaces allows for honest and sometimes critical dialogue between advisors as well as between advisors and advising administrators. Additionally, advisors who feel safe and are in positions that allow them to thrive are likely to provide increased benefit to the students they support and are certainly easier to retain.

Reflection Questions

1 What do you do (or could you do) to create psychologically safe and inclusive spaces in your advising unit?
2 What critically reflective practices do you engage in to examine your own social location and its influence on relationships with others?
3 Consider an extremely effective meeting you have participated in or led. What made it so effective? What were the goals? How were they met?

References

Bastian, B., Kuppens, P., Hornsey, M. J., Park, J., Koval, P., & Uchida, Y. (2012). Feeling bad about being sad: The role of social expectancies in amplifying negative mood. *Emotion (Washington, D.C.), 12*(1), 69–80. https://doi.org/10.1037/a0024755.

Beinart, H. (2014). Building and sustaining the supervisory relationship. In C. E. Watkins Jr., & D. L. Milne (Eds.), *The Wiley international handbook of clinical supervision* (pp. 255–281). Wiley-Blackwell.

Bloom, J. L., Hutson, B. L., He, Y., & Konkle, E. (2013). Appreciative education. *New Directions for Student Services, 2013*(143), 5–18.

Bloom, J. L., & McClellan, J. L. (2016). Appreciative administration: Applying the appreciative education framework to leadership practices in higher education. *Journal of Higher Education Management, 31*(1), 195–210.

Bowes, N.-K. E. (2017). *Culturally responsive academic advisement* [Unpublished doctoral dissertation]. John Hopkins University.

Brown, J. (2019). *How to be an inclusive leader: Your role in creating cultures of belonging where everyone can thrive.* Berrett-Koehler Publishers.

Brown, R., Desai, S., & Elliott, C. (2019). *Identity-conscious supervision in student affairs: Building relationships and transforming systems.* Routledge.

Cockell, J., & McArthur-Blair, J. (2012). *Appreciative inquiry in higher education: A transformative force.* Jossey-Bass.

Cooperrider, D. L., & Whitney, D. K. (1999). *Appreciative inquiry: A positive revolution in change.* Berrett-Koehler Communications.

Delizonna, L. (2017, August 24). High-performing teams need psychological safety. Here's how to create it. *Harvard Business Review.* https://hbr.org/2017/08/high-performing-teams-need-psychological-safety-heres-how-to-create-it.

Detert, J. R., & Treviño, L. K. (2010). Speaking up to higher-ups: How supervisors and skip-level leaders influence employee voice. *Organization Science, 21*(1), 249–270.

Edmondson, A. (1999). Psychological safety and learning behavior in work teams. *Administrative Science Quarterly, 44*(2), 350–383.

Edmondson, A. C., & Lei, Z. (2014). Psychological safety: The history, renaissance, and future of an interpersonal construct. *Annual Review of Organizational Psychology and Organizational Behavior, 1,* 23–43. https://doi.org/10.1146/annurev-orgpsych-031413-091305.

Edwards, K. E. (2006). Aspiring social justice ally identity development: A conceptual model. *NASPA Journal, 43*(4), 39–60.

Fook, J. (2007). Reflective practice and critical reflection. In J. Lishman (Ed.), *Handbook for practice learning in social work and social care: Knowledge and theory* (2nd ed., pp. 363–375). Jessica Kingsley Publishers.

Frey, W. H. (2018). *Diversity explosion: How new racial demographics are remaking America.* Brookings Institution Press.

Gallaher, L. (2021, February 10). *Avoiding toxic positivity is positively good for business.* HR Daily Advisor. https://hrdailyadvisor.blr.com/2021/02/10/avoiding-toxic-positivity-is-positively-good-for-business/.

Gallup. (2021). *Strengthsfinder 2.0: Discover your Cliftonstrengths.* Gallup Press.

Harro, B. (2000a). The cycle of liberation. In M. Adams, W. J. Blumenfeld, C. R. Castañeda, H. W. Hackman, M. L. Peters, & X. Zúñiga (Eds.), *Readings for diversity and social justice* (1st ed., pp. 463–469). Routledge.

Harro, B. (2000b). The cycle of socialization. In M. Adams, W. J. Blumenfeld, C. R. Castañeda, H. W. Hackman, M. L. Peters, & X. Zúñiga (Eds.), *Readings for diversity and social justice* (1st ed., pp. 15–20). Routledge.

Harvard Professional Development. (2019, August 26). How to improve your emotional intelligence. Professional Development: Harvard Division of Continuing Education. https://professional.dce.harvard.edu/blog/how-to-improve-your-emotional-intelligence/.

Kempster, S., Iszatt-White, M., & Brown, M. (2019). Authenticity in leadership: Reframing relational transparency through the lens of emotional labour. *Leadership, 15*(3), 319–338.

Kendall, F. E., & Wijeyesinghe, C. L. (2017). Advancing social justice work at the intersections of multiple privileged identities. *New Directions for Student Services, 2017*(157), 91–100.

Ladson-Billings, G. (1990). Like lightning in a bottle: Attempting to capture the pedagogical excellence of successful teachers of Black students. *International Journal of Qualitative Studies in Education, 3*(4), 335–344.

Ladson-Billings, G. (2014). Culturally relevant pedagogy 2.0: A.k.a. the remix. *Harvard Educational Review, 84*(1), 74–84.

Leach, D. J., Rogelberg, S. G., Warr, P. B., & Burnfield, J. L. (2009). Perceived meeting effectiveness: The role of design characteristics. *Journal of Business and Psychology, 24*(1), 65–76.

LeBlanc, L. A., & Nosik, M. R. (2019). Planning and leading effective meetings. *Behavior Analysis in Practice, 12*(3), 696–708.

Miller, W. R., & Rollnick, S. (2002). *Motivational interviewing: Helping people change* (3rd ed.). Guilford Press.

Neville, H. A., Gallardo, M. E., & Sue, D. W. (Eds.). (2016). *The myth of racial color blindness: Manifestations, dynamics, and impact.* American Psychological Association.

Pittenger, D. J. (1993). Measuring the MBTI...and coming up short. *Journal of Career Planning & Employment, 54*(1), 48–52.

Reed, A. M. (2021, May 24). The emotional tax of deficit thinking. *Stanford Social Innovation Review.* https://ssir.org/articles/entry/the_emotional_tax_of_deficit_thinking.

Richards, K. C., Campenni, C., & Muse-Burke, J. L. (2010). Self-care and well-being in mental health professionals: The mediating effects of self-awareness and mindfulness. *Journal of Mental Health Counseling, 32*(3), 247–264.

Riggio, R. E. (2014). A social skills model for understanding the foundations of leader communication. In R. E. Riggio, & S. J. Tan (Eds.), *Leader interpersonal and influence skills: The soft skills of leadership* (pp. 31–49). Routledge.

Rogers, C. R. (1965). *Client-centered therapy: Its current practice, implications, and theory.* Houghton Mifflin Company.

Rouse, J. E. (2011). *Social justice development: Creating social change agents in academic systems* [Unpublished doctoral dissertation]. University of North Carolina at Greensboro.

Saunders, S. A., Cooper, D. L., Winston, R. B., Jr., & Chernow, E. (2000). Supervising staff in student affairs: Exploration of the synergistic approach. *Journal of College Student Development, 41*(2), 181–192.

Scott, K. (2017). *Radical candor: Be a kick-ass boss without losing your humanity.* St. Martin's Press.

Spataro, J. (2020, July 8). The future of work—The good, the challenging & the unknown. *Microsoft 365.* www.microsoft.com/en-us/microsoft-365/blog/2020/07/08/future-work-good-challenging-unknown/.

Suarez, Z. E., Newman, P. A., & Reed, B. G. (2008). Critical consciousness and cross-cultural/intersectional social work practice: A case analysis. *Families in Society, 89*(3), 407–417.

Toor, S.-U.-R., & Ofori, G. (2008). Leadership for future construction industry: Agenda for authentic leadership. *International Journal of Project Management, 26*(6), 620–630. http://doi.org/10.1016/j.ijproman.2007.09.010.

van den Bosch, R., & Taris, T. W. (2014). Authenticity at work: Development and validation of an individual authenticity measure at work. *Journal of Happiness Studies, 15*(1), 1–18. https://doi.org/10.1007/s10902-013-9413-3.

Vrontis, D., Dib, H., El Nemar, S., & El-Chaarani, H. (2021). The relationship between managers' emotional intelligence and employees' performance. *Journal for International Business and Entrepreneurship Development, 13*(2), 177.

Winston, R. B., Jr., & Creamer, D. G. (1997). *Improving staffing practices in student affairs.* Jossey-Bass.

Winston, R. B., Jr., & Creamer, D. G. (1998). Staff supervision and professional development: An integrated approach. In W. A. Bryan, & R. A. Schwartz (Eds.), *Strategies for staff development: Personal and professional education in the 21st century* (pp. 29–42). Jossey-Bass.

Yosso, T. J. (2005). Whose culture has capital? A critical race theory discussion of community cultural wealth. *Race, Ethnicity and Education, 8*(1), 69–91.

21

CONCLUDING THOUGHTS AND FUTURE THOUGHTS FOR RESEARCH AND SCHOLARSHIP

Susan M. Campbell, Calley Stevens Taylor, and Mike Dial

Chapter 1 began with Grites' observation that the number of positions in academic advising administration (in title or function) has grown in the past five decades. Certainly, this indicates the importance of academic advising to student learning success and, in our opinion, the emerging professionalization of the field. The work to position academic advising—and academic advising administration—within the academy and as a profession continues to move incrementally forward. We hope that in the third edition of this book, future editors will be able to say unequivocally that advising administrators are recognized as important institutional leaders across the globe as a matter of fact and not as an aspiration. We also hope that research and scholarship continue to reinforce academic advising as an *academic function* that is inextricably connected to the curriculum and that to be effective, academic advisors must approach their work and "the curriculum in a holistic manner, exploring how the various pieces can fit together in ways that support both the goals of the curriculum and the goals of the students" (Darling, 2015, p. 94). Indeed, this statement has significant implications for us as advising administrators, particularly regarding requisite knowledge and skills, the scope of responsibilities, and commitment to inclusivity and social justice in a global world.

If academic advising plays a significant role in helping students connect the curriculum with their aspirations, then the work of advising administrators and academic faculty members is necessarily closely tethered, collaborative, and not siloed, with differences having more to do with institutional (administrative) or disciplinary (academic) allegiances. The chapters in this book have hopefully strengthened our case for the blurring

DOI: 10.4324/9781003437598-34

of these boundaries and the centrality of academic advising and, in turn, academic advising administration in the student experience. In this concluding chapter, we add our thoughts to what our colleagues have already introduced, particularly as they relate to expertise, an inherent obligation to equity, and the collaborative spirit required to successfully navigate an increasingly complex environment.

Knowledge and Skills

To be effective as an advising administrator requires an understanding of the internal and external higher education landscape, how policy and curricular decisions are made, and the wisdom to evaluate and anticipate the implications of decisions on the student experience. Contextualizing the implications of curricular and cocurricular decisions on the student experience demands understanding learning and development and how individual students translate those concepts within the circumstances of their own lived experiences. At this moment, the role of advising administrators as institutional leaders and champions of the student experience cannot be emphasized more. Academic advising is a relationship-based, learning-centered process that, when approached holistically, holds promise for advancing equity. As the "scholar-in-chief" for academic advising, administrators must explore, document, and interpret for others the relationship between learning-centered advising and the achievement of the student and institutional goals. Engagement in evidence-based planning, assessment, research, and scholarship is essential to document this relationship.

The higher education landscape is constantly changing and increasingly complex. Internal challenges, such as enrollment, shifting cultures and structures, and attempts to respond to changes in students' expectations concern most institutions, as do outward-facing metrics, such as expectations for persistence, retention, and graduation rates. As referenced throughout this volume, the relationship in the literature between academic advising and these institutional metrics shines a spotlight on the work of advising administrators as "student success experts." Even though we all know that student success is a team sport, the pressure for academic advising to deliver improvement, particularly regarding student persistence and completion, makes administrators sometimes feel like they are the only institutional representative competing in an individual event.

The ubiquity of technology has expanded the global reach of all colleges and universities and, with it, the need as administrators to engage beyond our borders and use new insights to inform practice, particularly as it relates more broadly to the whole of the student experience. For the field of advising administration to grow in reputation and prestige, not only on individual campuses but within the broader context of higher education research and literature, it is essential that advising administrators continue to push the envelope at home while simultaneously learning more about how advising and advising administration works in other contexts. While this book sought authors and presents some perspectives from contexts other than U.S.-based advising, we are barely scratching the surface in our understanding of how advising administration looks worldwide.

Using the canon of literature and the methodological techniques established in the field of comparative and international education (CIE) offers an opportunity to greatly expand our understanding of how advising works and deepen our perceptions of the roles and responsibilities of advising administrators. Like advising, CIE work and research are inherently multidisciplinary (Altbach, 1991). Admittedly, linguistic barriers are real regarding both the language of communication and publication, as well as in terms of differing terminology in the field (i.e., academic advising in the United States and personal tutoring in the United Kingdom). However, engaging in more comparative, cross-border, and cross-cultural research, program partnership and professional development will provide advising administrators with more nuanced and textured opportunities to reflect on their practice while exposing them to new ideas about what this role can be and do.

Commitment to Equity, Inclusion, and Social Justice

Advising administrators must develop equitable systems and services. In this regard, a commitment to inclusivity and social justice is a requirement and a mandate of the positions. As institutional leaders, advising administrators have a central role in breaking down systems, policies, and practices that prevent equitable participation in higher education. As a means of analysis and reflection, administrators should scrutinize who is and is not represented in institutional activities and intentionally create opportunities for inclusive and diverse engagement and voices. Equity-minded advising administrators use this critical lens in all facets of work with students, the curriculum, and other academic advisors.

To further these aims, rather than seeing students as somehow being flawed, equity-minded administrators should actively seek out, examine, and revise institutional systems, policies, and practices that currently fail students. This work includes advocating for funding, resources, and personnel, as well as hiring and developing culturally competent advising teams with members who recognize that the needs of an increasingly diverse student body are different than those of the past. In support of equity for students, socially just administrators:

- acknowledge a sense of belonging is critical to the success of college students (Gopalan & Brady, 2020; O'Keeffe, 2013),
- identify new modalities and means of offering quality academic advising to the many populations represented at our institutions (New, 2015),
- avoid deficit-based thinking and approaches (Hiemstra & Van Yperen, 2015), and
- advocate for the removal of institutional and societal barriers to student success (Barhoum, 2018).

For students, academic advisors are linchpins for the curriculum. They assist students in making meaning of the curriculum as a whole, similar to the way that faculty members lead students toward making meaning of individual course content (Lowenstein, 2005). Occupying a negotiated space between the administrative and academic domains, advising administrators should take advantage of opportunities to encourage the modernization of curricula to acknowledge and embrace the experiences, histories, and voices of previously ignored or minimized individuals. In addition, administrators committed to equity empower advisors to help students construct educational plans intentionally designed to expand understanding and engagement with the diverse and global societies of which they are a part.

As the profile of students in higher education continues to diversify, academic advising administrators must strive to ensure that advising personnel represent the identities of campus communities and constituencies. From the posting of positions to the way applications are reviewed to the types of questions asked in interviews to decisions about hiring, administrators must approach these processes with intentionality to ensure that various forms of cultural capital are valued in recruitment and selection processes (Yosso, 2006).

"Communities of practice are groups of people who share a concern, a set of problems, or a passion about a topic, and who deepen their knowledge and expertise in this area by interacting on an ongoing basis" (Wenger et al., 2002, p. 4). Advising units, as communities of practice, are strengthened by recruiting advisors with diverse personal and professional backgrounds who help infuse new ideas from various communities, cultures, professions, and disciplines into advising. It is thus incumbent on us, as advising administrators, to create and foster a learning organization whereby those in the existing advising community learn from newcomers and newcomers are given opportunities to act and learn among and alongside more seasoned academic advisors.

Integrated Practitioner

Our position is that academic advising is teaching: "If advising is teaching and the partaking of advising is learning, then it clearly behooves staff academic advisors to become more like faculty and it behooves faculty advisors to conduct advising in ways that are parallel to classroom teaching" (Hagen & Jordan, 2008, p. 29). In this regard, it makes sense that an important role for advising administrators is breaking down the wall between those in professional (or primary role) and faculty advising positions. While the metaphor of the wall is symbolic, in practice, it manifests in real and tangible ways. It is steeped in the traditions of the academy, where faculty members hold disciplinary expertise and operate autonomously and where allegiance is first to their discipline and secondarily to the goals of their employers (Henkel, 2010; McInnis, 2010; Whitchurch, 2010).

While these descriptors still are recognized, higher education, within the United States and internationally, has witnessed or is witnessing a diversification of the academic workforce (Rhoades, 2010), fueled in large part by a necessary shift toward entrepreneurialism as institutions engage in behaviors to generate revenue (Fredricks-Lowman & Smith-Isabell, 2020). This notion of academic capitalism, a term coined by Hackett (1990) and expanded by Slaughter & Leslie (1997), reflects the "engagement of faculty and universities in market-like behaviors such as competing for funds from external sources" (Fredricks-Lowman & Smith-Isabell, 2020, p. 22). This environment has given rise to a "category of professional employees with advanced degrees who lack the professional perquisites of professors and the positional power of senior administrators" (Rhoades, 2010, p. 41). Captured by Whitchurch (2010) as the Third Space, where professionals with academic credentials navigate between academic and administrative domains, this is the space where arguably most academic advising administrators live. Ironically, this positionality is being increasingly recognized as an underacknowledged—and invisible—resource that contributes to institutional interests in generating revenue and adds to the intellectual capital of the academic workforce (Rhoades, 2010). Our challenge is to build upon the infancy of this acknowledgment and continue to establish ourselves as integral to our institutions' teaching and learning missions and as active, visible, and intellectual partners with academic faculty members. We need to be unapologetic in our work as scholar-practitioners and actively navigate, negotiate, and legitimize our roles and positions as integrated practitioners.

In the end, legitimation of role and position is central to advancing our collective goal of student learning success and requires us to construct a cultural context for a position within the academy. The Third Space helps us understand that cultural context as one that bridges and navigates both the administrative and academic worlds of our institutions. The concept of integrated practitioner offers us a path forward to shape our professional identities as field experts, scholars, practitioners, and campus leaders.

A Research and Scholarship Agenda

Research and scholarship about academic advising hold much promise for its future. As Wenger (1998) suggested: "[Learning], in its deepest sense … concerns the opening of identities—exploring new ways of being that lie beyond our current state. … [Learning] is not merely formative—it is transformative" (p. 263). In this regard, the scholarship of advising should not only serve as a repository for where advising has been but as a catalyst to and springboard for what academic advising can become. The profession is strengthened by infusing new practices, ideas, and methodologies. As "scholar-in-chief," the advising administrator is responsible for encouraging and enabling all advisors to engage in the field beyond individual practice.

As a research focus, academic advising seems to be gaining traction and validity within traditional academic disciplines (Troxel et al., 2022). The influence of postmodern theories of an organization focused on change—such as critical theory, critical race theory, and feminist/queer theory—requires continued exploration, particularly regarding the implications for advising leadership and practice. The closely tethered relationship between advising administrators, as integrated practitioners, and academic faculty members needs to be articulated to secure the identity of advising administrators as campus leaders and contributors to the institution's intellectual capital. Finally, as advising administrators, we must continue to distinguish academic advising from other forms of advising that may exist at our institutions to clarify and strengthen academic advising's connection to the teaching and learning mission of higher education.

Final Thoughts

As many authors in this book have acknowledged—and celebrated—the work of advising administration is one that increasingly places the administrators at the intersection of numerous institutional functions. We intimately understand the ways that the design and delivery of the curriculum impact students and their curricular and cocurricular experiences. We see, every day, the relationships that advisors develop with their advisees and how those students come to rely on advisors as trusted mentors and guides for academic decisions—and, in many cases, as safe spaces to talk about the personal, structural, and societal challenges that they face. We have data and evidence to describe how institutional decisions, from academic to financial aid to student affairs policies, can either smooth students' paths toward graduation or establish new roadblocks that make it harder for them to reach their goals. Our place at these intersections makes advising administrators' perspectives on the relationships between students and their institutions exceedingly valuable and, as the chapters in this book have demonstrated, unique among other leadership positions in higher education.

References

Altbach, P. G. (1991). Trends in comparative education. *Comparative Education Review, 35*(3), 491–507. http://www.jstor.org/stable/1188427.

Barhoum, S. (2018). Increasing student success: Structural recommendations for community colleges. *Journal of Developmental Education, 41*(3), 18–25.

Darling, R. (2015). The academic adviser. *Journal of General Education, 64*(2), 90–98.

Fredricks-Lowman, I., & Smith-Isabell, N. (2020). Academic capitalism and the conflicting ideologies of higher education as a public good and commodity. *New Directions for Higher Education, 2020*(192), 21–27. https://doi.org/10.1002/he.20388.

Gopalan, M., & Brady, S. T. (2020). College students' sense of belonging: A national perspective. *Educational Researcher, 49*(2), 134–137.

Hackett, E. J. (1990). Science as a vocation in the 1990s: The changing organizational culture of academic science. *Journal of Higher Education, 61*(3), 241–279. https://doi.org/10.1080/00221546.1990.11780710.

Hagen, P., & Jordan, P. (2008). Theoretical foundations of academic advising. In V. N. Gordon, W. R. Habley, & T. J. Grites (Eds.), *Academic advising: A comprehensive handbook* (2nd ed., pp. 17–35). Jossey-Bass.

Henkel, M. (2010). Introduction: Change and continuity in academic and professional identities. In G. Gordon, & C. Whitchurch (Eds.), *Academic and professional identities in higher education: The challenges of a diversifying workforce* (pp. 3–12). Routledge.

Hiemstra, D., & Van Yperen, N. W. (2015). The effects of strength-based versus deficit-based self-regulated learning strategies on students' effort intentions. *Motivation and Emotion, 39*(5), 656–668.

Lowenstein, M. (2005). If advising is teaching, what do advisors teach? *NACADA Journal, 25*(2), 65–73. https://doi.org/10.12930/0271-9517-25.2.65.

McInnis, C. (2010). Traditions of academic professionalism and shifting academic identities. In G. Gordon, & C. Whitchurch (Eds.), *Academic and professional identities in higher education: The challenges of a diversifying workforce* (pp. 147–165). Routledge.

New, J. (2015). "Drive-up advising." Inside Higher Ed. Retrieved November 2, 2022, from https://www.insidehighered.com/news/2015/05/19/florida-atlantic-u-offers-academic-advising-parking-garages.

O'Keeffe, P. (2013). A sense of belonging: Improving student retention. *College Student Journal, 47*(4), 605–613.

Rhoades, G. (2010). Envisioning invisible workforces: Enhancing intellectual capital. In G. Gordon, & C. Whitchurch (Eds.), *Academic and professional identities in higher education: The challenges of a diversifying workforce* (pp. 35–53). Routledge.

Slaughter, S., & Leslie, L. L. (1997). *Academic capitalism: Politics, policies, and the entrepreneurial university.* Johns Hopkins University Press.

Troxel, W. G., Rubin, L. M., Grey, D., McIntosh, E., & Hoagland, I. (2022). *A content analysis of the scholarship of academic advising across global publications* [in development]. Research Report 221. NACADA Center for Research at Kansas State University.

Wenger, E. (1998). *Communities of practice: Learning, meaning, and identity.* Cambridge.

Wenger, E., McDermott, R. A., & Snyder, W. (2002). *Cultivating communities of practice: A guide to managing knowledge.* Harvard Business Press.

Whitchurch, C. (2010). Convergence and divergence in professional identities. In G. Gordon, & C. Whitchurch (Eds.), *Academic and professional identities in higher education: The challenges of a diversifying workforce* (pp. 167–183). Routledge.

Yosso, T. J. (2006). Whose culture has capital? A critical race theory discussion of community cultural wealth. In A. D. Dixson, C. K. Rousseau Anderson, & J. K. Donnor (Eds.), *Critical race theory in education* (2nd ed., pp. 113–136). Routledge. https://doi.org/10.4324/9781315709796.

CONTRIBUTORS

Editors

Susan M. Campbell, EdD, holds emerita status as chief student affairs officer at the University of Southern Maine (USM), where she worked in both student and academic affairs. While at USM, Campbell helped develop the student affairs concentration in the master's in Adult and Higher Education Program. Campbell has been actively engaged with NACADA for more than 20 years and is a recipient of the Virginia N. Gordon Award for Excellence in the Field of Advising. She also served as NACADA President from 2006 to 2007 and helped develop both the Assessment and the Academic Advising Administrators' institutes. Her scholarship and research interests include assessment and the administration of academic advising. She has authored and coauthored chapters in other NACADA publications and served as an editor of the *NACADA Journal*. Campbell received her doctorate from the University of Massachusetts at Amherst. Her dissertation focused on factors that influence the role construction of mid-level managers in student affairs.

Mike Dial serves as the associate director of Undergraduate Academic Advising at the University of South Carolina (UofSC). He leads the largest undergraduate advising program on campus, which supports 14,000 undergraduate students into and through the university. Since 2014, Dial has been involved in first-year and transition initiatives at UofSC including advising, the first-year seminar, early intervention, peer education, and student success programming. In addition to this publication, Dial served as the editor for *Academic Recovery: Supporting Students on Probation* and serves on the manuscript review board for *Building Bridges for Student*

Success: A Sourcebook for Colleges and Universities. He previously served on the editorial review board for *E-Source for College Transitions*. His other areas of scholarly interest include supporting students on probation, early alert programs, the first-year experience, academic advising, and the processes by which new advisors become academic advisors. Dial earned a BA in recreation administration from Eastern Illinois University and holds an MEd in higher education and student affairs from the University of South Carolina.

Calley Stevens Taylor, PhD, serves as the vice president for Student Success and Engagement and dean of students at Cedar Crest College, a private liberal arts college primarily for women. At Cedar Crest, she provides leadership for the division of Student Success and Engagement and supports college programs and initiatives that facilitate a successful student experience. Stevens Taylor has served as a mentor in the NACADA Emerging Leader Program and as chair of the NACADA Faculty Advising Community. She has presented and published on a wide range of topics related to advising, higher education, and student success. Stevens Taylor serves on the editorial boards of the *NACADA Review* and the *Journal of Access, Inclusion, and Retention in Higher Education*. She has been recognized as an Outstanding First-Year Student Advocate by Cengage and the National Resource Center for First-Year Experience and Students in Transition. She earned her PhD in international and comparative education at Lehigh University, where her dissertation research examined the impact of international engagement on the standards of U.S. regional accrediting agencies. She earned her BA in psychology from the University of North Carolina at Asheville and her MS in college student personnel from the University of Tennessee, Knoxville.

Contributors

Sharon A. Aiken-Wisniewski, PhD, is the assistant vice provost for Academic Advising at the University of Arizona and professor emerita in Educational Leadership and Policy at the University of Utah. Her service includes leadership roles with NACADA, a reviewer for various journals, and a NACADA Fellow for the Excellence in Academic Advising Initiative. Through rich narratives from students and colleagues as well as her previous roles as an assistant vice president for academic affairs, associate dean, faculty, and a primary-role advisor, she has developed an understanding of the scholar-practitioner identity. Her research agenda centers on questions that emerge from interactions between practitioners, leaders, and students as they create student success, which resulted in journal articles, book chapters, and a book on program development. Aiken-Wisniewski, a first-generation student, grew up in rural Vermont. She earned a BA in political science (University of Maine at Presque Isle), an MS in international studies (Troy State University), and a PhD in educational leadership and policy (University of Utah). Because of her love of nature, every weekend she hikes with her spouse, Alan, and Boston terrier Poppy.

Karen L. Archambault, EdD, has spent more than two decades in higher education and currently serves as vice president of Enrollment Management and Student Success at Rowan College at Burlington County. Archambault leads the college's efforts to grow student enrollment and oversees the college's retention efforts, including programs for honors students, low-income students, military and veteran students, and students with disabilities. A historian by training, Archambault teaches history of higher education at the graduate level, with a focus on historical equity in higher education. She writes on transfer students, first-year advising, and cultural competence for NACADA and has been an active member including past terms on the board of directors and as vice president and president. Archambault received her undergraduate degree in history from Salisbury University, master's degree in history from Old Dominion University, master's degree in counseling from Trinity Washington University, and her doctorate in educational leadership from Rowan University.

Laurie B. Baker serves as Director of the Office of Advising and Student Information Services at Rowan University. She and her energetic and creative team support graduate, post-baccalaureate, and certificate students, as well as "new majority" undergraduates pursuing degree completion online, in Camden, or through Rowan's community college partnerships. She completed her BA in English at Bucknell University and her MSEd in higher education management at the University of Pennsylvania. Baker is a doctoral candidate in the inaugural Leadership in Academic Advising cohort at Kansas State University, where her research is focused on the role of academic advisors in supporting student financial well-being. Having served for more than two decades in a variety of teaching, advising, and administrative roles at public and private institutions, she is grateful for the privilege of learning daily from her returning adult students and the emerging advising leaders on her team.

Amalauna Brock is the director of advising for the College of Agriculture at Auburn University. She has a BS in history from Tennessee Wesleyan University, an MA in history from Western Kentucky University, and is working on a PhD in history at Auburn University. She served as the chair of the LGBTQA Advising and Advocacy Community. She serves on the inclusion and engagement committee, global awards committee, and ELP advisory board.

Jennifer Brown, EdD, is the vice chancellor for Student Affairs at Windward Community College. She holds a bachelor's in political science from the University of California, Santa Barbara, and a master's in education, and a doctorate in educational leadership from the University of Southern California. She served as an academic advisor for 19 years, working with various student populations including professional programs, liberal arts, and transfer at her alma maters and the University of Hawai'i at Mānoa (UHM). She served as a transfer specialist advisor at UHM and was embedded on the community college campus to support a dual-admission, dual-enrollment transfer program for more than seven years. Her primary research interests are transfer student success and organizational change.

Scott Byington serves as Associate Vice President of Onboarding and Advising at Central Carolina Community College (Sanford, North Carolina) where he oversees institutional research, new student advising, and enrollment, and he facilitates a college-wide, faculty-based advising program. He holds a Bachelor of Science in biology from James Madison University, a Master of Science in biology from West Virginia University, and a Master of Science in Academic Advising from Kansas State University. He has served on the NACADA Summer Institute Advisory Board, as a Summer Institute faculty member, and on the Professional Development Committee. He was a founding member and inaugural chair of the North Carolina Community College Advising Association. He has worked as a Quality Enhancement Plan (QEP) consultant and reviewer for advising-based QEPs. He is most interested in advising assessment, first-year advising experiences, faculty advisor professional development, and advising for transfer students.

Rosanna J. Cabatic is the assistant director of International Student Services at Cedar Crest College. She has worked with international populations for the past 15 years as a student specialist, English language instructor, academic advisor, designated school official and academic administrator. In addition to working with international students, she provides guidance and support to faculty and staff who work directly with international populations and serves as an adjunct instructor to first-year students teaching first-year academic courses. She is active in diversity, equity, and inclusion work as a diversity educator to her campus community and coordinates book club discussions on different perspectives for college personnel. Rosanna received her undergraduate degree in political science from Hollins University in Roanoke, Virginia, a master's degree in TESOL from Seattle University, and an MBA from Cedar Crest College.

Lisa M. Cardello, EdS, NCC, BCC, is a national certified counselor, board-certified coach, and past president of the New Jersey Career Development Association. She serves as the executive director of Career Preparation and Experiential Learning at Rowan College at Burlington County in Mount Laurel, NJ. Previously, she served as director of the Center for Student Success at the Rowan University School of Osteopathic Medicine where she increased academic and career support services. Additionally, Lisa is an adjunct professor and teaches graduate-level career counseling courses. She earned her bachelor's degree in education and master's degree in counseling from The College of New Jersey, an educational specialist degree in counseling services from Rider University, and is pursuing a doctoral degree in counseling and supervision at Kean University. Cardello's research interests and past publications/presentations focus on career counseling for specific populations including physicians, medical students, transitioning teachers, and working mothers.

Helena E. Cole is the University of New Haven's director of the Center for Academic Success and Advising. She and her office provide advising assistance and academic support to students and faculty members and serve as primary-role advisors to undeclared majors in the College of Arts and Sciences. She received an AB in history and Italian from Bryn Mawr College, an MEd in College Student Personnel from the University of Maryland, and an MA in Humanities from Hood College. She is currently a doctoral candidate in the inaugural cohort for the PhD program in leadership in academic advising at Kansas State University. Her research interests center on how students make meaning of their advising experiences and best ways to identity and support at-risk students.

Erica R. Compton is the director of Student Advising & Success at the College of Western Idaho (CWI), with over 12 years in advising. In her role, she leads a team of 24 full-time professional advisors focused on proactive, intentional, and transformational interactions with their student body. She has previously worked at Central Texas College with experience in admissions, records and registration, financial aid, and international student services. In addition to her work in advising, Erica teaches first-year experience courses at CWI and the University of Arizona Global Campus.

She is extremely passionate about multiculturalism and enjoys working as an advocate with the refugee students and the community at CWI. Erica has been active in NACADA and recently served as the Idaho liaison to Region 8, 2023 regional conference cochair, and has previously contributed to the *NACADA Academic Advising Today*. She holds an associate degree from Central Texas College, a BS in sociology from Troy University, and an MS in international relations also from Troy.

Mary Carmel Etienne is the assistant dean and director of Advising in the School of Arts and Sciences at La Salle University. Spanning a 15-year career, she has served in various leadership roles in advising and program operations in higher education, including at Temple University, Trinity Washington University, and Hofstra University. Etienne has been an active member of NACADA since 2014. She participated in the 2018–2020 cohort of NACADA's Emerging Leaders Program and is currently a faculty member for the Assessment Institute. She holds a Bachelor's degree in sociology and economics from the University of Connecticut and a Master's degree in geography and urban studies from Temple University. In addition to presenting and writing about advising, she has also presented on facilitating dialogue to advance diversity, equity, and inclusion and has coauthored articles on faculty development.

Marian H. Gabra, PhD, is the director of Advisor Training and Professional Development and the University Studies Program at UCLA. In her role, she works collaboratively across campus to cultivate spaces of learning for students and personnel. She has created and implemented the Advising Communities of Excellence (ACE) Professional Development Program, offering interactive workshops and initiatives that bring together campus professionals to explore the relationship between advising theory and practice. Gabra and the ACE Committee have been awarded the 2018 NACADA Region 9 Advising Innovation award. Moreover, she leads an instructional team in curriculum design and innovative pedagogy and teaches courses under the University Studies program. She has been a featured keynote speaker at various programs and conferences. Gabra also advises students in the Center for Academic Advising in the College. She earned her BA in English from Occidental College in 2002 and her doctorate in comparative literature from UCLA in 2010.

Richie Gebauer, EdD, is the assistant dean for Retention and Student Success at Cabrini University and serves as faculty director of the IMPACT Living Learning Community. As the founding director of the university's first-year experience and learning community program, retention and persistence is at the center of Gebauer's work. He is a past president of the National Learning Community Association and has served on the editorial review board for the *Journal of the First-Year Experience and Students in Transition*, Learning Communities Research and Practice, and *E-Source for College Transitions*. His research focuses on the impact of learning communities on the integrative learning practices of students. Gebauer has authored publications advancing research and practice of learning communities; academic and professional advising; first-year experience and first-year seminars; academic recovery programs; and faculty learning communities. He completed a BA from Franklin and Marshall College, an MEd from James Madison University, and an EdD from Cabrini University.

Helen Gorgas Goulding has worked in higher education for 35 years in academic advising, professional development, and student affairs. Her areas of research and expertise are student development, student learning through curriculum/co-curriculum integration, career facilitation, professional development, retention initiatives and program assessment, academic support strategies, grit, growth mindset, authentic and adaptive leadership theories, and practice. She has taught courses on college academic success and career decision-making and community-building. She has been trained in relational coordination to help improve workflow issues within organizations and has contributed to the *NACADA Academic Advising Today* and to leadership studies literature.

Thomas J. Grites, PhD, served as Assistant Provost at Stockton University for 43 years managing academic orientation, first-year experience efforts, and transfer student initiatives. He continues to teach his transfer seminar course. He was a founding member of NACADA, served as its president, and serves as senior editor of the *NACADA Journal* and on the *NACADA Review* editorial board. Grites has written numerous professional publications and delivered more than 150 conference presentations, workshops, and program reviews on more than 100 campuses. He earned his BS and MS degrees from Illinois State University and his PhD from the University of Maryland. Both institutions have granted him alumni awards; he was inducted into the ISU College of Education Hall of Fame in 2007. He was recognized as a NISTS Transfer Champion in 2015. He received the 2021 NACADA Region 2 award for Outstanding Contribution to Scholarship. Region 2 now awards the Service to Region 2 award in his name.

Rebecca L. Hapes, PhD, is an associate registrar at Texas A&M University and oversees FERPA compliance and training for the university. Throughout her more than 20 years in higher education, she has advised undergraduate and graduate students, assisting in their institutional transition, working to build departmental community and foster belonging. She received graduate certificates in advanced pedagogy in agriculture and leadership education, theory, and practice and her doctorate in agricultural leadership, education, and communication, with a specialization in educational human resource development all from Texas A&M University. Her research interests focus on leadership development, student development, success, and thriving. Hapes has served in all divisions of NACADA: The Global Community for Academic Advising during her years of association involvement, including as a member of the board of directors, and as a mentor within the Emerging Leaders Program. Hapes serves on the editorial board for *Academic Advising Today: Voices of the Global Community* and *Strategic Enrollment Management Quarterly*. With more than 100 advising-related presentations and publications, Hapes has dedicated her career to enhancing and promoting the field of academic advising and the professional development of academic advisors.

Elizabeth M. Higgins, EdD, is the director of academic advising at the University of Southern Maine. She also teaches Foundations of Academic Advising and the Higher Education Capstone Seminar in the Adult and Higher Education Department. Higgins' research focus is the faculty and student relationship, student retention, assessment of academic advising, and process improvement. Higgins has more than 30 years of experience in academic advising. Throughout her years in the advising profession, she has implemented a dual advising program, developed advising assessment plans, coordinated professional development, led the University of Maine System-wide Advising Committee, and coordinated numerous retention and persistence initiatives. Higgins has been active in NACADA at the regional and national levels. In addition to facilitating numerous conference presentations, she has served on the NACADA Board of Directors and Academic Advising Consultants and Speakers Services and has contributed to the *NACADA Journal* and *Academic Advising Today*.

Cristy Holmes, EdD, serves as Dean of Arts and STEM at Central Carolina Community College, where she is actively engaged in advising transfer students. Holmes has worked in the North Carolina Community College System for 14 years, previously serving as associate dean of transfer and advising at Central Carolina Community College, department head of advising at Alamance Community College, and Spanish instructor and academic advisor at Rockingham Community College. Holmes earned her bachelor's degree in foreign languages from West Virginia University, her master's degree in Latin American literature from West Virginia

University, and her Doctorate of Education in executive leadership at Wingate University.

Brian Kapinos, EdD, holds a doctoral degree in Educational Leadership from the University of Hartford and currently serves as the Northwest Regional Advising Director for the Connecticut Community College System. Kapinos has worked in higher education for the past ten years, holding various roles in academic advising and academic affairs as well as several adjunct faculty roles within the Massachusetts Community College system. Kapinos is also an adjunct faculty member in the Doctoral Program for Educational Leadership at the University of Hartford. Finally, Kapinos' research focus is on advising systems, middle management, and the coordination of advising services and has published in several academic journals including both the *NACADA Journal* and *Review*.

Stephanie D. Kraft-Terry, PhD, is Director of advising for the College of Natural Sciences and Specialist within the School of Life Sciences. She is actively engaged in the undergraduate advising community at the University of Hawai'i at Mānoa. Kraft-Terry has served as chair for the NACADA STEM Advising Community, cluster representative within the Advising Communities Division, chair of the NACADA Administrators' Institute Advisory Board, and as a faculty member at the NACADA Administrators' Institute. Kraft-Terry has presented at regional and annual conferences on the topics of data-informed advising, advising assessment, and advising administration; she has coauthored chapters and articles in other NACADA publications. She received a Bachelor of Science from Pacific University and a doctorate from the University of Nebraska.

Katie Lackey, PhD, is the director of Advising for the College of Human Sciences at Auburn University. She has been involved in advising at Auburn for 17 years. Lackey recently was the Doctoral Winner of the NACADA Student Research Award based on her dissertation that completed her PhD program in Adult Education. Katie has also been the recipient of the regional and national NACADA Outstanding Advising Award—Primary Category. Her areas of expertise involve curriculum management, mentoring, and logistics. She is a firm believer in lifelong learning and truly enjoys working with college students who challenge her and humor her. She considers it an honor and privilege to work at her alma mater.

Keely S. Latopolski, PhD, serves as the director of professional development and engagement in the Culverhouse College of Business at The University of Alabama. Latopolski earned her PhD in higher education administration with a certificate in college teaching from The University of Alabama. She has extensive experience in academic advising, student success, and diversity, equity, and inclusion initiatives. Past coauthored journal publications include *Journal of Diversity in Higher Education*, *Journal of College Student Development*, and *Journal of the First-Year Experience and Students in Transition*.

Elaine Lewis serves as Director of the First-Year Center at Utah Valley University. In this role, she leads a team of 30 full-time academic advisors in providing proactive, holistic, and data-informed advising to approximately 6,000 first-year college students. Lewis aims to create a culture of exceptional care for students and the employees on her team. Her current professional interests include organizational design, hiring and onboarding practices, and employee motivation. In previous roles, Lewis' work focused on research, best practices, and program design to improve retention of first-year college students. She feels strongly about access to college for underserved and marginalized students and volunteers her time with GripTape, an American Achieves nonprofit project, which provides cocurricular and extracurricular experiences to students from socioeconomically disadvantaged high schools in urban and rural areas.

John Wesley Lowery, PhD, is Department Chair, Graduate Coordinator, and Professor in the Student Affairs in Higher Education Department at Indiana University of Pennsylvania. He previously served on the faculty at Oklahoma State University and coordinated the college student affairs program and higher education programs and at the University of South Carolina, where he taught in and coordinated the Higher Education and Student Affairs Program. He earned his doctorate at Bowling Green State University in higher education administration. Before beginning his doctoral work in 1996, he was director of residence life at Adrian College in Michigan and university judicial administrator at Washington University in St. Louis. He is a frequent speaker and author on topics related to student affairs and higher education, particularly legal and legislative issues (including Clery, FERPA, & Title IX), and student conduct, on which he is widely regarding as a leading expert.

Margaret Mbindyo, PhD, is an assistant professor in the Department of Academic Advisement and Student Development at Millersville University. She is also the advisement coordinator of the College of Arts, Humanities, and Social Sciences and the Lombardo College of Business. She holds a dual title PhD degree in curriculum instruction and comparative and international education from Penn State University. In 2019, Margaret was competitively selected to participate in the NACADA's 2019–2021 Emerging Leaders Program and in 2021 she won the new advisor certificate of Merit Award. Margaret has served on several NACADA committees and is currently the chair of the Global Engagement Community. A career educator, Margaret's areas of research include the academic resilience and academic persistence of low-income/first-generation and immigrant students. In addition, she has research interests in transformational leadership in academic advising. Among other peer-reviewed work, she has coauthored two journal articles about transformational leadership.

Emily McIntosh, PhD, has held a variety of senior management roles in learning, teaching and the student experience in several UK universities. She joined the University of the West of Scotland (UWS) as Director of Student Success in January 2023. Her expertise includes institutional leadership for learning, teaching, and student success, including student transition, technology-enhanced learning (TEL), academic practice, equality, diversity and inclusion (EDI), academic advising, and student engagement. Emily is a principal fellow of the Higher Education Academy (PFHEA, 2017) and a National Teaching Fellow (NTF, 2021). She was a founding board member and trustee of UK Advising and Tutoring (UKAT) from 2016 to 2021 and is also Academic Board Member of the NACADA Center for Research at Kansas State University, United States. She is a member of the executive board and trustee of the Heads of Educational Development Group and in October 2021 she was appointed as an independent board member of the Board of the Corporation for the Trafford College Group, sitting on the HE curriculum and quality committee. Emily has always had a keen interest in all things student success and has published monographs, chapters, and articles on a wide variety of topics from academic advising, personal tutoring, and peer learning to integrated practice. She is co-editor of the recently published monograph *The Impact of the Integrated Practitioner in Higher Education* (Routledge, 2022).

Paige McKeown serves as the assistant director for Undergraduate Advising and Academic Intervention at the University of South Carolina. She has been at UofSC in the advising field for six years and transitioned to a career in higher education from K–12 school counseling. She earned her bachelor's degree in social studies education from Wake Forest University and holds a master's in counseling from the University of Pennsylvania. She is a nationally certified counselor and career development facilitator. She is working toward her PhD in educational psychology and research at UofSC. Her research interests include students' self-regulation skills, mental health, social supports, and academic success strategies in the high school-to-college transition. She has been published in *Academic Advising Today* and has presented regionally and nationally on advising and intervention best practices.

Samantha Moreno, PhD, has served in higher education for more than 20 years as a senior leader in student affairs. She has a PhD in higher education and student affairs leadership and a master's in secondary/postsecondary school counseling. Dr. Moreno has a deep passion for student success, is an accomplished faculty member and author, and has years of experience in leadership roles centered on student success including oversight in residence life, dean of students, student life, counseling, and admissions. She has led, built, and guided the strategic direction of the online student success team at the University of Colorado.

Caleb Morris (he/they) is a faculty advisor in the Arnold School of Public Health at the University of South Carolina. In this role, Morris teaches first-year experience, career management, experiential learning, and senior capstone courses. Additionally, they advise upper level Exercise Science and Public Health majors, supporting degree progression, cocurricular engagement, and career preparation for future health care providers and educators. Morris has worked professionally in higher education for four years, with experience in college access, student success, and transitions. In 2022, they were recognized by NACADA with the Outstanding Advisor Award in the new advisor category. A champion of inclusion and equity, they have received institutional awards for leading DEI efforts in academic advising and have presented at conferences on the topic. Morris earned a Bachelor of Arts in history and a Master of Education in higher education and student affairs, both from the University of South Carolina.

Ankur Nandedkar, PhD, is an associate professor of management at Millersville University of Pennsylvania. He earned a doctorate in management from the University of Texas Rio Grande Valley in Edinburg, Texas. His research interest focuses on management pedagogy, leadership, and teams. He has published in the *International Journal of Organizational Theory & Behavior, Computers in Human Behavior*, the *Journal of Leadership Education.* He has presented his work at various national and international conferences. Currently, he serves as an associate editor for the *South African Journal of Economic and Management Sciences.*

Rubab Jafry O'Connor, EdD, is a distinguished service professor of Management at Tepper School of Business, Carnegie Mellon University (CMU). At CMU, she has created and teaches a unique longitudinal leadership development course to business students. In addition to leadership and student success, her interest is organizations and she teaches Organizational Design and Implementation at CMU. Before teaching, she held many management roles including director of Academic Advising, career consultant, and head of Career Center for both undergrads and MBAs nationally and internationally. She earned her EdD from the University of Pittsburgh, her MS in policy and management from CMU, and an MA in economics and BA in statistics and economics from Pakistan. Among other peer-reviewed work, she has coauthored two journal articles on transformational leadership.

Thomas Casey O'Connor has more than 20 years of corporate experience in various roles and holds an MS in public management from Carnegie Mellon University and Bachelor of Science in economics from Robert Morris University, Pittsburgh.

Yoshinobu Onishi, PhD, is a professor in the Institute for Excellence in Educational Innovation at Chiba University, Japan, and the advisor to the university's Rugby Football Club. He received a BA from Keio University, Japan; Master of Public Administration from Columbia University, USA; and PhD in higher education from Chulalongkorn University, Thailand. His research interests and areas of expertise include international student policy, liberal arts education, and academic advising focusing on study-abroad advising. His recent publication includes *A Theory for Study Abroad Professionals*, published by Toshindo in 2020. He previously held the positions of deputy director and professor in the International College at Osaka University, Japan, where all courses were taught in English. He also served as a sales representative at NHK (Japan Broadcasting Corporation) and as program officer, an international public servant, at the United Nations University headquartered in Tokyo.

Mary Anne Peabody, EdD, LCSW, RPT-S, is an associate professor in the Social and Behavioral Sciences Department for the University of Southern Maine, a licensed clinical social worker, and a registered play therapist supervisor. She is a prolific author in the play therapy field and remains actively involved as a foundation board member of the Association for Play Therapy and a reviewer for the *International Journal of Play Therapy*. As a faculty member, she views advising as central to her role. She has served as the department advising liaison, participated in the University's Excellence in Academic Advising process as a committee leader, is a member of the University Advising Council, and serves as co-lead for an internal advising-relational coordination grant. She has coauthored an article for NACADA and has an interest in relationally based andragogical practices with her undergraduate and graduate students.

Kristina Richards has been working in academic advising, mentoring, and coaching positions in various higher education settings for the past 13 years. She serves as the online student success manager in the Department of Continuing Education at the University of Colorado-Boulder. Specializing in fully online programs, she is passionate about working with diverse and nontraditional student populations. As an online learner herself, Richards recognizes the unique and rich experiences nontraditional learners bring to their programs and institutions. Richards is pursuing her Master of Arts in Leadership Organizations, Leading Change for Student Success in Higher Education at the University of Colorado-Denver and plans to graduate in August of 2023.

Rich Robbins, PhD, holds a doctorate in social psychology and is associate dean of Arts and Sciences at Bucknell University. He has performed more than 150 professional presentations and dozens of campus consultations; authored extensively on academic advising; and has developed advising programs at two separate institutions and directed advising programs at four institutions. Robbins has received various local, regional, national, and global advising awards, including the 2011 Service to NACADA Award and 2013 Virginia Gordon Award for Excellence in Advising. Among his NACADA leadership positions, he has served as a faculty member for the NACADA Assessment Institute, Administrators' Institute, Summer Institute, and Research Symposium; was a NACADA representative on the Council for the Advancement of Standards in Higher Education from 2011 to 2020; and was coeditor of the *NACADA Journal* from 2009 to 2016. In 2018, Robbins was selected as an Excellence in Academic Advising Fellow by NACADA and the Gardner Institute for Excellence in Undergraduate Education. Most recently, he was lead author for the 2021 and 2022 NACADA Pocket Guides on assessment of advising.

Claire Robinson, PhD, serves as Assistant Dean of Undergraduate Advisement and Director of the University Advising Center at the University of South Carolina. In her role, Robinson oversees campus-wide advising initiatives including first-year advising, transfer advising, exploratory advising, academic coaching, four-year curriculum mapping, advising technology, advisor career ladders, and advisor training and certification. In addition, several special initiatives fall within the purview of the Advising Center including faculty/student mentorship, the University Advisors Network, and academic recovery initiatives. Robinson has authored several publications evaluating academic advising and coaching and coauthored a book on appreciative college instruction. She has trained and consulted at more than 40 colleges and universities and served as the lead SACS Quality Enhancement Plan Evaluator for multiple institutions seeking to enhance their advising practices.

Katherine Schmidt, PhD, holds a split appointment as Writing Center director and professor of English Studies at Western Oregon University. In this capacity, her service has included change-making campus-wide roles, which include Faculty Senate president, faculty cochair of the University Budget Committee, and accreditation writing coach. Schmidt presents nationally and internationally on topics related to faculty advising, tutoring, and writing self-efficacy. Her publications include "The Empirical Development of an Instrument to Measure Writerly Self-Efficacy in Writing Centers" and creative works *Partitions* and *Awaken the Dawn*.

Ruthanna Spiers, PhD, serves as the director of University Advising at Auburn University. She completed her undergraduate studies in psychology at Presbyterian College and earned graduate degrees in counseling and higher education administration at Auburn University. Spiers formerly served as the coordinator of the freshman learning community program, as an academic counselor, and as director of the Exploratory Advising Center. She has been recognized as an Outstanding Advising Administrator at Auburn University, NACADA Region IV, and in the NACADA Global Awards program.

Billie Streufert oversees the Student Success Center at Augustana University in Sioux Falls, SD, and is pursuing a PhD from Kansas State University in leadership in academic advising. Before serving in this role, she worked at public and two-year institutions in academic and career advising capacities. She also is a teaching assistant in the master's and advising certificate program at K-State. While she earned distinction through multiple awards, publications, and certifications, she has most enjoyed collaborating with talented colleagues in a professional community of practice dedicated to transforming higher education. Her research focuses on first-year seminars, parallel planning, alternative advising, and career advising.

Karen Sullivan-Vance, EdD, is the associate director for Strategic Program Development in the Executive Office for NACADA: The Global Community for Academic Advising. Before coming to the NACADA Executive Office, Sullivan-Vance served as the associate vice provost for Student Success at the University of Tennessee-Knoxville, where she led student success initiatives and supervised First-Year Studies, National Scholarships and Fellowships, Student Success Center, TRiO, and first-generation student initiatives. Before Tennessee, Sullivan-Vance served as the director of the Academic Advising and Learning Center at Western Oregon University and was an academic advisor in the College of Liberal Arts and the College of Education at Oregon State University. Sullivan-Vance presents nationally and internationally on topics related to academic advising, first-generation college students, and student success. She is a proud first-generation college graduate and earned her bachelor's in English literature from the University of Puget Sound, her Master's in college student services administration from Oregon State University, and her doctorate in educational leadership at Portland State University.

Susan M. Taffe Reed, PhD, is an assistant dean of undergraduate students at Dartmouth College since 2015, where she has served as an undergraduate dean for the class of 2019 and class of 2023. A first-generation college student, she earned a BA from Colgate University, and an MA and PhD from Cornell University. Taffe Reed has taught in music departments at UNC-Chapel Hill and Bowdoin College where she completed postdoctoral fellowships. Her academic advising interests include assisting students with exploring majors and the liberal arts, supporting students in crisis, and advising first-generation and high-achieving students. Her current research involves arts-based advising and research, advisor development, and legal and ethical issues in advising. She recently authored chapters in two NACADA/Stylus Publishing books—a chapter on scholarly inquiry in academic advising using arts-based research methods in *Scholarly Inquiry in Academic Advising*, second edition, and a coauthored chapter on delivery systems for advisor training and development in *Comprehensive Advisor Training and Development*, third edition.

Deborah J. Taub, PhD, serves as Professor and Chair of the Department of Student Affairs Administration at Binghamton University. She has more than 25 years of experience as a faculty member in student affairs administration. Before coming to Binghamton University, she taught at Purdue University and the University of North Carolina at Greensboro. She earned her bachelor's degree in English from Oberlin College and her master's and PhD in college student personnel from the University of Maryland. She is an ACPA Senior Scholar and editor of *New Directions for Student Services*. She has been recognized frequently for her scholarship and teaching, including ACUHO-I's Research and Publication Award, NASPA's Robert H. Shaffer Award for Academic Excellence as a Graduate Faculty Member, ACPA Diamond Honoree, and ACPA's Annuit Coeptis Senior Professional

Award. However, she says that her only *real* claim to fame is that she was once a contestant on "Jeopardy!"

Jennifer Tharp, PhD, is a higher education leader with expertise in student success and thriving. Having held various roles from student support to cabinet leadership, Tharp currently serves as associate provost at The King's College in New York City. She founded the Office of Student Success at King's in 2014 and has since led student success and retention strategy. She holds a PhD in Higher Education with a concentration in Student Success from Azusa Pacific University, and her research interests include college student thriving, the cultivation of well-being, and holistic well-being among leaders of change. Tharp coauthored the chapter "Thriving in High-Risk Students" in the updated *Thriving in Transitions: A Research-Based Approach to College Student Success,* edited by Schriener, Louis, and Nelson. Tharp writes and consults on issues related to well-being and student success and also teaches in higher education leadership programs at the graduate level. She also serves as an executive coach with Novus Global.

Wendy G. Troxel, EdD, is the director of the NACADA Center for Research at Kansas State University, overseeing opportunities for research and professional development within academic advising. As an associate professor in the Department of Special Education, Counseling, and Student Affairs, she teaches graduate-level classes in research methods and assessment of academic advising and supports the scholarly work of students. She serves as the coordinator of the PhD in Leadership in Academic Advising program at Kansas State University. Her research interests revolve around the impact, context, and theories of academic advising; student learning and maturity throughout higher education; formative assessment techniques in the classroom; equitable program assessment processes; and implications for success for students and advisors. She earned her doctorate in educational leadership at the University of Alabama at Birmingham (UAB), with special emphases in both educational research and education law.

Isaiah Vance is Assistant Provost with The Texas A&M University System in College Station, Texas. He previously served as Director of Academic Advising and Retention at Texas A&M University-Central Texas in Killeen, Texas, and Chair of the Religion Department at Eastern New Mexico University in Portales, New Mexico. Vance served as president of the Texas Academic Advising Network from 2017 to 2018; he served on the organization's board from 2015 to 2019. He has presented at state, regional, national, and international conferences on issues related to assessment, transfer, technology, High-Impact Practices, adult and military learners, and advising administration. He has been a faculty member for the NACADA Assessment Institute since 2018 and serves as Institute chair from 2022 through 2024. Vance leads advising and transfer initiatives for the A&M System and works extensively on degree audit software, curriculum development, and multi-institutional partnerships.

Rich Whitney, PhD, is a professor and program director in the Organizational Leadership Doctoral Program at the University of La Verne in Southern California. He teaches courses in the phenomenology of leadership, team dynamics, leadership theory, and creativity in program development. His courses align with his interest and research in when one identifies as a leader. As a proponent of experiential learning theory, he believes that learning is a function of relearning with context. Teaching is a process of connecting the experience to the material. His research interests include the phenomenology of leadership, brain-based learning, and program development. Whitney is very interested and passionate about the topics and work within programming/program development. He has been training, facilitating, and speaking to groups on leadership for more than 20 years.

Beth Yarbrough, PhD, retired as Director of Student Services in the College of Sciences and Mathematics at Auburn University. She earned her BA and MA in communication and a PhD from Auburn University in educational psychology. She enjoyed a 26-year career in COSAM, 13 as an advisor and 13 as Director.

INDEX

Note: **Bold** page numbers refer to tables and *Italic* page numbers refer to figures.

NACADA The Global Association for Academic Advising

NACADA is a global association of professional advisors, counselors, faculty, administrators, and students working to enhance the educational development of students.

NACADA promotes and supports quality academic advising in higher education institutions to enhance the educational development of students. NACADA provides a forum for discussion, debate, and the exchange of ideas pertaining to academic advising through numerous activities and publications. NACADA also serves as an advocate for effective academic advising by providing a Consulting and Speaker Service, an Awards Program, and funding for Research related to academic advising.

NACADA evolved from the first National Conference on Academic Advising in 1977 and has over 12,000 members in over 30 countries around the world. Members represent higher education institutions across the spectrum of Carnegie classifications and include professional advisors/counselors, faculty, administrators, and peer advisors whose responsibilities include academic advising.

NACADA functions with volunteer leadership with support from the NACADA Executive Office and the Executive Director. Members have full voting rights and elect the global Board of Directors as well as other leadership positions within the association. NACADA is designated by the IRS as a 501(c)3 non-profit educational association incorporated in Kansas.

Diversity

NACADA: The Global Community for Academic Advising values and promotes inclusive practices within the association and the advising profession. NACADA provides opportunities for professional development, networking, and leadership for our diverse membership and fosters involvement and engagement across identity groups, geographic regions, and professional levels. NACADA promotes the principle of equity and respects the diversity of academic advising professionals across the vast array of intersections of identity, which includes but is not limited to age cohort, institutional type, employment role, location, nationality, socioeconomic status, faith, religion, ethnicity, ability/disability, gender identity, gender expression, and/or sexual orientation.

nacada.ksu.edu

NACADA: The Global Community for Academic Advising
2323 Anderson Avenue, Suite 225
Manhattan, KS 66502
Phone: 785-532-5717

Made in the USA
Columbia, SC
18 June 2024

37237737R00230